The Nearest Place That Wasn't Ireland

The Nearest Place

That Wasn't

IRELAND

Early Nineteenth-Century
Irish Labor Migration

RUTH-ANN M. HARRIS

Iowa State University Press / Ames

Ruth-Ann Harris is visiting professor of history and Irish studies at Boston College. She has taught at Tufts, Wesleyan, Boston, and Northeastern universities and is senior research fellow at the Institute of Irish Studies at Queen's University, Belfast, 1994–95. She is chief editor of *The Search for Missing Friends,* a series of books on Irish immigrants, and is currently working on a study of the letters, memoirs, and journals of Irish women in North America.

© 1994 Iowa State University Press, Ames, Iowa 50014
All rights reserved

Authorization to photocopy items for internal or personal use, or the internal or personal use of specific clients, is granted by Iowa State University Press, provided that the base fee of $.10 per copy is paid directly to the Copyright Clearance Center, 27 Congress Street, Salem, MA 01970. For those organizations that have been granted a photocopy license by CCC, a separate system of payments has been arranged. The fee code for users of the Transactional Reporting Service is 0-8138-1422-7/94 $.10.

♾ Printed on acid-free paper in the United States of America

First edition, 1994

"Murphy in Manchester" by John Montague is printed here by kind permission of Dolmen Press, which republished *Poisoned Lands and Other Poems* in 1976.

Library of Congress Cataloging-in-Publication Data
Harris, Ruth-Ann Mellish.
 The nearest place that wasn't Ireland : early nineteenth-century Irish labor migration / Ruth-Ann M. Harris. — 1st ed.
   p.   cm.
 Includes bibliographical references and index.
 ISBN 0-8138-1422-7
 1. Irish — England — History — 19th century. 2. Immigrants — England — History — 19th century. 3. Alien labor — England — History — 19th — Emigration and immigration.   I. Title.
DA125.17H37   1994
942′.0049162 — dc20   94-7403

Contents

MURPHY IN MANCHESTER

He wakes to a confused dream of boats, gulls,
And all his new present floats
Suddenly up to him on rocking rails.
Through that long first day
He trudges streets, tracks friends,
Stares opened-mouth at monuments
To manufacturers, sabred generals.
Passing a vegetable stall
With exposed fruits, he halts
To contemplate a knobbly potato
With excitement akin to love.
At lunchtime, in a cafeteria,
He finds his feet and hands
Enlarge, become like foreign lands.
A great city is darkness, noise
Through which bright girls move
Like burnished other children's toys.
Soon the whistling factory
Will lock him in:
Half-stirred memories and regrets
Drawn into that iron din.

JOHN MONTAGUE
Poisoned Lands and Other Poems

ERSKINE NICOL (1825–1
Irish Emigrant Landing at Liverp
Courtesy, National Gallery of Sco

Foreword

In popular imagination mass emigration from Ireland began with the Great Famine of 1846–49. Ruth-Ann Harris here ably draws attention to an important segment of an earlier, unduly neglected exodus. Though pre-Famine emigrants were greatly outnumbered by those of the late 1840s and 1850s, it should be stressed that the outflow of humans from Ireland in the generation between Waterloo and the Famine was vast by contemporary European standards. In those years over one and a half million people, mostly young and single, left Ireland for good. Most made their way to North America, but on the eve of the Famine "the nearest place that wasn't Ireland" contained about half a million of them.

These half-million Irish in Britain were highly concentrated regionally: the combined Irish-born populations of London, Manchester, Liverpool, and Glasgow accounted for almost one-half of the total. That together those four cities contained as many Irish-born in 1845 as Dublin says much about the nature of Irish participation in the Industrial Revolution. The pre-Famine Irish in Britain were highly urbanized, but most of them were country people, bringing many of their rural habits with them. The oft-quoted unsympathetic assessments of Frederick Engels and Thomas Carlyle reflected attitudes widely held among the host population. Discrimination in jobs and housing inevitably followed. In mitigation, however, two caveats are apposite. First, however unfriendly their reception in early nineteenth-century Britain, the Irish never shared the fate of unlucky Haitian or Asian boat people or Mexican illegals today. Second, the gap in living standards between those who left Ireland for Britain and their siblings who remained on probably widened at the expense of the latter in the decades before the Great Famine.

Ironically, despite the resentment against them, it seems that the economic impact of the Irish on the British labor market was small in aggregate, though it could be locally and fleetingly significant. On the other hand, the impact of the outflow on the country they left behind was important. If the Industrial Revolution marked the ruin of much traditional Irish manufacturing, that Britain acted as a safety valve for some of the ensuing population pressure was no small consolation.

Many of the best-known studies of the nineteenth-century Irish in Britain are based on statistical analyses of contemporary census manuscript forms. These exercises in "SPSS history" have produced many new insights, but they necessarily also have tended to produce a static "snapshot" image of the immigrant Irish. Ruth-Ann Harris does well to repeatedly stress the temporary, transient nature of much of the Irish immigration, vividly brought home by her judicious pen-pictures of Michael Sullivan and Owen Peter Mangan. Her insistence that most of those who left Ireland for Britain before 1845 did so with the firm intention of either returning home or moving on to greener pastures in America, and that the Irish migrants were very mobile within Britain, has several important implications.

Sidney Pollard has dubbed the pre-Famine Irish in Britain the "shock-troops" of the Industrial Revolution. Their transience is an important part of the story, and helps explain much about them. Typically, being casual labourers, they did not remain long enough in any one spot or employment to acquire skills or responsibilities, and, relative to their British peers, they were more likely to be found on a construction site than in a cotton factory. Nor, alas, did they become part of a united British working class: instead they were often resented for reducing wages and strikebreaking. Before the Famine, their integration into British society was minimal; intermarriage was unusual, and the Irish sought company and housing among their own kind, keeping in close contact with the old country. Being "on the move" and poor in turn meant that they were less likely to acquire their own homes, and their exaggerated reputations for sociability and criminality may have also followed from this. Highly concentrated in relatively few areas, the immigrants' failure (or, given the cold welcome they received, their inability) to integrate left them with little political clout. One result of all this was that the typical Irish immigrant in Britain in the 1830s or early 1840s probably had more in common with those compatriots who opted for temporary harvest migration than with those who chose America.

Ruth-Ann Harris's lively treatment of these issues will surely prompt some interesting comparisons with the better-known Irish diasporas in post-1845 Britain and America.

University College, Dublin   CORMAC Ó'GRÁDA

We are like wild geese, your honour.

—SEASONAL MIGRANT, 1881

Preface

The Irish were everywhere in England and Scotland in the nineteenth century, once you began to look for them. Irish migrants sought work wherever they weren't actively excluded by the local labor force, and in any employment which didn't prevent their returning regularly home to Ireland. In the burgeoning economy of nineteenth-century Britain the Irish occupied the niche of a work force which undertook employment spurned by others, whether it was strikebreaking or industry's least desirable tasks. Known as *lumpers* when they worked on the London docks, they could outwork and underlive their competition. Their speech and distinctive dress made them visible on every building site where they monopolized the job of bricklayers helpers. Ubiquitous throughout central London, they were the hawkers and traders who sold oranges to travellers and recycled old clothes to the poor. In Lancashire the low wages, which they accepted willingly, prolonged the death agonies of the handloom weaving industry in the textile districts. In sum, and to paraphrase a contemporary report on them, never before had a slave labor force imported itself so willingly.

There had never been much doubt but that England was the best place for ambitious persons living anywhere in the British Isles to make a name for themselves. Dr. Samuel Johnson was well aware of this when he remarked that "the noblest prospect which a Scotchman ever sees, is the high road that leads him to England!"[1] While this had always been true for the Anglo-Irish, now, as England emerged as the nineteenth-century world's most vigorous economy, Irish persons of less privileged origin also started to achieve distinction in English public life. Among the most prominent of these were Feargus O'Connor, the member of

Parliament for Cork, and Bronterre O'Brien, the Chartist writer. The London stage had its Irish actors like Dion Boucicault, and Fleet Street had its Irish journalists like John Denvir. Furthermore, just as Irish brain power had always flourished with greater advantage abroad than at home, so too did Irish muscle find greater reward working abroad than at home.

The stimulus for studying this migration of Irish workers abroad grew out of my interest at discovering large numbers of Irish workers choosing to work as temporary migrants in England and Scotland, seemingly in preference to emigrating farther abroad. In choosing to study the dynamics of the migration I sought to understand why Irish men and women chose to improve their living standards only temporarily when, it appeared, they could have bettered themselves permanently had they emigrated to America—and later in the nineteenth century—also to Australia. The result of my exploration is an examination of the work world of Irish temporary migrants, in Ireland and in Britain in the first half of the nineteenth century; looking at why Irish people chose temporary employment abroad and were content with a style of life which benefitted them only briefly.

The elements of similar migrations have been repeated many times over since those early years of industrialization, particularly in the twentieth century as rural men and women in Africa and Asia and Latin America have found that the only way to maintain life in rural areas was to supplement their poor standard of living with earnings gained elsewhere. The teeming cities of Africa and Asia today have their equivalent of the early nineteenth-century Irish migrant worker. In Indonesia he may be the *becak* (bicycle pedicab) driver who keeps his family and his farm in Central Java but commutes to Jakarta for from six to ten months of the year to earn enough to remain a farmer and pay his children's school fees. In Kenya he may be the up-country farmer who migrates into Nairobi, seeking any work which will enable him to support his family back in Kitui or Narok or Nyeri. But they find, as Irish seasonal migrants found earlier, that the economic benefits do not last forever, and the social costs in terms of fragmented families and altered roles for female heads of household ultimately result in fundamental social and economic transformation of rural communities.

Since beginning this search I found that what once had seemed a unique pattern of migration was really not uncommon, and that Irish temporary migration was only part of a wider pattern of a European structure whereby Poles migrated to Germany, and French from the Massif Central went to Spain. The life-patterns of such temporary migrants also tended to be similar. Just as energetic Irish migrants, after working abroad for a few years, sometimes found their lives so little improved that they used their earnings to finance permanent emigration, so did many of the Polish immigrants studied by Thomas and Znaniecki work as temporary migrants in Germany before leaving for America.[2] It appears that short-term migration has often functioned as the prelude to permanent emigration. Thus for many Irish persons, whether they intended it or not, working in Britain was a way station on the journey to America.

British cities today still have their equivalent of the Irish temporary migrant of the nineteenth century. It is no longer necessary to supplement Irish rural incomes from cash earned abroad; the Irish government sees to that when it subsidizes Irish farmers with grants obtained through Ireland's membership in the European Economic Community. But the habit of going abroad has become so thoroughly ingrained in Irish life-patterns that an expected stage of life for energetic young people is to leave to seek work in London or Glasgow or Liverpool—with the result that their education and training benefit every country but their own.

Among the aftereffects of the Famine years that catapulted Irish society into the modern age, temporary migration lost the original function, which had been to provide short-term relief for a cash-starved rural population. And while some sectors of the far western regions of Galway and Mayo were still largely sustained by the cash earnings of temporary migrants well into the late nineteenth century, by and large those persons who might in the years prior to 1845 have been seasonal migrants, saving their earnings in order to lease more land to farm, had by now lost their faith in the land. They were more likely to have become permanent fixtures of the English or Scottish labor force, or to have gone to America. Although migrants abroad still sent their earnings home in generous amounts, their statements indicate that more often the money was intended to persuade their brothers and sisters to join them overseas than to sustain their ancient parents at home. Meanwhile, regions of Ireland where seasonal migration still remained a way of life became more immured in poverty as migrants were trapped by a tempo of life which dictated that they migrate or starve.

Acknowledgments

During the years when this study was under way I incurred many debts to persons who have encouraged or aided its development. Among those in America are Donald Akenson, Eric Almquist, Frank Carney,

Ballard Campbell, Perry Curtis, Adele Dalsimer, James Donnelly, Tim Guinnane, Pierre Laurent, Lynn Lees, Bruce Logan, Bill Lowe, Deirdre Mageean, Howard Malchow, Michelle McAlpin, Rosemarie McDonald, Clay McShane, David Miller, Leslie Moch, Joel Mokyr, Maureen Murphy, Kevin O'Neill, Lisa Peattie, Michael Piore, John Post, David Schmitt, Howard Solomon, Barbara Solow, Mary Helen Thuente, Tom Truxes, and Jeffrey Williamson. Thanks are due Charles Kindleberger whose seminar in economic history at MIT influenced my thinking and whose excellent advice helped give this study its present form.

In Ireland, England, and Scotland I am greatly in the debt of many who gave generously of their time and advice to aid my study of these invisible migrants. Among them I acknowledge many thanks to Tom Bartlett, John Belchem, Michael Burns, Brenda Collins, Sean Connolly, Bill Crawford, Louis Cullen, Mary Cullen, Fergus D'Arcy, David Dickson, David Doyle, Ruth Dudley Edwards, Marianne Elliott, David Fitzpatrick, Alan Gailey, the late Rodney Green, the late Joseph Hamling, Carmel Heaney, John A. Jackson, Joseph Lee, Margaret MacCurtain, Brid Mahon, the late Aiken McClelland, Catherine McCullough, John Montague, Íde O'Carroll, Anne O'Dowd, Sean O'hÉochaidh, Kevin O'Rourke, Patrick O'Sullivan, Géaroid Ó'Tuathaigh, Trevor Parkhill, George Thompson, Brian Trainor, Brendan Walsh, and Sophia, Patrick, and Michael Ferry. Special thanks to Janet Harris Fraser and the late Barclay Fraser for drawing my attention to the painting of the Irish emigrant landing at liverpool that appears at the beginning of the book. In particular I would like to acknowledge the great debt I owe to Austin Bourke and Cormac Ó'Gráda who befriended me in Dublin, offering advice and encouragement, and convincing me that with effort there was sufficient material to make a study of this pre-Famine migration.

I wish also to thank the following who read or commented, or in other ways made this manuscript possible: Stella Coughlin, Meg Courtney, Nuala Eastwood, Lynn Fiducia, Jerrine Larsen, Bridget Knightly, Athena Kokas, Eliza McClennan, Maurice Rahilly, Lois Randall, Solveig Turner, and Pat Woo. To my editors at Iowa State University Press, Jane Zaring and Bill Silag, I say thank you for the encouragement and admirable attention given to the production of this book; it was a pleasure to work with them. Thanks also to the Danforth Foundation for supporting my research in the early stages. Their willingness to encourage women to continue educations interrupted by family responsibilities through their Graduate Fellowship for Women Program was a substantial contribution.

Finally, I wish to express my gratitude to my family. My parents, Catherine Hartley and Gordon Mellish, gave me an enviable start in life in Liberia, West Africa. And to my husband, John Rees Harris, whose own studies of migration in the less-developed contemporary world made him a good companion, a rigorous critic, and an exciting colleague, I say special thanks. There are a number of persons this study could have been dedicated to because they made a special contribution, either to this study or to my life, but historians are concerned with first causes so that it is to my grandmother, the late Martha Ann Beresford Watkins Hartley, that I dedicate what is written here. As a child she told me about the Irish whom she remembered while she was growing up in Penarth, walking barefoot through Wales on their yearly search for work. Most of all it was my grandmother, as a former factory girl, who taught me that the Industrial Revolution was not an unmitigated disaster but had offered opportunities to those who knew how to make use of them.

COUNTY MAP OF IRELAND

--- BOUNDARY OF NORTHERN IRELAND
—— PROVINCE BOUNDARIES

The Nearest Place That Wasn't Ireland

The Irish

[The migration was] . . . an example of a less civilized population spreading themselves as a kind of substratum beneath a more civilized community; and, yet without excelling in any branch of industry, obtaining possession of all the lowest departments of manual labor. So long as the emigration could not take place, as the working classes were not at liberty to choose the place of their residence; and, as it has been in general more profitable to import than to breed slaves, the working population of the more civilized states was recruited either by captives taken in war, or by foreigners kidnapped in barbarous or half-civilized districts. In many countries likewise in which slavery has been abolished the existence of strict policy regulations with respect to pass-ports, and other measures of the Government, have proven a powerful obstacle to the diffusion of a poor and frequently mendicant population over richer and more civilized regions.

Report on the State of the Irish Poor in Great Britain, 1836

in Ireland and England

By the fifth century, while the last Roman garrison was evacuating England, the Britons underwent the first of a series of invasions of Germanic peoples. The Angles and Saxons, many of whom eventually settled, contributed to what would become the British peoples. More invasions followed. Beginning in the eighth century, Norsemen and Danes, arriving for plunder, often remained; once more invasion was followed by adaptation. Family names are a constant reminder of the mixed origins of the British, making them among the "most ethnically composite of the Europeans."[1]

The Normans, arriving in the eleventh century, established a powerful centrally organized state in southern England a century before they sought to conquer Ireland. Following this last great invasion other peoples also arrived in England—Flemings, Walloons, Germans, Huguenots—some ejected from their homelands because they held dissident religious beliefs, some attracted by economic opportunity, all welcomed because they were skilled artisans. The arrival of these immigrants foreshadowed future developments in the British Isles because their skills contributed significantly to Britain's future reputation as the workshop of the world.

By the eighteenth century a series of technological changes, known collectively as the Industrial Revolution, created greater demands for labor in agriculture and industry than could be supplied by surrounding populations. Meanwhile the people of Ireland, once known for the ferociousness of their attacks on Saxon England, now mounted a new assault on the sister island. Irish laborers, armed only with reaping hooks, descended upon the British countryside looking for work, returning to

3

Ireland weeks or months later with their earnings to settle their debts, pay the landlord, the priest, the moneylender, or the tithe proctor. The frequency with which these migrants returned, as well as the brief duration of their stay, precluded assimilation into British life. As an invasion it posed certain problems because this latest group of raiders would not be easily digested. Near enough to England so that return was always an option, yet sufficiently distinctive in their way of life so as to deter successful assimilation into British society, the Irish were and are in Britain, but often scarcely of it.

This book is an examination of the Irish invasion in the first half of the nineteenth century, its antecedents and consequences; how and why temporary migration became an option; and why most chose not to remain. Fundamental changes occurred with the collapse of the potato economy after 1845. Potatoes were central to the household economy of most seasonal migrants, so that the cataclysmic ruin of their main crop four years in succession also removed a primary impetus for seasonal migration, which was the need to earn cash income in order to retain access to land. This is not to say, however, that temporary migration ceased. Western regions of Ireland continued to be characterized by early age at marriage, continued subdivision of property holdings, heavy dependence on the potato, and grueling poverty—a persistence of pre-Famine conditions that could only be alleviated by supplementing with an outside income. But what changed after 1845 was that the migrant stream bifurcated, so that while some migrants continued to go to England and Scotland, the majority now went west instead of east—to America rather than Britain.

A new custom also developed to mark a changed attitude toward the leave-taking—the American wake, a symbolic death—marking the belief that the emigrant was now lost to their family and community because the prospect of return was so remote.[2] However, despite all the trappings of this symbolic death of its migrating members, rural Ireland remained a society in which family claims on each other persisted, so that whether migrants went east to Britain or west to America they were still burdened with heavy obligations to contribute to the support of those still at home. Patrick MacGill, a seasonal migrant who eventually settled in America, explained the economic link between migrants and the family at home when he said:

> I never for a moment thought of keeping all my wages for myself. Such a wild idea never entered my head. I was born and bred merely to support my parents, and great care had been taken to drive this fact into my mind from infancy. I was merely brought into the world to support those who were

responsible for my existence. Often when my parents were speaking of such and such a young man I heard them say, "He'll never have a day's luck in all his life. He didn't give every penny he earned to his father and mother."[3]

The dynamics of the migration are made more clear with an inquiry into why it began.

Why Did They Migrate?

Adam Smith once observed that man of all creatures was the most difficult to transport, but what the father of classical economics may not have foreseen was that some conditions — such as ensuring the option of return — could persuade people to uproot themselves. Seasonal migration was one way of ensuring freedom of movement because it made migration reversible.

Irish wanderers in England had since the fifteenth century been a minor feature of English life, but by the eighteenth century large numbers of Irish laborers began arriving for work in the harvest fields surrounding London. Their need for work mirrored conditions in Ireland, whose economy was by the late eighteenth century so closely tied to that of England that it was said that when England sneezed Ireland caught pneumonia. This situation, in conjunction with growing opportunities in a newly industrial England and the possibility of relatively easy return, made for a compelling combination. The Irish people soon discovered the economic side of the political maxim that said "England's difficulty is Ireland's opportunity,"[4] when they learned that the greater the shortages of labor abroad, the greater the opportunities for the Irish to fill them.

While migrants sometimes settled permanently, for most it was primarily a sojourner migration, one in which they left home with an intention to return. Most returned in six weeks or from three to four months. Others stayed for a few years, some for their work lifetime, and some fewer remained permanently. The extent to which people lingered depended upon such factors as the employment they found, the trade cycle that determined whether they flourished or not, and the ties of kin and community which commanded their return. Most importantly, however, decisions to return or remain depended critically upon an individual's access to land. Ireland's industrial base had never been large, but after the cutbacks consequent upon the end of the French Wars, there were fewer non-agricultural opportunities every year; and, as the industrial base shrank, access to land assumed greater importance.

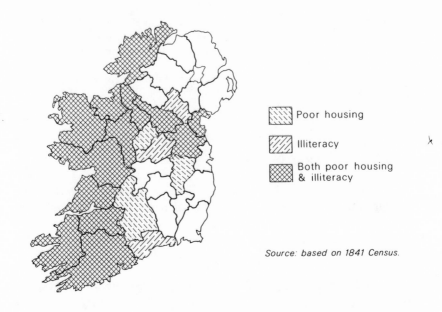

Poor housing

Illiteracy

Both poor housing & illiteracy

Source: based on 1841 Census.

FIGURE 1.1.   Distribution of poverty, 1841.

Of notable cause for concern was Ireland's phenomenal poverty, which when coupled with an increasing casual labor force, meant that increasing numbers of Irish were unable to find sufficient employment to prevent them from falling further into poverty. As early as the first decades of the nineteenth century it was widely believed that population growth in Ireland, encouraged by the custom of early marriage and sustained by dependence upon the potato, was at the root of Ireland's problem of poverty. By the 1830s it appeared that the age of marriage was rising, pointing to greater caution in marriage custom, but the most vulnerable portion of the population was, if anything, more dependent upon the potato than ever before. The potato, which in good years nourished the population extraordinarily well, was tending over time to decrease in both reliability and quality. The result was that every year more persons shared smaller portions of the economic pie.

The struggle to survive in Ireland was exacerbated by additional factors: among them were the decay of domestic industry, withering in the cold blast of competition from more efficiently produced British goods; the increased pressure of population on the land, accelerating the

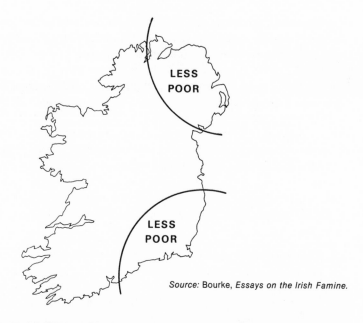

FIGURE 1.2. Arcs of prosperity in pre-Famine Ireland.

division of family farms and greater competition for leaseholds; and an iniquitous social system that the landed gentry were unwilling—or possibly unable—to change, despite warnings from those who foresaw in it the eventual disintegration of their way of life.

Technological changes in Britain throughout the eighteenth century increased production, first in agriculture and then in industry, and in doing so created demands for new forms of labor. Difficulties arose, however, from an inefficient geographical distribution of the population, so that while the southern regions of England were growing, the resident population appeared largely immobile; whereas areas like industrializing Lancashire to the north were starved for workers. The growing rural proletariat appeared to resist incentives to relocate, sustained in their intransigence by the operations of the poor laws.[5] These laws, established during Elizabethan times, pegged the price of labor to the price of bread and provided a safety net for the poor that mitigated the possibility of their falling into real destitution.

Change began to be discussed when the English landed classes protested the high cost of the poor rates financing the system. Manufacturers, beginning to emerge as a political force, lamented scarcities of labor as hampering their productivity. While undoubtedly labor shortages did exist at certain times and in some industries, scarcity was more perceived than real. At the heart of the problem for manufacturers was that employers wished to have workers to whom they could dictate terms, rather than being forced to deal with a work force that had alternative resources and thus could dictate the terms under which it was willing to work. Industrial output requires a high degree of predictability, while regular schedules and predictable work habits are hard-learned lessons for persons whose lives have been timed by the rhythm of rural life. The British labor force was notoriously intractable, asserting both its rights and its unwillingness to submit to the new industrial discipline.[6] Daniel Defoe described the English working population in the early eighteenth century:

> There's nothing more frequent than for an Englishman to work till he has got his pocket full of money, and then go and be idle, or perhaps drunk till it is all gone and perhaps himself in debt: and ask him in his cup what he intents, he'll tell you honestly, he'll drink as long as it lasts, and then go to work for more.[7]

The Irish were to be the work force which would temper the habits of the recalcitrant English. Ireland had the supply and England had the demand. Thus it is hardly surprising that as communication between the two countries accelerated, so did the Irish rush to seize the opportunity for work. There was no poor law to restrain their movement as existed in England. Leaving Ireland for shorter or longer intervals in search of work, they became that ideal labor force so desired by English capitalists: one to whom employers could dictate terms. Arriving, frequently as wage cutters and strikebreakers, the Irish were prepared to accept whatever would enable them to earn enough to fulfill their aspirations, chief of which was to earn enough to remain in Ireland.

Developing links between Ireland and England encouraged market-oriented agriculture in the eastern counties surrounding Dublin. Owners of large farms preferred to avoid the cost of maintaining a resident labor force by employing seasonal migrants. Small farmers, who had once employed laborers year-round, now preferred to rely on their own families and immediate neighbors for help. Wherever the application of capitalist methods to agriculture enabled large farmers to grow grain primarily for export, the labor force grew increasingly redundant because of diminished demands for farm labor. The result was that the number of workers in casual employment increased and a stagnant surplus continued to grow which in Marx's words, "continued to form a self-reproducing and self-perpetuating element of the working class."[8]

Prior to 1850 those who sought work in England, and to a lesser extent in Scotland,[9] did so not necessarily because they were unable to go to North America but because they did not wish to cut their ties to Ireland. A few migrants giving evidence to parliamentary commissions declared that they would consider going to America only if work in England or Scotland became less remunerative. Emigration to North America was not a widely sought option during the early nineteenth century, except in areas of Ulster among those whose ancestors were themselves relatively recent migrants to Ireland and more accustomed to regarding land as a capital investment. Greater risks were inherent in the longer journey, which implied permanence. Cutting ties was anathema to the Irish who preferred instead to retain the ability to reap benefits from two countries, travelling either between regions within Ireland, or between Ireland and England or Scotland.

While landlords might bewail the redundant populations cluttering their estates, in many cases it was the money remitted by migrant workers which sustained the relatively high cost of leases. Contemporaries believed that it was the increasing cost of those leases which drove people to seek work abroad. John Trotter, a writer, recalled a discussion with two farmers who were preparing to leave their farms for work. When he asked them why they were doing this since they appeared to be prosperous, Trotter received the reply: "Because I can never be better than I am [here]. Times promise to be worse, and such farmers as we are cannot possibly stand it long."[10] Thus, as the noose of economic opportunity tightened, those who had once known moderate prosperity sought to ensure its preservation.

Studies of migration patterns to the New World have often deliberately, if unconsciously, distorted the nature of conditions in the Old. By adopting the rhetoric of the Americas as lands of golden opportunity there has been a tendency to exaggerate conditions that prompted the emigrants to leave. Though why, if European conditions were so bad, did considerable numbers of immigrants wish to return and succeed in doing so?[11] Answers may lie in the economic motivations of individuals, because with the exception of those fleeing social or political persecution, most migrants are economic migrants, people leaving to earn more money and have a more satisfactory life than is possible at home. It may be then asked whether those who succeeded in returning did so because they had gained what they sought without developing ties that would bind them to life in America.

Unless the motivation is understood, it is difficult to comprehend the hardships which the Irish people were willing to endure in order to retain some hold on the land. But were they, as Winston Churchill once said, "persistent peasants?" Or were more of them like the Roscommon laborer who travelled every year to England for work, and told a parliamentary commission in 1835 that "[I] would have a veneration for the soil if I could get support from it."?[12]

From an economic viewpoint short-term migration may have been wrong. In the regions where most migrants lived subsistence farmers could plant sufficient potatoes for a family of six for a year on one acre of land, a system of cultivation hardly conducive to modern agricultural production, but for the migrants it was right because it left them with some degree of control over their lives. In the words of David Thomson, a twentieth-century observer of Irish behavior, "They want the gamble of working for themselves."[13] Casual labor for low wages in Britain, labor for the landlord in return for land — each was sufficiently exploitative for Karl Marx to call these workers "part serfs," but each made it possible to maintain and preserve a cherished autonomy of action. Unfortunately, when the potato crop failed four years in succession after 1845, those who had supplemented their income by working abroad lost the control over their lives that seasonal migration had given them. In doing so they were faced with a whole new set of choices, of which permanent leave-taking was the most viable.

Thus it was both the push of conditions in Ireland as well as the pull of opportunities in Britain which explain why the Irish chose to go there. Migration has been termed "an arrangement for making maximum use of persons with special qualifications."[14] If this is so, then the Irish were maximizing and enhancing the total resources available to them by migrating and returning on a regular basis.

Why Did They Return?

Understanding the motivation for migration poses some complex questions. They concern the nature of conditions in Ireland leading to decisions to leave, the continuum of the migration process resulting in increasing numbers leaving for shorter or longer periods of time, and the nature and function of the conditions in Britain that attracted them. One must attempt to understand the sometimes separate, sometimes complementary roles of Irish men and women in the migration process, a fact that social scientists have only recently begun to explore. Stephan Thernstrom's study of immigrants in Boston is only one of many which errs in this regard.[15] While temporary migration was overwhelmingly male (in a sample year the male/female ratio in the migrant stream was six to one), the roles which Irish females played in supporting and sustaining it have left their mark even to the present day.

Migration is a complex process which, if it is to be fully understood, must be examined from all aspects, including gender roles. For that reason, we need to understand why few females who left Ireland returned; either they remained in Britain or re-emigrated to America. There remains a largely inconclusive question as to how migration may have changed male/female roles, thereby engendering and influencing subsequent changes in the structure of the Irish family.

Attitudes toward land, again, are crucial to a general understanding of what motivated people to leave only temporarily. John Revans, a political economist and an assistant commissioner during the 1835–36 inquiry into the condition of the people of Ireland, concluded this when he said that an understanding of the importance of land to the Irish people was crucial to a comprehension of the social dynamics of the countryside:

> The possession of land is of immense importance, without it he [the peasant] must lead the life of a mendicant. The only way in which a woman can get an interest in land is by marrying, and the only chance of protection from beggary when she loses her husband, or when his powers fail, is to have children. The poorest Irish peasant is therefore always married.[16]

Revans was largely correct: The majority of Irish farmers were really peasants in the sense described by Robert Redfield, in which the production of individuals was primarily for their own consumption and in fulfillment of their duties to those who held political and economic power.[17]

As previously indicated, the Great Famine forms the cataclysmic divide in changing the nature of the migration, and indeed much of Ireland's history as well. After 1850 migrants were more likely to become emigrants, most appearing to lose their veneration for the land, while at the same time showing a new political militancy in their efforts to gain rights to it. But this raises a question as to what role may the migration have played in the changes in Ireland prior to the Famine, since it is now clear that the Famine only accelerated changes which were already under way. To what extent may the economic system of the countryside have become dependent upon these injections of cash from elsewhere? As early as 1827 a witness at a parliamentary enquiry noted changes in the behavior of migrant laborers. He believed that among some who had previously returned because they possessed small farms there was an increasing tendency to remain abroad for longer periods of time. If this was so, what was happening? Might conditions in the various counties of Ireland explain differential migration?

It is also instructive to look at the role of the Irish as a minority group within Britain. Misunderstandings of cultural differences between these two peoples have long caused friction and clearly endure to the present day. Their experiences in Britain caused Irish people to change in more than an economic sense. The history of Irish nationalism demonstrates that almost all late nineteenth-century nationalists had either lived or worked abroad at some time in their lives, suggesting that the experience of living out of Ireland transformed them. And if the presence of the Irish had not been so visible and so frequently resented in England and Scotland, the history of Anglo-Irish relations might have been very different.

Conversely, what role may the juxtaposition of two so very different peoples have played in Britain's development? James Edmund Handley, one of the first historians of the Irish abroad, explained an early source of misunderstanding between the two peoples when he observed the behavior of Irish harvest migrants:

> The natural vociferousness and sprightly temper of the immigrants often lent themselves to a mistaken interpretation; and the sight of a gesticulating Irishman brandishing wildly a reaping hook in the exuberance of argument could convey as one meaning to a people unaccustomed to a strictly literal construction of words and actions.[18]

Why Ireland and Why the Irish?

Since this migration was the first industrial migration of modern history, an understanding of the processes involved in such a movement contributes to our awareness of similar contemporary phenomena operating at present. Since the end of the Second World War, Mediterranean peoples have been migrating in great numbers to fuel the industries of northern Europe; and Hispanics and other Caribbean peoples have been moving into and out of the harvest fields and industries of North America in much the same way that the nineteenth-century Irish travelled between Ireland and Britain.

In the nineteenth century, Ireland had what may be either the good or the bad fortune to live next to the wealthiest and most dynamic country in the world. It was a proximity which created certain unavoidable dilemmas for healthy economic growth in Ireland. The two countries were too near to ignore each other, but their inhabitants were so unlike as to be uncomfortable with the proximity. Various problems deserving investigation arise from this juxtaposition of two such different peoples and economies. The result makes for an interesting case study of the inherent difficulties which arise when a primarily agricultural country must coexist in contact with an industrially voracious neighbor. Is the increase of peripheral poverty necessarily the result of, or only an aspect of centralizing industrial development elsewhere? Michael Hechter's study of the British Isles sees the growing regional inequalities of peripheral regions as leading to subordinate roles for Ireland, Wales, and Scotland. Each region was limited in its development, being able only to export either people or labor-intensive products to the dominant region.[19] An examination of the interaction between the two societies suggests some interesting conclusions.

The migration process is best seen as a two-way flow of people, a migration which because it was reversible permitted the Irish to benefit from conditions on both sides of the Irish Sea. British stereotypes of the Irish saw them as feckless "paddies," persons whose job commitment was brief and whose willingness to undertake work spurned by their Scots or English counterparts made them somewhat less than human. Closer examination suggests that this was an uninformed judgement. Explanations for the behavior lie in the proximity of the two counties, and the ease of passage which enabled Irish migrants to maximize what they valued in both places: in Ireland a way of life and in England the opportunity to earn a living. Migration to Britain was a substitute for migration within Ireland and it delayed the necessity to migrate to North America or elsewhere—an undesirable prospect because it was far less reversible.

Agricultural adaptation and adjustments were necessary in facilitating the movement of migrants. In Ireland this was facilitated by the rundale system of shared cultivation of land, which ensured the migrants' access to land by enabling them to leave for shorter or longer periods of time without jeopardizing their claims to land. In addition, the lazybed system of potato cultivation enabled cultivators to plant as early as St. Bridget's Day on the first of February, fulfill whatever contractual labor obligations existed with the landlord in return for land, and still arrive in Britain in time for the planting or construction seasons. At the end of the work season, return to Ireland could be delayed until as late as November because the potato crop need not be lifted before that time. The Irish countryman was thus able to be at home for the winter months, which had always been the social season, when there was time to relax from farm chores to enjoy dancing, drinking, or matchmaking around the fire.

This study underlines the necessity of integrating the history of the development of Ireland, a labor- and food-exporting economy, into the history of the development of Great Britain, which in the early nineteenth century, was in the pioneer phase of its industrialization. Unless developments in the two islands are regarded as contributing to and resulting from complementary activities, we are limiting perspective and foreshortening our knowledge of the history of the whole region.

Difficulties in Research on Migration

The most obvious problem is a lack of systematic data on seasonal migration during the period. Thus the detailed texture of data necessary to make good estimates of magnitudes, timing, and dating of specific migration flows is missing. And even when some data exists, it is impossible to connect migrants directly with such factors as their access to land, ownership of assets, occupational history, marital status, or any of the other variables important to an understanding of why specific categories of people move. For that reason it is necessary to use fragmentary pieces of data, some of which are sometimes inconsistent; and indeed, much useful data cannot be reconstructed. Historians, unlike sociologists and anthropologists, do not have access to the richness of a detailed series of interviews with persons involved in the migration process.

All too often the public records pertaining to the migrants are left by those whom they have inconvenienced: magistrates or poor-law administrators. And while useful observations on the state of what were then called the lower classes can be gained from traveller's accounts, parliamentary investigations, and the like, all too often migrants do not come to the attention of such people because they were not physically present to make an impact on contemporary observers.

Even more unfortunate for historians is the fact that temporary migrants rarely left the kind of personal records which make their lives real to us—diaries, letters, or books. I was fortunate in that my other research indicates that many North American immigrants had first worked in England or Scotland. Included here are accounts from two temporary migrants who later went to America and one whose poverty was so great that initially he couldn't even consider emigrating.

The first task of a historian is to try to tell a plausible story with the evidence available, however fragmentary, asking whether the fragments are consistent with other evidence. I found it reassuring that isolated pieces of the puzzle, even if they do not fit perfectly, frequently do have that consistency with the other evidence.

Background Studies of Pre-Famine Migration

My discovery of Friedrich Engels's classic investigation of the condition of the working classes of England in the early period of industrialization first sparked my interest in trying to discover why so many Irish went to England. This middle-class German manufacturer's son exhibited great respect for the English worker, but he did not extend this respect to Irish workers. While it cannot be denied that the Manchester Irish lived in the worst possible conditions, Engels's judgement failed to take into account why this may have been so. Of them, he said:

> These Irishmen who migrate for fourpence to England, on the deck of a steamship on which they are often packed like cattle, insinuate themselves everywhere. The worst dwellings are good enough for them; their clothing causes them little trouble, so long as it holds together by a single thread; shoes they know not; their food consists of potatoes and potatoes only; whatever they earn beyond these needs they spend upon drink. What does such a race want with high wages?[20]

In sharp contrast to Engels's attitude was that of Henry Mayhew, a mid-century journalist whose examinations of the working poor of London have been plundered by historians as a rich source of data for many years,[21] receiving little acknowledgement until relatively recently.[22] Mayhew's contribution as an objective observer of the working classes, despite origins as middle class as those of Engels, has contributed immeasurably to my understanding of these rather invisible immigrants.

A relatively unknown source, but a keen observer of the Irish was the same Alexis de Tocqueville who left such a prophetic account of democracy in America.[23] This French nobleman's understanding and objectivity regarding such matters as the role of the Catholic Church in Ireland, the functions that the aristocracy in Ireland fulfilled (or failed to fulfill), and the condition of the laboring poor make his judgements an invaluable resource. De Tocqueville's writings on England and Ireland have not had the circulation they deserve, possibly because, as he says, he was less willing to pass judgement on a society as old as that of Britain, in contrast to that of the United States which was still in a formative stage.

While scholarly recognition of the social history of the Irish in Britain has been surprisingly slow to emerge, the political history of the "Irish Question" has been well plumbed. The oversight can be explained partly by the fact that once in England, Irish migrants tended to be invisible except when their presence caused annoyance. The English have always found it difficult to acknowledge that the Irish are truly different, not just obstinate and arbitrary in their insistence upon separate recognition and a degree of autonomy within the larger entity. Once in England the Irish tended to retain the habits and customs of people who didn't intend to remain. John Jackson's study of the sociology of the Irish in Britain was a pioneer work which while it broke important ground did not lead to an outpouring of further scholarship.[24] Roger Swift and Sheridan Gilley ended a long silence on the history of the Irish in urban Britain with their volume of essays on the Irish in the Victorian city which brought together in one place a number of previously inaccessible local studies in the social history of the Irish.[25] In Ireland among Irish scholars there was, as in Britain, a preoccupation with political history. A shift has happened in the last twenty years with the founding of the Irish Economic and Social History Society and the emergence of a generation of scholars committed to the social and economic history. Enlightened by new methods and research tools, this new generation is undeterred by factors which kept an older generation from examining the topic. Géaroid O'Tuathaigh's analytical review article on the Irish in England broke new ground on the Irish side, and all subsequent studies must take his into account.[26]

In the nineteenth century, the first general study of the Irish community abroad was undertaken by an emigrant Irish journalist, John Denvir.[27] Denvir, writing in the 1890s, pointed to "a vast change for the better in the surroundings of our people. . . . Irishmen are gradually emerging from the ranks of unskilled labour and becoming more numerous among the artisans, shopkeepers, merchants and professional classes."[28] However, he still felt that his countrymen would never fit into English society until they forgot that they were Irish. Early in this century, Handley's studies of the Irish in Scotland broke important ground.[29] His interpretation, based as it is on the writings of the economic historian, George O'Brien, saw in the political relationship with England the primary reason for the lack of healthy economic growth in Ireland. While eminently readable, his accounts lacked the impact of scholarly analysis which mark later studies. Brenda Collins, more recently, has studied the Irish in Dundee and Paisley, documenting that in 1851 the proportion of Irish-born in the Scottish population was more than twice their proportion in England.[30]

Lynn H. Lees' landmark inquiry into the lives of the London Irish leads to the conclusion that the London Irish were more likely to be permanent migrants because they were more likely to have lost their ties with Ireland.[31] She concluded that the urbanization which strained their institutional and social relationships tended to intensify existing problems. The nature of job opportunities in the London economy would indeed suggest that the person who remained was more likely to become trapped and thus less able to return to Ireland than persons in Manchester and Liverpool. While conceding that Ireland's proximity made migration reversible, her study does not emphasize this factor as important in the social structure developed by the London Irish.

I owe much to William Lowe's study of the Lancashire Irish.[32] Bill was generous in sharing with me his data on aspects of the post-Famine emigration period, data which I used for comparative purposes. Based on an analysis of data from census enumeration books, his study depicts considerably changed conditions following the Famine, including a greater tendency for the Irish to settle permanently in England. Since Lowe's analysis placed little emphasis upon return migration, this would suggest that the Irish had begun to develop their own institutions within the new society. The founding of political clubs such as the Fenians were a result of more permanent settlement patterns. While earlier generations of the Irish willingly provided vocal contributions to political rallies, with notable exceptions, they did not remained sufficiently long in one place to form their own political institutions.

Among general studies of migration there are only a few which recognize the significance of return migration. Among them is that of Thistlethwaite, cited previously. But in the amount of time which has passed since his work appeared, surprisingly little new work has emerged on the subject. An exception to this was Arthur Redford's classic work on labor migration within Britain which first appeared in 1926. While his work was as important as that of Engels in directing my early researches, it does express the view that Irish labor played a crucial role in depressing workers' living standards in the period under consideration.[33] This view has recently been challenged by Jeffrey G. Williamson in a revisionist article which concluded that the Irish did not play a significant role in accounting for rising inequality, lagging real wages, or rapid industrialization.[34]

Michael Piore's study of circular migration between Hispanic regions of the Caribbean and North America was an important influence on the conclusions which I reached regarding the behavior of Irish emigrants.[35] His analysis of the role of temporary migration underpins the structure of this study when he sees the horizon of migrants as temporary because they do not intend to remain, which thus explains why migrants were willing to undertake undesirable jobs in England, but not in Ireland. To those at home the migrant who remained abroad, even if highly successful by the standards of the new society, was a failed migrant because he or she had abandoned their original aim, which was to earn sufficient money to return.

Research on the role of agricultural adaptation in facilitating migrants' ability to rotate seasonally was rare. I was fortunate, however, in finding similarities to what I saw in my research in that of Anand Yang who examined migration into the Bombay textile industry.[36] The decision-making responses of migrants to expected income was examined by John Harris and Michael Todaro in their investigation of rural-urban migration in Kenya.[37] It was shared observations with my husband, John Harris, which first alerted me to the role which temporary migration plays in the lives of agriculturally bound people.

Brinley Thomas's classic study of the relationship between migration and economic growth, an excellent piece of economic analysis, contributed substantially to my theoretical and methodological knowledge of the subject,[38] as did the studies of E.P. Thompson[39] and Eric Hobsbawm[40] which contributed greatly to my understanding of British economic history. I consulted Hobsbawm's works fairly thoroughly, and I am particularly indebted to him for contributing the quotation from which the title of this book is derived. He said that the Irish went to Britain because it was the nearest place that wasn't Ireland, which struck me as apt. Thompson's *The History of the English Working Class* will endure as a classic. His death in 1993 came too soon, but those like myself who owe so much to him will not forget his dream that "causes which were lost in England might, in Asia or Africa, be won."

Among general economic histories of Britain are those of J.H. Clapham[41] and Carlo Cipolla.[42] Each in its own way helped me to understand the processes of industrialization in a modernizing economy. While generally useful, George O'Brien's economic history of Ireland[43] reflected the atmosphere of the post-Independence and Civil War period in Ireland, a viewpoint which saw all Ireland's wrongs as deriving from the connection with Britain. Louis Cullen's[44] wide range of studies in economic history have been valuable reference sources for this study, while T.W. Freeman's study of pre-Famine Ireland contributed regional information and data, and his utilization of mapping techniques influenced me in the visual presentation of my own data.[45] Any study of Ireland's population growth still begins with Kenneth Connell's work.[46] Other scholars will add to his contributions, but it will be a long time before his studies cease to be the first source for scholars wishing to understand the dynamics of Irish population.

Edward Baine's contemporary study of the role of the cotton industry within England's industrializing economy contains careful evaluations of data relating to that industry, as well as some recognition of the role of the Irish working within it.[47]

Potatoes are central to Ireland's nineteenth-century economic history, despite an attempt by Cullen to challenge the significance of their role.[48] For that reason P.M. Austin Bourke's studies of the potato blight and the Irish Famine have been of immense value to me, as was his generosity in sharing his unpublished writings with me and advising my researches at an early stage.[49]

While the concept of economic dualism can be a quagmire I have ventured to make a contribution. First applied to Irish economic history by Patrick Lynch and John Vaizey in their study of the role of the Guinness Brewery in the Irish economy, they were the first to suggest that Ireland had not one, but two distinct economies.[50] J. Joseph Lee countered this, arguing rather the existence of a kind of strata dualism, where he said, money was more or less important according to the necessity for its use.[51] Lee's explanation is now the more accepted one.

Raphael Samuel's studies of the role that ancillary occupations in Britain played in the industrial revolution merit wider recognition than they have received in North America.[52] He and his colleagues at the Historian's Workshop in Cambridge, England, have done valuable work in the field of the social history of individuals for whom the artifacts are so scarce as to discourage the usual forms of scholarship.

The mid-1830s parliamentary investigations of the condition of the poor of England[53] and Ireland[54] provided both a qualitative and quantitative basis for my researches. Both reports were the product of meticulous examination and evaluation of conditions of the Irish in Ireland and England. In Ireland their purpose was to seek to determine whether the extension of a poor law to Ireland would mitigate the deteriorating social condition of the country. There were some misgivings, since it was believed that the English poor law prevented the free mobility of labor, thereby starving the industrial midlands of an adequate labor supply. Despite such warnings, there was a prevailing belief that Irish property should be made to bear the cost of Irish poverty. Irish landlords had become extremely unpopular among the well-informed public as a result of their extravagant living and exploitation of their tenantry, so that it was generally held that this class should be forced to bear more responsibility for deteriorating conditions in Ireland.[55]

Hobsbawm paid tribute to the careful investigation of the report on condition of the Irish poor in Great Britain which is part of the larger English report, terming it a remarkable sociological document deserving of a study itself. Directed by George Cornewall Lewis, the report has the unmistakable stamp of early nineteenth-century Benthamite laissez-faire liberalism, a belief which sought to find utility in "putting the poor to work." Despite what appear now as slightly condescending general attitudes toward the poor, the good sense induced by the teachings of people like Edward Wakefield, permeate its conclusions regarding the role and importance of Irish labor in British society. It is to the credit of these early political economists that the migration was valued eventually for its utility rather than its perceived untidiness. Thomas has pointed out[56] that it is to Edward Wakefield[57] that we must be grateful for converting the early political economists to the belief that a free market for labor should be encouraged, so that emigration from Ireland should not only be encouraged, but that any restrictions on the emigration of skilled labor to the New World should be lifted. He persuaded such as John Stuart Mill, John Revans, Nassau Senior, and George Cornewall Lewis to the belief that emigration must be looked at in a positive sense as a contribution to the growth of a country's economy.

Of particular value to the researcher on migration is the collection of reports on harvest migration contained in the Poor Inquiry.[58] While the evidence collected is relatively systematic, it is not sufficiently consistent to permit any kind of satisfactory reconstruction regarding the incidence and extent of harvest migration. For that reason I have been content to utilize J.H. Johnson's analysis of the parish data on seasonal migration.[59] S.H. Cousens made a series of studies of the demographic data in the pre-Famine period which illuminate regional variations in emigration, emphasizing for the first time the important differences in regional demographic patterns.[60] For the post-Famine period he was able to show that overextended parts of the country population did not diminish, and in fact in parts of western Ireland population was greater in 1871 than it had been in 1851. His explanation for this lay in the persistence of pre-Famine conditions in those regions, conditions such as early age at marriage, continued subdivision of holdings, heavy dependence on the potato, and a persistent grinding poverty.[61] Brendan M. Walsh, writing later, developed these issues further, but was more concerned with the breakdown of the traditional structure of society, particularly after 1870.[62] Both overlooked the significance of seasonal migration, a factor which Cormac Ó'Gráda saw as important in explaining post-Famine differences between the eastern and western regions of the country.[63] Barbara Kerr's largely narrative account was the first to examine Irish seasonal migrants prior to the Famine.[64]

Parliamentary blue book reports, such as those on emigration and handloom weaving, have contributed, although possibly not so much as might have been desired in the area of migration because of the confusion in the public mind between temporary migration and permanent emigration. Two other studies of the late 1830s and early 1840s however must be mentioned. The first, the *Drummond Report,* was a feasibility study for the introduction of a railway system. Ireland in the 1840s was experiencing some degree of healthy economic growth, but so unevenly distributed among the population that the Commissioners warned of the consequences of ignoring the deteriorating condition of the majority of the population.[65] The second, the *Devon Enquiry,* was also helpful.[66]

Ireland's 1841 census was the first in Britain to be carried out along well-planned, thorough, and accurate lines.[67] Most of the quantitative data contained here derives from that report which was the first attempt to assess and measure numbers of Irish seasonal migrants. The Commissioners are to be applauded for the accuracy of their calculations in those days before the computer and calculator. Information derived from the census report made it possible to develop some distributional maps of the country to provide more graphic evidence of the condition of Ireland in this period than could have been obtained from the tables alone.

A valuable source of data on economic conditions in Ireland is found in *Griffith's Valuation Report,*[68] the first of its kind to attempt to document the rental values of Irish property following the introduction of the poor law into Ireland. This report, measuring the rental value of land alone, does not include such items as farm stock. To my knowledge the 1843 version of the report has not been employed for such purposes before, although Kenneth Connell used the next five-year valuation report to indicate the extent of subdivision of land. Since the information contained in it correlates highly with other measures, such as that of the incidence and spread of Class I housing, wage rates, and literacy, I am confident that it is a useful measure for estimating the relative wealth of Irish counties.

The Halliday Collection of pamphlets in the Royal Irish Academy were utilized but proved to be of limited value; as with many other reports, the problem is that one is looking for evidence of people who were almost invisible.

Evidence of conditions in nineteenth-century Ireland appear in the many accounts left by travellers so that it was instructive to study their observations of the people and conditions in the Irish countryside. Some travellers were acute observers, notably H.D. Inglis,[69] the Halls,[70] and Caesar Otway.[71] Other accounts were impressionistic and influenced by the biases of the observers. From Giraldus Cambrensis[72] in the twelfth century to the present, the inquiring tourist in Ireland may be unwittingly subjected to the ancient Irish custom of leg-pulling.

I do not include material from Irish newspapers here because pre-Famine newspapers did not prove as valuable as at first thought. The migrants were after all, mostly invisible to the reading public and newspapers did not, as yet, play an important role in most people's lives. British newspapers reflected both ambivalence and a hostility which many felt toward Ireland and the Irish, a situation which diminished their value as objective sources of information. In L. Perry Curtis's study of the Irish in Victorian caricature, he notes the transformation of the Irish from early depictions as drunken, harmless "paddies" to simianized, threatening creatures, ultimately scapegoats for the anxieties of the Victorians.[73] Newspapers do not appear to have been a possible source of job information for the migrant. Their information network was more informal; one in which the successful worker returned to encourage kin and friend to try their luck next spring. Ireland's "bush telegraph" was far more effective in transmitting information about conditions and opportunities than any newspaper could have been. William Lowe did, however, research newspapers and found them useful in conveying information for the later generation of migrants, a story consistent with the fact that migration after 1850 assumed a far different character than in the earlier period.

In any study of Ireland or of the Irish it is important to understand the role and influence of the Catholic Church, and that is particularly true of those who were Catholic because the Church was the sole institution charged with responsibility for their social and spiritual needs. In order to meet the challenge of the emigrant flock, All Hallowe's College in Dublin was founded in the 1830s to supply the English and Scottish mission field with priests.[74] Their archives yielded some valuable information on the attitudes of the Catholic clergy toward political activity among Irish immigrants, and deserve wider attention from anyone wishing to understand the role of the clergy in the lives of the Irish in Britain.

The Irish Folklore Commission collection deposit at University College, Dublin, was a most useful source, but at times difficult to use because of the idiosyncratic nature of the method of cataloging. What I gained from my study of the material collected there influenced me because the archives were often one of the few windows into the lives of real people who had been themselves seasonal migrants. Desmond McCourt drew attention to the value of such oral history accounts when he said that in a country like Ireland, where continuity has been the basis of peasant life and lore and where the folk memory probes deep into the past, the systematic study of oral tradition recorded from live informants in the field can, if used with circumspection, not merely help to corroborate conventional sources of historical evidence but enhance our knowledge of those aspects of the past barely touched by documentary history.[75] Utilization of the collection requires either intimate and intricate knowledge of the country or advice from someone who can interpret information.[76] For example, an account from Longford indicated that the first thing a harvest worker did in England was to join a society like the Molly McGuires or the Fenians. "If he didn't he wouldn't be let work."[77] Since there was no evidence of such activity prior to 1850 what conclusions can be drawn? And to what extent was it typical of migrants to organize, or was this true only of harvesters from that locality? Furthermore, what does this say about the organization of harvest work among Irish laborers in Britain?

Another account told of a harvester who failed to return on schedule and was reported dead. Not knowing that the news was untrue, his wife remarried rather quickly. On his return one night, he found himself locked out, and so he went to the barn to sleep with the pigs. When the priest came that night to collect a pig that had been promised him, and saw the former husband, he ran in terror because he thought he'd seen a ghost.[78]

Migrants were sometimes recruited through a contract labor system, called the "gaffer" system, after the leader who was called the gaffer. An eighty-nine-year-old man from Clare in 1939 remembered the following story about them:

> [It was the gaffer's custom to] go around to so many farmers and enquire if they had any hay to cut. He'd make bargains to cut their hay and be paid by them directly. He'd then go to the hiring market and get 20–40 spalpeens and "knock all the work out of them." He used to set them against each other to see who could last the longest. He took most of the money for himself and the spalpeens would be badly paid—sometimes he'd knock off work in the morning and they would lose a day's wages.[79]

His story may be an indication that the system was losing its former useful function because we know that prior to the 1840s the gaffer, by assuming some of the risk, facilitated harvest migration for individuals who otherwise could not afford to go, either for lack of money to finance the journey or lack of language in which to negotiate terms.

Contemporary literature was another useful but cautionary source. While few seasonal workers appear in literary accounts, two early nineteenth-century authors, Maria Edgeworth and William Carleton, illuminated Irish peasant society, the former from above and the latter from below. Edgeworth reflected the concern of landowners who cared about the well-being of their tenants. She writes reflecting viewpoints of the ascendancy class looking downward and outward, with a remarkable ability to portray the complexities of Irish cultural life in such books as *Castle Rackrent* (1800), *The Absentee* (1812), *Ormond* (1817), and in her father's *Memoirs* (1820). Edgeworth saw the problems inherent in the absentee syndrome, one that resulted in feckless behavior on the part of landlords and uneasy relations between that class and their tenants. Her ability to do this effectively presented the deteriorating condition of Ireland to a literate public throughout the English-speaking world. Carleton was born a peasant. His interest was also in the Big House (but from the outside) and in the peasantry from within. He wrote about his class because, as he said,

> I found them [the peasantry] a class unknown in literature, unknown by their own landlords, and unknown by those in whose hands much of their destiny was placed. If I became the historian of their habits and manners, their feelings, their prejudices, their superstitions and their crimes; if I have attempted to delineate their moral, religious and physical state, it was because I saw no persons willing to undertake a task which surely must be looked upon as an important one.[80]

Carleton also depicted the darker, uglier side of peasant life, where protest against conditions gave rise to the agrarian secret societies whose members sought to teach responsibility to those who controlled the land, societies which, to paraphrase Hobsbawm, functioned as the collective bargaining of the poor in the early nineteenth century.

Both sought through their writings to improve the system of land tenure by educating landlords to their responsibilities. At a time when there was an absence of effective political leadership in Ireland both writers sought effectively through literary means to draw attention to Ireland's wrongs.

Conclusions

Most studies of the Irish in England have not been concerned with their role as temporary migrants, nor with the migration as a rational response to conditions. In a historiographical survey of the Irish in Victorian cities, Sheridan Gilley and Roger Swift state that the Irish who went to England were those least able to afford the trip to America. While I will not dispute that this may have been true following the Famine, it is my belief that the majority of migrants prior to 1845 either did not remain or did not intend to remain and thus were temporary migrants. They saw themselves as taking best advantage of the nearest opportunity, but were ready to go to America when opportunities shrank.

In England the Irish were well-known as wage cutters and strikebreakers. They out-worked and under-lived the native English, working harder and longer than they had at home because of the temporary nature of the employment and the reward of better wages. The result of this was that by the 1840s what may have appeared in Ireland as a rural population firmly attached to the land, was in fact a rurally based labor force with widespread seasonal or recurrent participation in a foreign labor market. The effects of the Famine fractured this attachment to the land and transformed the nature of the migration. While this pattern of ready mobility and response to opportunity among the Irish transformed them into a labor group quick to respond to new and changing opportunities, migrants were on the whole prevented from entering into or remaining in jobs which encouraged upward mobility, so that they tended not to integrate into British industrial life.

Migration also provided the capital to emigrate to North America, and many persons who were initially temporary migrants emigrated permanently when the differences between what they could earn in Ireland and what they could earn in England narrowed, thereby making seasonal shifts less profitable. Evidence here suggests the need to look again at the picture of the American Irish as arriving with no prior experience of urban industrial life. Seasonal migrants who re-emigrated were no longer really in the class of peasant portrayed in most studies of the American Irish, but were already familiar with taking risks, and well able to calculate the costs and benefits of emigration.

Thus migration to England contributed both to the transformation of the Irish countryside and of its people, which in turn also influenced the nature and experience of the Irish who came to America. This study seeks to tell the story of the migration by placing it in a coherent context.

Profile of the

There are a great many hundred who go every year to England, we call them spalpeens, in England Cokers, to get in the harvest. . . . There is one thing remarkable of these men, they are the most industrious of our people, those who return generally bring home from three to six to seven guineas, and it has been observed that when in England they have once converted their labour into gold, they will almost perish with hunger rather than change a guinea for their relief. Their economy is this, they plant their potatoes before they set out, then lock up their cabin door with a padlock, the husband goes to England (they pay six shillings for their passage). The wife and children set out upon their travels in Ireland and subsist by begging. When they return their winter stock of potatoes is ready for their subsistence. He pays his landlord from L3 to L4.10 for the rent of his cabin and potatoes and the keep of a cow, the most enormous price, and if he has had a good harvest perhaps there is something left toward buying a porket or a goat.

EDWARD WILLES
Chief Baron of the Exchequer, on circuit, Ireland, c.1759

Migration: Those Who Left

Migration optimally is a mechanism of adjustment which functions to reduce inequalities between two areas. This chapter examines the extent to which seasonal migration functioned in this way for the Irish people who migrated between Ireland and England prior to 1850. By following a regular pattern of temporary migration to England, the rural people of Ireland were, at least temporarily, able to preserve valued aspects of their existing social system. For the migrants, this early nineteenth-century migration was more positive adjustment than forced choice.

Those who left were not hapless peasants fleeing to Britain out of dire necessity because the evidence confirms that most were well aware of the range of choices available, and that they chose those options which produced the greatest number of desired benefits. Chief among such benefits was the ability to continue to live on the land; to maintain valued ties of kinship and community; and to continue to exercise autonomy about decisions affecting their welfare.

Increasingly, however, the decision to migrate was forced upon many of the Irish by the decline of options and opportunities available at home. Cormac Ó'Gráda has made a conservative estimate that perhaps two-thirds of those working in the agricultural sector of Ireland in the 1830s and 1840s were dependent primarily on wage labor for their living.[1] This means that the majority of persons engaged in agriculture in Ireland were vulnerable to the vagaries of a fluctuating market system because in the majority of Irish counties wage labor was available from only two to at the most about seven months in the year.[2] It is clear then why so many had to seek income from other sources and why migration became such a vital component of Irish life. Unemployment and under-employment took their toll, causing the majority of the population as well as the country to slide further into becoming an economic slum, a situation which reached its nadir by the 1840s, culminating in the cataclysm of the Great Famine.

A decade later, the results of the Famine had transformed expectations so drastically that what previously had been temporary migration for most persons was now more likely to be a permanent leave-taking. By the end of the nineteenth century, Ireland was a demographic abnormality, a country in which the most enterprising and energetic of its young were reared to emigrate. Seasonal migrants still existed, and indeed continued to play an important, if negative role on the western seaboard,[3] but by now permanent emigration to North America, and later to Australia, began to be the norm. The result was that every census but one between 1841 and 1961 recorded population decrease.

Why did this change in migration patterns happen, and what did it mean? I will attempt to answer these questions by looking at the broader picture of conditions in Ireland in the years of accelerating decline before the Famine. Two aspects of conditions in this period relate directly to this study: (1) The development of connective ties between Ireland and Britain, fostering Ireland's development as an export economy and making survival increasingly dependent upon conditions abroad; and (2) the fundamental social changes taking place between those who controlled the land and those who occupied it. Both the landlord class and their tenants were heading toward a crisis which would determine Ireland's future, although few would have predicted that an event as catastrophic as widespread successive failures of the potato crop would create the conditions effecting that final transformation.

Historical Antecedents of Migration in Ireland

Reconstructing the situation which led to and sustained the outflow of persons in this pre-Famine period is hampered by a relative lack of substantive regional information on conditions in Ireland. In England enumerations of the numbers of Irish persons present prior to the collection of official counts vary so widely as to be unreliable. Nevertheless, Irish laborers appear to have been a distinctive presence there from early times, but it was not until they began to be considered a threat to the wages and living standards of the indigenous work force that serious attention was focused on their presence. This was in the form of a governmental commission established in the 1830s to discover whether limits should be placed on the Irish coming to England. Their report concluded that this was the first time in history that such a "poor and mendicant population," had spread themselves as a kind of substratum beneath a more civilized community, monopolizing all the lower departments of manual labor.[4] If the Commissioners' recognition of the extent and nature of the population movement they were examining was somewhat rudimentary, this was even more true of Ireland where seasonal migrants were almost invisible to the official world until the 1841 census.

It is not possible then to ring these birds of passage, these seasonal migrants. As individuals they eluded detection, and as groups their effect was distorted. It is possible, however, to trace patterns of their movement to help explain the nature of the migration.

Movement of some sort or other was hardly a new phenomenon for the Irish people. Historically there is the unmistakable impression that migration was resorted to more often by the Irish than by the English.[5] On the European continent and in America the westward movement of peoples developed into a frontier tradition, offering greater opportunities for the exercise of talent to restless but otherwise thwarted individuals. Movement was usually followed by the establishment of settled institutions. The Celtic peoples, the root stock of those who eventually became the Irish, had participated in such movements centuries earlier when they sought to evade the expanding Roman Empire by migrating to its outer fringes. But possibly because they never developed settled institutions they were without the means to fully satisfy the frontier mentality within their small island nation, and so retained the need to be on the move.

The arrival of Christianity in Ireland provided an outlet for their transient nature when it preached the idea of a martyrdom of exile for Christ. Irish Christians accepted the precept to go forth and preach the gospel with such vigor that in pre–tenth-century Europe Irish scholars were known to ask for no more than food and lodging in exchange for sharing their learning.

When the Normans attempted to subdue and pacify their Irish neighbors, between the twelfth and fifteenth centuries, many Irish responded by abandoning grassy lowland areas to move up into more mountainous regions, preferring an impoverished liberty to assimilation on the conqueror's terms. This may to some extent have been because they desired to escape the proximity of their new neighbors, or it may have resulted from either an inability or an unwillingness to exercise two other alternatives: to give voice (dissent) to their frustration, or to be loyal (submit) to authority.[6]

By the sixteenth century the English sought once again to impose their Elizabethan form of civility on the Irish. The Gaelic way of life appeared as barbarous to the Elizabethans as that of the North American Indians with whom they were also then coming into contact, and conflict between warring tribal factions within Ireland made the country increasingly difficult as well as expensive to control. Nonetheless, the English provoked resentment with their cruel treatment attempting to bring their form of modernization to Gaelic Ireland.[7] A series of rebellions against the crown, beginning among the descendants of the Normans, began to make retaining the sister island an unremittingly costly undertaking for the English crown. There was an international aspect to their fears also with the development of a network of trade links between Anglo-Norman families and the French, and Gaelic families and the Spanish, both of whom were traditional enemies of England. Determined to curtail the great expense of governing the country and allay the fears of trade links, Henry VIII persuaded the Gaelic chieftains to surrender their titles, exchanging them for English titles.[8] As Henry well knew, holding title from the crown implied its loss after unsuccessful rebellion. What followed were extensive confiscations of both Anglo-Irish and tribal lands, resulting in the first extensive escapes to Europe of Irish titleholders.

Resentment against the behavior of the English crown so accumulated throughout these years that by the seventeenth century, rather than submit to English authority, the Irish gentry class fled in increasing numbers to the continent, thereby reinforcing a pattern whereby exile was preferred to submission. Those who fled Ireland usually joined foreign armies or the bureaucracies of foreign governments where they were commonly known as Wild Geese, echoing the theme of temporary residence. Trade connections between Ireland and the continent facilitated this exit, as well as increasing the fears of the English merchant classes, now becoming a significant force in parliamentary affairs. Despite leaving Ireland, however, the Wild Geese never abandoned their intentions to return, and as they fought in foreign battles or served foreign monarchs, their songs reinforced their belief that they would eventually return to liberate the homeland.

Although most of these persons were either decayed gentry or their retainers, and as such were hardly representative of the kind of person who sought work in Britain during the period of this study, the Wild Geese were a symbol that flight from oppression was possible. So a sense of historical tradition further embedded exit as an option into the consciousness of the Irish people. Irish folksongs and stories, especially those called *aisling* or vision poems, popular in the eighteenth century,[9] were constant reminders of the glorious past and the promise of eventual future liberation from oppression.

By the eighteenth century liberation was more likely to come from economic than political causes because this was a generally promising time for the Irish economy. The flourishing English market drew increasingly on Ireland, giving promise of continued prosperity for Anglo-Irish trade. It was an unequally distributed prosperity, however, both geographically and socially, and within that factor lay a fundamental unsoundness in the Irish economy.

Nineteenth-century population growth, primarily concentrated in areas which could no longer support the old economic order, would be the underlying force which would accelerate migration patterns established in the previous century. By the late eighteenth century there were already sizeable Irish settlements, particularly in London and to a lesser extent in industrializing Lancashire. After 1815, outflows from Ireland of persons seeking work increased tremendously as a result of cutbacks in Irish agricultural production resulting from the cessation of hostilities with the French.

Kinds of Migrants

Pre–Industrial Revolution changes in agricultural technology resulted in modifications in the hiring practices of farmers in both Ireland and in England. Substantial farmers sought to minimize their expenditure on farmhands by hiring seasonal laborers, and smaller farmers drew on their families and neighbors rather than having to feed a household of farmworkers year round. The new hiring pattern served to encourage the development of networks among potential workers, and this in turn facilitated the continuation of seasonal migration by establishing information networks on job opportunities. So while accounts of Irish persons migrating to England for work in the eighteenth century tend to suggest that their numbers were not great, the slack created by a generally uneven demand for laborers in Ireland was taken up by growing demands for seasonal workers in England. In view of the fact that all that was required of workers was that they have strong backs and be willing to work, the sector in which they worked was determined by the availability of work, so that in the eighteenth century, Irish seasonal workers were primarily in agriculture and in the nineteenth they tended to be in construction-connected employment.

Seasonal harvest laborers were target workers in the narrowest sense of persons who work abroad until they had saved a desired or targeted sum of money, a sum which would be used to purchase a farm, additional land, or—as the noose of economic necessity tightened—to repay the debts contracted before leaving in the spring: monetary obligations to the landlord, the tithe proctor, or the moneylender. A County Mayo landlord testified before a parliamentary committee in 1833 how he collected debts from those of his tenants who were seasonal laborers. "I have sometimes been holding an office at the period of their return in a town upon their way, and they have come and paid me what they owed before they went home to their families."[10]

A fictional account of a work party of sixteen cottier farmers (smallholders who owed labor in return for their land) from Athlone in Connacht seeking work suggests both the manner in which seasonal migrants sought work and how decisions about return were made.[11] Arriving at Holyhead, eight sought industrial work in Chester, Lancashire, and the rest walked through Wales toward Lincolnshire, the most frequently cited destination for Irish harvest workers. Their destination was a landowner, "known to be kindly disposed toward Irish Catholics." On the way through the town of Denbigh they joined a hiring fair.

> The next morning they placed themselves on the circular steps of the great market cross. . . . Their purpose was made known by the seats they occupied, for such is the practice of labourers who want employ. They received the usual greeting of contemptuous looks and sneers; but remained not otherwise molested, till a farmer came up who wanted two men to assist him in a press of work. He chose the father and son whose name was Moylan; agreed with them for wages at his hay and fallows; "And then," he said, "I will let you some wheat to reap if we can agree, if not, you will be no worse off than now; for you will be in time for harvest in the fens, where I take it, you are going."[12]

The Moylans decided to remain, so the remaining six Irishmen continued their journey toward the fen country. In Newcastle under Lyme they were offered employment in the potteries; three refused because they wished to return home following the harvest. The remaining three were brothers who decided to work there for a while. Calculating that "by laying by half of their wages for three years, they might return three of the richest men in their humble neighbourhood. They departed for Etruria after requiring a promise from the others that they would return that way to the port whence they should sail for Ireland."[13]

While fictitious, the story illustrates the fact that migrants probably should not be bracketed into tightly differentiated categories. Those who went toward the industrial north were probably accustomed to doing so every year, since the rest, headed for the fens area, were going to a farmer who had employed them before. The fact that five of those were willing to take other employment offered along the way suggests how open migrants were to opportunity.

Work-life migrants, much like the seventeenth-century and eighteenth-century Wild Geese, were influenced by a strong drive to return, always buoyed by the hope that conditions at home would change. Irish persons resident in Britain customarily sent their children back to be reared by grandparents, as can be seen by considerable numbers of English-born children resident in Ireland appearing in the census.[14]

One conclusion that does seem clear is that the temporary character of the migration flow appears to have created a sharp distinction between work on the one hand and the social identity of the worker on the other. The work performed in the other community was purely instrumental, a means to gather income to be taken back to Ireland and used to fulfill or enhance the migrant's role within Ireland's social structure. For that reason, work was purely a means to an end. Noting this of more recent temporary migrants, Michael Piore has said, "In this sense, the migrant is initially a true economic man, probably the closest thing in real life to the *homo economicus* of economic theory."[15]

The Implications of Growing Trade Links between Ireland and Britain

A generally improving standard of living in late eighteenth-century Ireland was encouraged by market ties developing between the two countries as early as the mid seventeenth century. At that time the demand for Irish goods in Britain was stimulated by two factors: the growth of London as a city, and the expansion of the woolen industry in England.[16]

The provisioning of London was secured by an elaborate structure of economic institutions and activities and many of the farmers who sent their produce to the London market geared their land to commodity production in a thoroughly "modern" fashion. In short, whereas pre-industrial cities might grow large and powerful without any way undermining the structure of traditional society, a city like London in the later seventeenth century was so constituted sociologically, demographically and economically that it could well reinforce and accelerate incipient change. What might be called the demonstration effect of London's wealth and growth, for instance, played an important part in engendering changes elsewhere.[17]

This effect was recognized early, and is well illustrated by the remark of a contemporary, John Houghton, who wrote, "The bigness and great consumption of London doth not only encourage the breeders of provisions and higglers thirty miles off but even to four score miles."[18] Deane and Cole suggest that the rise in agricultural productivity per head in the first half of the eighteenth century in southern England alone may have been as high as 25 percent.[19] London as it grew was supplied by cattle from Ireland, brought there to be fattened in the grain-producing counties on the periphery of the city. Growing demand for cattle for export led both to the development of economic interrelationships between the two countries and to a greater shift away from cultivation to livestock rearing in the southeastern counties of Leinster and the southern province of Munster. The port cities of Waterford and Cork had, throughout the eighteenth century, a vigorous export trade in salted beef, hides, and butter to the West Indies and to North America.

Ireland's potential as a competitive cattle-producing country had since the second half of the seventeenth century been of concern to merchant interests in the English parliament. They sought to limit Irish trade by imposing restrictions on exports of certain goods which were perceived to be in competition with those of England. Thus the intention of the Cattle Acts of 1663 and 1667 was to keep Irish cattle out of England, and the Navigation Acts of 1663 and 1671 to curtail the nascent export trade by redirecting all shipping through England and on English ships.[20] Attempts to restrain Irish trade led to flourishing smuggling enterprises, from ports on the southern coast to Spain, Portugal, and France; countries whose merchants and governments were always more than willing to inconvenience their British rivals. The imposition of these laws in turn provided escape hatches for Irish rebels and also encouraged disrespect for laws not seen to be in Ireland's best interests.

By the midpoint of the eighteenth century most of the economic restrictions were either lifted or largely ignored, and Irish landlords sought ways to participate in the growing export industries. Eric Almquist's work on County Mayo indicates that in the seventeenth and eighteenth centuries rural industry tended to locate in regions where the peasants were relatively landless, encouraged by landlords who wished to ensure the steady payment of their rents.[21] The new export industries played an important role in supplementing incomes, already becoming increasingly precarious where population growth was straining the resources of the general population.

Despite implied restrictions on trade and navigation, the laws were largely either circumvented or ignored so that the 1730s mark the onset of a long period of growth and further development of Anglo-Irish trade. Beef exports rose, as did grain, which by the 1780s had become an essential export to urban regions of England. Grain and butter exports soared both in volume and price during the French Wars. The linen trade, which had never undergone restrictions, grew and flourished, accounting for about half of total exports by the end of the century.[22]

The increasing market orientation of the economy meant that it was closely allied with and tied to market conditions elsewhere. It is hardly surprising in a situation where survival depended increasingly on external demand that food producers in Ireland sought to shift more of their production into export products, and their domestic consumption away from grain and into a more productive foodstuff. That food was, of course, the lowly potato. And what developed from the shift to a potato diet was a most striking paradox in Irish social history, as Kenneth Connell has remarked, that a people whose wretchedness was so widely acknowledged and known were so remarkably well nourished.[23]

Stages in the Adoption of the Potato Diet

Ireland's social history cannot be written without focusing upon the role of the potato economy in the development and eventual deterioration of the physical well-being of the Irish people. Cullen has demonstrated that while possibly too much stress has been placed upon it as an active agent of change, the potato diet played a significant role, although it was somewhat more passive than others have believed. He argues that the widespread adoption of the potato was a response to population increase, not a cause of it.[24]

Austin Bourke explains the adoption of the potato diet in four stages. In stage one, dating roughly from 1590, when it was probably introduced into the country, to 1675, the potato came into use as a supplement to cereal foods. Its most obvious advantage at that time was as a standby against famine, because the potato was most abundant in wet seasons when grain crops were poor in quality and quantity. Potatoes had a definite advantage over grain in that they could be eaten without processing, whereas the miller had to be paid in cash or kind for converting oats to meal or wheat to flour.[25] Bourke says, "Climate and soil, per se, were well suited to the potato over much of northwest Europe, but the meteorological differential which favoured the potato against cereal crops in wet years operated most strongly in Ireland's humid climate."[26]

In stage two, from 1675 to 1750, the potato came into general use as a winter food for the increasing numbers of poorer people. Now the potato showed obvious advantages aiding its adoption: food production per acre of potatoes was approximately four times greater than that of grain crops, and that, combined with the fact that potatoes could also be consumed without further processing services, made a winning combination. At this time evidence shows that the general population ate potatoes only a part of the year, from August to March or April, because storage was difficult beyond that time. But as time passed and population grew, economic pinch became squeeze for the peasantry, and the period when the potato crop in the spring was exhausted posed greater dangers to people's survival if they had no alternative food crop to shift to during what is called in African countries today, the Hungry Time. The midsummer distress varied in intensity from year to year, but it was a regular feature of the Irish social scene for at least thirty years before the great failure of the potato crop in 1845. Where it occurred in areas of widespread dependence on a potato diet, people were forced to purchase their food, forcing them into greater dependence upon cash income supplements. Where local opportunities to earn from such supplements as domestic industry, or stock raising, or even poteen making[27] diminished, people were forced to resort to credit at rates of interest sometimes as high as 75 percent.

The third stage, when as Bourke says the Irish advanced in the "sinister trend toward monoculture," occurred in the years from 1750 to 1810. During this period potatoes became the staple diet of small farmers for the greater part of the year and an important part of the diet for all classes.[28] Arthur Young, the agricultural economist who travelled through the country in the late eighteenth century, noted that the cultivation of the potato had increased greatly during the twenty years prior to his 1776–79 tour.[29]

It may also have been during this period that changes in the cultivation of the potato aided new aspects of Irish social development. By lengthening the interval between planting and harvest would-be seasonal migrants were able to leave their home plots earlier and return later in the agricultural season from work elsewhere, either in Ireland or in England. The practice of transhumance, called *booleying* and long-practiced in Ireland, may also have encouraged cultivators to plant their crops earlier to enable them to take the cattle to more fertile upland pastures earlier in the year. A writer in 1794 observed that cottiers were planting their potatoes earlier in the season because of their obligations to their landlords.[30]

Planting potatoes in the technique known as "lazybed," considered elsewhere in Europe to be characteristically Irish, also facilitated seasonal movement.[31] Although some consider the term the scornful epithet of the English, Bourke says it is far more likely that it was derived from the French *laisser* meaning to do least damage to the soil. In this form of cultivation, the earth was piled in ridges with trenches between. This technique required more intensive cultivation in the initial stages, but then needed almost no maintenance until the potatoes were harvested in October or November. Estyn Evans suggests that the name may derive from the fact that the sod under the ridge is not dug and so undisturbed; the bed is built up on top of the grass with sod and soil dug from the trenches between the ridges.[32] Not only does this method make full use of the humus and decaying grasses, but it prevents the potato sets from becoming waterlogged and rotting by raising the bed above the water table. In addition, the unbroken sod checks the downwash of valuable plant nutrients. Trenches or furrows between the ridges provide open drains and the lazybeds are always carefully aligned with the slope of the land, thus providing for minimal soil erosion.

The years between 1810 and 1845 mark the fourth and last stage, a period of decline down to the Famine. Potato varieties deteriorated, the crop failed more often, and suffering increased with each failure.[33] By now the unappetizing lumper potato was in widespread use, as can be seen in Figure 2.1, so that the full disadvantages of the potato diet were evident.[34] Edward Wakefield, on tour in 1812, noted that the "belly full"

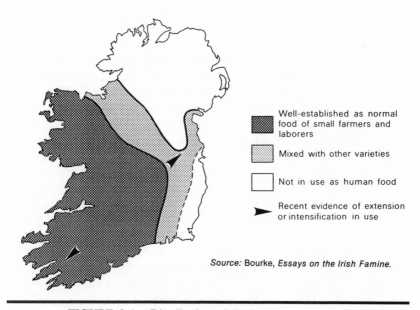

Well-established as normal
food of small farmers and
laborers

Mixed with other varieties

Not in use as human food

Recent evidence of extension
or intensification in use

Source: Bourke, *Essays on the Irish Famine.*

FIGURE 2.1.   Distribution of the lumper potato as human food, c.1835.

of potatoes which had been the portion of country people thirty years before, was now a thing of the past.[35]

Other aspects of the agricultural economy strongly influenced Irish social conditions as well. The shift to production for an export market, beginning between around 1760 to 1770, changed the relationship between tenants and laborers to their landlords. As the importance of rural persons as laborers increased, this lessened the restraints on population growth which had existed under the previous system of subsistence agriculture. Another influence lessening restraints on population growth lay in the deterioration of the land-tenure system, a system which had its roots in the sixteenth century when the Brehon system of law was abolished. Effacing old titles to the land placed the peasant's claims to land on a purely contractual, albeit modern basis.

Relations within the family also changed. Until the 1760s a father's control of the land ensured his dominant position both in the household and in the prevailing farming system; a son only obtained his share at his father's death. But by the mid-eighteenth century the source of patriarchal power was eroded with the expanding number of capitalist farming males who could earn income through wage labor without directly controlling land. This broke a socially necessary preventive check on marriage and thus on population growth.[36] Because there existed no other rights than those contractual rights in the land, after 1760 a young man with only a laborer's income could rent land to grow potatoes and, subsisting on them, pay rent as high or higher than his father. In this way the ability to pay rent conferred on the son the same right to the land as the father.[37] The shift in the son's role vis-à-vis that of his father undoubtedly also contributed to the release of traditional restraints on physical movement, which in turn facilitated an energetic and ambitious young person's desire to migrate when opportunity offered.

The land-tenure system, aimed at maximizing the returns of landlords, resulted in rentals quadrupling between 1760 and 1815, although agricultural prices increased in that period by only half that amount. While exports rose by 40 percent between 1779 and 1815, Cullen says that the rise in prosperity was due more to the rise in prices than to an increase in volume.[38] Wartime demands, inflation, and poor harvests in the first decades of the nineteenth century kept prices at artificially high levels, setting the stage for an economic slump consequent on the termination of hostilities on the continent by 1815. Prices fell sharply and by 1820 there was major economic crisis throughout Ireland.

Serious monetary deflation added to the depression in some regions. With the suspension of payments in gold in 1797 had come an increase in the circulation of bank notes.[39] Then, in 1819, when the gold standard was reinstated, the Bank of Ireland restricted credit. Merchants who were already vulnerable because of falling prices caused many of the banks to fail when, suspecting that their banks were not solvent, they demanded Bank of Ireland notes. Notes that were already in short supply. This action may also have provided a stimulus to migration. It was said at the time that the deflation caused some landlords to insist upon payment in coin, best obtainable in England.

The province of Munster was particularly hard hit by events. The banking crisis was largely confined to this province when wartime prices, which had been at their highest there, then fell most sharply after 1815.[40] After 1821 the Munster counties experienced some degree of demographic stagnation due to a steady trickle of emigrants. What appears to have occurred is that landlords ejected unprofitable tenants, thereby increasing the numbers of redundant laborers. In 1841 persons from the province of Munster were the least likely to migrate elsewhere in Ireland, suggesting that reduced opportunity there twenty or thirty years earlier resulted in permanent out-migration from Munster earlier than from all the other counties except Ulster.[41]

Agriculture was dominated by farmers who held their leases from landlords or middlemen, so that when prices fell these farmers contracted their tillage acreage, shifted to pasturage and thus lessened their demand for labor. With the onset of economic hard times the payment of rents declined, defaults being most common in regions of predominantly tillage farms. There was an additional incentive for farmers with capital to increase their profits by shifting to raising pasturage stock with improvements in transport. Steamshipping facilitated trade between Ireland and Britain when it was introduced after 1819; and the building of railroads and to some extent the Grand and Royal Canals in the 1820s resulted in the reduction of inland transport costs. With improved transport it was no longer necessary to walk cattle and sheep to their destination, although the stories of William Carleton suggest that the custom continued long after this period. Delayed journeys because of unfavorable winds were practically eliminated by steamshipping. Improved transport clearly also encouraged the exodus of people as well as stock. Seasonal migrants were now able to travel to England or Scotland for rates as low as sixpence.

Despite improvements in some sectors of the economy, the general population did not appear to benefit. As Bourke says, "Every improvement in transport facilitated the movement of agricultural products so much in demand in Britain and forced the Irish tenant to fall back more and more on a poor potato diet."[42] Severe privation was in no way unusual in early nineteenth-century Europe, but Irish poverty, involving as it did such a considerable proportion of the population, drew the attention of many who sought its cause and cure. In 1841, 70 percent of the rural population of Ireland consisted of laborers and smallholders with less than five acres of land, although there were regional variations ranging from 60 percent in the eastern counties to 75 percent in County Mayo in the far west.[43] Indeed Ireland was to Europe of its day what sub-Saharan Africa has become in the present century—a region with intractable problems. And as with Africa's problems in the present, analyses and proposed cures kept scholars busy. Indeed, as T.W. Freeman, the geographer, has suggested, the weight of ink expended upon the accumulation of evidence examining Ireland's ills and proposing cures should have sunk that island into the Atlantic long before now. Studies proliferated, from continental travellers such as Alexis de Tocqueville to parliamentary committees; but all condemned the system of land tenure as bearing primary institutional responsibility for the deterioration glaringly obvious by the second decade of the nineteenth century. Exaggerating only slightly, De Tocqueville said of the system of land tenure, "Here there is no yeomanry—no agricultural capitalist; no degree between landlord and labourer; the words 'peasantry' and 'poor' synonymously employed."[44] He believed that the fault lay with an irresponsible aristocracy: "If you want to know what can be done by the spirit of conquest and religious hatred combined with the abuses of aristocracy, but without its advantages, go to Ireland." Nevertheless he did observe changing attitudes, noting that while Irish peasants in the past had never been known to love their landlords, they had previously "submitted with a patience they no longer possess."[45] This indication of changing attitudes toward authority showed a people who were beginning to implement new strategies to ameliorate their condition.

The faults of Irish landlords, as the fair-minded historian, W.E.H. Lecky, has pointed out, were really more negligence than oppression. Notwithstanding that, to most estate owners their stock of cattle, horses, and hounds were more important to them than was the welfare of their tenantry. Hely Dutton, writing in 1824 condemned the landlords who knew the names, dam and sire, of every one of their hounds, but knew nothing of their tenants.[46] Priority for most great landlords was to be sure of their rents, to get them punctually, and with as little trouble as possible. To achieve this with minimal expenditure of capital and energy, they had in earlier times divided their estates, letting them out to middlemen who in turn often sublet, so that between the owner of the soil and the actual occupier there might be as many as three or four persons, each obtaining a portion of rentals which grew higher at every succeeding transaction.[47]

The question arises then as to how or why land tenure relationships between owners and renters differed from that of England where the ownership of private property was concentrated in at least as few hands as it was in Ireland. The middleman system may have made the difference because as long as it appeared to function well — and by well I mean that landlords got their rents more or less regularly — the gentry had no incentive to improve the condition of their tenants. But the system exacerbated existing population problems when it encouraged a fee-paying tenantry to multiply.

On the positive side, James Donnelly says that in a system where few estate owners wished to be resident on their properties, these middlemen were the next best thing to landlords with capital to invest in property improvements.[48] To its credit, the middleman system also reduced the degree of risk incurred from the wide fluctuation in prices and yields characterizing eighteenth-century Ireland because when long-term investment prospects seemed poor, farms were granted to middlemen on leases of from two to three "lives," or thirty-one years as the best return available to the landlord class.[49] Arthur Young explained that the middleman "would at least improve a spot around his own residence, whereas the mere cottar can do nothing."[50] Young, did however, have a very low opinion of the efforts of middlemen which often amounted, he said, to little more than keeping a pack of wretched hounds on which they wasted their time and money.

When prosperity collapsed in the wake of an end to the French Wars, many landlords refused to lower or abate rentals of middlemen who were in financial difficulties. This contributed to the system's eventual demise and set the stage for better management of Irish estates. As long as a general uncertainty about markets had prevailed, the largest landholders advocated long leases as a means of encouraging property improvement, but when conditions changed so did their opinions about retaining the system so that many landlords began to regard long leases as a disincentive to investment. It was by now apparent that the middlemen holders of long leases often took little interest in the management of their lands and that longer leases also prevented landlords from profiting by raising rents so as to benefit from market upturns. Donnelly says that real reforms of estate management began in the 1830s when, in order to increase rentals or make payments more certain, the owners began to consolidate small farms and make improvements.[51]

While scholars do not as yet agree as to whether Irish rentals in general were unjustifiably high in this period, Ó'Gráda found for the post-Famine period that rents in areas of high seasonal migration were higher than elsewhere in the countryside, suggesting that returns from migration may also have had an impact in raising the level of rents prior to the Famine also.[52]

Middlemen were the *squireens* portrayed in scornful words by contemporaries such as Arthur Young and the novelist, Maria Edgeworth — persons who let their undertenants multiply by subdivision among a land-hungry population, while they lived extravagantly and often elsewhere.[53] Edgeworth's didactic novels of Irish life supplement the picture of mismanaged Irish estates. In *Castle Rackrent* she portrayed, in comic fiction, the declining fortunes of the Rackrent family through several generations. The Rackrent family were drunken, slovenly, ignorant, and excessively fond of ruinous litigation. "As for the law," relates their estate steward, the narrator of the story, "no man dead or alive, ever loved it so well. He had once sixteen suits pending at a time. . . . He used to boast that he had a lawsuit for every letter of the alphabet." In her novel, *The Absentee,* Lord and Lady Clonbrony preferred to make their way in fashionable London society rather than attend to their Irish estates. While they spent beyond their means, their tenants were ground down by a corrupt agent under pressure to meet the pressing financial needs of his employers. Their son and heir, determined to make his father recognize his responsibility, eventually forced him to return to Ireland to right all wrongs and free the tenants from oppression.

While statistics and testimony in parliamentary blue books multiplied, novels such as these were having their influence on the reading public, so that by the 1830s readers were well aware that Ireland was a social and economic basket case. So effective were they that Sir Walter Scott sought to do the same in his Waverly novels, writing them with the conviction, he said, that "something might be attempted in my country of the same kind as Miss Edgeworth so fortunately achieved for Ireland."[54] Ivan Turgenev, the Russian writer, claimed to be "an unconscious disciple of Miss Edgeworth in setting out on his literary career," seeing in the exploitation of the Irish peasant a parallel to the treatment of Russian peasants.[55] John Ruskin declared that there was more to be learned of Irish politics from *The Absentee* than from a thousand volumes of blue books. Even George III, after having read *Castle Rackrent,* said, "I know something now of my Irish subjects."[56]

A kind of requiem for the middleman system was pronounced in 1839 by Caesar Otway, when he said,

> Let people say what they will, they [the middlemen] were in their time useful, and without whom, bad as Ireland is, it would be worse than it is. They expended capital which either the owners of the soil could or would not expend. They became the stock-farmers of the country, and introduced

the fine breed of long-wooled sheep. . . . It is the hunting, racing, duelling, punch-drinking carousing squireen middleman that has been, and is, a nuisance in the land; who takes ground on speculation and sublets it, who gambles in lands as he does on the cards.[57]

In England the gentry may have been equally alienated in their sympathies from the "swinish multitude" who paid them rent, but there were more alternatives for the English poor in the rapidly expanding industrial and agricultural economy. Urbanization and industrialization offered opportunities (even when resisted), and dissenting religions such as the chapel sects offered a scale of values by which the poor could outdo the rich in piety. As Hobsbawm has said, the chapel sects dealt with proletarian problems, not by solving them for a class, but for the individual, or a chosen group of the elect.[58] Latitude in the form of migration into England's regions of expanding opportunity did exist, but it meant physically leaving Ireland, an option which even though most did it more or less willingly and perhaps even cheerfully, their exposure to Britain did little to endear either England or the English to the Irish. And the counterpart for the influence of the chapel sects for the Irish may have been to encourage an expanded role for the Catholic Church in their lives. Irish migrants in England expressed no great love for Protestantism, considering it a heathen religion. One of Henry Mayhew's informants, an Irish costermonger from Limerick, was critical of the people he lived among. "I don't go much among the English streetdealers. They talk like haythens. I never miss mass on a Sunday, and they don't know what the blissed mass manes."[59]

The spirit of the penal laws, enacted in the late seventeenth century to prevent Catholics from being disloyal citizens, also exacerbated differences between the usually Protestant landlord and his usually Catholic tenant.[60] Relationships between different classes in Irish society were often acrimonious. Hely Dutton, from his position as the representative of the Royal Dublin Society, observed the frequently harsh relations between landlord and tenant:

Irish farmers are not that race of obstinate fools that they are sometimes called by absentees, or their disinterested or ignorant agents or stewards; they are no more wedded to the customs of their forefathers than the English, or those of any other country of the same rank. I have even found them ready to listen, and willing to be instructed, if gentle methods are used; but the language of petulant reproach, so often used to them, is by no means calculated to make proselytes: how quietly an English farmer would bear such language from a stranger riding along the road, as "Damn you, you stupid rascal, why don't you use two horses to your plough?" He certainly would return the compliment, and perhaps might make some additions to it.[61]

Furthermore the historical denial of their religion rankled the Catholic population in Ireland, so that many were not prepared to forget old injuries. The spirit of conquest's lingering heritage poisoned relationships between farmers and their hired laborers so that distrust and acrimony were frequent. De Tocqueville called attention to this when he said, "Here it happens that those who want to get are of one religion, and those who want to keep of another. That makes for violence."[62] Old religious grievances joined with land grievances to create extreme tension.

But it was problems which arose within the cottier system of labor which lay at the root of tensions between landlord and tenant because it was an economic system based primarily on an exchange of land for work. The landlord, in exchange for receiving labor, usually provided a house, a potato garden of from one-half to one acres, a couple of sheep, some bog land for turf, or tillage land for raising flax. This was the cottier system in its entirety and it was most common in parts of southern and southwestern Ireland. There were, however, regional variations where the laborer could make separate arrangements for shelter and for his potato ground, called conacre.[63] The rent for a cabin, a kitchen garden, and the right to cut turf and collect dung could cost from one pound ten to two pounds or as high as three pounds a year. Potato ground, if manured, cost from four to six pounds per acre, or if unmanured, from two to three pounds per acre.[64] In return, laborers in some areas were obliged to work whenever summoned by the landlord. Population pressures in such regions tended to drive rentals exorbitantly high, amounting, Donnelly says, in the 1840s in Munster, to almost 50 percent of the market value of potato ground.[65] In the eyes of one observer in 1824, the tragedy of the system was that the class which had the least means had proportionately the highest rents to pay.[66]

Whenever a failure of the potato crop made it difficult to gather these conacre rents, farmers at the next level of leasing, hard pressed themselves to pay their own rentals, demanded payment of whole or part of the crop before it was harvested.[67] Grievances also accumulated when poorly constructed houses were kept in poor repair by the landlord. (These houses, built of mud and wattle, were truly biodegradable, because when the tenants vacated them, as they did in large numbers during the Famine, the houses disappeared without a trace.) The fact that a majority of the disputes brought to petty sessions courts were over such issues as farmers withholding wages or failing to rethatch cabins or provide manure, illustrates the declining relationship between landlord and tenant.

While the condition of this "tied" laborer was far more secure than that of the casually employed laborer or cottier, the numbers of the former decreased and the latter increased greatly in the critical years after 1815 with spiralling population growth. And as the supply of rural labor increased, so did the demand for it continue to shrink. The number of days in a year when laborers could get work varied regionally, from as low as seventy-five days work per year in Sligo to 210 days per year in Louth.[68] Figure 2.2 presents a regional picture of the number of days per year when agricultural work was available, which when correlated with average wages per week in Figure 2.3, indicates the relative poverty of the west and northwest. An important factor in the lives of laborers was the fluctuation in demand for their labor throughout the year, and a correlation can be seen between this and seasonal migration where the areas in which the fluctuations were greatest were also the areas of highest seasonal migration to Britain.

Surplus labor coincided with increased subdivision of farms, and as farms became smaller farmers cut labor costs by depending on their families and neighbors for an exchange of work.[69] An enquiry in the 1830s found that "in spring and harvest the neighbors assist each other, giving an interchange of work."[70] Table 2.1 shows a sampling of agricultural employment in a number of parishes of four counties in 1836, figures which paint a general picture of underemployment.

Casual laborers were extremely vulnerable in this system of declining employment. Donnelly estimates that from one-third to one-half of all laborers in County Cork were hired as casual laborers.[71] Bourke estimated that throughout the country landless laborers represented more than one-quarter of the entire population by 1841,[72] while Ó'Gráda says that "During the 1830s and 1840s perhaps two-thirds of those working in the agricultural sector was dependent primarily on wage-labor for a living."[73] The source of their vulnerability stemmed from the fact that wages were rarely paid in money, but in conacre land, or provisions, or daily diet. If diet was provided by the farmer, wages were from fourpence to sixpence per day. This tends to lend some substance to the Lynch and Vaizey argument that parts of the country were hardly in a market economy, so scarce was the need for coinage there.[74] Wherever casual laborers could not exchange their labor for land, it meant that they had to have cash in order to lease conacre land on which to grow potatoes for subsistence. And if this group was able to supply only about 75 percent of their food intake from potato land set in conacre, as

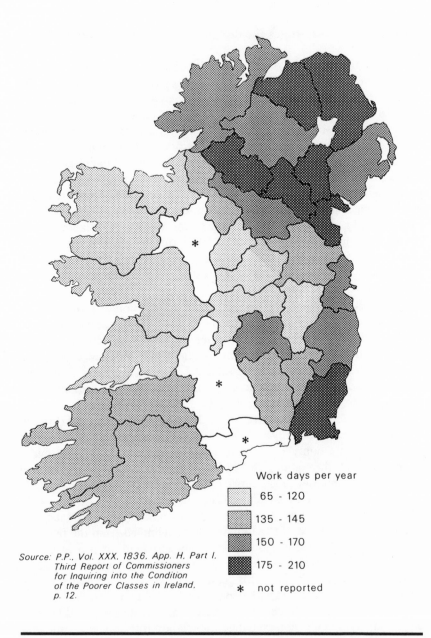

Work days per year

65 - 120

135 - 145

150 - 170

Source: P.P., Vol. XXX, 1836, App. H, Part I,
Third Report of Commissioners
for Inquiring into the Condition
of the Poorer Classes in Ireland,
p. 12.

175 - 210

* not reported

FIGURE 2.2. Average number of days when agricultural work was available, 1836.

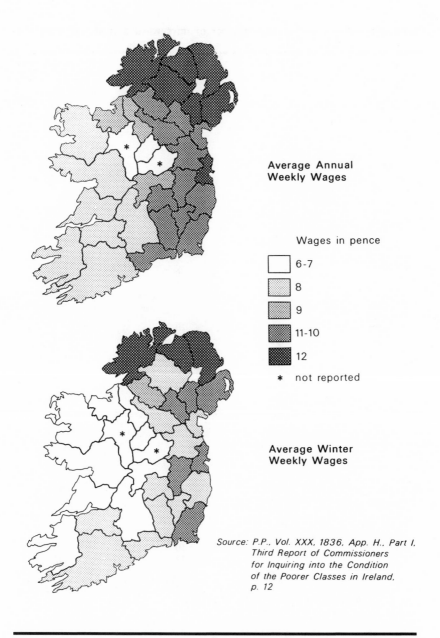

Average Annual
Weekly Wages

Wages in pence

6-7

8

9

11-10

12

*   not reported

Average Winter
Weekly Wages

Source: P.P., Vol. XXX, 1836, App. H., Part I,
Third Report of Commissioners
for Inquiring into the Condition
of the Poorer Classes in Ireland,
p. 12

FIGURE 2.3.   Agricultural wages, 1836.

Table 2.1. **Wages and average number of days when agricultural work was available, 1836**

	Winter wages (shillings)	Rest of year wages (shillings)	No. of days work available per year
Leinster			
Dublin	10	12	160
Carlow	8	10	145
Kildare	10	10	100
Kilkenny	8	10	145
King's	7	9	100
Longford	6	6	80
Louth	8	10	210
Meath	8	10	135
Queen's	8	10	155
Westmeath	..	..	..
Wexford	10	10	190
Wicklow	8	10	170
Average	8.27	9.72	140
Munster			
Clare	6	8	100
Cork	8	8	135
Kerry	6	8	145
Limerick	8	10	140
Tipperary	6	8	..
Waterford	8	10	..
Average	7.00	8.66	130
Connacht			
Galway	6	8	120
Leitrim	7	9	140
Mayo	6	8	65
Roscommon	..	..	..
Sligo	6	9	75
Average	6.25	8.50	100
Ulster			
Antrim	12	12	180
Armagh	10	12	175
Cavan	8	10	150
Donegal	12	12	170
Down	10	12	160
Fermanagh	9	11	190
Londonderry	12	12	180
Monaghan	10	10	180
Tyrone	8	12	150
Average	10.11	11.44	170

Source: PP, Vol. xxx, 1836, App. H. pt 1; *Third Report of Commissioners for Inquiry into the Condition of the Poorer Classes of Ireland,* p. 12.

Table 2.2. Sample employment of agricultural laborers, 1836

County	Total laborers	Permanently employed
Dublin	1783[a]	578
King's	1288	880
Queen's		790
Kerry	2139	(about half)

County	Occasionally employed	Almost always unemployed	Permanently disabled
Dublin	1081[b]	124[c]	
King's	(very few employed)		
Queen's	1238		245
Kerry			

SOURCE: *Poor Inquiry,* Sup. to App. C., pp. 15, 23, 37, 48.

[a]The County Dublin barony from which the figure is taken (Balrothery) is in the northern area of the county, immediately adjacent to County Meath, and so can be said to be a reasonably accurate representation of primarily agricultural conditions.

[b]Employed 6–7 months per year.

[c]Income gained only from harvest work and begging of wives and families.

estimates suggest, how did they make up the remaining 25 percent? The only apparent answer is from supplementary income.

Income supplements assumed increasing importance as conditions declined. As long as there were some small factories in an area, and the domestic industry of female members of the household brought some small returns for cottier and laborer families in areas where goods could be sold. These efforts blunted the worst times, but as industry in Ireland imploded so did such opportunities dwindle, and the need to look elsewhere for income accelerated.

Pig breeding was a common survival strategy of many country people. Its importance in the lives of cottiers and laborers is apparent by the numbers of pigs per capita listed in the 1841 census; there was an average of 1.4 pigs per farm for all farms up to fifteen acres in size, at an average value of one pound seven pence per pig.[75] The Munster Irish kept the most pigs, averaging 1.8 per farm; Leinster had 1.7 per farm; Connacht had 1.1; and Ulster people kept only 1.0 per person. Donnelly says that one-third of the 177,500 pigs in Cork were kept on holdings of one acre,[76] which is consistent with their role as the banking system of the poor. Often referred to respectfully as "the Gentleman Boarder" the pig fed the family in a good year, or could pay the rent in a bad one. One informant from Galway testified of this. "They must keep the pig to pay the con-acre; one-quarter do not pay their con-acre in labour, they must pay in ready money, the farmers take work, but the landlords never do."[77] When some harvest migrants testified that they were forced to sell the pig to pay their passage to England, it was generally regarded as a measure of more extreme poverty than was usual—a last resort because, if harvest income was also less than expected, there was no future cushion against adversity. Another, more optimistic migrant, however, testified at the same parliamentary commission, that, "I sold my pig myself, to enable me to go (to England). I thought little of my pig when I had the good English wages before me."[78]

It is difficult to ascertain the degree to which persons who had some land were likely to become seasonal migrants as a way of supplementing inadequate incomes. In 1828, an informant from Erris said that small landholders in Mayo were the class which "most commonly seeks work in England—mostly unmarried young men."[79] The English political economist, Harriet Martineau, described in a highly moralistic tale a cottier family for whom migration was a way of life:

> It was feared that Dora Sullivan would disappear [from school] when her brother departed for England in hopes of making a little money to bring back to his father [to pay for the lease of the land]. . . . Dan Mahoney [whose father shared the lease] . . . had been long in love with Dora, and who would have married her out of hand, if he had had so much as half an acre of ground to marry upon. All parties approved of the match; but would not hear of its taking place till Dan had a roof of his own to lodge a wife under, by keeping Dora at school, and encouraging Dan to go and seek his fortune at a distance for a while; which the young man, after much murmuring, consented to do.[80]

Lord Dillon's estate agent in England testified that he often received small sums of money for safekeeping and transmittal to Ireland for the lord's tenants, and that the same people came every year, leaving Ireland in the middle or end of May and returning in October.[81] His testimony would tend to corroborate that it was not totally landless persons in the earlier period who were leaving, but those with some access to land which gave them ties and thus some incentive to return. Another testified to this effect when he said, "The small tenantry in Ireland pay more rent than any regular farmer would pay, and they pay it not out of the produce of the land but out of their labor in England."[82]

As times worsened, so did the character of the migration tend to change. One authority testified to this, saying that "formerly those who went over came for the harvest and returned because they were possessors of small farms but the New Emigration [emigration of persons who had lost their farms] has a tendency to produce settlement."[83] An informant from Leitrim believed that many of the residents of villages in his area were harvest migrants, because they were dependent upon occasional employment. He said that most of these village dwellers were ejected tenants who preferred to migrate elsewhere for seasonal work rather than take local employment on roadwork at wages of eightpence per day.[84] Preferring to work elsewhere rather than take demeaning wage employment in home areas is consistent with other evidence about Irish behavior in this period. Everyone who has travelled in the west of Ireland has heard people speak of the humiliation of forced employment on "Famine roads"; work provided for cash income during the worst years of the Great Famine, and to this day the humiliation of having such work forced on them rankles in the very soul of their descendants.

Raymond Crotty has noted changes occurring from 1820 to 1850: "As the tenure system conduced to population explosion in the late eighteenth century, it now worked powerfully to implosion in the nineteenth century."[85] Between 1780 and 1821, there was an estimated total population increase of 17 percent per decade, slowing down in the 1830s to 14.9 percent, and in the next decade falling dramatically to 5.25 percent.[86] As Brendan Walsh has summarized, "No basic population pattern changed as a consequence of these (the Famine) years,"[87] bearing out the belief that the rate of population growth was already slowing down prior to the Famine, playing down its role as the great watershed in population history. But while the demographics were changing in Ireland, primarily in response to changes in the British market after Waterloo, new marriage trends which found women marrying later and later, did not have an immediate effect. In the 1820s the population was still growing fairly rapidly without any evidence of a drop in the death rate, a situation suggesting that the continuing increase in population was resulting from an increase in the proportion of younger people of child-bearing age; that is, that the population was growing younger on the average as well as larger. A youthful population, denied opportunity at home, was also more likely to seek emigration as a safety valve.

By this time, too, it was becoming more difficult to mask the effects of bad years by resorting to income supplements, so that the disadvantages of potatoes as a total diet became glaringly apparent. They could not be stored from one year to the next because they were too bulky, and they were too easily bruised and too heavy to transport easily in order to alleviate regional famines. Disaster was inevitable for the swollen and underemployed population living upon this very precarious diet.

Potato varieties had changed and deteriorated by this time, as well. At the time of Arthur Young's visit, a variety of potato known as the Apple was the best for taste, yield, and keeping quality, but by 1800 yields of this species had begun to decline, and was now 10 to 15 percent less than that of the Cup potato, the next in order of importance.

Bourke suggests that the Cup could have been introduced no earlier than 1800 and was adopted enthusiastically for its hardiness and high yield.[88] However, the keeping qualities of the Cup were inferior, a fact that had important social consequences in the period before the Famine because it was soon challenged by a variety known as the Lumper, whose yield was 10 to 15 percent more, even though contemporaries described it as "watery and ill-flavoured." Its arrival coincided with the end of the boom period following after the French Wars, where one witness described the effect of its advent:

> Our gentry who fed upon turtle and wine
> Must now on wet Lumpers and salt herrings dine.[89]

By the mid-thirties investigators found that Apple varieties were consumed in large towns, Cups in small, and Lumpers fed to cattle and the poor.[90] Austen Bourke believes that the Lumper variety most likely came from England, where it was developed for stock feeding, and brought to Ireland, quite possibly by returning dock workers.[91] Henry Mayhew described these casual dock laborers, known as "lumpers," coming to London in the Cork boats for summer employment as workers in the seasonal lumber import trade.[92] Bourke's evidence suggests that the Lumper potato was first introduced to Ireland in the counties of Clare and Galway, and later in the south and east of Ireland. In Britain, the Lumper was known under that name in areas most frequented by migrant workers from the west of Ireland.[93] The susceptibility of this potato to disease would later be the major cause of the devastation of the Famine.

But by this time, other factors had begun to align into a trajectory toward disaster. The numerous tenantry, which in periods of rising prices had augmented rents and increased the landlord's prestige at the polls, now became a liability.[94] Landlords needed little convincing by now that though a stock of capital could make a profit, a stock of unemployed human beings did not. The Devon Commission, recognizing that changed conditions were beginning to take effect, noted that if the very small farmers could be cleared from land it could be re-let to graziers at higher and more certain rentals. Although grain crops continued to increase during this period, the increase was the result of an extension of tillage into less-productive bogland, on hillsides, and on the sides of mountains, all of which also increased the danger of a population already poised precariously on the knife edge of ecological disaster. Because potatoes, the diet of the poor, were well adapted as a crop to break new ground, it was said that landlords encouraged their tenants to cultivate marginal land, offering rentals at low rates, and then, the next year when the ground had been prepared, raising the rent sufficiently high so that cottiers had to move elsewhere. An observer noted this when he said, "The poor manufacture the waste lands, then the landlord will turn them out and add their farms to his estate and send them elsewhere on the mountain."[95]

Much current research on Ireland is directed at detailed examination of the country's actual condition in the pre-Famine period, and while the overall picture is that of a country in such a desperate state that only a disaster the proportion of the Great Famine could cure its problems, this picture is now being balanced with micro evidence indicating that positive changes were taking place. The decelerating rate of population growth was an important aspect of slowly improving conditions and emigration undoubtedly played an important role in reducing the numbers of persons. Certainly the Census Commissioners believed this when they computed total emigration from Ireland between 1831 and 1841 as 403,459 persons.[96] Legislative changes such as a poor law (1838), a national school system (1838), and a model police force (1836) also contributed to the amelioration of conditions.[97]

In 1838, the drafters of the Drummond Report drew attention to improving conditions when they pointed out that

> From north to south indications of progressive improvement are everywhere visible . . . but these signs of growing prosperity are, unhappily, not so discernible in the condition of the laboring people, as in the amount of the produce of their labour. The proportion of the latter reserved for their use is too small to be consistent with a healthy state of society. The pressure of a superabundant and excessive population (at least with respect to the resources as yet developed for their maintenance and occupation), is perpetually and powerfully acting to depress them.[98]

If this is an accurate assessment of the country's condition at that time (and other evidence would support that it is), then Ireland was improving substantially overall but unequally because while the demand in Britain for Ireland's grain and stock output continued, gains from this did not filter down to the laboring population in the form of higher wages and an improved standard of living. Instead, as a result of their determination to retain land rights by seeking income supplements earned increasingly through seasonal migration, large sectors of the population achieved their immediate goals, but did not substantially improve their overall condition. The pressure on the land was such that the margin of safety was always small. Carlyle may have foreseen this in 1840 when he said, "The time has come when the Irish population must either be improved a little, or terminated."[99] Thus, until the Famine intervened, the laboring people of Ireland were winning their battle to stay on the land but losing the war by failing to materially improve their overall condition.

MICHAEL SULLIVAN was one of those whose survival was precariously balanced. A laborer from Cork, he testified before the Devon Commission, which in 1843 began to collect evidence on conditions in the countryside. Appointed by Sir Robert Peel under the chairmanship of Lord Devon, the Commission was charged with investigating conditions in the following areas: relations between landlords and tenants, the mode of occupation of the land, cultivation of the land, need for improvements, and conditions and habits of the laboring classes. It heard one thousand witnesses, one of whom was Michael Sullivan. The widespread investigations contained in the Commission report, finally issued in 1847, were rendered academic by the onslaught of the Great Famine of 1845–49 and the subsequent dislocation of the Irish economy.[100]

Michael's story may be taken as typical of the situation experienced by the very poorest Irish families before the Famine. When asked how much ground he held, his reply was that he held no ground. "I am a poor man. I have nothing but my labour." He held his house and an acre of ground under a farmer called Daniel Regan for which he paid three pounds; two pounds for the acre of ground, and one pound for the lease of the house. The location of his acre of ground varied from year to year. "The acre I have this year I cannot have it next year; he will have it himself. I must manure another acre."[101]

Sullivan worked as a daily laborer for Daniel Regan for a wage of sixpence a day and meals. When that work wasn't available he said that he went farther south in Cork or north to Tipperary or Limerick where he earned one pound or thirty shillings, according to the local wages there, at the harvest or in digging potatoes.

He and his wife had five children, the eldest of whom had turned twelve the sixth day of the previous May; the next, nine; and so on down. None of the children were employed by farmers.

> They do not employ any of the children—not one; and even we must go ourselves into the country for the want of employment here: and I blame much the landlords of the country for that, though they are very indulgent.

When asked how he managed to support a family of seven on sixpence a day he said that he could make a little more from road-making for the landlord. But the family's food consisted only of dry potatoes. Did he ever eat fish? "No," he said, "not one, except they may bring a pen'orth home in a month. If my poor wife sells her eggs, or makes up a skein of thread in the market, she may take home with her a pen'orth or two pen'orth of something to nourish the children for that night; but in general I do not use 5s. of kitchen from one end of the year to the other."

Did he ever have milk with his potatoes?

> Not a drop. I have no means of getting it. I would think myself middling happy if I could give the five children that; and if they were near a National School, I could give them schooling. I have an idea of giving them schooling as well as I can. A better labouring man than what I am cannot afford his children any schooling, and even some of the people called farmers in the same place.

He testified that while there were some free schools none were convenient to where he lived. Was he anxious for his children to be taught to read and write? "Yes; and so I am striving, but without the assistance of my good friends I could not do it."

His wife made a small contribution to the family income from raising chickens but he did not know how much. He had a small garden attached to the house in which he raised about four hundred cabbages. He had a pig, but not a pig house, so that the pig lived in a corner of their house with the family. He could not build a pigsty outside because he did not know if he would have the same house next year. Of what did his household goods consist?

> I have a chaff bed and bed-clothes that would do my own business, but I am in want of a second one. I cannot afford to have it. I cannot complain myself, but I could complain for others. There are others of the poor working class, as I am myself, who have no beds, nor more than a gentleman or even a wealthy farmer would think too good for his pig, and they may lie in the clothes they wear by the day.

Even the farmers in his district were badly off. Of them he said,

> One out of 100 cannot drink a pint of sour milk among five in family from about Christmas until about the 17th of March or so; and then generally they are forced to sell the sour milk in order to meet the rent, or pawn their clothes. I know in different places three women in one house trusting to one cloak, and for a time, perhaps, it might be in the pawn office.

He was asked what was the smallest quantity of land upon which a man could support himself and his family, to which he replied, "They could, I know, where they are encouraged in that place support themselves by ten acres, properly cultivated, of good light land, better than what they are doing by thirty acres, from the want of capital and means."

Did people of his class ever emigrate to America? His reply was, "Not many in the place, not in the very neighbourhood." And why did they not emigrate? "For want of money." "Supposing the means of emigration were given to them, would they be willing to emigrate?" Sullivan answered, "They are not anxious for it — they have not the courage." The questioner continued: "Those people you describe as being so wretched in their condition — supposing lands were supplied for them in America, would they be willing and anxious to emigrate?" Answer: "It is hard for a man to account for another man's mind, but of course they would."

Michael Sullivan's life by present standards seems incredibly bleak, yet he still aspired to have his children educated and would have considered going to America if he could receive assistance. His aspirations mirror the social changes transforming life in the decades prior to the Famine, changes which paralleled the changing economic conditions. The people of Ireland were already well on their way to being the cautious, conservative people who would take little pleasure in either country dances or marriage later in the nineteenth century. The picture of the hapless, improvident peasant of earlier times, living cheerfully in an extortionate society, was possibly always something of a fiction, but it is certain that the people of Ireland in general had developed more forward-looking attitudes about their lives. One example of this was recorded by a traveller in Donegal who, noting the unusual length of the haft of the shovels used by local laborers (4 feet) was told that this kept them from developing a stoop which would have disqualified them for army service.[102]

Seasonal migration played a significant role in the transformation of rural Ireland. Work abroad enabled Irish workers to retain a hold on their right to live in Ireland, but it could not deter the worker's inevitable transition to another way of life. And although the disruption was not as painful as it was for those who migrated permanently to North America, it was just as certain.

Provincial and Regional Disparities within Ireland, and Urban Industrial Decline

To understand the nature of conditions in Ireland preceding the Famine, it is important to see how the country's various regions were affected, because Ireland's countryside was more varied and complex than may be apparent in the preceding discussion.

According to Cullen, pre-Famine Ireland can be broadly divided into three distinct regions[103] (see Figure 2.3). The first, running from the north diagonally toward the southeast, was most prosperous and comprised the eastern counties of the provinces of Leinster, and Ulster (exclusive of Donegal and Fermanagh). In these regions, wage employment on tillage farms in areas of intensive tillage or supplementary incomes from spinning or weaving in the traditional textile districts made the condition of the smallholder and laborer somewhat less precarious than elsewhere in Ireland. The second region consisted of the more western provinces of Leinster, Munster (exclusive of Clare and southwest Cork, and the Kerry peninsula), east Galway and parts of Roscommon, Leitrim, and Sligo in the province of Connacht. This region was, on the whole, poorer than the first region. Supplementary textile income was smaller and had declined more rapidly than elsewhere in the country, adversely affecting the lower levels of society and causing distinctions between farmers and other rural classes to be sharper here than elsewhere. The third region included the districts along the west coast of the country.

Even though Ireland can be divided into these clear-cut regions, it is still difficult to find adequate assessments of the condition of the country. Figures 2.4 and 2.5 present a range of measures in an attempt to flesh out the picture of conditions in the period, keeping in mind however that what may have appeared as the direst poverty to the statisticians who measured it, the census collectors, and travellers who observed it, or the parliamentary commissioners assembling evidence on it, may not have been entirely the case.

While much has been said of landlords who chose not to reinvest their profits in the land, less attention has been paid to the peasant who dressed in rags but could dower his daughter with two hundred pounds or so of cash. Caesar Otway noted that one of the only ways to release the cash which farmers hoarded was for their daughters to run away with young men, and then, to keep the good name of the family, the father gave the cash to make his daughter an honest woman. In Erris, Otway noted that the people there were great hoarders of coin though they had few comforts. "They exhibit outwardly a poverty which is far from real."[104]

Unfortunately it was not in the best interests of the poor to look anything but as poor as possible. Property improvements could result in leases being bid higher at the next auction, and appearing to the neighbors to have money could be dangerous, given the general state of lawlessness prevailing in much of the country. On the other hand, if the

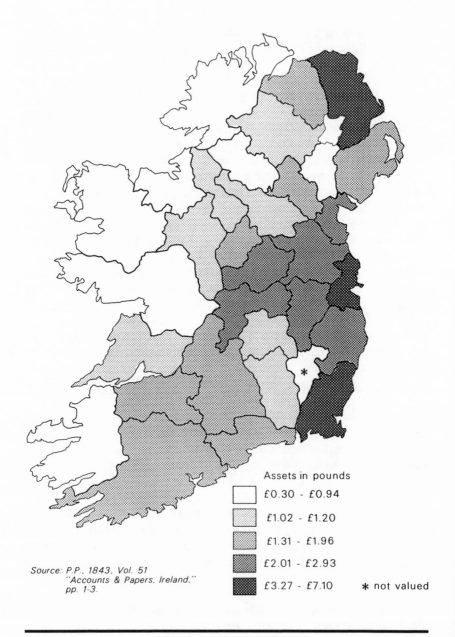

Assets in pounds

£0.30 - £0.94

£1.02 - £1.20

£1.31 - £1.96

£2.01 - £2.93

£3.27 - £7.10   * not valued

Source: P.P., 1843, Vol. 51
"Accounts & Papers, Ireland,"
pp. 1-3.

FIGURE 2.4.   Valuation of assets per capita, 1843.

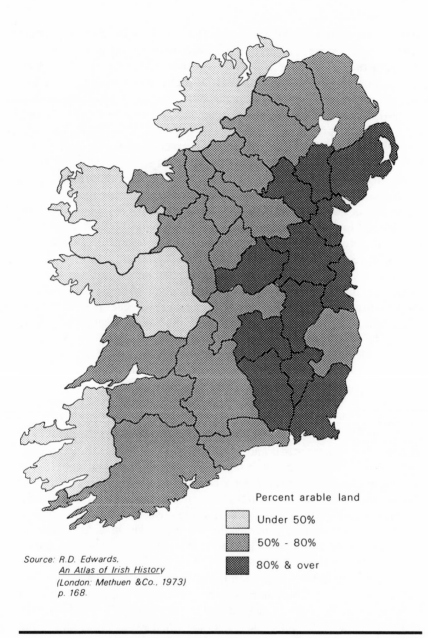

Percent arable land

Under 50%

50% - 80%

80% & over

Source: R.D. Edwards,
An Atlas of Irish History
(London: Methuen &Co., 1973)
p. 168.

FIGURE 2.5.   Proportions of arable land per county, 1841.

peasant dressed in rags and ate his potatoes from the same pot as his pig, then the gentry were reassured that he was as degraded as he appeared, and both they and the neighbors were reassured that it was not worth preying upon him. The evidence of H.D. Inglis, who testified at a parliamentary commission tends to bear this out. He said, "I would not always judge the condition of an Irish farmer solely by the way in which he lives; because some live like paupers who could live in greater comfort."[105] The Rev. Hall, like Inglis, an observer of conditions in Ireland, noted that, "The cottagers in Ireland are often so wretchedly poor; yet some of them have often 50 or 100 pounds in their house . . . some choose to appear this poor, to save themselves from being murdered."[106] As Williams Forbes Adams says, "The custom of the country favored deterioration and the state of the law did nothing to check it."[107] The disincentive to spend on improvements is an important factor in assessing the picture of pre-Famine Ireland.

Figure 2.4, showing the value of assets per capita, has been used as a measure of the wealth of the country on a regional basis.[108] In general, the map bears out Cullen's picture of three fairly distinct regions. Counties Dublin, Antrim, and Wexford present the highest wealth per capita, closely followed by those counties contiguous to Dublin in Leinster, (Louth, Meath, Westmeath, Longford, King's [now Offaly], Kildare, and Wicklow). The northern counties of Derry, Monaghan, and Down are next in order of wealth, as are all the counties of Munster with the exception of Kerry. The poorest regions are those of the far west and north: counties Donegal, Fermanagh, and Armagh in Ulster (although as returns for Fermanagh and Armagh were incomplete, the per capita assessment is understated); and County Kerry in Munster; Sligo, Mayo, and Galway in Connacht (with under-representation in Galway).

Figure 2.5 indicates that the areas with the highest proportions of arable land were also the richest in income valuation; and that figure, together with Figure 2.6, illustrates that the areas with the highest population densities were in general also the areas which were poorest in arable land. These were chiefly the counties of the far west and north: Donegal, Mayo, Galway, and Kerry. Income supplements such as domestic industry and harvest migration in the southeastern counties of Ulster (Down, Armagh and Monaghan) permitted greater population densities in those areas.[109] Wages in these counties (see Figure 2.3) were relatively high, as were the number of days per year when work was available (see Figure 2.2).[110] Armagh and Monaghan were both areas of relatively high harvest migration, as Figure 2.7 shows.

Additional information for the four provinces provide some regional and historical contrasts having some bearing on emigration from

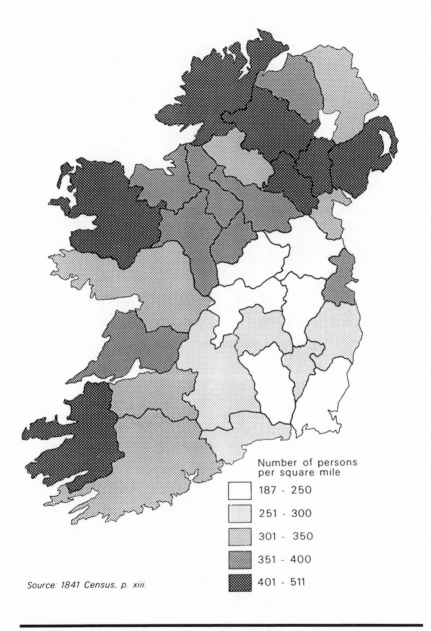

Number of persons
per square mile

187 - 250

251 - 300

301 - 350

351 - 400

401 - 511

Source: 1841 Census, p. xiii.

FIGURE 2.6.   Persons per square mile of arable land, 1841.

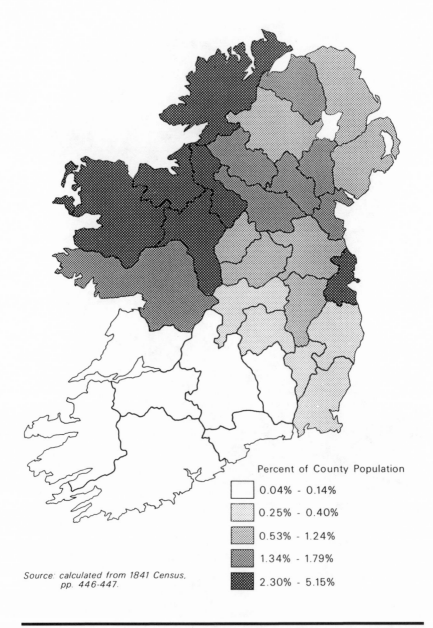

Percent of County Population

0.04% - 0.14%

0.25% - 0.40%

0.53% - 1.24%

1.34% - 1.79%

2.30% - 5.15%

Source: calculated from 1841 Census, pp. 446-447.

FIGURE 2.7. Males migrant to Britain, May–August 1841.

them. A parliamentary commission of the 1840s called Leinster the "least poor province of Ireland." Centered on Dublin, it was traditionally the market-oriented sector of the Irish economy, the center of the flourishing grain export trade, employing the largest number of landless laborers, and closely attuned to the demands of the British market. The province covers 23 percent of Ireland and in 1841 had a population of 1,973,731 persons or 24 percent of the total population.

Munster, in the south and southwest, was a province of intermingled lowlands and uplands, with three main towns: Waterford, Cork, and Limerick, each of them port cities dealing in the agricultural produce of a farmed and generally fertile countryside. Covering slightly more than one-quarter of the total acreage of Ireland (29 percent), Munster had 2,396,161 inhabitants in 1841, 29 percent of the total population. Of the 162,386 farms in the 1841 census, 35 percent were of less than five acres, and a further 38 percent were from five to fifteen acres. The fragmentation of farms here led to land hunger. It was here also that farmers in the northerly counties of Tipperary and Limerick switched from tillage to grazing when the price of wheat fell, thereby lessening the need for laborers and thus the incentives to keep a numerous tenantry. These regions had the greatest number of agrarian outrages which, though generally confined there, caused people to think all of Ireland was in a disturbed state.[111] Ever since the eighteenth century, southern Ireland and the city of Cork, in particular, had been engaged in the provision trade, first with the colonies, and then for the British navy during the period of the French Wars. The contraction of this trade after 1815 resulted in greater distress in that region. As a further indication of increasing poverty, Munster had the largest proportion of ratepayers per capita with a property valuation less than one pound, 17.22 percent of total.

Connacht, in the west, had the highest incidence of poverty, both then and now, but its distribution was more even than that of Munster. A total of 86 percent of the population were valued at five pounds or less (see Table 2.3). (Ulster had the lowest percentage of population under five pounds valuation, 59.03; Leinster was next with 66.05; and Munster had 66.53.) In land area Connacht is 21 percent of Ireland, and had an 1841 population of 1,418,973, or 17 percent of the total. With the worst weather in Europe, the smallest farms, the lowest yielding soil for farming, and dangerous coastal waters, this province was the last area to undergo out-migration. But in the 1830s, with the decay of the domestic industries which had formerly supplemented inadequate incomes,[112] increasing numbers of persons from Connacht sought an alternative supplement in seasonal harvest labor. In every county of the province, with

Table 2.3. Valuation of assets per capita

County	Total pop.	Rate-payers	Persons per rate-payer (2 ÷ 1)	Total assess-ment (£)	Assessment per rate-payer, (4 ÷ 2) (£)	Value of assets per capita (4 ÷ 1) (£)	Ratepayers under £5 valuation	% rate-payers under £5 (7 ÷ 2)	Ratepayers under £1 valuation	% ratepayers under £1 (9 ÷ 2)
Leinster										
Dublin	372,700	44,915	8.29	1,219,526	27.15	3.27	13,485	30.02	3,299	7.34
Carlow	86,200ᵃ									
Kildare	114,500	12,356	9.26	265,957	21.52	2.32	6,823	55.22	2,821	22.83
Kilkenny	202,400	16,560	8.18ᵇ	242,817	14.66	1.20ᵇ	5,836	35.24	1,401	8.46ᵈ
King's	146,900	25,175	5.83	295,108	11.76	2.01	15,168	60.25	6,381	25.34
Longford	115,500	22,511	5.13	226,869	10.08	1.96	11,815	52.49	2,687	11.94
Louth	128,300	19,610	6.54	325,866	16.62	2.54	9,104	46.43	1,687	8.60
Meath	183,800	26,507	6.93	537,869	20.29	2.93	15,896	59.97	7,237	27.30
Queen's	153,900	19,334	7.96	168,749	8.72	1.10	12,422	64.25	5,291	27.37
Westmeath	141,300	22,635	6.24	300,924	13.29	2.13	12,558	55.48	4,739	20.94
Wexford	202,000	37,302	5.42	1,434,262	38.45	7.10	18,892	50.65	6,855	18.38
Wicklow	126,100	19,290	6.54	314,576	16.31	2.49	8,799	45.61	2,604	13.50
TOTAL	1,887,400	266,195	7.09	4,112,997	15.45	2.18	130,798	49.14	45,002	16.91
Connacht										
Galway	422,900	45,504	9.29ᵇ	396,183	8.71	0.94ᵇ	28,518	62.67	5,385	11.83
Leitrim	155,300	29,296	5.30	162,551	5.55	1.05	18,593	63.47	3,931	13.42
Mayo	388,900	61,506	6.32	268,898	4.37	0.69	50,170	81.57	11,414	18.56
Roscommon	253,600	41,438	6.12	282,272	6.82	1.11	28,779	69.45	7,573	18.28
Sligo	181,000	17,774	10.18	145,959	8.21	0.81	10,710	60.26	3,356	18.88
TOTAL	1,401,700	195,518	7.17	1,255,863	6.42	0.90	136,770	69.95	31,659	16.19
Munster										
Clare	286,400	30,788	9.30	292,982	9.52	1.02	14,553	47.27	3,843	12.48
Cork	854,100	66,337	12.88ᵇ	1,123,202	16.93	1.32ᵇ	30,447	45.90	11,558	17.42
Kerry	293,900	26,823	10.96	209,040	7.79	0.71	16,490	61.48	7,888	29.41
Limerick	330,000	40,407	8.17	647,820	16.03	1.96	18,862	46.68	5,324	13.18
Tipperary	435,600	48,369	9.01ᵇ	601,563	12.44	1.38ᵇ	25,393	52.50	9,095	18.80
Waterford	196,200	16,130	12.16	290,122	17.99	1.48	7,099	44.01	1,704	10.56
TOTAL	2,396,200	228,854	10.47	3,164,729	13.83	1.32	112,844	49.31	39,412	17.22
Ulster										
Antrim	276,200	69,952	3.95	1,344,771	19.22	4.87	28,919	41.34	10,167	14.53
Armagh	232,400	13,569	17.13ᵇ	88,118	6.49	0.38ᵇ	9,050	66.70	3,109	22.91
Cavan	243,200	27,559	8.82	260,175	9.44	1.07	10,544	38.26	1,604	5.82
Donegal	296,400	19,224	15.42	120,450	6.27	0.41	10,361	53.90	1,331	6.92
Down	361,400	77,003	4.69	581,815	7.56	1.61	41,963	54.50	12,421	16.13
Fermanagh	156,500	4,957	31.57ᵇ	46,940	9.47	0.30ᵇ	1,968	39.70	335	6.76
Londonderry	222,200	29,157	7.62	331,861	11.38	1.49	12,096	41.49	1,325	4.54
Monaghan	200,400	34,470	5.81	262,033	7.60	1.31	16,813	48.78	4,023	11.67
Tyrone	313,000	35,976	8.70	321,333	8.93	1.03	16,287	45.27	1,772	4.93
TOTAL	2,301,700	311,867	7.38	3,357,496	10.77	1.46	148,001	47.46	36,087	11.57
ALL IRELAND										
TOTAL	7,987,000	1,002,434ᶜ	7.97	11,891,085	11.86	1.49	528,413ᶜ	52.71	152,160ᶜ	15.18

ᵃCounty Carlow omitted from return.
ᵇReturns on ratepayers incomplete; therefore household size is overstated and per capita assessment is understated.
ᶜTotals differed inexplicably by moderate amounts in original report.
ᵈSmaller proportion classified as very poor.

the exception of Leitrim, at least three-fifths of all farms were of less than five acres, a fact that forced most of the farming population to seek supplemental sources of income.

Ulster, the northern province, varies in landscape and resources, from the industrialized Lagan Valley in the northeast, to the barren, rocky shores of Donegal, which were (and are) as poor as the worst areas of Connacht. Ulster covers 26 percent of Ireland and in 1841 had a total population of 2,386,373 persons, 29 percent of the total. Separated by a series of natural barriers from the rest of the country, Ulster has stood apart both historically as well as geographically.[113] Contact was in fact easier with Scotland and it was there that the earliest people of Ulster turned for trade and contact. Differences between Ulster and the rest of the island were accentuated when the linen trade and ship building accelerated the economic development of Ulster after about 1860, causing the province to sprint ahead of the rest of the country.[114] Emigration from Ulster differed from that of the rest of the country; a stream of permanent emigration from Ulster left for North America early in the eighteenth century.

Differences between town and countryside in Ireland corresponded with problems in the country's low level of industrial development. In 1841 only one-fifth of the Irish population lived in towns or villages.[115] Only eighteen towns had populations larger than 10,000, of which all but five were port towns. Throughout the nineteenth century Dublin was the largest town and the unquestioned metropolis of Ireland, having grown from about 172,000 in 1801 to 232,726 persons by 1841.[116] While the city remained a commercial, administrative, military, educational, theological, and political center of no mean importance, its vitality as an economic and industrial center became a casualty of changes taking place elsewhere in the British Isles.[117] Twenty-five percent of Dublin's 1841 population had been born elsewhere, indicating that a considerable part of the city's growth was through in-migration, but approximately 63 percent of those migrants were in non-industrial occupations (compared to a national figure of 46 percent). The only town with any potential for industrial development was Belfast, with a population of 75,308 persons.[118] Belfast and the lower Lagan Valley of County Antrim served as a collection center for the agricultural and domestic industrial production beginning to develop by the 1840s in the surrounding regions. Cork, in the south, with 80,720 persons, was the great agricultural center of the country, and the regional capital of the province of Munster. Limerick, in the west, on the River Shannon, was the meeting place of sea, canal, and road communications, with 48,391 inhabitants. Waterford, in the southeast, with 23,216 people, was busy, as was Cork, in the provision trade. These five towns composed the major urban areas of Ireland in 1841, but only Dublin and Belfast have grown significantly since then.

Although a nascent growth of industry had affected Ireland considerably in the eighteenth century, what happened later, says Cullen, "was not because Ireland was a non-industrial country but because she was an industrial country that she had so much to lose in the great economic transformation which affected all countries in one way or another, but Ireland perhaps more than most."[119] Despite early signs of positive development there was weakness in industry's growth. Most industrial firms were on such a small scale that they could not meet the demands of the Irish market, and that, with the competition from more efficient British industry eventually resulted in stagnation and decay of industry throughout most of the country.

However, in the closing decades of the eighteenth century, Ireland's economic prospects still seemed generally healthy. As indicated earlier, prices of agricultural products had risen sharply relative to industrial prices. In industry, some new technological features were rapidly being adopted, although sufficient capital was always a problem. There was even talk of some English manufacturers considering investment in Ireland. (Chapter 4 discusses the industrial connections which resulted in Manchester manufacturers investing in Irish textile mills.) The expansion of the linen industry in the 1780s gave reason for optimism, especially as much of the expansion of domestic manufacturing was located in impoverished regions such as Mayo. Contemporaries thought that industry might regenerate poor and backward regions which lacked the potential for sustained agricultural prosperity. Indeed, the healthy prospect of Ireland's industrial development so alarmed British manufacturers that they launched a campaign against a 1785 proposal for a free market interchange of goods between Britain and Ireland, arguing that Irish manufacturers would flood the British market with cheap goods and that British capital and artisans would then flock to new industrial centers of Ireland.[120] Proposals for a free market area came to nothing when members of the Irish parliament opposed it, seeing in the arrangement a surrender of important parts of Ireland's legislative independence.[121]

Notwithstanding, the political union of the two countries on January 1, 1801, gave birth in its economic clauses to what had been aborted in 1785. William Pitt, the British prime minister, held out the prospect that free entry into the British market would facilitate Irish industrial development by encouraging a flow of British capital into Ireland. Those in Ireland opposed to the union, however, cared little for economics; their opposition was on political grounds. Dublin and districts in the north strongly influenced by Orangeism were against the union, though opinion in much of the rest of the country favored freedom from the threat of internal rebellion and external invasion by France promised by direct control from London. Thomas Newenham, the political geographer, was one of those who opposed union. He saw the decline of trade in the post-1801 period as a direct consequence of the free trade measures.[122] Newenham was, however, hardly representative of public opinion at the time which tended to see only good in the union of the two economies.[123]

Structural weakness in the economy became more apparent after the turn of the century as Ireland began to appear a less credible rival to Britain. That weakness lay in her dependence on the textile industry which was in direct competition with that of England. Ireland was also handicapped by the chaotic state of her currency and the lack of a sound banking system.[124] Since early in the eighteenth century, when the importation of English gold and silver coin was forbidden, there was a constant lack of coin and a flood of paper notes.

Another factor of economic weakness was that the investment capital of middle-class Catholics in Ireland was being channelled elsewhere than business. Earlier, when the penal laws had excluded Catholics from investing in land, they had channelled their enterprise into industry and commerce, especially in the southern and southeastern port cities.[125] Barred from the professions of law, the army, and the navy, as well as from positions in central and local government, middle-class Catholics in the eighteenth century could choose between emigrating (which Arthur Young says almost none did "being so tied to their parishes") or remaining at home to make the best of whatever occupations remained available to them. Although it was galling for Protestants in direct competition with them in trade to see them flourish despite the no-popery laws, the strength of Catholics, especially in Cork, Waterford, Limerick, and Galway, was sufficiently great as to make it impossible to debar them from enterprise. It is ironic, then, that the Catholic Relief Acts of 1778 and 1782, permitting them to take longer leases and to buy land outright, changed their pattern of investment and way of life. Prior to the lifting of the laws their opportunities for ostentatious consumption had been circumscribed. Now, with the strictures on the use of their capital removed, they diverted their money away from commercial investments, preferring instead to send their sons into the professions rather than family businesses. As Maureen Wall has suggested, it was singularly unfortunate for Ireland that this came about at a time when that country was, for the first time, to meet the challenge of free trade.[126]

With industrial development in a nascent state and frequently precarious, trade was the somewhat shaky mainstay of most towns and villages, many of which had small craft and workshop industries, and a few had grain mills, breweries, and distilleries. Nevertheless, far less work existed than did the demand for it.[127] Perhaps the greatest weakness and longest-lasting effects of the union were in textiles, but for different reasons than believed by Newenham.

The years of the Napoleonic Wars had certainly concealed difficulties already inherent within the Irish economy, as the previous discussion has illustrated. After the wars, agricultural prices fell sharply and the

Irish had less money to spend on consumer goods. Herein lay the real difficulty of the infant Irish cotton industry, which was that the domestic market for cotton goods was too small, thereby guaranteeing its demise. If it had been export based, the industry could possibly have taken advantage of the overseas market for cheap machine-spun yarn. Instead, before the union and for some time after, it was cushioned against outside competition by protective legislation, not withdrawn until 1824, and thus had no incentive to do anything but continue to produce inferior goods inefficiently and at high cost. Irish manufactures simply could not keep pace with its highly efficient Lancashire rivals, whose size enabled them to cut costs and sell more cheaply.[128] Home spinners and weavers still existed, but the growth of modern textile factories first reduced earnings from these industries and later drove many of the workers to emigrate for longer periods of time to the textile regions abroad.

General declines in the early part of the century were exacerbated by postwar shrinkages after 1816. Worse was to come when a kingdomwide depression in 1825 and 1826, concurrent with, although not caused by, the 1824 repeal of protective tariffs on wool and cotton from England, caused serious dislocation on both sides of the channel.[129] An immediate result of widespread depression was that "some thousands of artisans and work people, hitherto employed in England . . . returned to their own country in a state of frightful penury."[130] By April of 1825 some 19,000 textile workers were idle in the Liberties section of Dublin: 11,000 woolen weavers, 1,860 silk weavers, 480 cotton weavers, and 5,600 unspecified branches.[131]

Dublin, which had been one of the outstanding cities of Europe in the eighteenth century still retained much of its outward splendor, but Inglis, travelling through Dublin in 1834, pointed out that the approaches to the city were so squalid as to spoil its charm.[132] Within the city, houses appeared attractive, but inside were often broken up into tenements. Density was high, reaching 250 persons per acre according to the 1841 census.

Dublin was also directly affected by changes in the linen industry. In the early 1700s Dublin has been the natural distribution center for linen manufactured throughout the country, so that by 1710, 1,688,574 yards of linen cloth were exported, much of it to America. Linen was free from export restrictions placed on other Irish industries, and the linen trade had received extensive manufacturing grants. By the time of the Union, 18,863,042 yards per year were being exported, much of the gain from earlier times having taken place in the previous two decades. A splendid Linen Hall had been erected in Dublin in 1728 to encourage the industry, and until 1816 the volume of trade passing through it amounted to three-eighths of the total exports from Ireland. However by this time Belfast was developing as a port and the northern linen merchants had begun to trade directly with England, which resulted in a gradual transfer of the industry's center to the north.[134] Trade from Dublin gradually fell off, and by 1828 the hall was no longer a market. In his *Irish Sketch Book,* William Thackery wrote with scorn of the deserted hall. "We went to see the Linen Hall of Dublin—that huge, useless, lonely place, in the vast windy solitudes of which stands the simpering statue of George IV, pointing to some bales of shirting, over which he is supposed to extend his august protection."[135]

Aggressive trade unionism may also have encouraged decline by discouraging prospective investment. Dublin's artisan trades and industries were organized into powerful guilds with long histories. The Weavers, being one of the most powerful, first received its charter in 1446. In Fergus D'Arcy's study of Dublin artisan activity he said that as trade associations, the Dublin guilds had been in decline since at least 1750, threatened on the one hand by the spread of industrial enterprise with its emphasis on wage labor, and on the other by discontent among workmen who formed "combinations" to press their demands.[136] Combinations of workmen were effective in gaining higher wages for Dublin workmen than their counterparts in England received. Table 2.4 illustrates comparative wages in the two areas. In both cases Manchester artisans improved their money wages slightly during the period, whereas Dublin workers, although consistently higher than their counterparts, simply returned, by the late 1850s, to their approximate position at the beginning of the century.

Table 2.4.   Comparative wages in Dublin and Manchester (shillings per week)

	1810	1815	1825	1838	1840	1859	1869
Carpenters							
Manchester	25/	25/	24/	26/	27/	28/	32/
Dublin	30/	26/	26/	28/	28/	30/	30/
Bricklayers							
Manchester	22/6	22/6	24/	27/	27/	31/6	32/
Dublin	30/	20/	27/	26/	25/	28/	30/

SOURCE: D'Arcy, "Dublin Artisan Activity," pp. 178–79.

Dublin wages may have been higher, but industry there was subject to recurrent trade depressions causing the wages to appear to be less stable over time than were English wages, as illustrated in Table 2.5.

The figures point to a general decline in money wages over the period from 1810 to 1840, although less in the building trades than in the

Table 2.5.   Average wage of Dublin artisans (shillings per week)

	1800s	1810s	1820s	1830s	1840s	1859
Building trades	9/	25/1	26/3	26/	27/4	29/7
Textile trades	5/	26/9	21/7	17/6	11/8	28/
Leather trades	8/4	22/6	19/10	19/4	14/	---

Source: D'Arcy, "Dublin Artisan Activity," pp. 168–75.

other two. During this period there was a general fall in the price of bread and, if one can generalize from bread prices, the position of artisans, although particularly poor in the years 1816–25, showed some gradual improvement after 1826.

At a time when in all of the United Kingdom there were laws against combinations of workmen to prevent trade union activity among industrial workers, Dublin artisans were singularly agile in circumventing such laws. So insistent in their demands were they, and so violent in their methods that it has been suggested they often managed to kill the industries which supported them, and so incidentally ruined themselves.[137]

Shipbuilding in Dublin suffered particularly from the effects of this militancy. Here the demands made by the men, both with regard to wages and the conditions of apprenticeship, were considered unreasonable by one master ship broker who declared before a government commission in 1838:

> Ireland is the dearest country in the world for labour. Every description of artisan demands at least one-third more than in England . . . I am resolved never to drive another nail here, if I can possibly avoid it. . . . If you find any fault, they strike directly.[138]

The tyranny of the workers was also apparent in the silk industry. Charles G. Otway, the Hand Loom Weaver Commissioner, certainly believed that the tyranny of workman combinations was harmful to trade. He reported in 1840:

> It cannot be doubted that illegal and dangerous combinations among workmen have operated most injuriously on the trade, driven many of the most extensive manufacturers out of it, and deterred others from directing that capital and intelligence towards it by which alone it could be preserved or enabled to compete with the other silk-weaving districts of the Empire. If not checked, this system will speedily drive away the portion of the trade which now remains.[139]

One Dublin manufacturer informed Otway that he was giving up his business because the workers would not permit him to use newly purchased jacquard looms and a silk-winding machine. They also limited the numbers of employees who were to work for him and refused to pay what he considered an economic price for the use of the looms. The Commissioner also noted that many Irish silk weavers had emigrated to Manchester and other silk-weaving districts in England where they were glad to obtain employment at a lower rate than that fixed by trade in Dublin.[140]

Dublin attracted large numbers of paupers. Poor relief was relatively easy to obtain through the various charitable agencies, whereas the countryside offered only the hospitality of the slightly less poor until the introduction of a poor law in 1838. The Mendicity Institute in Dublin indicated in 1836 that silk weavers and cotton weavers were by far the highest proportion of those given relief. However, the Institute's figures suggest that Dublin was to some extent also a magnet for migrants. Of the total of 247 persons in that institution in 1841 (the total number of migrant persons returning themselves as paupers in Dublin in 1841 was 198), nine counties were represented by fourteen or more persons. These were: Kildare, 21; Dublin, 19; Carlow, 15; Wicklow, 21; Westmeath, 16; King's County, 14; Meath, 20; Cork, 15; Wexford, 14.

Such information does not tell much more than that indigent paupers came primarily from the counties surrounding Dublin, but then so did the remaining population of migrants.[141] Thus, while the availability of poor relief may not have been the initial attraction for migrants who later became paupers, it may very well have tended to keep persons either from going elsewhere, or from returning to their home areas.

Dublin had a regular city mob, as did London and other large cities. There were said to be constant feuds between the Butchers and Weavers guilds, conducted with great bitterness to the point of regular battles between the groups. Nevertheless, contemporary observers may have been perhaps too quick to call attention to the culpability of street rowdiness and union activity as the important factor in the decline of Dublin industries. The excesses of Dublin street life as well as its industrial life were similar to those of eighteenth-century London, and while that city's capitalists may have been dismayed and even inconvenienced by the militant demands of the mob, few could claim that it kept London from thriving.

Dublin industry did receive a severe blow, however, when in 1801 it lost its position as the political center of Ireland, causing the nobility and gentry to withdraw their business from Dublin trades because they no longer spent a season there. This exodus severely hurt Dublin industries, many of which were based on servicing the luxurious habits of extravagant spenders. Eighty-two Irish peers kept their accounts at the La-

Touche Bank, Dublin's most important bank in the eighteenth century,[142] and the ledgers of this bank show that these people spent 624,000 pounds a year in that city.[143] When the gentry left, so did their capital. While opinions may differ on the overall economic results of the union, the removal of bank balances such as these to London was a serious loss to Dublin as well as to the country as a whole.

Overall, one can conclude that conditions of urban life in Ireland in general, and in Dublin in particular, were hardly conducive to encouraging persons to settle there in preference to Britain. John Harris and Michael Todaro suggest that migration is a response to expected income where the expected income depends on both the wage offered and the probability of finding a job at such a wage.[144] All evidence suggests that the pool of persons contemplating migration were knowledgeable about conditions, calculating costs and benefits very carefully, and thus more attracted to regions with steadily expanding opportunities where there was a greater probability of obtaining employment and expected income was thereby higher. Dublin wages may have been kept high by the threat of militant trade union activity, or as in the case of weaving, by legislation, but as long as industry in the rest of the country was in decline and subject to fairly drastic periodic downturns, the overall effect was a deterrent to continued economic growth. Conditions in Dublin imply that the probability of migrants obtaining those high expected wages was not great — hence expected income was low. In contrast to this, Manchester wages, though generally lower, grew steadily throughout the period, making Manchester a much more attractive, because surer prospect. The table of Dublin wages (Table 2.5) demonstrates that although they stayed roughly constant, they were maintained above their potential market level artificially, without the possibility of an expansion of opportunities. On the other hand, Manchester manufacturers, with their steady expansion, required a growing labor force and wages that grew over time as the labor force continued to be attracted by opportunity. Dublin thus served as a funnel, to direct the flow of migrants out of Ireland through its port facilities, and was not a city of job opportunity.

Underlying the primary factors retarding the sustained growth of Irish industry countrywide were a lack of investment capital, the scarcity of natural resources such as coal and iron, competition with more efficient English industries, and a general lack of trade, but the negative effect of labor militancy must also be taken into account when one is totting up the balance sheet to explain why Ireland failed to keep pace with her competitors. Worker militancy, both among themselves and toward their employers, and an unwillingness to compromise on demands may tend more toward a sociological explanation than an economic one. It may be that it was the intransigence of Irish workers in their relations with their compatriots which resulted in decisions to migrate abroad rather than to seek opportunities where (sometimes) wages were higher but terms and conditions less tolerable.

Regional Patterns of Migration

Emigrants in general should be seen as leaving, not from vaguely defined "countries of origin," but from particular provinces and regions, each with its own kind of response, or lack of it, to the forces shaping that movement.[145] Regional differences help to explain varying responses to opportunities posed by the attraction of migration to Britain.

Patrick Lynch and John Vaizey provided the first explicit alternative to O'Brien's contention that Ireland failed to thrive after 1800 because of the malevolence of British policy.[146] In their argument they see a lack of healthy economic growth as proceeding from the lack of an integrated economy, where instead of one economy, Ireland had two. In the east, a relatively healthy economy, focused on supplying the agricultural needs of the English economy; and in the west a desperately poor subsistence economy based primarily on an exchange of land for labor. It is their contention that it was a lack of coinage in the subsistence sector which was the critical factor in explaining sectoral differences. Herein also lies the root cause of the country's failure to develop along healthy lines, so that only a catastrophe of the magnitude of the Famine could effect any transformation of such an unhealthy situation. J. Joseph Lee, while accepting their essential argument, disagrees regarding the nature of the non-monetized sector. Where Lynch and Vaizey see geographically distinct dual sectors, Lee suggests that in reality in the west there existed a strata dualism in which money was more or less important according to the necessity for its use.[147] Ó'Gráda contributed to the debate, saying that the central question should be, not the extent of the use of money, but its role. "Did the Irish peasant of the 1820s or the 1830s sell his produce when the price was right, or merely because, say, the rent was due?" he asks.[148]

Large sections of the west were indeed still enmeshed by the restrictions of a barter economy. An 1823 account, written in a period of distress, noted the situation:

> How seldom it happens in this country, that the labour of the poor man is requited with ready money. He gives labour for his garden, rent, and tythe.

He gives labour in exchange for horses to draw out his manure, or draw home his turf. He labours for the taylor, the weaver, the smith, and even for the priest and justice, in payment of the benefits derived from their various callings. In a word, he works for everything but ready money. In general the poor people here [Co. Limerick] have no money dealings, but in buying and selling their pigs, and paying their bog money. This system answers very well as long as the poor man has potatoes enough raised by his own labour, but where, as in the present instance this resource totally fails him, his embarrassment and difficulty is greater than can be conceived. He may be surrounded with plenty, but in this plenty he cannot share without paying the price.[149]

"Paying the price" was increasingly important as demands for hard cash began to replace barter in the fulfillment of rural obligations. The importance of monetization of obligations made it increasingly necessary for Irish county persons to raise cash to meet their obligations. Cash was becoming more necessary to pay the landlord, the tithe proctor, the moneylender, and the priest, so that when tenant farmers were unable to raise sufficient money to pay these obligations, they were forced to seek temporary employment elsewhere.

It was generally believed that preoccupation with the size of their rent rolls hindered eighteenth-century landlords from introducing the kind of good estate management which might have made farming in Ireland more productive.[150] If so it also robbed tenants of the incentive and capital to become progressive farmers, but they did become more inventive in discovering ways to raise cash to pay the rent. Marx said that Irish peasants were part serfs — because of their custom of paying the rent by their labor — but this became less true as the demand for their labor diminished. As Figure 2.2 illustrates, the number of days per year by county when agricultural work was available varied from county to county. Figures were lowest in the western counties of the province of Connacht, regions which were also areas of highest seasonal migration.

Agricultural innovation in the technology of potato cultivation has already been cited as an important factor in facilitating migrants from some regions to leave early in the year so as to arrive earlier than their competition in the labor market. While transhumance or booleying had once been an important part of rural life in southern and eastern Ireland, the practice commenced to disappear with the confiscations and land settlements of the sixteenth and seventeenth centuries. It lingered on, however, in some poor and hill areas in Kerry, Donegal, Connemara and the Mournes in Ulster.[151] In an article on transhumance in the Wicklow mountains south of Dublin, F.H.A. Aalen has suggested that various forms of the word *booley* (which was an anglicization of the Irish word *buaile*—a cattlefold or milking place) which appears in place names throughout Ireland may provide clues to the earlier extent of the practice.[152] Since we know that lazybed cultivation in Ireland preceded the advent of the potato in the country, we can assume that by adopting it people had for a long time provided themselves with the means whereby they could be absent from their farms for considerable lengths of time.

Population shifts within Ireland appear to have been fairly localized, however, according to Edward MacLysaght, even today Gaelic surnames are still to be found primarily in the part of the country to which their sept belonged.[153] While this is not absolute proof of fairly minimal inter-regional migration, the information contained in Figure 2.8 and tables 2.18 (Propensity to Migrate within Ireland), 2.19 (Gaining and Losing Counties), and 2.20 (Movement out of County of Birth, 1841) tend to bear out that internal movement followed by any kind of permanent settlement was fairly insignificant prior to the Famine. In the tables and the map it can be seen that the number of persons who migrated within the country in 1841, other than to Dublin, is not great. The largest loser, Wicklow, had a net loss of 11 percent of the total population (12,690 persons) because of its proximity to Dublin. The largest gainers were Dublin and Antrim (which contains Belfast) with 18 percent (67,890 persons) and 7 percent (19,385) respectively. This is consistent with Dublin's position as the capital of the country and chief entrepôt for goods and people during that period. In addition, as Freeman indicates, it was the focus of the system of canals, roads, and newly planned railroads, thus assured of a continuing importance.[154] Belfast was evolving into the principal industrial center of Ireland by midcentury.

What then was the nature of permanent internal migration? Tables 2.6, 2.7, and 2.20 indicate by gender the destinations of those migrating out of the county of their birth. A breakdown of regional migration by county is contained in tables 2.8, 2.9, 2.10, and 2.11. Movement thus, when it took place at all, was primarily short range and within provinces. Leinster migrants had the lowest propensity for movement outside that province: only 17 percent of male migrants and 19 percent of female migrants moved outside the region. Ulster persons who migrated within Ireland tended to move within the province (68 percent of all male migrants and 73 percent of female migrants moved only within the province), which is consistent with other factors. Among them were that the majority of Ulster residents were distinctly different from the remainder of the population and thus less likely to seek opportunity among strangers; the economy of the region was already quite different from that of the rest of the country; and thirdly, that Ulster already had a well-established pattern of permanent emigration to North America. Mi-

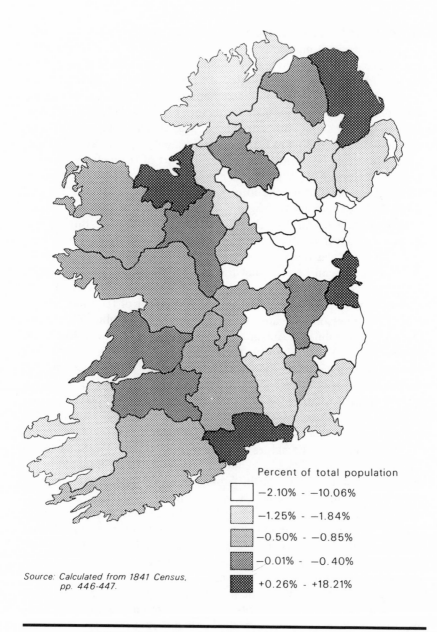

Percent of total population

☐	−2.10% - −10.06%
▨	−1.25% - −1.84%
▨	−0.50% - −0.85%
▨	−0.01% - −0.40%
▨	+0.26% - +18.21%

Source: Calculated from 1841 Census, pp. 446-447.

FIGURE 2.8.   Net migration as percent of total population, 1841.

Table 2.6. County origins of migrants into Sligo, 1841

	Males		Females	
County	No. of migrants to Sligo	Total from county to all destinations	No. of migrants to Sligo	Total from county to all destinations
Mayo	956	4,758	1,081	4,967
Leitrim	699	4,117	770	4,453
Roscommon	625	5,571	671	5,393

SOURCE: Calculated from 1841 Census.

Table 2.7. County origins of migrants into Waterford, 1841

	Males		Females	
County	No. of migrants to Waterford	Total from county to all destinations	No. of migrants to Waterford	Total from county to all destinations
Cork	2,759	10,482	2,515	9,753
Tipperary	2,125	10,790	2,230	10,422
Kilkenny	1,070	5,132	1,228	5,393

SOURCE: Calculated from 1841 Census.

grants in Munster were also unlikely to move beyond the region, supporting a conjecture that permanent emigration from that province was already well under way, borne out by information from the Boston *Pilot* "Missing Friends" data in which almost half of those leaving Ireland between 1831 and 1850 were from the province of Munster.[155] Migrants from Connacht, when they moved, were more likely to move greater distances within Ireland: 55 percent of male and 48 percent of female migrants moved outside the province.

Dublin was clearly the magnet for much of the country, so that it is worth examining in detail some of the characteristics of migration to and from the capital. Tables 2.12, 2.13, 2.14, 2.15, and 2.16 show the distribution of occupations of the migrants.[156] Reference to the occupational groupings in Dublin provides clues as to why that city was so high in skilled occupational categories. One example will illustrate: More than half of all migrants reporting themselves as one variety or another of dealer or shopkeeper came from Dublin (33,611 persons out of a total of 63,808 throughout the country).

The majority of those women with a reported occupation and living outside their county of birth were domestic servants (14 out of 30 percent). This was certainly true of Dublin-born female migrants (15 out of 29 percent). As the largest proportion of female migrants into Dublin were from the surrounding counties and went into domestic service, it

Table 2.8.   Leinster natives living outside county of birth (1841)

Born	Dublin	Leinster	Munster	Connacht	Ulster	Total
		Place of residence in 1841				
Males						
Carlow	1,898	3,198	204	60	119	5,479
Dublin	--	6,909	1,436	799	1,537	10,681
Kildare	4,165	1,981	170	105	154	6,575
Kilkenny	1,053	1,695	2,203	95	86	5,132
King's	1,486	1,907	1,307	583	211	5,494
Longford	785	1,118	155	874	454	3,386
Louth	1,512	1,233	92	97	1,151	4,085
Meath	5,674	2,468	128	130	662	9,062
Queen's	1,599	3,119	827	113	160	5,818
Westmeath	2,144	6,517	191	425	267	9,544
Wexford	2,535	2,350	506	96	184	5,671
Wicklow	6,853	3,173	292	83	138	10,539
TOTAL	29,704	35,668	7,511	3,460	5,123	81,466
Females						
Carlow	1,996	2,761	214	71	110	5,152
Dublin	--	6,630	1,618	934	1,710	10,892
Kildare	4,521	1,942	150	89	161	6,863
Kilkenny	1,080	1,579	2,548	90	96	5,393
King's	1,738	1,799	1,327	633	169	5,666
Longford	845	1,177	113	1,064	530	3,729
Louth	1,457	1,259	63	51	1,248	4,078
Meath	5,789	2,205	90	128	772	8,984
Queen's	2,170	3,604	990	151	194	7,109
Westmeath	2,355	3,064	171	510	237	6,337
Wexford	2,748	2,212	761	95	242	6,058
Wicklow	7,901	3,084	279	89	214	11,567
TOTAL	32,600	31,316	8,324	3,905	5,683	81,828

Source: Calculated from 1841 Census, pp. 446–47.

Table 2.9.   Munster natives living outside county of birth (1841)

Born	Dublin	Leinster	Munster	Connacht	Ulster	Total
		Place of residence in 1841				
Males						
Clare	488	383	2,453	899	94	4,317
Cork	1,321	1,146	7,371	300	344	10,482
Limerick	796	526	5,640	378	167	7,507
Tipperary	1,438	3,628	4,926	593	205	10,790
Waterford	449	1,074	2,122	62	73	3,780
TOTAL	4,492	6,757	22,512	2,232	883	36,876
Females						
Clare	382	435	2,584	926	82	4,409
Cork	1,372	748	6,981	311	341	9,753
Limerick	871	412	5,594	350	159	7,386
Tipperary	1,442	2,928	5,260	605	187	10,422
Waterford	559	752	2,445	65	80	3,901
TOTAL	4,626	5,275	22,864	2,257	849	35,871

Source: Calculated from 1841 Census, pp. 446–47.

Table 2.10. Connacht natives living outside county of birth (1841)

Born	Place of residence in 1841					
	Dublin	Leinster	Munster	Connacht	Ulster	Total
Males						
Galway	1,294	1,755	1,939	2,423	184	7,595
Leitrim	313	809	135	1,647	1,213	4,117
Mayo	501	448	301	3,271	237	4,758
Roscommon	874	1,627	288	2,524	258	5,571
Sligo	391	295	179	1,926	521	3,312
TOTAL	3,373	4,934	2,842	11,791	2,413	25,353
Females						
Galway	1,239	1,235	1,619	2,370	201	6,664
Leitrim	254	765	70	1,991	1,373	4,453
Mayo	475	327	202	3,716	247	4,967
Roscommon	839	1,441	197	2,694	222	5,393
Sligo	368	202	110	2,204	436	3,320
TOTAL	3,175	3,970	2,198	12,975	2,479	24,797

Source: Calculated from 1841 Census, pp. 446–47.

Table 2.11. Ulster natives living outside county of birth (1841)

Born	Place of residence in 1841					
	Dublin	Leinster	Munster	Connacht	Ulster	Total
Males						
Antrim	663	357	209	116	3,283	4,628
Armagh	581	913	135	140	4,315	6,084
Cavan	1,364	2,079	131	903	1,931	6,408
Donegal	294	262	151	501	3,146	4,354
Down	572	470	165	154	6,808	8,169
Fermanagh	562	544	154	653	2,765	4,678
Londonderry	339	253	117	138	3,897	4,744
Monaghan	672	1,167	75	234	3,603	5,751
Tyrone	495	391	165	255	6,043	7,349
TOTAL	5,542	6,436	1,302	3,094	35,791	52,165
Females						
Antrim	665	317	191	110	3,919	5,202
Armagh	663	706	97	130	4,937	6,533
Cavan	1,310	2,099	114	711	2,353	6,587
Donegal	251	162	107	545	3,605	4,670
Down	654	437	140	127	7,304	8,662
Fermanagh	520	303	101	677	3,052	4,653
Londonderry	320	168	77	139	4,200	4,904
Monaghan	632	987	51	196	4,387	6,253
Tyrone	491	271	95	225	6,643	7,725
TOTAL	5,506	5,450	973	2,860	40,400	55,189

Source: Calculated from 1841 Census, pp. 446–47.

Table 2.12. Percentage distribution of occupations of male migrants, 1841

Born	Farm servants and laborers	Clothing	Construction	Police	Domestic servants	Paupers	Other	Up to 15 years	15 + years unspecified occupation
	%	%	%	%	%	%	%	%	%
Leinster									
Dublin	14.09	5.61	9.68	1.30	5.97	0.64	19.25	27.38	16.08
Carlow	29.24	7.17	9.40	2.45	6.32	0.82	19.71	13.98	10.91
Kildare	30.45	7.19	9.22	2.16	7.14	0.40	18.46	13.93	11.05
Kilkenny	25.44	8.21	9.74	3.11	5.17	0.75	18.88	18.44	10.26
King's	26.76	7.96	8.35	5.61	5.27	0.58	18.16	17.03	10.28
Longford	27.82	7.16	7.27	6.38	5.20	1.75	19.07	15.94	9.41
Louth	26.38	10.21	9.38	2.54	4.94	0.38	20.34	17.66	8.17
Meath	35.94	5.55	7.56	2.48	2.05	0.72	22.81	12.98	9.91
Queen's	26.07	6.96	8.80	5.68	7.20	0.36	19.15	15.07	10.71
Westmeath	32.47	6.35	7.99	3.23	6.03	0.81	18.03	14.48	10.61
Wexford	27.14	8.69	11.64	2.86	5.66	0.46	20.24	12.54	10.77
Wicklow	33.48	5.94	8.21	2.11	6.73	0.62	17.98	15.86	9.07
Munster									
Clare	27.01	6.37	6.69	5.77	5.49	1.00	18.71	19.38	9.57
Cork	28.58	7.76	9.37	3.99	4.17	1.20	17.37	18.06	9.50
Kerry	30.47	6.53	5.97	7.55	4.49	2.80	16.23	17.48	8.48
Limerick	24.47	7.25	7.91	4.17	4.34	1.19	17.95	20.94	11.78
Tipperary	28.46	7.71	7.74	4.08	5.34	0.65	18.34	17.52	10.16
Waterford	26.06	7.94	8.92	1.75	4.66	1.27	19.50	17.20	12.70
Connacht									
Galway	28.14	6.73	7.22	5.65	5.83	1.41	16.08	18.60	10.34
Leitrim	28.22	6.63	6.00	6.07	4.88	2.28	17.60	20.45	7.87
Mayo	29.34	7.55	5.00	7.23	4.14	3.26	14.49	20.58	8.41
Roscommon	27.12	6.93	7.34	4.16	5.56	1.56	16.40	20.03	10.90
Sligo	21.20	8.03	7.55	7.76	4.44	1.36	22.16	17.78	10.72
Ulster									
Antrim	11.69	13.66	10.85	4.60	5.21	0.93	19.20	23.62	10.24
Armagh	19.87	16.32	8.33	2.53	4.24	0.77	19.13	20.71	8.10
Cavan	27.56	8.01	7.19	4.37	5.17	1.98	19.58	18.09	8.05
Donegal	26.00	7.60	8.66	4.07	4.43	0.78	19.16	21.93	7.37
Down	14.18	16.59	13.59	1.86	3.75	0.13	20.44	22.18	7.25
Fermanagh	20.31	8.19	7.42	8.38	5.28	0.90	21.09	18.77	9.66
Londonderry	19.58	13.72	9.00	3.23	4.70	0.84	22.71	18.38	7.84
Monaghan	26.46	9.95	7.58	2.96	4.43	0.99	20.00	19.61	8.02
Tyrone	24.08	13.70	8.44	2.12	4.98	1.63	17.36	20.59	7.10
All Ireland	25.89	8.70	8.52	4.18	5.18	1.11	18.54	18.39	9.49

SOURCE: Calculated from 1841 Census, pp. 448–51.

can be assumed that these were supplying vacancies created by female servants leaving Dublin for domestic employment elsewhere. As will be seen later Irish women in England did not as yet enter domestic service in significant numbers, presumably because the local supply was sufficient. This would also suggest that adequate demand for their services still existed within Ireland.

The largest number of Dublin-born female migrants reported themselves as having unspecified occupations, which would indicate that they were probably housewives (7,755 persons out of a total of 10,892 females born in Dublin but living elsewhere, or 71 percent). Dublin then, it would appear, was a training ground for housewives as well as domestic servants. Movement of females out of Dublin was, as indicated previously, not far; 61 percent of Dublin-born female migrants were still within the province of Leinster; 16 percent were in Ulster; 15 percent in

Table 2.13. Percentage distribution of occupations of female migrants, 1841

Born	Farm servants and laborers	Clothing	Domestic servants	Paupers	Other	Up to 15 years	15+ years unspecified occupation
	%	%	%	%	%	%	%
Leinster							
Dublin	0.59	6.07	15.09	1.19	5.86	25.13	46.07
Carlow	2.23	7.08	17.93	2.23	3.40	16.05	51.07
Kildare	1.11	5.67	21.97	1.37	4.84	13.89	51.15
Kilkenny	3.33	5.66	14.25	1.64	4.10	18.10	52.92
King's	1.44	6.30	17.49	1.46	3.29	17.45	52.57
Longford	1.56	14.32	12.39	2.92	2.62	16.73	49.46
Louth	1.10	7.35	15.98	1.15	3.91	19.54	50.97
Meath	1.61	5.51	18.64	1.34	6.09	13.97	52.84
Queen's	2.42	6.86	17.33	1.01	4.45	14.45	53.48
Westmeath	1.03	6.56	17.58	1.78	3.69	15.12	54.24
Wexford	1.34	5.66	18.74	0.69	5.43	13.12	55.02
Wicklow	1.00	3.92	20.06	1.00	4.91	14.62	54.49
Munster							
Clare	0.75	7.16	16.65	1.95	3.94	21.00	48.55
Cork	1.74	7.69	12.52	2.28	3.09	18.64	54.04
Kerry	1.89	5.75	18.65	6.12	2.83	18.77	45.99
Limerick	0.61	6.70	12.92	2.14	3.35	21.38	52.90
Tipperary	1.65	6.33	13.37	1.58	3.22	20.02	53.83
Waterford	1.51	4.41	16.07	1.79	4.31	16.46	55.45
Connacht							
Galway	1.45	6.80	12.56	2.91	2.61	20.77	52.90
Leitrim	0.36	13.56	11.23	3.86	2.49	21.92	46.58
Mayo	0.81	10.01	9.76	6.56	1.83	20.15	50.88
Roscommon	0.85	10.09	12.61	3.69	2.72	19.51	50.53
Sligo	0.27	12.29	9.64	3.10	2.47	20.30	51.93
Ulster							
Antrim	0.33	14.30	14.26	1.58	2.98	21.47	45.08
Armagh	0.43	17.01	13.59	1.03	6.09	20.14	41.71
Cavan	0.83	12.16	13.56	3.15	2.97	19.54	47.79
Donegal	0.34	14.03	13.19	1.46	2.74	20.32	47.92
Down	0.38	16.80	12.13	0.43	1.88	21.96	46.42
Fermanagh	0.58	17.24	11.67	2.49	2.60	20.09	45.33
Londonderry	0.18	17.39	12.56	1.59	1.68	18.35	48.25
Monaghan	1.15	14.82	11.98	2.86	2.01	19.94	47.24
Tyrone	0.47	17.41	9.95	2.12	2.52	22.14	45.39
All Ireland	1.13	9.86	14.25	2.22	3.03	20.53	48.98

SOURCE: Calculated from 1841 Census, pp. 448–51.

Munster; and 9 percent in Connacht. (See Table 2.20.)

From Table 2.8 it can be seen that the majority of migrants to Dublin came from Wicklow and Meath, counties contiguous to Dublin (7,901 females and 6,853 males, and 5,789 females and 5,674 males respectively) with Kildare next in order of importance (4,521 females and

Table 2.14. Emigrant farmworkers as percent of population, 1841

County of origin	Farm servant and laborer		% total county population	% migrant population for county
	Male	Female	Male	Male
Leinster				
Dublin	1,505	64	0.88	14.05
Carlow	1,602	115	3.77	29.23
Kildare	2,144	82	3.69	30.44
Kilkenny	1,620	215	1.63	25.44
King's	1,661	92	2.28	26.76
Longford	937	58	1.62	27.51
Louth	1,165	47	2.13	26.38
Meath	3,257	145	3.52	35.92
Queen's	1,517	172	1.98	26.07
Westmeath	2,051	65	2.91	32.46
Wexford	1,539	81	1.57	27.13
Wicklow	3,528	116	5.55	33.43
Subtotal	22,526	1,252		
Munster				
Clare	1,166	32	0.80	27.19
Cork	2,996	170	0.71	28.54
Kerry	1,480	81	1.00	30.44
Limerick	1,837	45	1.13	24.19
Tipperary	3,071	172	1.41	28.45
Waterford	935	59	0.97	24.72
Subtotal	11,485	559		
Connacht				
Galway	2,137	91	0.97	28.31
Leitrim	1,162	16	1.49	28.32
Mayo	1,396	40	0.71	29.06
Roscommon	1,511	46	1.18	27.11
Sligo	792	9	0.88	23.89
Subtotal	6,998	202		
Ulster				
Antrim	541	17	0.31	11.67
Armagh	1,209	28	1.06	19.82
Cavan	1,766	57	1.46	27.53
Donegal	1,132	16	0.77	25.97
Down	1,158	33	0.66	13.98
Fermanagh	950	27	1.23	20.29
Londonderry	929	9	0.86	19.50
Monaghan	1,522	72	1.55	26.40
Tyrone	1,770	36	1.15	23.96
Subtotal	10,977	295		
ALL IRELAND TOTAL	51,946	2,314	1.29	25.89

SOURCE: Calculated from 1841 Census.

Table 2.15. Persons "ministering to clothing" as percent of population, 1841

County	Spinners and winders Male	Female	Weavers Male	Female	Shoemakers Male	Female	Dress-makers Female	Tailors Male	Total migrants in clothing Male	Female	"Ministering to clothing" as % total county population Male	Female	% total emigrants Male	Female
Leinster														
Dublin	39	119	78	24	206	13	375	83	559	661	0.32	0.32	5.61	6.07
Carlow	6	91	35	15	188	16	172	98	393	365	0.92	0.83	7.17	7.08
Kildare	22	81	79	12	206	26	196	71	506	418	0.87	0.74	7.70	6.09
Kilkenny	23	101	71	23	233	10	148	96	523	365	0.52	0.38	10.19	6.77
King's	15	139	112	7	174	6	184	80	494	402	0.67	0.54	8.99	7.09
Longford	10	375	60	3	80	7	112	40	241	534	0.41	0.92	7.16	14.32
Louth	14	142	175	3	122	5	123	42	451	314	0.82	0.54	11.04	7.70
Meath	10	211	98	5	173	10	179	80	503	495	0.54	0.54	5.55	5.51
Queen's	19	144	71	38	171	19	196	73	405	488	0.53	0.62	6.96	6.86
Westmeath	14	185	93	16	140	7	134	67	402	416	0.57	0.58	6.35	6.56
Wexford	9	75	29	10	231	16	157	114	493	343	0.63	0.32	8.69	5.66
Wicklow	12	121	46	23	291	14	210	127	626	454	0.98	0.72	5.94	3.92
Subtotal	193	1,784	947	179	2,215	149	2,186	971	5,596	5,255	0.58	0.52		
Munster														
Clare	4	135	38	7	105	7	116	81	275	305	0.19	0.21	6.37	6.92
Cork	29	348	175	30	276	12	242	121	813	750	0.19	0.17	7.76	7.69
Kerry	4	143	65	2	85	1	78	31	317	247	0.21	0.16	6.53	5.75
Limerick	4	224	126	3	184	13	170	106	544	495	0.33	0.29	7.25	6.70
Tipperary	39	248	116	83	366	13	217	132	832	660	0.38	0.30	7.71	6.33
Waterford	4	33	34	7	145	11	90	43	300	172	0.31	0.17	7.94	4.41
Subtotal	84	1,131	554	132	1,161	57	913	514	3,081	2,629	0.26	0.22		
Connacht														
Galway	8	224	77	3	177	7	177	134	511	454	0.24	0.20	6.73	6.81
Leitrim	10	502	68	1	87	1	77	60	273	604	0.35	0.77	6.63	13.56
Mayo	4	272	121	8	116	7	137	76	359	497	0.18	0.25	7.55	10.01
Roscommon	10	342	57	2	169	2	162	83	386	544	0.30	0.42	6.93	10.09
Sligo	3	290	38	0	85	3	91	61	266	408	0.29	0.44	8.03	12.29
Subtotal	35	1,630	361	14	634	20	644	414	1,795	2,507	0.26	0.36		
Ulster														
Antrim	29	352	315	60	102	10	221	26	632	744	0.36	0.39	13.66	14.30
Armagh	121	686	472	64	116	15	246	63	993	1,111	0.87	0.93	16.32	17.01
Cavan	15	590	179	9	161	2	166	65	513	831	0.42	0.67	8.01	12.62
Donegal	6	449	87	4	88	7	138	59	331	655	0.22	0.15	7.60	14.03
Down	167	637	519	56	245	12	513	84	1,351	1,455	0.77	0.77	16.59	16.80
Fermanagh	13	492	125	8	123	6	193	60	383	802	0.49	1.00	8.19	17.24
Londonderry	52	513	286	16	98	5	178	53	651	853	0.60	0.73	13.72	17.39
Monaghan	49	655	185	9	154	2	194	63	572	927	0.58	0.90	9.95	14.82
Tyrone	107	921	417	36	197	13	256	87	1,007	1,345	0.65	0.84	13.70	17.41
Subtotal	559	5,295	2,585	262	1,284	73	2,105	560	6,433	8,723	0.57	0.74		
ALL IRELAND TOTAL	871	9,840	4,447	587	5,294	298	5,848	2,459	16,905	19,114	0.42	0.47	8.70	9.33

Source: Calculated from 1841 Census.

Table 2.16. Dublin migrant occupations, 1841

Males	All Ireland % migrants — mean	Born in Dublin migrant elsewhere
Farm servants and laborers	25.89	14.09
Clothing	8.70	5.61
Construction	8.52	9.68
Police	4.18	1.30
Domestic servants	5.18	5.97
Paupers	1.11	0.64
All other	18.54	19.25
1–5 years	18.39	27.38
15 + years (unspecified occupation)	9.49	16.08

Source: Calculated from 1841 Census data.

4,165 males). Despite Louth's proximity to Dublin, only 1,457 females migrated from there (versus 1,512 males). Freeman indicates that in that period Louth bore more resemblance to Ulster in the north than it did to the counties to the south, with numerous grain mills, flax mills, bleaching greens, and arable farming,[157] which suggests that domestic industry provided an alternative to migration, encouraging people to remain. When landlords in counties Kildare and Meath shifted from cultivation to grazing and fattening cattle from the west for the export market, they sought to eject smallholders to make room for large grazing farms. Laborers, also, were poorly paid (normally eight shillings per day in winter and ten shillings per day in summer, see Figures 2.2, 2.3 and Table 2.1), and the number of days per year when agricultural employment was available was low (Meath 135, Kildare 100, Louth 210, Wicklow 170, both factors providing incentives to leave these counties. In contrast, while wages in Louth were low, the number of days work available was considerably more, which would tend to encourage potential migrants to remain.

Wicklow supplied the largest number of migrants to Dublin; Table 2.17 shows 6,853 males (Meath was next with 5,674). Conditions in Wicklow varied fairly widely, according to the terrain. While lowland areas were prosperous with well-farmed estates, in the mountainous areas poverty and scarcity were endemic. (Furrows can still be seen which follow the slope of the land as high as 1,000 feet in the Wicklow hills, an indication of land pressures so great that the poor were forced to grow potatoes to that height.) When the Rev. Hall visited Wicklow early in the nineteenth century, he recorded that land in that county let for eleven pounds per acre (double the cost of land in the vicinity of London) but that produce such as potatoes brought only very low prices.[158] While the days per year when work was available were fairly high overall (160) and wages per week resembled those of Kildare and Meath, reference to valuation figures in Table 2.3 indicate a smaller percentage of the very poorest ratepayers in Wicklow than in Meath or Kildare (Wicklow 14 percent of total; Kildare 23 percent; Meath 27 percent; Louth had only 9 percent). Wicklow had somewhat less than the average proportion of the poorest ratepayers for the province (14 as opposed to 17 percent), but Kildare and Meath are considerably above it.

Reference to tables 2.12 and 2.13 indicates the occupations of migrants from Wicklow. It seems safe to assume that the occupational distribution of Wicklow migrants should be dominated by their occupational distribution in Dublin since Dublin was the destination for the majority of them, 6,853 out of a total of 10,539 of all migrants from Wicklow. (All figures are for males, unless otherwise stated.) Most

Table 2.17. Migration from counties contiguous to Dublin as percent of total migrant population, 1841

	Louth		Meath		Kildare		Wicklow	
	Male	Female	Male	Female	Male	Female	Male	Female
Migrant to Dublin	1,512	1,457	5,674	5,789	4,165	4,521	6,853	7,901
Total migrant pop.	4,416	4,078	9,062	8,984	6,575	6,863	10,539	11,567
% of total	34.2	35.7	62.6	64.4	63.3	65.9	65.0	68.3

SOURCES Computed from 1841 Census data.

Wicklow migrants were laborers connected with food production (33 percent) which was 7 percent more than that of the average for the whole country (26 percent). Only 6 percent were connected with the production of clothing, which was less than the national average of 9 percent; 8 percent of the migrants were in construction, equal to the national average; 2 percent went into the police force (national average 4 percent); slightly more than the average went into domestic service, 7 percent versus 5 percent (more than three times as many female migrants as males from Wicklow went into domestic service — 2,320 versus 709 — and in fact Wicklow was also the largest supplier of female domestics to the rest of the country). Only .62 percent of all migrants from Wicklow were paupers, less than the 1.11 percent mean. Forty-three percent of all Wicklow migrants fell into the unspecified class which included a large proportion of males who were dealers, shopkeepers, and writing clerks (the mean was 46 percent).[159] Children under the age of 15 years were 16 percent of the total number (mean was 18 percent) which would indicate that it was primarily a family migration. Only 9 percent of those reporting themselves as fifteen or more years of age had unspecified occupations (which I take to be either gentlemen or students), which is consistent with the mean for that category (9 percent).

Table 2.18 presents a gender breakdown for the propensity to migrate within Ireland for all persons. As there are no great disparities between the propensities of the two sexes to migrate it can be assumed that overall internal migration was probably a family movement, and thus fairly likely to be followed by permanent settlement. Reference to this table as well as Table 2.19 show that when taken as a percentage of total population, all four provinces showed little male-female difference in the relative propensity to migrate (the total for the country was 4.9 percent for males and 4.8 percent for females).

From Table 2.19, which breaks down propensities to migrate into counties within provinces, it can be seen that when the total number of persons in-migrant are subtracted from those out-migrant, Connacht's loss of males was primarily from Galway and Leitrim (1,609 males ver-

Table 2.18. Propensity to migrate within Ireland

Province	Population	Out-migrants	Percent migrants
Males			
Dublin County	170,900[a]	10,681	6.2
Leinster	792,800	70,454	8.9
Munster	1,182,200	36,876	3.1
Connacht	699,900	25,353	3.6
Ulster	1,122,600	52,165	4.7
TOTAL	3,968,400	195,529	4.9
Females			
Dublin County	201,800[b]	10,892	5.4
Leinster	808,100	70,936	8.8
Munster	1,210,000	35,871	3.0
Connacht	701,800	24,797	3.5
Ulster	1,179,000	55,189	4.7
TOTAL	4,100,700	197,685	4.8

SOURCE: Calculated from 1841 Census, pp. 446–47.
[a]25.2% of Dublin male population born elsewhere (¾ native born). 7.8% born outside Leinster.
[b]22.8% of Dublin female population born elsewhere. 6.6% born outside Leinster.

sus 572 females for Galway, and 1,108 males versus 833 females for Leitrim). Mayo showed a net loss of more females than males (436 more females; 1,870 versus 1,434); one can assume from this that with the decline of domestic industry, which had been an important supplement to family incomes there, women were losing the economic importance within the family that they had once enjoyed, and were tending to seek employment elsewhere. If that was so, then it explains why Roscommon and Sligo were total gainers in in-migrant women; Mayo women were migrating to contiguous counties. (Roscommon stands out, as it lost 608 males and gained a total of 578 females.) Mayo females went primarily to Galway (1,694), Sligo (1,081), and Roscommon (864).

Sligo was a net gainer in total population, one of only four counties in Ireland which gained in population in this period. While the amount is small, only .26 percent of total population, the gain was primarily from female in-migrants (391 as opposed to 98 males). While the total figures are not large they do invite the question of what attracted women to a county which was already overcrowded and desperately poor. The valuation of assets per capita was less than a pound per person (.81) which was slightly less than the average for Connacht (.90) but considerably below the average for the whole country (1.49). In the barony of Carbery in Sligo, considered representative for purposes of the question being asked (it was in the northeast corner of the county and bordered Sligo city) the 1841 laboring population was said to number 6,206, of which

Table 2.19. Gaining and losing counties, 1841

County	Net totals				Net in-migration[a]			Net migration as percent of population		
	Emigrant		Immigrant							
	Male	Female	Male	Female	Male	Female	Total	% Male	% Female	% Total
Leinster										
Dublin	10,707	10,920	43,424	46,093	+32,717	+35,173	+67,890	+19.14	+17.43	+18.21
Carlow	5,479	5,224	3,163	3,492	− 2,316	− 1,732	− 4,048	− 5.46	− 3.95	− 4.70
Kildare	7,042	7,374	7,937	6,243	+ 895	− 1,131	− 236	+ 1.54	− 2.00	− 0.21
Kilkenny	6,367	6,447	5,025	4,399	− 842	− 2,048	− 2,890	− 0.85	− 1.98	− 1.43
King's	6,206	6,380	5,714	5,832	− 492	− 548	− 1,040	− 0.68	− 0.73	− 0.71
Longford	3,406	3,761	3,236	3,046	− 170	− 715	− 885	− 0.30	− 1.23	− 0.77
Louth	4,416	4,273	3,842	3,579	− 574	− 694	− 1,268	− 0.92	− 1.05	− 0.99
Meath	9,065	8,987	5,365	4,959	− 3,700	− 4,028	− 7,728	− 4.00	− 4.41	− 4.20
Queen's	5,818	7,109	5,204	4,498	− 614	− 2,611	− 3,225	− 0.80	− 3.36	− 2.10
Westmeath	6,317	6,337	4,086	3,865	− 2,231	− 2,472	− 4,703	− 3.17	− 3.48	− 3.33
Wexford	5,671	6,009	4,552	4,055	− 1,119	− 1,954	− 3,073	− 1.14	− 1.87	− 1.52
Wicklow	10,552	11,591	4,987	4,466	− 5,565	− 7,125	−12,690	− 8.76	−11.36	−10.06
Subtotal	81,046	84,412	97,035	94,527	−15,989	−10,115	−26,104	+ 1.66	+ 1.00	+ 1.38
Munster										
Clare	4,288	4,258	3,866	3,887	− 422	− 371	− 793	− 0.29	− 0.26	− 0.28
Cork	10,496	9,791	7,148	6,938	− 3,348	− 2,853	− 6,201	− 0.80	− 0.65	− 0.73
Kerry	4,862	4,305	2,543	2,356	− 2,319	− 1,949	− 4,268	− 1.57	− 1.32	− 1.45
Limerick	7,592	7,425	6,931	7,667	− 661	+ 242	− 419	− 0.38	+ 0.14	− 0.13
Tipperary	10,791	10,422	9,858	9,175	− 933	− 1,247	− 2,180	− 0.43	− 0.57	− 0.50
Waterford	3,782	3,901	7,978	8,038	+ 4,196	+ 4,137	+ 8,333	+ 4.39	+ 4.11	+ 4.25
Subtotal	41,811	40,102	38,324	38,061	− 3,487	− 2,041	− 5,528	− 0.29	− 0.16	− 0.23
Connacht										
Galway	7,546	6,672	5,937	6,100	− 1,609	− 572	− 2,181	− 0.76	− 0.27	− 0.52
Leitrim	4,103	4,419	2,995	3,586	− 1,108	− 833	− 1,941	− 1.43	− 1.07	− 1.25
Mayo	4,803	4,932	3,369	3,062	− 1,434	− 1,870	− 3,304	− 0.73	− 0.96	− 0.85
Roscommon	5,572	5,394	4,964	5,972	− 608	+ 578	− 30	− 0.47	+ 0.45	− 0.01
Sligo	3,314	3,322	3,412	3,693	+ 98	+ 371	+ 469	+ 0.10	+ 0.40	+ 0.26
Subtotal	25,338	24,739	20,677	22,413	− 4,661	− 2,326	− 6,987	− 0.66	− 0.33	− 0.50
Ulster										
Antrim	4,634	5,206	14,073	15,152	+ 9,439	+ 9,946	+19,385	+ 7.08	+ 6.95	+ 7.02
Armagh	6,099	6,408	4,096	4,623	− 2,003	− 1,785	− 3,788	− 1.75	− 1.50	− 1.63
Cavan	6,414	6,836	3,425	3,820	− 2,989	− 3,016	− 6,005	− 2.47	− 2.46	− 2.47
Donegal	4,358	4,679	2,628	2,379	− 1,730	− 2,300	− 4,030	− 1.18	− 1.53	− 1.36
Down	8,278	8,805	5,093	5,857	− 3,185	− 2,948	− 6,133	− 1.83	− 1.56	− 1.70
Fermanagh	4,681	4,655	3,968	5,054	− 713	+ 399	− 314	− 0.92	+ 0.50	− 0.20
Londonderry	4,762	4,950	4,026	4,803	− 736	− 147	− 883	− 0.68	− 0.12	− 0.40
Monaghan	5,765	6,260	2,783	3,165	− 2,982	− 3,095	− 6,077	− 3.03	− 3.02	− 3.03
Tyrone	7,386	7,741	4,444	4,939	− 2,942	− 2,802	− 5,744	− 1.91	− 1.75	− 1.84
SUBTOTAL	52,377	55,540	44,536	49,792	− 7,841	− 5,748	−13,589	− 0.70	− 0.49	− 0.59
ALL IRELAND TOTAL	200,572	204,793	200,572	204,793	0	0	0			

SOURCE: Calculated from 1841 Census, pp. 446–47.
[a]Total immigrant minus total emigrant population.
Note: Leinster excluding Dublin had a net loss of 16,728 males and 25,058 females, for a total of 41,786 persons.

one half were engaged in agriculture. (Since the total numbers of persons engaged in agriculture resemble areas such as County Dublin with its demand for non-agricultural labor as porters, etc., it may be safely assumed that a similar situation existed in Carbery.) It was reported that most of the tenantry there who had been dispossessed from there had emigrated to America.[160] This evidence contrasts with that of a noted unwillingness of cleared tenants to emigrate from other surrounding baronies. Carbery's proximity to Sligo, a port city with passenger ships travelling regularly to America, certainly must be part of the explanation for why persons from there were more likely to emigrate. In an area where emigration had been considerable, may this not also have created sufficient labor shortages to attract persons to the area?

It is not possible to distinguish between migrants who went to the city and those who went to the country because the census information for Sligo does not differentiate. However, the city of Sligo with an 1841 population of 12,272 persons, was described by Inglis as "the chief mart of the northwest of Ireland."[161] He says also that it was the only town of note in the whole area (and it was only after the Famine that the port trade of Galway exceeded that of Sligo). Since the city attracted more female migrants than male, and as there was always a larger proportion of females than males in Irish cities (as well as in Ireland), one can assume that it was an urban migration. It is not possible to attempt a similar reconstruction to that of Dublin of the occupational distribution of migrants which would tell something about the nature of the occupational attractions of the county because the proportions of persons migrating to Sligo was too small to permit accuracy (see Table 2.6). The same also is true for Waterford (Table 2.7), suggesting the same question as to why that county was a total gainer in population.

If migration into County Waterford was primarily an urban migration (and it seems likely, based on evidence of the three other areas which were growing in population), then explanations for why this was so are not readily apparent. (What comes to mind is that if Waterford city with a population of 23,216 persons was growing why was there not comparable growth in Cork city with a population of 80,720 persons?) The 1831 census, which may have overestimated population, returned Waterford as having 28,821 persons and Cork 107,041.[162] Valuations for County Waterford are fairly high for the province, 1.48 per capita, higher than the 1.32 for Munster, and similar to that for the country as a whole, 1.49. Freeman indicates that the success of Waterford as a port resulted in declines for nearby southeastern ports such as Passage and Dungarvan.[163] Could the extent of decline have been greater than Freeman recognized? Manufactures were of minor significance in Waterford at the time, so growth would have been confined to the export trade in grain products, livestock, and dairy products. Furthermore, Waterford is within Bourke's southeastern arc of "less-poor" areas (see Figure 1.2) which means that the port city may have been sharing in the general prosperity of the whole region.

All of the preceding evidence, taken together, makes it clear that the degree of internal migration within Ireland was really quite small. The picture emerges of Dublin and Belfast urbanizing at fairly moderate rates, with Dublin primarily a government and service center; slight growth in Sligo and Waterford, which can be explained by their role as port regions serving their hinterlands. The minimal amount of migration between provinces, and particularly minimal movement out of the poorest western counties, is consistent with the belief that there were serious barriers to major permanent movement within Ireland. This, then, would suggest that external migration of a temporary nature was much more important in the Irish economy than was internal migration.

However, it is important to keep in mind that the preceding is no measure of seasonal migration within Ireland. Instead, the statistics catch people at only one particular point in their lives, and because the census was taken in early June, when the seasonal movement to Britain was well underway, the persons enumerated were more likely to have been relatively settled.

The history of migration then goes as follows: historically, the continuum of migration began earliest with a seasonal removal of persons with their livestock to higher pastures. As the demand for temporary employment developed within Ireland it attracted seasonal migrants for harvest work or relatively permanent movement to nearby urban areas. This in turn encouraged movement to England and Scotland when greater opportunities developed there and improvements in marine transportation minimized the time and risk involved in the journey.

The problem of measuring harvest migration within Ireland in the pre-Famine period remains tantalizingly difficult, if not impossible. The main source of information for reconstructing the areas supplying harvest migrants is the collection of parish reports submitted in 1836 to the *Royal Commission on the Condition of the Poorer Classes of Ireland*.[164] Information contained in this report is extremely difficult to use because of inconsistencies and vagueness in the responses. Even the wording of the questionnaire gives some indication of the difficulty of using this source. For example, the following question sought to discover what areas were contributing migrants, but as can be seen, it could give rise to ambiguous responses: *What number of labourers are in the habit of leaving their dwellings periodically to obtain employment, and what proportion of them go to England?*

While one can feel confident about the integrity of the people collecting the information, drawn as they were from the middle classes (including a large number of parish priests) and having real local knowledge, few responses clearly distinguished between internal and external movement. In addition, the interpretation of numbers mentioned needs clarification. For example, some persons reported "a few" which cross-

Table 2.20. Movement out of county of birth, 1841

Place of birth	Dublin		Leinster		Munster		Connacht		Ulster		Total	
					Area of residence in 1841							
Males												
Dublin	..		6,909	(64.7)	1,436	(13.4)	799	(7.5)	1,537	(14.4)	10,681	(100.0)
Leinster	29,704	(42.2)	28,759	(40.8)	6,075	(8.6)	2,661	(3.8)	3,255	(4.6)	70,454	(100.0)
Munster	4,492	(12.2)	6,757	(18.3)	22,512	(61.0)	2,232	(6.1)	883	(2.4)	36,876	(100.0)
Connacht	3,373	(13.3)	4,934	(19.5)	2,842	(11.2)	11,791	(46.5)	2,413	(9.5)	25,353	(100.0)
Ulster	5,542	(10.6)	6,436	(12.3)	1,302	(2.5)	3,094	(5.9)	35,791	(68.6)	52,165	(100.0)
TOTAL	43,111	(22.0)	53,795	(27.5)	34,167	(17.5)	20,577	(10.5)	43,879	(22.4)	195,529	(100.0)
Females												
Dublin	..		6,630	(60.9)	1,618	(14.9)	934	(8.6)	1,710	(15.7)	10,892	(100.0)
Leinster	32,600	(46.0)	24,686	(34.8)	6,706	(9.5)	2,971	(4.2)	3,973	(5.6)	70,936	(100.0)
Munster	4,626	(12.9)	5,275	(14.7)	22,864	(63.7)	2,257	(6.3)	849	(2.4)	35,871	(100.0)
Connacht	3,175	(12.8)	3,970	(16.0)	2,198	(8.9)	12,975	(52.3)	2,479	(10.0)	24,797	(100.0)
Ulster	5,506	(10.0)	5,450	(9.9)	973	(1.8)	2,860	(5.2)	40,400	(73.2)	55,189	(100.0)
TOTAL	45,907	(23.2)	46,011	(23.3)	34,359	(17.4)	21,997	(11.1)	49,411	(25.0)	197,685	(100.0)

SOURCE: Calculated from 1841 Census, pp. 446–47.
Notes: (1) 50.5% of all male migration is within provinces and becomes 69.2% when Dublin is included as part of Leinster. (2) 51.1% of all female migration is within provinces and becomes 71% when Dublin is included as part of Leinster.

checking revealed as in one case was about two hundred; other persons say "many" which when compared with other evidence revealed to be fewer than fifty.

Two useful attempts to reconstruct a pattern of seasonal migration based on the evidence collected at the Poor Inquiry have been made by J.H. Johnson and Anne O'Dowd.[165] The problem in using this material is that it is difficult to distinguish sufficiently between regional and long-distance migration. If systematic information was available about the areas from which the earliest harvest migrants came, it would provide evidence concerning the areas from which there was seasonal migration to Britain in a later period. In other words, as regional movement tended to break the ties with the land (which had formerly limited farmers' activities by confining them to a more evenly distributed agricultural cycle) laborers were enabled to move locally into areas where there was seasonal demand. The result of their expectations being raised by the attraction of opportunities elsewhere, or of their displacement by persons willing to undercut their wages (a constant in Irish labor history), the migrants who travelled to Britain came from the earliest areas where capitalized farming was prevalent (regions of eastern Leinster and southeastern Munster). In turn, these people were replaced by migrants from adjoining counties. For such a pattern to develop a ready supply of available labor was necessary, and this was assured by the increasing population throughout the country and a general narrowing of opportunities for employment. If this hypothesis is correct, then the areas from which the seasonal migrants departed for Britain in 1841 were once regions of local harvest migration.

Regions within Ireland which had once generated a demand for harvest migrants were those where market-oriented production resulted in landlords clearing uneconomic tenants, thereby reducing the size of the total labor force and creating a demand for seasonal workers. By the 1830s, laborers from Connacht, particularly those known as Black Irish from Mayo, were being hired to harvest in Leinster. The cost or availability of transport within the country was not a deterrent to movement (since all migrants were said to walk to their destinations), but there was reported to be a great deal of hostility to workers from Mayo in areas of northern Munster. The supply of laborers for that area was met by people from adjacent counties to the south.

As was also true of conditions in the city of Dublin, it is difficult to measure whether hostility to outsiders was worse in Ireland than elsewhere. Certainly Irish harvest migrants in England were frequently on the receiving end of a good deal of hostility as the account earlier in this chapter will attest, but they were reported as being unaffected by it.

Some respondents in the Poor Inquiry reported that hostility was highest toward harvesters from Connacht and that for that reason they preferred to seek work in England.

The available evidence indicates that potential migrants were extremely cautious in calculating the costs and benefits of the trip, either within Ireland or abroad. It took careful planning to make the substantial journey from the more remote areas of Ireland such as Connacht and Donegal across to England. It was said to cost at least a pound for the journey to England: an average of eight shillings for food for the journey within Ireland, another four shillings for the ship passage, and another eight shillings for food in England or Scotland. The food of choice, potatoes, was too bulky to carry so those workers who did not beg their way customarily carried oaten bread on the journey. In spite of their dire financial straits, very few people who were or had been migrant laborers said that they begged along the way (although there were some reports from informants in Leinster that migrant harvesters always begged); others testified as to the pride of seasonal workers who preferred to pay their own way. Apparently, few of them took their wives and families, citing as their reasons that women could earn more by begging in Ireland than they could in England where there was believed to be not only little demand for Irish women's labor at the harvest, but that begging there was discouraged.[166]

Despite the absence of a leader in the fictional account of the Irish work crew which appears earlier in this chapter, seasonal workers usually journeyed in a kind of padrone system, led by a leader, himself usually a seasonal worker of long experience. The system minimized the risk for people departing from more traditional regions where they would have been unfamiliar with the English language, the money system, or wage negotiations and terms of employment. In some cases, where the migrants were too poor to pay the cost of the journey, the leaders were said to advance the cost of the journey. Leaders of work gangs even negotiated with ship captains for a group rate, thus reducing fare.[167]

The novelist William Carleton's character, Phelim O'Toole, was the grandson of the leader of one such gang of harvesters. He was able to lease a small piece of land at home with the proceeds from eight guineas, "won from the Sassenach [Englishman] at the point of his reaping-hook, during a descent once made upon England by a body of spalpeens in the month of August."[168]

The departure of these harvest laborers did little to raise the price of labor in the regions from which they departed because the abundance of available labor was usually sufficiently great to preclude it. A Galway clergyman testified, "When large numbers go to England during the summer months preceding the harvest, wages remain as usual and only suffer a slight rise during the actual harvest."[169]

The poet Synge, who spent considerable time at the turn of the century investigating conditions in the congested districts of the northwest and west, left a description of seasonal workers. He was sufficiently observant to make a clear distinction between those poorer districts where persons went reluctantly because they were unable to live on the local resources, and places which were relatively better off, but which the younger, brighter, and more ambitious men and women abandoned. He described migrants from Belmullet in north Mayo as having "many harvestmen with scythe handles and little bundles tied in red handkerchiefs, walking into Ballina to embark for Liverpool or Glasgow."[170] Watching them, he confessed to "an indescribable feeling of wretchedness." (Was it possibly a particularly bad year, or was this a particularly deprived district?) While Synge had the humanist's empathy for their difficulties, he was not blind to some of the advantages of the seasonal migration which may have kept some from going to America, when he said, "This migratory labor has many unsatisfactory features; yet in the present state of the country it may tend to check the longing for America that comes over those that spend the whole year on one miserable farm."[171]

Information in Figure 2.7 and Tables 2.21 and 2.22 drawn from the census count of migrants taken from May to August of 1841, shows that this was overwhelmingly a migration of males (six males to every female). The extent to which the numbers reported may have been harvest migrants or permanent migrants is covered in Chapter Four, but it can be assumed that the migration was primarily seasonal.

According to the information by county, Connacht males had the highest propensity to migrate seasonally (3.35 percent) and Mayo the highest in the province of Connacht (5.15 percent), which is consistent with other evidence indicating that the area sent the largest number of seasonal workers abroad in that period. Ulster harvesters were next in propensity to move seasonally (1.54 percent) with the preponderance from Donegal (3.18 percent) and the least from Down (0.78 percent). County Down is a region of excellent farming, which explains why persons from there did not have to seek work abroad. The sample enumeration shows that Dubliners had a surprisingly high propensity to migrate (2.3%). It may be that the majority of those who would become relatively permanent migrants were from there, although seasonal demands for laborers in construction in England may have attracted Dubliners. The proportion of labor force in construction in Dublin was high relative to the rest of the country: 7.11 percent for Dublin compared with 2.91 percent for Leinster and 2.01 percent for all of Ireland.[172]

Table 2.21. Male migration, internal and external, 1841

County	1841 population	Males out-migrant within Ireland	% of total population	Males going to Britain May-Aug. 1841	% of total population
Leinster					
Dublin	170,900	10,681	6.2	3,980	2.30
Carlow	42,400	5,479	12.9	104	0.25
Kildare	58,000	6,575	11.3	357	0.62
Kilkenny	99,100	5,132	5.1	142	0.14
King's	72,700	5,494	7.5	291	0.40
Longford	57,600	3,368	5.8	661	1.15
Louth	62,300	4,085	6.5	928	1.49
Meath	92,500	9,062	9.8	494	0.53
Queen's	76,400	5,818	7.6	226	0.30
Westmeath	70,400	6,317	8.9	475	0.67
Wexford	97,900	5,671	5.7	361	0.37
Wicklow	63,500	10,539	18.4	171	0.27
SUBTOTAL	963,700	78,221	8.11	8,190	0.85
Munster					
Clare	144,100	4,317	3.0	127	0.09
Cork	420,600	10,482	2.4	347	0.08
Kerry	147,300	4,858	3.3	61	0.04
Limerick	176,100	7,507	4.2	192	0.11
Tipperary	216,600	10,790	4.9	252	0.12
Waterford	77,500	3,780	4.8	34	0.04
SUBTOTAL	1,182,200	41,734	3.53	1,013	0.09
Connacht					
Galway	211,600	7,595	3.5	2,882	1.36
Leitrim	77,500	4,117	5.3	2,641	3.41
Mayo	194,200	4,758	2.4	10,008	5.15
Roscommon	127,000	5,571	4.3	4,945	3.89
Sligo	89,600	3,312	3.7	2,958	3.30
SUBTOTAL	699,900	25,353	3.62	23,434	3.35
Ulster					
Antrim	133,200	4,628	3.4	1,650	1.24
Armagh	113,900	6,084	5.3	1,539	1.35
Cavan	120,800	6,408	5.3	1,623	1.34
Donegal	145,800	4,354	2.9	4,635	3.18
Down	173,500	8,169	4.7	1,348	0.78
Fermanagh	77,000	4,678	6.0	1,085	1.41
Londonderry	106,800	4,744	4.4	1,915	1.79
Monaghan	98,100	5,751	5.8	1,575	1.61
Tyrone	153,500	7,349	4.7	1,904	1.24
SUBTOTAL	1,122,600	52,165	4.64	17,274	1.54
ALL IRELAND TOTAL	3,968,400	197,473	4.97	49,911	1.26

SOURCE: Calculated from 1841 Census, pp. 446–47.

Table 2.22. Female migration, internal and external, 1841

County	1841 population	Females out-migrant within Ireland	% of total population	Females going to Britain May-Aug. 1841	% of total population
Leinster					
Dublin	201,800	10,892	5.4	1,645	0.82
Carlow	43,800	5,152	11.7	57	0.13
Kildare	56,500	6,863	12.1	159	0.28
Kilkenny	103,300	5,393	5.2	71	0.07
King's	74,200	5,666	7.6	176	0.24
Longford	57,900	3,729	6.4	201	0.35
Louth	65,900	4,078	6.1	195	0.30
Meath	91,300	8,984	9.8	99	0.11
Queen's	77,500	7,109	9.1	117	0.15
Westmeath	70,900	6,337	8.9	202	0.28
Wexford	104,100	6,058	5.8	212	0.20
Wicklow	62,700	11,567	18.4	80	0.13
SUBTOTAL	1,009,900	81,828	8.10	3,214	0.31
Munster					
Clare	142,300	4,409	3.1	79	0.06
Cork	433,500	9,753	2.2	319	0.07
Kerry	146,600	4,294	2.9	70	0.05
Limerick	168,100	7,386	4.3	170	0.10
Tipperary	218,900	10,422	4.7	149	0.07
Waterford	100,600	3,901	3.8	17	0.02
SUBTOTAL	1,210,000	40,165	3.31	804	0.06
Connacht					
Galway	211,300	6,664	3.1	423	0.20
Leitrim	77,800	4,453	5.7	219	0.28
Mayo	194,700	4,967	2.5	422	0.22
Roscommon	126,600	5,393	4.2	477	0.38
Sligo	91,400	3,320	3.6	143	0.16
SUBTOTAL	701,800	24,797	3.53	1,684	0.23
Ulster					
Antrim	143,000	5,202	3.6	297	0.21
Armagh	118,500	6,533	5.5	149	0.13
Cavan	122,300	6,587	5.3	281	0.23
Donegal	150,600	4,670	3.1	280	0.19
Down	187,900	8,662	4.6	207	0.11
Fermanagh	79,500	4,653	5.8	177	0.22
Londonderry	115,300	4,904	4.2	193	0.17
Monaghan	102,400	6,253	6.1	262	0.26
Tyrone	159,500	7,725	4.8	192	0.12
SUBTOTAL	1,179,000	55,189	4.6	2,038	0.17
ALL IRELAND TOTAL	4,100,700	201,979	4.9	7,740	0.018

SOURCE: Calculated from 1841 Census, pp. 446–47.

Table 2.23. **Migrants and their occupations from counties contiguous to Dublin, 1841**

Occupations	Mean	Louth		Meath		Kildare		Wicklow	
		Male	Female	Male	Female	Male	Female	Male	Female
Farm servants and laborers	25.8	28.5	1.1	35.9	1.6	32.6	1.1	33.4	1.0
Clothing	8.7	11.0	7.7	5.5	5.5	5.6	6.1	5.9	3.9
Construction	8.5	10.1	..	7.5	..	9.6	..	8.2	..
Police	4.8	2.7	..	2.4	..	1.3	..	2.1	..
Domestic service	5.1	5.3	16.7	2.0	1.0	5.9	23.6	6.7	20.1
Paupers	1.1	0.4	1.2	0.7	1.3	0.4	1.5	0.6	1.0
All other	46.3	20.3	3.9	22.8	6.1	18.5	4.8	18.0	4.9
1–15 years	18.3	19.0	20.5	12.9	14.0	14.9	14.9	15.8	14.6
15 + years (unspecified occupations)	9.4	8.8	53.4	9.9	52.8	11.8	55.0	9.0	54.5

SOURCES: Computed from 1841 Census data.

A number of Spearman rank order and Pearson correlation coefficients were computed to investigate whether there were systematic relationships between several of the variables in Table 2.24. These are summarized in Table 2.25. In addition, a number of different measures were used to show economic conditions in the various counties. These included valuation, first-class housing, literacy, winter wages, summer wages and number of days when agricultural work was available. Nonetheless, these variables were not without error and, in fact, the basis from which they have been calculated is not well documented.

Valuation, which is a measure of average wealth per capita in a county, seems to be somewhat reliable as shown by the fact that it has a high positive correlation with the percentage of first-class housing. However, while this may show differences in the total wealth and prosperity throughout the country, it does not necessarily show what is available to migrants, nor does it affect the distribution of wealth.

The analysis of winter wages, summer wages, and days worked shows that all three were positively correlated so that any one of these three measures gives the same results. For that reason only summer wages are used. It is important to note that while the degree of association is not overwhelming, there is a positive correlation between valuation and wages, suggesting that where there was greater wealth, opportunities were also greater.

A seemingly paradoxical result is that wages and population densities appear positively related. However, when the six Ulster counties with significant amounts of domestic industry were removed from the calculation, the correlation became negative. This is highly significant because it reinforces the usual expectation that population pressures reduce

Table 2.24. County rankings, 1841

County	Rental valuation per acre (£)	Days worked per year	Wages per week	Emig. % of total pop.	Internal migration Emig.	Internal migration Immig.	Persons per sq. mi. arable land	Arable land per 100 acr.	Persons per acre orchard planting	Vested means	First-class accommo-dations	Literacy	Persons employed in agric. per 100	Persons employed in trade, mfg. per 100
1. Wexford	7.10	2	10	22	14	18	22	5	30	10	5	7	22	9
2. Antrim	4.87	5	2	16	30	3	21	21	23	14	16	1	32	1
3. Dublin	3.27	10	5	6	11	1	12	6	1	1	1	4	31	7
4. Meath	2.93	23	16	20	4	12	31	1	30	26	8	20	12	15
5. Louth	2.54	1	16	9	8	9	17	5	10	20	12	23	1	6
6. Wicklow	3.27	8	16	24	1	7	24	26	17	2	3	6	26	10
7. Kildare	2.32	26	10	18	3	2	32	7	21	5	2	9	27	21
8. Carlow	…	17	16	25	2	5	26	9	20	14	5	5	21	13
9. Westmeath	2.13	29	29	17	5	13	29	11	16	5	10	19	20	17
10. King's	2.01	26	20	21	6	6	27	20	19	3	8	13	24	22
11. Kilkenny	1.20	17	16	27	9	14	28	2	28	20	6	16	11	25
12. Queen's	1.10	12	16	23	7	8	25	11	13	6	10	8	19	16
13. Limerick	1.96	20	16	26	21	15	20	15	25	20	17	21	7	29
14. Longford	1.96	30	29	13	10	11	14	17	3	8	20	15	10	18
15. Down	1.61	10	5	19	18	24	7	8	11	12	14	2	30	2
16. Londonderry	1.49	5	2	7	22	20	10	25	15	8	19	3	29	3
17. Waterford	1.48	17	22	32	24	4	22	19	31	26	10	30	15	20
18. Tipperary	1.38	20	29	28	19	17	23	13	26	30	14	14	17	19
19. Cork	1.32	23	22	29	32	32	19	19	24	16	14	27	13	23
20. Monaghan	1.31	5	10	8	13	26	4	3	12	30	23	17	14	11
21. Roscommon	1.11	26	24	2	23	16	15	16	7	12	29	26	4	32
22. Cavan	1.07	14	16	11	16	23	8	14	9	20	26	18	9	14
23. Leitrim	1.05	20	24	3	17	19	9	23	6	14	29	22	1	28
24. Tyrone	1.03	14	7	15	20	25	5	27	22	26	21	11	25	5
25. Clare	1.02	26	29	30	28	28	11	28	8	31	23	25	6	26
26. Galway	0.94	24	29	12	26	27	16	29	5	26	26	31	3	30
27. Sligo	0.81	31	21	4	25	21	13	24	2	20	31	28	8	24
28. Kerry	0.71	17	29	31	27	30	6	31	18	26	26	29	5	27
29. Mayo	0.69	32	29	1	31	29	2	30	4	32	32	32	2	31
30. Donegal	0.41	8	2	5	29	29	3	32	14	26	23	24	18	8
31. Armagh	0.38	7	5	14	15	22	1	11	32	20	19	10	28	4
32. Fermanagh	0.30	2	8	10	12	10	18	23	27	8	29	12	16	12

SOURCE: Computed from 1841 Census.

Table 2.25. Rank order correlations

Variables[a]	V_s	P<
Valuation × first-class housing	.89	.001
Wages × population per arable sq. mi.	.19	.25
Wages × population per arable sq. mi. (six counties with highest % mfg. empl. removed)	−.35	.07
Valuation × wage	.21	.25
Valuation × % immigration	.71	.001
Wage × emigration within Ireland	−.24	.20
Valuation × emigration within Ireland	.58	.002
Wage v. emigration to Britain	.23	.20
Valuation v. emigration to Britain	−.28	.15
Emigration within Ireland v. emigration to Britain	−.12	.40

[a]Spearman rank order correlation variables.

wage levels in agrarian counties. It also follows that urbanizing areas could support higher population densities because of the relatively high industrial wages available there.

Conventional economic theory suggests that people should move from poorer areas to richer areas to better their lot. This is examined in the several correlations between emigration, immigration, valuations, and the wages of agricultural laborers. It is evident from Table 2.25 that within Ireland people were, in fact, moving to counties with high valuations and wages. However, those counties with high valuations also were sources of emigration to other counties, as evidenced by the positive and highly significant correlation between valuations and emigration. There is, however, a negative but weak relationship between wages and emigration. This apparent paradox is explained in part by the fact that wealthy counties (particularly Dublin) were producing skilled and professional personnel who were quite mobile (e.g., schoolteachers, clergymen, justices). And it is this effect that gives rise to the positive correlation with valuation, and largely offsets the effects of wages on emigration which is presumably more important for the less skilled.

It is quite clear from other evidence that labor in Ireland was not freely mobile and able to respond to economic incentives within the country. In fact, most of the internal movement took place within the limits of provinces, and most movement took place within the relatively prosperous provinces of Leinster and Munster. Mobility within Ireland was particularly low in the impoverished west and in parts of Ulster. Among the important reasons for this may be that domestic industry, whose purpose it was to supplement inadequate incomes from the land, had declined more recently there than in other areas. In addition, these areas were geographically separated from the areas of higher valuation, posing barriers to mobility. Finally, such factors as discrimination, resulting from such differences as language, offered other barriers to mobility.

However, it is likely that while people from the west did not move permanently, they were heavily involved in seasonal migration. (There is no direct evidence on seasonal migration within Ireland because census data is only for permanent migration.) This is evidenced by the fact that emigration to Britain for the three-month sample enumerated for 1841 was a predominantly temporary migration and that the migration is inversely related to valuation and wages. And, correspondingly, migration to Britain is inversely correlated with emigration to other Irish counties. Nonetheless, the straightforward correlation analysis misses the point that movement to Britain was highly concentrated in the counties of the far west and northwest (see Figure 2.8).

Conclusions

A number of conclusions can be drawn regarding the migration process as it affected Ireland and the Irish.

1. The first of these is that permanent internal migration was of minimal importance within the country, as had been suspected. Some characteristics of interest regarding internal migration do emerge, however, which is that those counties where there was the largest number of migrants from elsewhere in Ireland were also those characterized by high valuations and higher agricultural wages.

2. In addition to being fairly minimal, most internal migration was fairly short range. At least half was within provinces, and this became more than 70 percent when Dublin was included as part of Leinster.

3. It can be assumed that movement to Britain was a substitute for movement within the country. Counties of low valuation and low wages were also the counties from which there was the most seasonal migration to Britain, and the least internal migration.

4. In areas where industry was either absent or minimal, wage and population densities were inversely correlated. That is, a high density of agricultural population was consistent with low wages. Conversely, where domestic industry was important, such as in areas of Ulster, a high population density was consistent with high wages.

What we are unable to determine with any degree of certainty are the factors that determined harvest migration, or the characteristics of the seasonal migrants. Why did some persons go and not others? Was it really only a movement of the casual redundant population, or did small farmers from some areas, as some evidence suggests, leave seasonally in order to earn enough to remain on their farms? If so, then was the internal seasonal migration dominated by small farmers wishing to preserve whatever they had, and the external migration dominated either by persons from Connacht and Donegal with relatively secure access to land, or by the redundant casual laborers?

Appendix

Occupational Groupings

Some clarification is necessary to explain how the occupational groupings were devised. All occupations in the census were grouped according to eight categories which were as follows: 1 Ministering to Food, 2 Ministering to Clothing, 3 Ministering to Lodging, Furniture, and Machinery, 4 Ministering to Health, 5 Ministering to Justice, 6 Ministering to Religion, 7 Unclassified, and 8 Unspecified. From these I chose those occupations in which I would most expect to see the kind of migrants covered in this study. They appear as the first six and last two categories in Table 2.12 (males) and the first four and last two in Table 2.13 (females). The breakdown within these categories and my choices for them are as follows:

1. *Ministering to Food:* Under this I chose from the twelve occupational categories only that of servants and laborers which, as survey revealed, included about three-quarters of the total occupations in that grouping. For example, in Dublin 1,505 of the total 2,107 males who "ministered to food" returned themselves as either servants or laborers; in Wexford, a primarily rural area, it was 1,539 out of 2,019; in Mayo, it was 1,396 out of 1,664. It is of interest to note that in Leinster more women returned themselves as either farm servants or laborers than in the other provinces. The only clue to why this may be so is that in the late nineteenth century increasing numbers of women returned themselves as farmers, which has been interpreted to indicate that these were widows who considered themselves the primary owners of the property and were reluctant to turn

the family farm over to their inheriting sons. (Could the incidence of this in Leinster in the earlier period be an indication that the trend was beginning there earlier?)

2. *Ministering to Clothing:* Under this I included all 21 occupational categories for two reasons: first, the occupational spread was wider, and, secondly, they reflect occupational groupings relatively available to all migrants. Note, however, that few men returned themselves as spinners (which would have been factory spinning) and few women returned themselves as weavers.

3. *Ministering to Lodging, Furniture, Machinery, etc.:* This was somewhat of a catchall category because it included those in construction as well as in crafts and industries such as blacksmiths. However, all these occupations can be considered skilled or semi-skilled, so for that reason I included all 27 occupational categories. There was a concentration of persons in three categories: "carpenters, etc." (carpenter's helpers?); "masons, slaters"; "blacksmiths, brassfounders." For example, in Dublin 551 persons were in these three categories out of a total of 1,034; in Wexford it was 449 out of 660, and in Mayo it was 163 out of 238. I did not include this category for female occupations as their numbers were minimal.

4. *Ministering to Health:* These were counted with the miscellaneous category in Tables 2.12 and 2.13 as the numbers were minimal and not immediately applicable to the purpose of this study.

5. *Ministering to Justice:* In this grouping I counted males in the police force. My reason for doing this did not apply to this study but it will be of future interest to know to what extent police officers were migrating within the country. For example, Tipperary supplied the greatest number of police officers elsewhere in Ireland (440) and Waterford supplied the least (66). (Tipperary also had the highest incidence of agrarian unrest; why was this producing a surplus of police officers?)

6. *Ministering to Religion:* The number of those in this grouping were minimal and were included in the miscellaneous category in Tables 2.12 and 2.13.

7. *Unclassified:* In this grouping I separated the category of domestic servants and paupers from the rest. They were the largest categories and most pertinent for my purpose. As I expected, female paupers far outnumbered male paupers among outmigrants. This is mostly because it was considered less shameful for a woman to beg; and begging was one of the few alternatives to domestic industry for females. The remaining persons in this grouping were included under "other" in Tables 2.12 and 2.13.

8. *Unspecified:* This category was divided by age into those "under 15 years" of age and those "15 and upwards." I take the males in the latter category to include primarily those of either vested means (gentlemen) or students with no specific occupation. I take the females to be housewives who, as the census indicated, were "though occupied in several ways, do not consider themselves as having any occupation in the meaning which a Census attaches to the term" (1851 Census).

Temporary employment elsewhere could result in a permanent leave-taking but when it happened it was because the attractions elsewhere outweighed the advantages of remaining at home.

The Demand

Good husbandry is no English
virtue; it may have been brought
over; and in some places where it has
been planted it has thriven well enough;
but it is a foreign species, it neither loves
nor is beloved by an Englishman; and it is observed, nothing is so universally hated, nothing
treated with such a general contempt.

DANIEL DEFOE, 1703

for Labor in England

The Act of Union, when it came into effect in January of 1801, passed the responsibility for the management of Irish affairs onto the English parliament. One wonders if the optimism of the authorities in assuming responsibility for Ireland's problems would have been as great had they known the blame which would be attached to their efforts in the future. Nevertheless, accept responsibility they did, and set about the task with some zeal, establishing investigative commission after investigative commission in their energy to get to the root causes of Ireland's problems. It was a problem-solving era, and the English still had the optimism to believe that if the correct mechanisms could be discovered, Ireland could be made as productive as England. Even had they wished to they could not have ignored the deterioration of conditions in Ireland because every boat arriving from Ireland brought swarms of Irish laborers seeking work, willing to outbid, outwork, and underlive any English worker against whom they were pitted by employers. The testimony of one employer was as follows:

> The Irish are employed in this town [Manchester], not because they are preferred to the English, but because they are necessary, or perhaps because they are here. There are not English enough to supply the demand. The English from the country parishes would not be suited to the work of the towns; the Irish adapt themselves more speedily to it, and are more importunate: they thrust themselves forward more.[1]

By the 1830s public pressure to ascertain why the Irish were arriving in such great numbers culminated in a number of investigations of their conditions, both in Ireland and in England and Scotland. Confronted with the task, the Commissioners could only conclude that "nothing seems more natural than that labourers should go from places where they are not wanted and wages are low, to places where they are wanted and wages are high."[2] This was conventional economic theory, and well understood by the early political economists such as Nassau Senior, John Stuart Mill, and Revans who dominated the thinking of the age. However, while the theory of supply and demand worked in the case of Irish workers flooding eagerly into every job from which they weren't actively excluded, it did not work so well for the English work force, immured in poverty as they appeared to be in the southern counties of England, while ignoring a constant demand for their labor in the industrializing textile regions to the north. This was widely believed by contemporary observers. The question arises then as to why the Irish were more mobile than were the English, and what constraints prevented the English from taking advantage of job opportunity? This chapter will examine the nature of that dilemma.

Among the problems addressed are: the conditions of work organization in Britain; the specific features of conditions in the industrializing areas which explain the concentration of Irish persons there; and the significance this may have for British social and economic history.

Work Organization in Early Nineteenth-Century England

New sources of energy and new inventions developed in eighteenth-century Europe, as they were adapted to fit the English situation, made their impact on a society still encumbered by the most primitive and elementary forms of industrial organization. David Landes's summary of the transforming ability of steam power and machinery subsumes the process of urban industrialization under three principles: the substitution of machines for human skill and effort; the substitution of inanimate for animate sources of power; and the use of new and far more abundant raw materials, specifically the substitution of mineral for vegetable or animal substances.[3] Inherent in this view of the new technology was the picture of machinery dispensing with human toil. But a closer look at the history of industrialization from the viewpoint of labor processes, rather than only of machine technology, reveals that the new technology did not dispense with human toil. Instead, it accelerated drudgery for larger numbers of laborers to supply the new industries which had been created. Consequently, as mechanization increased in one department of production, reducing a demand for human toil there, it tended to increase sweated labor in another. And paralleling the development of every large firm was the need for a multitude of small production units to supply and support it. Developments in sugar refining illustrate this.

Candy consumption soared along with urbanization as the public developed a phenomenal sweet tooth; and while the machines of such as the Tate and Lyle factory refined sugar, for a long time the process of making it into sweets was still carried on in the kind of squalid backstreet kitchens and courts which Henry Mayhew portrayed so vividly in his examination of the lives of underclass Londoners.[4] Likewise, while timber was sawn by steam-driven machinery, it was ultimately shaped by hand by carpenters working pretty much as they had for centuries. The giant furnaces of England's Black Country, their production benefitting from the utilization of the most recent technologies, coexisted with backyard smithies. Textiles, the first industry to benefit from newly mechanized processes, continued to employ handloom weavers on a large scale well into the 1850s; and the clothing trades continued to depend upon needlewomen's fingers rather than utilizing the newly available sewing machine, developed in the 1840s in Boston, Massachusetts.[5] Thus it can be said that the Industrial Revolution, rather than abridging human toil as is generally believed, created a whole new world of labor-intensive occupations necessary to support the new technology.

Dual technologies also continued to coexist within large industrial establishments because goods produced by the early machines often couldn't compete in quality with labor-intensive production. The hand mule spinners held their own in the cotton mills right down to the 1870s alongside steam-powered spinning machine operators, because only a hand spinner could achieve the finest quality textiles. In newspaper printing steam-powered machinery was installed by the *Times* as early as 1814, but typesetting continued to be done by hand until the 1890s. In transport, while goods hauled by the new railways increased in volume, so did those carried by one- or two-horse carts and wagons. With adequate supplies of both technology and energy sources to abridge human toil, then what explanations are there for why British manufacturers continued to utilize these dual technologies?

In 1851, the great Crystal Palace Exhibition in London's Hyde Park was widely celebrated as the absolute pinnacle of British industrial civilization, although even the architecturally innovative structure of the Palace building itself illustrated the dichotomy of the dual technologies in Britain. For example, while the mahogany of the galleries of the Palace was turned by steam power, the 300,000 panes of glass which gave the building its distinctive appearance were all handblown.[6]

The primary cause underlying delays in shifting to machine technology lay in the fact that labor was still cheap relative to machinery; and despite regional complaints regarding scarcities of labor, there was always a sufficient work force available to deter manufacturers from switching to less labor-intensive processes. Furthermore since many of the new technologies utilized cheaper, less-skilled labor, this gave employers increased opportunity to balance investments in capital production against investments in human resources.

Daniel Defoe was not alone in maligning the willingness of workers to avail themselves of new opportunities to submit to the yoke of industry, but he did express the recalcitrance better than anyone else.

> There's nothing more frequent than for an Englishman to work till he has got his pocket full of money, and then go and be idle, or perhaps drunk, till it is all gone and perhaps himself in debt: and ask him in his cups what he intents, he'll tell you honestly, he'll drink as long as it lasts, and then go to work for more.[7]

The result was that employers in few industrial regions claimed to be happy in having a sufficient supply of labor. For workers, the process of submission to the new industrial capitalism was both painful and protracted, so that workers who still had more to lose than to gain from submitting themselves to the new discipline, showed no hesitation in demonstrating opposition to changes which disrupted their way of life. Luddite methods of bargaining[8] still lingered on into the 1830s as both agricultural laborers and industrial workers protested against the intrusion of unskilled workers at lower wages. Resistance against mechanization lingered on in some industries so long after the introduction of new technologies that as late as 1898 a steam sawmill was blown up by skilled workers opposed to the loss of their livelihood.[9]

Nor was opposition to the new technology confined to potentially displaced workers. The old gentry classes, whose political authority was being eroded by the rising manufacturing classes, also expressed their opposition to change. Edward Baines, describing their opposition, noted regretfully "that they still publish solemn lamentations over the growth of machinery."[10] This class still bore the main burden of support for the poor rates, so that their opposition is hardly surprising; they feared that those put out of work by machinery would increase their tax burden. In one instance, in Blackburn in 1779, the local gentry were so opposed to the introduction of textile machinery that they protected from punishment a mob which had smashed looms and water frames. Baines said that after this the atmosphere in the district was so hostile to machinery that many spinners and small manufacturers left the district.[11]

As was also true in industry, the first technological changes activating the agricultural revolution necessitated greatly increased demands for laborers. For example, the turnip, a vegetable which played a pivotal role in the transition to modern agriculture, required intensive cultivation of the soil prior to planting, and repeated weedings during the growth stage, all of which necessitated farmers keeping access to large numbers of laborers. Increased numbers of persons living in urban areas required larger supplies of food, and these could only be produced by an increased number of market gardens, and market gardening was the most labor intensive of all agricultural processes. The ground had to be hand dug by spade and seeds dropped by hand. Weeding had to be done by women and children with a knife rather than a hoe so as to protect the tender shoots; and harvesting tended to be done with baskets rather than wheelbarrows.[12] Donegal-born Patrick MacGill worked as a labor contractor with a gang of men and women for a potato farmer in Buteshire, Scotland. The men would dig potatoes from the ground with short three-pronged "grapis," a kind of fork, and the women followed behind on their hands and knees, dragging two baskets apiece into which they lifted the potatoes dug out by the men.[13]

Small farmers often tend to be the most traditional of all groups in resisting technological innovation—that is, until they can be assured of the benefits—and English farmers in the market garden regions contiguous to London, long accustomed to a readily available local labor force, resisted technological innovations well after their introduction. As late as 1822 no farmer could be found who was willing to go to the expense of trying the newly developed reaper after its invention years earlier by a Northumbrian schoolmaster.[14] Apparently as long as a ready supply of labor existed there was no pressure to substitute capital. The writer Rider Haggard was in 1899 still echoing objections to the reaping machine expressed a generation earlier. It was a mistake to suppose, he believed, that reapers would be willing to cut corn if it was badly laid and twisted by a machine.[15] Later, when the mechanical reaper displaced hand labor in the cutting process, there was a consequent greater demand for hand labor in the shocking and tying process. But farm laborers tended to resist intrusions of new technology, whether it be machinery or lower-paid workers, much as did the artisan classes. The following incident, which took place in the early 1880s in Berkshire, illustrates how intransigent farm laborers could be. When laborers saw their employer assembling his new combined mowing and reaping machine they protested, but the farmer refused to be dictated to. Equally uncompromising, his laborers left him, to go "uppards" to work for another farmer. Later the machine was found broken up in the field after it was left out overnight. Further trouble erupted during the wheat harvest for this farmer when his workers demanded not only more pay but also beer money, and then refused to work after six o'clock if they weren't paid overtime.[16] In such a situation any farmer would have preferred a labor force more willing to be dictated to.

There were many obstacles to full mechanization in nineteenth-century Britain. Among these was the irregularity of consumer demand for goods and the irregularity of the market. During the period of the French wars in the early nineteenth century, Britain geared up for a war economy which accelerated industrialization, but after the monster of Europe, Napoleon, had been successfully exiled to the island of Elba, the decreased demands consequent on a return to peacetime production resulted in a slack economy, leaving manufacturers to absorb their losses and lick their wounds. The fact also that machines often failed to perform satisfactorily and required skilled technicians to maintain them — technicians who were themselves often in rare supply — compounded the difficulties of entry into full industrialization. Furthermore, productivity gains were often insufficient for the manufacturer's investment in machinery. Each of these made the availability of an abundant and available — if largely unskilled — labor force very attractive, encouraging capitalists to utilize capital-saving rather than labor-saving investments. This was in direct contrast to the situation in America. America was sparsely populated with immigrants, with the result that labor was in short supply; wages were relatively higher than in Britain, thus making it worthwhile for employers to invest in machine technology rather than be handicapped by deficiencies in the labor market. Karl Marx knew this when he observed that machines invented in England were often employed only in America.

Constraints on the English Working Force

Eighteenth-century changes in the market for agricultural productivity in England and Ireland which caused farmers to prefer to employ a temporary labor force rather than supporting workers all year-round produced what R.H. Tawney has termed "a residual population of propertyless free labour."[17] Contributing to the production of this labor force, which was free to maximize returns from their individual productivity but also free to starve, was a shift in attitudes toward land where it began to be regarded as a source of capital production by a new breed of entrepreneurs seeking to invest in it for the purpose of generating income. The Duke of Bridgewater was one of this new breed when he developed the coal resources on his property by building a canal, named after himself, to transport coal to the industrializing regions of Lancashire.

In order to shift to capitalized farming landowners consolidated small acreages which had become less profitable for small farmers when they lost common rights as a result of the enclosure of waste land.[18] These changes transformed the traditional fabric of rural society, forcing small landholders into the wage labor class if they wished to remain on the land. The effort to survive forced a choice between working for a larger farmer or migrating to a manufacturing region. Persons displaced by these developments felt a loss of autonomy, resulting in a sense of grievance and alienation. Eric Hobsbawm and George Rude say that "The only thing which could have held English agricultural labourers above the level of even partial independence was a traditional system of mutual aid and collectivity such as existed in Ireland."[19] But by the end of the eighteenth century, England was becoming less and less of a traditional society; now a poor law administered by the rulers of the countryside replaced reliance on mutual aid and social obligations; and instead of the patronage of the local gentry and village custom to cushion shocks in the economy, there was the straightforward nexus of cash wages.

It was widely believed that restrictions, both formal and informal, prevented a market for free labor from operating as freely as manufacturers would have wished, and that the poor laws were an important restraint on this creation of a free and competitive market for labor. Poor relief was only given on the basis of settlement, so that when individuals moved they lost their entitlement, and this had the effect of tying people to areas of already abundant population by discouraging their taking the risk of leaving.[20] The poor law was basically a subsidy whereby the individual received assistance even if employed, as long as his wages amounted to less than the family income granted to him by an established scale.

The first deliberate attempt to create a free market for labor occurred with the enactment of the new Poor Law of 1834. By this time, extensive subsidization of rural inhabitants had finally became too politically explosive, too expensive for the ratepayers, and too demoralizing for the poor.[21] But while its intention was to release constraints on the freedom of the poor, the choice which they now had was between independence with the freedom to starve and the complete loss of their personal freedom and civil rights. Instead of subsidy they had the workhouse.[22]

The old system of poor relief based upon settlement had undoubtedly been an important factor in reducing mobility, but this does not provide the whole explanation for lack of mobility because the introduction of the new poor law was not followed by a rush of workers into the factories. Manufacturers continued to lament the lack of an adequate labor supply. It is necessary then to consider what additional factors could have either reduced the mobility of the labor force, or perhaps even have made mobility unnecessary. As previously indicated, redundant or surplus labor was most apparent in the agricultural districts of southern and eastern England, where agricultural innovation in response to the needs of the growing London market transformed the region earlier than the rest of the country. An improved food supply led to better diets, which in turn led to greater health and lower mortality rates; all of which then resulted in the population growth which created surplus supplies of labor. Meanwhile the industrializing regions of the northwest offered the greatest employment opportunities, but employers testified repeatedly that they never had persons from the southern counties seek work from them.[23] "I have reason to know that persons have come from Staffordshire to Manchester, and probably others have come from other neighbouring counties. I have never heard of any coming from the South of England, nor do I think that any come."[24] One official believed that this was due to the relatively comfortable state of the English laborer compared with his Irish or Scottish counterpart, which

> makes him more unwilling to change his place of abode: he risks more and gains less by the enterprise, and suffers more from temporary privation and inconvenience. Moreover, he is less accustomed to look for assistance in difficulties from neighbours and persons in his own class; on such occasions he looks to the parish.[25]

While there may have been a perceived reluctance to relocate, this is not to imply that no movement whatsoever took place. However those who moved tended to go only short distances in a risk-minimizing process whereby laborers from the south and east of England went to nearby towns; thus it was London rather than Manchester which drew them. As stated by John Saville, the Industrial Revolution did not consist of simple transfers of population from the south and east of England to the north and west, but followed a wavelike pattern of short-distance moves which eventually culminated in reaching industrialized areas.[26] The cumulative effect was a protracted process of transfer which restrained the development of a ready supply of English workers willing to respond to opportunities. English laborers knew that there might be employment, but they were also well aware of the greater risks of periodic unemployment. In contrast, laborers from Ireland or Scotland, because they came from societies with far fewer alternatives, in facing the same risks had far less to lose in responding to opportunities for employment.

Emigration was believed by some to be the answer to the problem of redundant labor. But efforts to promote emigration faced considerable opposition because the authorities knew from experience that assisted emigration for paupers had proven costly and had been largely unsuccessful.[27] Not only were the poor reluctant to be moved, but there were many instances when, after having been packed off abroad at considerable cost, they returned when their funds and supplies were exhausted, only to once again become parish charges. In an 1826 emigration inquiry it was estimated that approximately one-quarter of all assisted emigrants eventually returned.[28]

Assistance programs to encourage persons to move within the country were even less successful. For example, in 1835 it was estimated that about 90,000 people would be required from outside Lancashire to fuel expansion of work in the cotton industry, but after some were assisted to move north, two years later there was a collapse of trade resulting in massive cutbacks of factory employment.[29] Those most recently hired lost their jobs, and many families returned home voluntarily or were sent by charity overseers, with the result that future plans for more assistance schemes were cancelled.[30] Any form of induced migration was unpopular because people confused it with transportation, which was the system of penal servitude to the colonies. Opposition was widespread, not only from those who were to be assisted to emigrate, but by spokesmen for the lower classes. William Cobbett, one of the latter, raged in the 1830s against "the folly, the stupidity, the insanity, the presumption . . . the barbarity, of those numerous wretches who have now the audacity to propose to transport the people of England upon the principle of the monster Malthus."[31]

At the same time there is reason to believe that a redundant population was not entirely unwelcome in some areas of the country. Landowners might have complained about the poor rates; but they may not have been as anxious as they seemed to have the community's paupers shovelled out because they might need them at the next harvest, which always created special demands for extra helpers. The 1851 Census gives a figure of 1,077,627 persons reporting themselves as agricultural laborers in England and Scotland, but the number of people needed for harvesting was certainly larger than that. Industrial workers in agricultural areas contiguous to manufacturing regions sometimes functioned as harvest workers during slack periods. Working in the harvest was also one of the few ways in which industrial workers could afford a holiday. A factory inspector told of a London enameler who went to the hop pick-ing "for the purpose of cleaning himself from chalk."[32] But in the pri-marily agricultural southern regions of England an additional labor force was necessary at certain seasons of the agricultural year, which also explains why there existed a demand for Irish seasonal migrants in these areas as early as the mid eighteenth century.

The growth of Britain's population created tremendous demands for food production. For that reason, by the middle years of the nine-teenth century more land in England was cultivated than ever before (or since) reaching a maximum of three million acres by 1869.[33] The staple food of most people was still bread so that wheat acreages were contin-ually being increased to meet the demands of the rapidly increasing population. Changes were however taking place in the distribution of peak workloads throughout the agricultural year, peaking primarily in the harvest season, even though such crops as turnips and market garden farming still required considerable numbers of additional laborers in the planting season as well. Mayhew noted the changes that an influx of Irish labor had created when he found, in one parish of 1,800, areas that there were

> Seventeen farmers who occupied, upon the average, 100 acres each, and who, previous to the immigration of Irish harvest men, *constantly* employed 6 men a-piece, or, in aggregate, upwards of 100 hands. Now, however, the farmers in the same parish occupy to the extent of 300 acres each, and respectively employ only 6 men, and *a few extra hands at harvest time.* Thus, the number of hands employed has decreased one-half.[34]

Utilizing labor in such a fashion enabled farmers to economize on their total labor costs. "The term of hiring has been cut down to the finest possible limits, so that the labourer may not be paid for even a second longer than he is wanted."[35] The consequence of such changes was that the farmer needed and welcomed an available surplus of labor, whether it be from Ireland or from the supply of local paupers. Com-plaints against the idle thriftless poor were heard more frequently in the slack months of winter than in the spring and summer, so that it may be assumed that there was a real need for a reserve army of the willing when the demand for labor increased, a factor balancing the grim picture of burdensome poor rates.

Even when successful in having attracted a factory labor force, early nineteenth-century employers often complained of the problem of accustoming workers to a regular output, a crucial element of productiv-ity. E.P. Thompson drew attention to this when he said that wherever men were in control of their own lives (i.e., working for themselves, such as artisans, small farmers, or craftsmen), their work pattern alternated between bouts of intense labor followed by periods of idleness.[36] English workers were known to honor what was called Saint Monday. Even in periods of full employment, such as the French Wars, one witness complained that Saint Monday was still religiously kept and often followed by Saint Tuesday as well.[37] The pre-industrial way of life encouraged autonomy, but it did not necessarily breed habits of diligence in the work force. It would take severe adversity and the whip of machine technology discipline to tame workers into becoming the automatons that employers desired. Some artisans foresaw the coming changes and welcomed the need for a disciplined work force. An old potter, who was also a Methodist lay preacher and so undoubtedly subject to more advanced views, said that the slothful behavior of other potters was the consequence of a lack of mechanization in the pottery industry. Expressing the very essence of Methodism, he argued that the same indiscipline in daily work influenced the entire way of life. "Machinery means discipline," he said grimly.[38]

It is not entirely fair to blame only the workers. The rhythm of pre-industrial work habits were not entirely at fault because the nature of employment opportunity in the early years of industrialization tended not to encourage habits of work commitment. Work in the textile mills was often irregular because employers preferred a more fluid work force as a way of adjusting more easily to the fluctuations in market supply and demand. In consequence the workers such employment attracted had to be willing to undertake the risk of irregular employment. Persons such as this were more likely to value some degree of autonomy or control over their lives by being able to choose what they would work at rather than having to tolerate the tedium of remaining in one place.

Employers sought to overcome resistance to factory work, according to Arthur Redford, by hiring whole families to work for them.[39] Farmers were even offered employment as road builders in nearby areas, or as construction workers, in order to obtain the more valued labor of their wives and children inside the factory. Within the factory, incentives to work included a subcontract system whereby spinners, rovers, and power-loom weavers were paid by the piece and then encouraged to hire their own assistants. In this way employers could maximize worker satisfaction by enabling workers to assist relatives. This system reduced the risks of sporadic unemployment by increasing the claims families would have on each other.

Until well into the third decade of the nineteenth century, manufacturers were often persons who had themselves once risen from the laboring classes through skill, their own industry, and the good fortune to be in an expansionary business climate. Such individuals tended to reinvest all of their profits in their businesses with the result that they faced constant shortages of ready capital to continue employing workers in slack times. Having risen by their energies from the very ranks of those they employed, they also may have been less likely to be sympathetic to retaining an uneconomic work force during the frequent periods of lessened demand. Overproduction was particularly rife in the textile industry, so that workers frequently had to fend for themselves. Entrepreneurs such as these were squeezed even further when the Factory Acts placed restrictions on the number of hours worked, thereby diminishing the already slender profits of small factory units.[40] Another limitation on profits came with competition from abroad when American factories, which had the advantage of being relative latecomers to the process of factory industrialization, competed successfully against British manufacturers in exporting to the Indian and South American markets. A contemporary noted that, "The Americas have this advantage, that all their establishments being new they have the most improved machinery, whereas many of our mills are working with machines 30 or 40 years old."[41]

Thus while wages might be good when workers were in full employment, when there were business cutbacks, when factories were retooling, or when there were supply problems, workers were thrown on their own resources, and life became very insecure. It is hardly surprising then that workers showed no great alacrity to risk moving into industrialized areas.

Michael Anderson's study of the effect of industrialization on the family in nineteenth-century Lancashire reveals that trends in the cotton industry explain both why textile regions offered optimal opportunities for a mobile work force, and why the textile areas were unattractive to a work force with alternative employment opportunities. Before the Factory Acts limited the profitablility of female and child labor, there was almost no demand in early factories for adult males which meant that fathers could often get only casual employment; this was an important disincentive for some families to uproot themselves. There were few skilled jobs and workers in those which existed usually restricted the entry of newcomers into their trade, which made also made it difficult for individuals to gain training for skilled employment. This was particularly true of machine spinners. Working conditions in textile mills were in general considered quite undesirable, so that there was a tendency for persons employed there to abandon such employment whenever other opportunities arose. As Anderson has noted, textiles thus tended to lose labor to other occupations.[42]

Informal restraints on labor mobility are often difficult to detect. England had, and still has, regions in the south and east where people remain extremely localized. Movement out them was relatively rare throughout the nineteenth century. Even long-standing economic stagnation in these regions was insufficient to persuade many persons to go elsewhere looking for employment. Movement when it did take place late in the century was usually a permanent shift, which often meant emigration to Canada or Australia or South Africa.

The life of the typical rural laborer in regions such as this is portrayed in Flora Thompson's book, *Lark Rise to Candleford,* describing her childhood and youth in Juniper Hill, an Oxfordshire village in the 1880s. It illuminates the contrast between those who were willing to migrate and those who were not.[43] Almost all of the men in Juniper Hill worked for the local farmer for a wage of ten shillings a week during the 1880s and 1890s, which was hardly a living wage and only two shillings more than they would have received fifty years earlier. As in Ireland, then, it meant that their wages had to be supplemented by the hard work of the whole family working as an economic unit. People liked to keep some degree of independence from the farmer, so most preferred to rent their own homes, paying anywhere from two to three shillings a week rather than living in cottages supplied as a perquisite of employment by the farmer. While living in a "tied cottage" ensured a more predictable income, it cost the inhabitant the right of freedom of choice to go to either church or chapel, or to vote either Liberal or Tory. With the rental of each house came rights to a vegetable garden plot close by the house and an allotment of field land elsewhere in the village.[44] The garden plot was reserved for green vegetables and fruit bushes (with a few flowers if the gardener had the time and inclination), while the field allotment plot was divided into two parts: one-half planted with potatoes and the other with wheat or barley. Potatoes were the special pride of the householder who had to grow enough to last the whole year.[45] The village women's special contribution to the family budget came from gleaning for grain in the farmer's field; such was their pleasure in the effort to collect what they called the "leazings" that the wheat (when milled usually about two bags per family) was displayed with pride on a chair in the front room for a few days and the neighbors stopped by to visit and admire.[46] All the home-produced flour went for the daily pudding served at the beginning of the evening meal, whose purpose it was to blunt the appetite. Few housewives had ovens, so bread, still the staple of the family diet, had to be bought from the baker.

As in Ireland the pig played an important role in the family's survival strategy. "The family pig was everyone's pride and everybody's business."[47] If it was a good year the meat would provide the family with bacon for a winter or longer. The pig was also collateral in a bad year when portions of it were pledged to the baker or the miller and, upon slaughtering, that portion would go for payment.[48] Thus the saying, "Us be going to kill half a pig," meaning that the other half was already pledged away.

Thompson's book gives substance to the picture of the general unwillingness on the part of a proletarianized population to undertake further risks by moving elsewhere. She says that the town of Oxford, nineteen miles away, was considered by the villagers as a possible place to go for work.[49] Wages were higher—twenty-five shillings a week—but where, they asked, could you have a garden or keep a pig in Oxford? That is, what supplement could tide you over a lean time? While unafraid of hardship at home, few were willing to risk moving there.

The picture of Juniper Hill may be taken as representative of certain parts of rural England in the late nineteenth century, as well as earlier times. Information regarding the outside world as a place to look for employment extended to scarcely more than Oxford. The support system to tide a person over lean times could fail if they left the village. Families aided each other when they were nearby, but little help was possible beyond the immediate area, Thompson relates. The postal system was still rudimentary and expensive, and most were unlikely to consider it as an opportunity to keep in contact. The situation she portrays is one in which there were few incentives to encourage migration elsewhere in England.[50]

Earlier in the century a reluctance to move may in part have been a very rational weighing of the the costs and risks of what was a fairly rudimentary transport system. The journey from the south or east of England to Lancashire was a far more expensive and difficult one than was the journey from Ireland to Lancashire, despite the fact that the Irish migrant had farther to travel. Although evidence points to both the Irish and the Scots showing a greater preference for walking than did the English, overland transport was both less convenient and more costly than transport by sea and canal.

In addition, as contemporary observers have noted, in England social and economic dislocation, and the consequent distress which would eventually induce English workers to leave home areas, was fairly recent. The last two decades of the previous century were an Indian summer period for the working classes in England when wages were rising in most sectors yet still keeping pace with the cost of living. And although wages continued to rise in the next two decades, the prosperity was false because the cost of living, inflated by wartime prosperity, failed to keep pace and indeed had risen to alarmingly high levels by the end of the second decade of the nineteenth century. Between 1819 and 1826 real wages began to rise once again, but they failed to reach 1789–98 levels again before 1849. What is significant is that the greatest period of distress followed what had been a period of rising incomes. A Manchester cotton manufacturer contrasting the situation of the English working classes and that of the Irish in 1834 said,

> The reason why no English come from the pauperized parishes in the southern counties is the distress is more recent; in Ireland, the poverty is of long standing. Perhaps the greatest reason is that the English are settled in their parishes, and the Irish are not.[51]

Composite wage trends are deceptive inasmuch as they give the impression of full employment, whereas, as has already been noted, employment in this period was extremely irregular. (Also, the combining of rural and urban industrial wages creates distortions.) In addition, indices of real wages present an incomplete picture of what may have been the real cost of surviving at such a time. There are no surveys of the extent and incidence of poverty before those of Charles Booth and Seebohm Rowntree in the late nineteenth century. Booth's study of London in the 1880s and that of Rowntree of York in the 1890s were both conducted during times of depression and thus may be somewhat distorted. Nevertheless, Booth found that 31 percent of the total population and about 40 percent of the working classes were in poverty; and Rowntree found comparable proportions of about 28 percent and 43 percent respectively.[52]

It seems likely then that the fluctuating nature of employment would have made Lancashire poverty before the mid-century greater and more widespread. To illustrate, Anderson cites a study of the incidence of poverty in 1847 and 1849 in Oldham, one of the Lancashire textile towns. 1849 was considered a "normal" year, yet 20 percent of the population was below the line of subsistence; and in 1847, a distress year, about half the population was in real poverty.[53] His own calculations, based on Rowntree's scale of the cost of subsistence, indicate that in 1851, 17 percent of single persons could be expected to live at a level where they were anywhere from less than four shillings above the poverty line to four shillings or more below it. By the time of having reached the life-cycle stage of married with one child the figure of those in the same relationship to the poverty line jumps to 52 percent. In this study he also found that nearly 20 percent of all families for whom data could be obtained were below the poverty line, which correlates well with other findings for a nondistress year.[54]

Taking into consideration the differences between a "good" and a "slump" year, where 20 percent of the population always lived at the brink of poverty, a percentage which could increase to 50 percent in a year of distress, it can be concluded that there had to be a relatively high degree of risk taking on the part of the working population to be willing to migrate to urban industrial areas at all. Such uncertainty also suggests why a working population which did not consider itself permanent would be more willing to make itself available. The risk was far less for temporary workers who had the option of return.

In Ireland, although the general fluctuations in economic trends followed those of England, rewards went primarily to a landed upper class, and there was no poor law to blunt the bite of under- or unemployment. Unlike their counterparts in England, the Irish laborers' standard of living did not keep pace with the general prosperity of the late eighteenth-century period when exports were expanding. Instead of their food becoming more varied (as had that of the English working classes), it became more monotonous. In addition the potato, while far more productive than wheat, was subject to periodic failures and was extremely difficult to transport to overcome regional failures of the crop. As was indicated in the previous chapter, the 1841 Census pointed out Ireland's precarious situation when it reported that 70 percent of the population of Ireland consisted of laborers and smallholders with less than five acres.[55]

An important factor in the transformation which finally produced a disciplined labor force in Britain was the competition produced by the Irish in their willingness to substitute themselves for the localized, less-willing English workers.[56] Employers were mostly concerned with profits, so that a willing and available work force such as the Irish, offered obvious advantages, chief of which was their eagerness for work and a willingness to move to where the work was located. Cornewall Lewis, in the tone of a reproving Benthamite, observed in his report on the Irish in England that if English laborers had not intelligence or ambition enough to seek employment at the good wages offered by manufacturers, they deserved to be replaced by the Irish.[57] Manufacturers tend to be an unsentimental group when it comes to employee relations. A manufacturer echoed the economist's dictum when he remarked, "Wages have always gotten the man." If this is so, then one can assume that the wages which English manufacturers wished to pay were inadequate to induce sufficient numbers of English workers to take the risk implied by movement into labor-starved industrial districts.

In spite of recurring complaints of shortages of labor, by the 1830s there was an impressive output of manufactures in some sectors. But to ensure output it was necessary to ensure a steady supply of workers, and the work lives and inclination to work of those in industrial areas were brief, and thus in constant need of replenishment. Informants at Royal Commissions were stunned by the sight of those who had worked in factories from childhood: evidence of stunted growth and disabling injuries were graphic demonstrations of the unhealthy nature of factory work.[58] While labor scarcity persisted as a theme throughout the first half of the nineteenth century, the fact is that the population almost doubled between 1800 and 1850—from 11 million to 22 million—despite extensive out-migration to the Americas and Australia from Scotland, from Ireland, and from parts of England.[59]

In all probability then the scarcity was more apparent than real. In a contemporary study, manufacturers in the Bombay textile industry voiced similar complaints about the quality and supply of labor available to them, including a widespread notion that labor was not firmly committed to industrial work, even when the evidence showed that it was available in abundant quantities.[60] D. Mazumdar, examining this, questioned whether there was a true scarcity or whether there was merely a scarcity of skilled workers coexistent with a surplus of unskilled labor. This, he concluded, was less plausible when one reflects upon the fact that more than 90 percent of the occupations were unskilled.[61] This is, he says,

> the normal response to the market conditions one would expect in a newly industrialized area. When there is a potential shortage of skill, the volume of machine work, instead of being carried through by a small group of carefully selected and trained operatives, tends to be spaced out over a large number of workers with lower skills.[62]

Concluding from this, it seems not unlikely that Britain's textile industry may have been hampered less by real shortages of labor than by shortages of certain kinds of labor which employers would have preferred. In other words, scarcities of labor were a function of the need for employers to dictate terms to those they employed.

Casual Laborers in the Work Force

As late as the 1830s manufacturers in Britain were said to be seeking to eliminate "that restless and migratory spirit which is one of the peculiar characteristics of the manufacturing population and perhaps the greatest obstacle to permanent improvement among them."[63] It may be necessary to revise some earlier assumptions about the nature of the labor force during the early period of industrialization if we accept the fact that it appeared at the time to be extremely transitory. This was partly the result of and in response to the difficulty of recruiting and retaining an adequate work force.[64] To achieve production goals factories in the earlier period were forced to rely on migratory tramp labor, often considered disreputable, probably because of the independence a migrating work force often displayed in bargaining for wages and terms. Our understanding of the nature of employment in the nineteenth century is as incomplete, as has been previously demonstrated, as is our knowledge of the kinds of employment available.

Just as we are mistaken when we assume that technology swiftly became a substitute for human toil, we are equally mistaken in thinking that the labor market for the new technology followed the lines of rationalized employment. In fact fundamental changes in society produced large supplies of casual labor, but few understood it at the time. For that reason, the journalist, Henry Mayhew devoted considerable study to the subject of casual labor, believing that it had been "utterly ignored by economic writers and unheeded by the public."[65] It was his belief that "in almost all occupations in Britain there was a *superfluity of laborers,* and this alone would tend to render the employment of a vast number of the hands of a casual rather than a regular character."[66] The situation was, he believed, a phenomenon of the changes taking place in Britain and thus unique to that country.[67]

Seasonal employment was a boon for the manufacturer wishing to economize on his labor force, as has already been demonstrated. The London gasworks economized when they employed seasonal workers. When questioned about what became of the extra men who left in the spring, an official of the Gas, Light & Coke Co. replied, "They are only too ready to leave us in the spring."[68] Some gas workers gave their notice while others were discharged in mid February or March. He estimated that only one-third of the total force was employed throughout the year. In winter extra hands were recruited from migratory laborers who spent the summer as brickmakers, builder's laborers, navvies, and farm workers.[69]

Seasonal demands resulted in the months of August and September being the dead months of the year for many urban indoor trades, especially those which depended on the world of fashion or those in heavy industry where heat was a factor. This was true of the the tailoring trades where employment depended on the London social season, causing many women to be thrown out of work periodically. One large Bethnal

Green factory was said to sack about one-quarter of their girls each summer.[70]

The docks were another place where seasonal demands skewed the continuity of the work year. In Liverpool there were greatly increased demands for labor whenever bales of cotton arrived from America; at such times as many as 2,500 extra porters were taken on. Of these men it was said that "a certain number . . . systematically follow another trade in one season or go to sea and come back for the busy period between October and March."[71] Elsewhere winter was the season when there was extra demand for persons to repair the ships in dry dock.

What did persons in seasonal employment do during the rest of the year? Mayhew's studies would indicate that they dovetailed employment into the local network of odd jobs to keep themselves in more or less constant employment. A person might be a navvy, a tramp, a peddler, or a harvester, all in the same year, or at different stages of their work life.

There were different kinds of job migrants. Some were habitual wanderers with no regular settlement; some kept winter quarters in town, but spent most of the year in the country; and others made regular short tours, never moving far from home. Some people did a variety of jobs, all within a single district; and others visited a variety of places, often doing the same job. The building trades were typical of the latter class of workers. For example, some stonemasons and carpenters were known to emigrate seasonally from England to the United States, leaving in the spring and returning every autumn having earned anywhere from five hundred to seven hundred dollars for the summer's work.[72]

Mayhew, who called such individuals "the wandering tribes," says that they found indoor shelter in winter. For most of them the City of London was the lottery of prizes, and the capital city's Christmas season was a veritable paradise of odd jobs. He says that street trading was a frequent resort of such persons in slack times, detailing a multitude of occupations done by such persons, from street cleaning, to working in the pantomime, to puppet shows.[73] The nature of available work in London goes far to explain why the Irish who went to London appear to have fared so poorly, because while the variety of employment available was likely to attract the venturesome, there appears to have been little opportunity to prosper. At the same time, the excitement of the capital city must have been a strong inducement for the young and adventurous to linger, and to an extent get caught.

Temporary jobs appear to have been less at that time the prerogative of social outcasts than they are sometimes considered today. And indeed, many of them were considered a normal phase in an entirely respectable work life. Some persons migrated or perambulated from desire, being "fond of a change"; some were forced into a wandering life when settled occupations failed; while others chose it from the beginning as a result of their experiences at home. Many of Mayhew's wanderers spoke of stepmothers or stepfathers, and brutal and abusive fathers as causing them to leave home and take up the casual life.

Casual work was also undoubtedly a standby for out-of-work laborers; this was so in York when Rowntree made his study. It could also enable workers to support themselves during a strike. Hay making in the nearby countryside enabled weavers from Padiham to support themselves during a long strike in 1859.[74]

When Mayhew investigated temporary workers, he estimated that there were about four laborers employed in summer for every three employed in winter.[75] Using the most recent census (1851) he computed the following numbers of those employed.

Agricultural laborers (not including Irish harvest labor)	1,000,000
Carpenters	163,000
Builders	92,000
Brickmakers	18,000
Painters	48,200
Coal whippers	92,000
Coal miners	110,000
Total	1,523,200

From this he calculated that if one-fourth of this total were casual laborers; this meant that approximately 380,650 persons were employed on a casual basis. Additional utilization of his findings could well contribute to a further study of the whole nature of casual labor in early industrialization.

Hobsbawm asks whether the tramping system, which was one aspect of casual labor in nineteenth-century Europe, was an expression of a newfound mobility on the part of the artisan, or derived from older traditions.[76] He concluded that tramping was a carryover and systematization of old habits, habits which were functional in overcoming seasonal and irregular employment. It would appear then that casual labor was a functional adaptation of workers to the rigors of the early stages of industrialization, enabling them to adjust their own needs to those of employers.

Conditions in Industrial Lancashire

Long-established links between Dublin and Liverpool made that port city and its hinterland of the industrializing region of Lancashire, an obvious choice for Irish migrants searching for work. Steam packet service, inaugurated between Dublin and Liverpool after the close of the French wars, facilitated passage when fares were drastically reduced, as were the risks and the time involved in what had previously been a relatively arduous trip by sailing vessel.

Liverpool was both a window to the New World as well as a reminder that the new focus of European trade would be away from Europe and toward the Americas. As such, the Atlantic trade represented a new age and a new importance for northwest England. For centuries London had been and would continue to be the political and commercial heart of Britain, but the Liverpool-Manchester nexus was assuming new and greater importance in an expanding industrial age. This importance called upon a combination of resources and skills to be readily available if expansion was to continue unchecked. There were other important west coast seaports such as Bristol and Glasgow, but none had such a close concentration of natural and physcial advantages as did Liverpool.

Lancashire was the cradleland of England's Industrial Revolution, a situation made possible by a number of advantages which it possessed in abundance: namely waterpower, fuel, and iron. A fourth advantage was its access to a fluid labor force on the other side of the Irish Sea.

Lancashire led industrializing Britain in typifying the advantages of the new age. In 1851 the Lancashire textile area contained, in an area of about seventy miles from north to south and between ten and fifty miles from east to west, almost one-quarter of all the adult male industrial employees of Great Britain, but it possessed less than 3 percent of the country's agricultural population.[77] Many more residents of the region depended directly or indirectly on factory-based industry for their livelihood, and a majority were employed in it at some period of their lives.[78]

W.E.H. Lecky, the nineteenth-century historian of Ireland who provided the first objective account of Ireland's development as a nation within the British context, drew attention to the new economic role which Ireland assumed in her relationship with England. He noted Ireland's position as a "back door larder" for the English market to draw upon.[79] The decade between 1760 and 1770 marked a change in the relationship between the two countries when England, previously self-sufficient in grain and in good years even an exporter of grain, became an importer, much of it from Ireland.[80] Some of the implications of this relationship were covered in Chapter Two, while others are beyond the scope of this study. In terms of drawing the two economies together into an integrated network, understanding the role played by the transport system in facilitating linkages is vital to understanding the dynamics of the period. Lancashire was by that time enabled "at very small expense, to appropriate to its use the natural advantages of the whole kingdom."[81]

The cotton textile manufacturing industry had at first localized around the Manchester area, a region approximately twenty miles inland from Liverpool but connected to it by the Duke of Bridgewater's canal. Manchester and its environs were a synonym for the manufacture of cotton goods. In earlier times trade had been essentially a handicraft undertaking, providing a source of additional cash income to persons living in an area of small farms where the poor quality of soil and wet climate made oats and barley standard but unreliable crops.[82] Most cottagers drew wage income from agriculture only during the harvest season and so had to depend on supplemental income from the spinning and weaving. Thomas Baines's contemporaneous description of the parish of Mellor, located fourteen miles from Manchester, illustrates how people were drawn away from agricultural production into industry. In 1770 the township had consisted of fifty or sixty farmers, of whom only six or seven could be said to be primarily dependent on income from the produce of their farms. The rest gained it from some form of industry: spinning or weaving wool, linen, or cotton. Every cottager had a convenient loom shop and garden attached, and the rentals for these ranged from one to two-and-a-half guineas per year.[83] A weaver could earn from eight to thirteen shillings per week, and his sons could each earn from six to eight shillings. (It took six to eight persons to prepare and spin yarn sufficient to supply one weaver before the introduction of the spinning jenny.[84] While it is difficult to estimate the female contribution to family income, Baines estimated that spinsters received from one to three shillings per week.) During the eighteen years between 1770 and 1788 linen and wool production disappeared in Mellor and cotton took over, thereby increasing the impact of the foreign import trade upon the area. From 1788 to 1803, the period which he calls "the Golden Age of the Trade," many new weavers' shops "rose up in every direction and were immediately filled." Wages also rose, some families bringing home forty, sixty, ninety, and even 120 shillings a week. Rentals for farms, once about ten shillings per acre prior to 1770, now "doubled and in many instances trebled."[85] While Mellor may not have been typical of the entire Lancashire area, because its proximity to industrialized Manchester undoubtedly explains the unusually high wages there, it is representative of the process whereby an area, once relatively self-sufficient in agriculture was transformed into the industrial environ of a nearby city.[86]

It is clear from the evidence about Manchester and its environs that it had long profited from a welcoming attitude toward outsiders arriving with needed skills. During the reign of Edward III, Flemings were encouraged to settle in York, Kendal, Halifax, and Manchester. The king, after his marriage to the Flemish Philippa of Hainault, brought over many woolen manufacturers from there, "granting them letters of protection, and tempting them with well-founded hopes of large profits and good living."[87] Prior to their arrival, it was said that English woolen products had been of the coarsest sort, but since English manufacturers expressed a desire not only to export raw wool but to compete with the finished product, to do this meant upgrading their level of skills—and this made them more willing to accept strangers.

The first evidence of Irish persons arriving in Manchester comes in a sixteenth-century statute of Henry VIII:

> many strangers, as wel of Ireland as of other places within this realme, have resorted to the saide towne with lynnen yarne, wooles, and other necessary wares for making of clothes, to be solde there, and have used credit & truste the poore inhabitants of the same towne, which were not able to and had not redy money to paye in hande for the saide yarnes, wooles and wares . . . wherein hath consisted much of the common welth of the saide towne, and many poore folkes had lyvynge.[88]

Market ties between the Manchester region and Ireland were known to exist as early as 1641. Yarn was brought from Ireland to Manchester "in great quantity" and when made up, returned to Ireland for sale there.[89] Such ties increased in the next century when that country began to supply much of the linen yarn then used for the warp thread in cotton weaving. This affected weavers in both Scotland and Ireland who complained of their yarn being bought out of their hands to be sold at a high price in Manchester.[90] The Dublin Linen Board made official note of such complaints in 1734, 1736, and 1738, estimating the value of yarn exports at 40 or 50,000 pounds a year. Quantities rose, from 13,734 cwts. in 1731 to 18,519 cwts. in 1740, to 22,231 cwts. in 1750.

The welcoming atmosphere of Manchester also proved a boon for persons driven out by the protests of those who saw threats to their livelihood posed by machinery. When a riot occurred in Blackburn in 1779 mobs scoured a wide area of the country demolishing spinning jennies, carding engines, and water frames. Every machine turned either by water or horsepower was destroyed and the spinners and small manufacturers were driven from the neighborhood; but they found a welcome in Manchester.[91] Mr. Peel, the father of the future prime minister, had been a refugee from such mob violence, and was typical of the small manufacturer who by dint of hard work rose into prosperity from having been a skillful and enterprising spinner. When his machines were broken up and thrown into the river it was said that he removed himself in disgust to Manchester where it was known that he could work unmolested.

Manchester's continued growth amazed visitors. In 1720 an observer said of its trade that it was "incredibly large . . . and dispersed all over the kingdom, and to foreign parts."[92] The next twenty years of almost uninterrupted peace gave commercial towns like Manchester the opportunity to make rapid strides in manufacturing. By 1787, when a census was taken of cotton mills in Great Britain, the Midland and western Midland counties clearly predominated in industrial location, with 99 out of a total of 119 textile mills situated in that area.[93] The same census gave 80,000 as an official count of the number of persons engaged in cotton manufacture in 1785 but Baines believed that because it was a year of low imports (only 11,482,086 lbs.), the figure was a vast underestimate. Taking the year 1787 (when imports were 23,250,268 lbs.), he estimated that at least 162,000 persons would have been engaged in the manufacture of cotton.[94] The great discrepancy in figures between those employed in 1785 and those estimated to be employed two years later provides a clue that there had to be an extremely mobile labor force available to adjust to a fluctuating demand of such proportions. And that, given the situation where the native labor force was both relatively immobile and insufficient to meet the demand, Ireland was in the position to provide the nearest available additional labor force.

Attention has been drawn to the pattern whereby factories were built initially in the countryside and drew their labor force from nearby villages, producing a pattern of cluster urbanization and industrialization. Manchester itself was the most important center of this cluster in Lancashire since it retained its early function as the principal marketing nucleus for the region. Despite this growth, or even perhaps because of it, Manchester lacked almost all public amenities, a situation very like contemporary Liverpool, so that by the early nineteenth century many of the difficulties characteristic of other industrialized towns prompted social reformers to call for action. The poor were "crowded in offensive, dark, damp and incommodious habitations, a too fertile source of disease."[95]

Not surprisingly, persons from elsewhere came to look and record their opinions of Manchester. One who suffered acute culture shock was the son of a German manufacturer, Friedrich Engels, whose father suggested that if he was critical of living conditions in Germany he might examine the much worse conditions of England. Engels' conversation with a Manchester manufacturer suggests both why immigrants found their way to the town and why their living conditions there failed to improve while they were resident there.

> I spoke to him of the miserable, unhealthy method of building that is to be found in the working-class districts and of the atrocious, disgraceful conditions of those districts. I declared to him that never in my life had I seen so badly built a town. He listened to all this patiently and quietly, at the corner of the street at which we parted he remarked: "And yet there is a great deal of money made here. Good morning, Sir."[96]

Conclusions

Technological changes taking place in Britain in this period created heavy demands for labor to transform what had been a largely agrarian society into an urban industrial society. But the changes were of both a qualitative as well as a quantitatively different nature than may have been previously understood. It may not have been as necessary as contemporaries often asserted that all workers be disciplined and hardworking. Fluctuations in production demands, in the supplies to maintain them, as well as the vast number of subsidiary occupations created by industrialization, point to a great need for laborers willing to take any work and on any basis to meet these fluctuations.

English workers did move into industry. They had to or they would have starved. But they did so with insufficient alacrity from the viewpoint of their employers. The result was that workplaces were staffed primarily by women and children, and by Irish laborers, far more eager for employment than were their contemporaries. For the English working person there was the cushion of a poor law, a safety net which the Irish did not have. In addition, the Irish had a history of migratory movement, and coming as they did from an economy increasingly on the edge of crisis, were willing to take any job which offered a degree of security because it would be an improvement on their alternatives in Ireland.

John Milton said, "What is freedom but choice?" In a real sense then, both the English and the Irish laborer had choice, but English laborers had more options, and thus more freedom. In contrast, choice was forced upon Irish laborers by his or her narrower range of total options.

Irish Migrants

The rapid extension of English industry could not have taken place if England has not possessed in the numerous and impoverished population of Ireland a reserve at command. The Irish had nothing to lose at home, and much to gain in England; and from the time when it became known in Ireland that the east side of the Irish Sea offered steady work and good pay for strong arms, every year has brought armies of the Irish hither.

FRIEDRICH ENGELS (1844)

DATE DUE

in England: The Reserve Army

Politics has made England and Ireland strange bedfellows; their labor market relationship has been even more complicated, if less known. Engels' remark that the Irish had nothing to lose at home, and much to gain by seeking work in England, cannot be disputed. Despite this harsh judgement on the connection between the two countries, a positive aspect of it was that the proximity also kept alive the possibility that the decision to migrate could be reversed relatively easily.

Seasonal workers whose custom was to return yearly to their plot of potato land, were buttressed by a safety net of cash earnings so that they could spend the sociable winter months at home, living in a slightly more comfortable level of poverty. Migrant workers who sought earnings in order to secure the lease of a farm or establish some business enterprise, customarily spent two, three, or more years abroad, but always with the option of return if conditions proved adverse. For either group, the decision implied relatively little risk as long as their access to land at home remained secure. England functioned then as an outlet, a safety valve which enabled the Irish to continue to live in Ireland.

But were these migrants the same persons who after a few years in England or Scotland joined the stream of emigrants to North America? Evidence allows us to surmise that many formerly temporary migrants then became permanent migrants to America. When successive failures of the potato crop between 1845 and 1849 brought the years of optimism to an end for most persons at the bottom the economic ladder in Ireland, we know that the disaster hit hardest at the class of persons who had less than five acres of land. The Census of 1851 told its own story when it recorded a population decline of 20 percent in the ten years, and when those persons with holdings of one to five acres dropped from 45 percent of the population down to 15 percent.[1] It is certain that many smallholders whose survival depended on work abroad calculated their gains and losses as did the migrant who told a parliamentary commission that times had been bad for about two years, and that if he made as little this year as last, he would take his money and go to America. The following letter from an otherwise anonymous Irishman from Drogheda tells a typical story of someone who was weighing the costs and benefits of emigrating to America in 1846, one year after the first evidence of the disastrous potato blight hit. He probably would not have qualified as a temporary migrant as it is defined in this book, although he travelled there regularly, but he would have been fairly typical of a Famine emigrant from the eastern seaboard of Ireland. He was not among the very poorest because he refers to "the poor" as other than himself. Familial obligations played a large part in his decision to go, but his father's recent death had freed him of obligation to his natal family, so that he could now consider emigrating. The letter was to his brother, John Lawless, living somewhere in Patch Grove, Wisconsin:

Collystown [Drogheda, Co. Louth]
30 July 1846

My dear brother,

In reply to your letter of 8th March 1846, I have to say I was in England . . . at the time it came from Drogheda and I did not return from England for four months after. . . . I really cannot say how long we will live in this country. The potato crop has failed in this country this year as it did in 1845 with this different that the distemper of infection set in this year about the end of June before the late crop planted in May had time to form. The early ones are very much infected in places but the disease is progressing and we all consider that there will not be a potato to put in November. We have also had great rains and severe gales of wind which it is feared has injured the cash crops so that you see there is a poor look-out for the ensuing spring and summer. Should the potato crop fail as anticipated my business falls to the ground. . . . Wheat rates from 25–24 shillings per barrel of twenty stone. Oatmeal 14–15 shillings per cask. We need not speak of potatoes for it is on Indian corn that the poor Irish live on. What I suppose you feed your pigs on. . . . I may perhaps make up my mind to go to America either this winter coming on or in spring. I cannot yet speak positively on Jenny's account. [Jenny was his wife whom he wished to remain in Ireland with their children until he sent for her.] I might however surprise you by calling to see you before you might be aware of it.

I remain, my dear brother
ever affectionately,
Lawless[2]

His attitude was typical of the many enterprising individuals who, having lost their faith in the land, then focused their attention on America. Four years of successive failure of their main subsistence crop broke the dream that it was possible to remain in Ireland.

This chapter addresses a number of issues raised by the migration on the English side. Among them are: who came? once there, what happened to them? how did they adapt to urban industrialization? what was the nature of their impact? and why was there the persistent belief that their stay was temporary?

In addition to illustrative material from contemporary and modern secondary sources, the study draws upon the reports of parliamentary commissions which sought to determine what effect the Irish were having upon working conditions in England. William Lowe's study of the post-Famine Lancashire Irish is drawn upon for comparative purposes because it focused upon the region which attracted the majority of the migrants.[3] Much of the strength of his work rests on the analysis of the census enumerator's notebooks for the years 1851, 1861, and 1871. Since 1851 was the first year in which such information was collected and made accessible to scholars, study of the years prior to this period must rest largely on analysis of the qualitative information which is available.

The Magnitude of the Migration

Reliable figures measuring the number of Irish persons resident in England are not available earlier than the 1841 Census, which was the first to collect statistics classifying persons in each parish according to whether the person was native to the parish or not. This census also recorded the nativity of each person in a hundred,[4] but not until the next census was detailed information on birthplaces collected. The information was unrepresentative of actual numbers of Irish persons in Britain because it caught persons at a fixed time, with no information to indicate why they were there, nor how long they had been resident; in other words, we cannot know much about their status.

According to the published census figures of 1841 there were 520,000 Irish-born persons resident in England and Wales. Thirty-seven percent of them (191,500) were resident in the county of Lancashire, which made that Irish community the most numerically significant in England. However these figures were skewed by having been collected in the period of crisis following the Famine when Irish persons were leaving, not from choice, but because they had lost choice. The concentration of famine-distressed population was located in Liverpool, Manchester-Salford, Oldham, Preston, St. Helens, and Widnes. These towns contained over 77 percent of Lancashire's Irish-born population in 1851, an indication that the nature of the migration was both urban and industrial.[5] Figure 4.1 indicates the concentration of Irish migrants in Britain in 1841.

Prior to the 1840s some attempts were made to provide estimates of the number of Irish persons in Britain, although the accuracy is in some doubt. One of the more careful examinations, Cornewall Lewis's 1836 *Report on the State of the Irish Poor in Great Britain* attempted to illustrate the growth of the Irish population by utilizing Roman Catholic registers. This method of estimating the size of the whole Irish settlement by calculating so many persons to every baptism was not satisfactory because it supposed that the number of baptisms to a certain number of persons would have remained constant for over thirty years, whereas changes in conditions in Ireland or in conditions attracting persons abroad tended to cause fluctuations in the supply of those migrating over the period of time. David Miller's work on church attendance in Ireland prior to the Famine indicates that large numbers of Irish persons did not observe the sacraments, with the result that many Catholic parents would not have sought to register their children.[6] Others avoided registering their children so as to evade uncomfortable questions about the child's age when they sought to send them to work. Furthermore, evidence from those giving testimony at hearings is that many Irish persons working in the Lancashire textile regions were Protestant and thus would not have been enumerated in this count.

Nevertheless, the numbers of Irish in England raised the anxiety levels of all who commented on the phenomenon. The sight of work gangs of Irish persons searching the countryside for work alarmed public authorities whose responsibility was the well-being of their parish, so that their estimates would tend to exaggerate total numbers. One attempt to produce an accurate count was made by the Statistical Society of London in 1837, which said that between 1821 and 1830, 12,000 persons per year emigrated to Britain. Another estimate gave 1,500,000 as the number who had settled in Britain in the thirty years between 1810 and 1840.[7] The 1841 Census acknowledged the problem of accurate counts when it reported:

> We have not the means of ascertaining the exact numbers of Irish who were in Britain in 1831, so as to compare them with their present numbers; still the whole number of persons of Irish birth dwelling in Great Britain on the 7th June 1841, was 419,256, which, of course, does not include their chil-

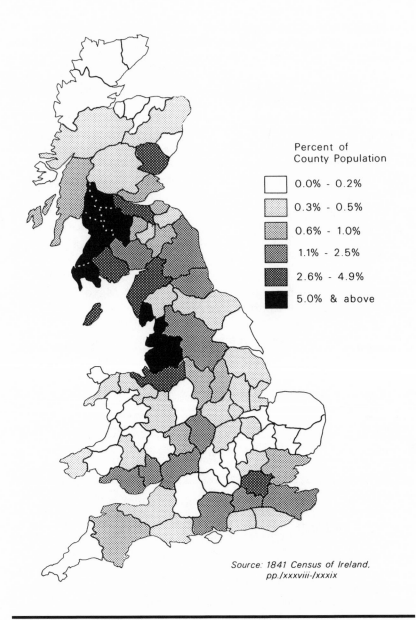

Percent of
County Population

☐ 0.0% - 0.2%

▨ 0.3% - 0.5%

▨ 0.6% - 1.0%

▨ 1.1% - 2.5%

▨ 2.6% - 4.9%

■ 5.0% & above

Source: 1841 Census of Ireland,
pp./xxxviii-/xxxix

FIGURE 4.1.   Irish-born population in Great Britain, 1841.

dren born there; and we may perhaps assume that one-fourth of this number have been added since the census of 1831, in which case we have 104,814 as a result.[8]

An important concern of the Census Commissioners in Ireland was that seasonal migrants would not be included in the enumeration, because the tally was collected too late in the agricultural season to catch them before their departure. Their intention was to count all the persons leaving Ireland that summer, especially those before the enumeration on the 7th of June. For that purpose, enumerators were stationed at all packet offices in the ports listed in the following table to collect from each person as he or she received their ticket of embarkation information concerning their county of origin. Before the sixth of June, when the enumeration was collected, 5,481 persons departed. Between that date and the first of July, another 13,997 persons left. For the whole summer a total of 57,651 persons left to work abroad. Almost half of these individuals came from the western province of Connacht (25,118 persons), while well more than a third were from Mayo (10,430 persons).[9] A breakdown by port was reported as follows:

Table 4.1. Port departures of Irish migrants, May–August, 1841

	Male	Female	Total
Londonderry/Portrush	10,545	772	11,317
Belfast	6,490	987	7,477
Warrenpoint	1,621	119	1,740
Dundalk	1,841[a]	353	2,194[a]
Drogheda	13,321[a]	465	13,786[a]
Dublin	15,303[a]	4,388	19,691[a]
Wexford	304	182	486
Waterford	47	2	49
Cork	439	472	911
TOTAL	49,911	7,740	57,651

SOURCE: *1841 Census of Ireland*, p. xxvi.
[a]Dublin was the main port of departure for migrants. During the 1841 sample enumeration the flow of persons reverted quickly fourteen miles north to Drogheda when departees heard that passage rates had been reduced there. Thus it may be assumed that the combined figure (33,477) represents what may have flowed through Dublin in a normal year.

Two-thirds of those who left were between sixteen and thirty-six years of age, an indication that they were of working age, implying also that they were accompanied by only a small number of dependents — again an indication that the majority of those leaving probably intended to return.

While it is difficult to determine the extent to which seasonal workers became longer term migrants, the data collected by the Census Commissioners seeking to learn how many of those who left returned at the end of the season, permit us to draw some tentative conclusions about characteristics of the migration on the basis of differential sex ratios. Table 4.2 shows the sex ratios of those Irish resident during the census enumeration in Britain, permitting a number of conclusions to be drawn. In the enumeration of those departing, the male-female sex ratio was six to one. However the census of population of England for that year reported an approximately even male-female ratio of those born in Ireland. Since the census procedures counted only those with relatively permanent settlement, it is reasonable to assume that, since few females were involved in the short-term temporary migration, males and females had the same propensities to migrate on a permanent basis. Thus, for each female departing, there would also be a male who would become relatively permanent.[10] This suggests that approximately six men left temporarily for each one moving on a longer-term basis. From this it is possible to estimate that between five and six migrants would return to Ireland within the year for every migrant who left on a more or less permanent basis. From the testimony given by seasonal migrants we know that only a few women migrated seasonally, so one can assume that the majority of females enumerated would remain abroad for a longer time.[11] From this, then, it can be assumed that between five and six males in the count would return to Ireland within the season.[12]

Table 4.2. Male-female ratios of Irish in Britain in 1841

Total Irish in Great Britain	Males	Females	Sex ratio M/F
England	148,151	135,977	1.09
Wales	3,180	2,196	1.40
Scotland	66,502	59,819	1.11
Total	217,733	197,922	1.10

SOURCE: *1843 Population Enumeration* (abstract), Parliamentary Papers, vol. 22, London: Her Majesty's Stationary Office; *Report of Census of 1841,* pp. 14–17.

The overwhelming significance of temporary movement is apparent from the above figures (see also Figure 2.7). The Irish Census Commissioners reported surprise that the figures for the Irish resident in Britain were not larger; this may be explained by the fact that close perusal of the British census suggests that harvest or temporary migrants were not enumerated (although they would be in the 1851 Census).

The proportions of emigrants from each county in Ireland was as follows:

When sex ratios are broken down by province, a seen in Table 4.4, they are most even in Munster (which also had the least total migrants in

Table 4.3. Proportion of migrants per county, May–August, 1841

Counties	Emigration	Population	Emigrants as % of total population
Mayo	10,430	388,887	2.7
Roscommon	5,422	253,591	2.1
Leitrim	2,860	155,297	1.9
Sligo	3,101	180,886	1.7
Donegal	4,915	296,448	1.7
Dublin	5,625	372,773	1.5
Londonderry	2,108	222,174	1.0
Monaghan	1,837	200,442	0.9
Louth	1,123	128,240	0.9
Fermanagh	1,262	156,481	0.8
Cavan	1,904	243,158	0.8
Galway	3,305	440,198	0.8
Longford	862	115,491	0.7
Armagh	1,688	232,393	0.7
Tyrone	2,096	312,956	0.7
Antrim	1,947	360,875	0.5
Westmeath	677	141,300	0.5
Kildare	516	114,488	0.5
Down	1,555	361,446	0.4
Meath	593	183,828	0.3
King's	467	146,857	0.3
Wexford	573	202,033	0.3
Queen's	343	153,930	0.2
Wicklow	251	126,143	0.2
Carlow	161	86,228	0.2
Limerick	362	330,029	0.1
Kilkenny	213	202,420	0.1
Tipperary	401	435,553	0.1
Cork	666	854,118	0.1
Clare	206	86,394	0.1
Kerry	131	293,880	0.04
Waterford	51	196,187	0.03
TOTAL	57,651	8,175,124	0.7

SOURCE: *1841 Census*, p. xxvii.

the 1841 sample period), an indication that emigration from Munster was more likely to have been either relatively permanent or long term. The ratio was only slightly more for the province of Leinster; that province also had the largest number of migrants living elsewhere in Ireland, suggesting that these individuals were relatively skilled. Since persons leaving Connacht and Ulster were mostly male, it may be concluded that the seasonal movement was primarily from these provinces.

Irish children born elsewhere than in Ireland were enumerated by the country of their birth, so that most of the 30,137 persons enumerated as being of English and Scottish birth resident in Ireland presumably were the children of Irish persons born during their parents' residence in Britain. The total population of Great Britain was 18,656,414 and that of Ireland 8,175,238; so that the natives of Ireland resident in Britain was one in forty-four of the population (while that of the natives in Ireland one in 379, and of Scotland, one in 952, making together one in 271).[13]

Table 4.4. Provincial origins of migrants to Britain, by sex, May–August, 1841

Provinces	Males	Females	Ratio M/F
Leinster	8,190	3,214	2.55
Munster	1,013	804	1.26
Ulster	17,274	2,038	8.48
Connacht	23,434	1,684	13.92
TOTAL	49,911	7,740	6.45

SOURCE: *1843 Population Enumeration* (abstract), Parliamentary Papers, vol. 22, London, Her Majesty's Stationery Office; *Report of Census of 1841*, pp. 14–77.

Although occupations of the Irish migrants were not collected, their concentration in urban regions of Britain provides clues to the nature of the migration as being primarily urban-industrial rather than rural. However, the majority of males enumerated as Irish were located in the English agricultural counties of Cumberland, Durham, Kent, Lincolnshire, Northumberland, Southampton, Warwick, and York West Riding, an indication that these were most likely migrant harvesters.[14] Liverpool and Manchester contained one-third of the entire number of those in England. (Liverpool had 49,639 Irish persons out of a total urban population of 286,487 or 17 percent; and Manchester had 30,304 Irish persons out of a total urban population of 242,983 or 12 percent.[15]) There was a total of 79,943 Irish persons in the two cities out of a total population of 529,470 (15 percent). The total numbers for the county of Lancashire was 105,916 persons, and for the county of Cheshire was 11,577 persons, making a total of 117,492, or 28 percent of the total Irish persons in Britain.[16]

There is little quantifiable evidence regarding the numbers of Irish persons in various occupations and what exists is based on estimates and thus open to prejudice. For example, the Poor Law Commissioners' estimates say that there were approximately 24,000 Irish persons in Liverpool and 30,000 Irish in Manchester in the 1830s. Yet other estimates inflated the numbers in Liverpool and underestimated those in Manchester. The most reasonable explanation for this relates to Liverpool's role as a primary port of entry, where persons arriving there, unless already contracted to work elsewhere, would tend to search for jobs before proceeding elsewhere. This means that there would tend to be a superabundance of persons for every job opportunity.[17] In contrast, Manchester manufacturers complained that there was a constant need to replenish their supply of labor, which would have resulted in greater opportunities for employment for migrants.[18]

Only after the 1851 Census, when for the first time occupations were classified and distinguished, is it possible to form an accurate picture of the kinds of labor at which Irish persons were employed. However, despite this, testimony given at the 1836 Parliamentary Enquiry, as well as scattered evidence from other sources, indicate general patterns and trends in the occupational choices of the migrants.

Types of Migrants and their Occupations

In 1671 a group of persons in Lancashire convicted for their Catholic faith included thirty-eight websters (the feminine form of weaver) and thirteen weavers, which a history of Catholics in England after the Reformation suggests may have been migrants from Ireland.[19] Chapter Two drew attention to early connections between Irish and English industries, and certainly ties such as this undoubtedly served to establish a recruitment network of attraction to opportunity. However, the earliest solid evidence of Irish persons seeking work in Manchester is from the mid eighteenth century when a writer in 1749 boasted of the small numbers of "Papists" in Manchester, saying "those we have are of no note or condition being chiefly poor Irish brought here to settle by our manufacture."[20] By 1784 a definite connection had been established between Manchester and Ireland when attempts were made by manufacturers in that city to promote the manufacture of cotton in Ireland.[21] Ireland was attractive for investment because it was free from duties on the cotton industry, duties which manufacturers considered vexatious, and which were a holdover from the period when the British government wished to discourage the domestic manufacture of cotton to protect its own woolen industry. At that time, Manchester manufacturers investigated the possibility of manufacturing in Ireland to take advantage of plentiful waterpower and an abundant labor force. While little can be discovered about the outcome of this venture, this and others like it served to establish connections between the two markets, the one with a demand for labor and the other with a more than ample supply.

Ties such as these opened a network of opportunities for industrial workers to leave declining or vanished industries in Ireland. Dorothy George notes connections between the silk trades of Dublin and London, believing that the first Irish settlement in London was the result of the decline in the silk and linen industries in Ireland.[22] One such example of decline in the first decade of the nineteenth century was the existence of an extensive cotton-spinning industry around Belfast employing about 13,500 persons.[23] Two decades later, competition with English steam power had defeated Irish waterpower, resulting in severe distress among cotton spinners when the trade was replaced with flax spinning, which utilized an entirely different technology. Displaced weavers were encouraged by opportunity abroad to emigrate into the cotton-weaving districts around Manchester. Wage differentials between the two regions would probably answer why persons chose to migrate rather than seeking to adapt to the new technique. A *Handloom Weaver's Report* states that by 1830 a flourishing area of cotton manufacture which had existed in Queen's County (now Leix) was extinct and the weavers and spinners gone. At Bandon, in Cork, another colony which had 1,500 weavers in 1829 was reduced to 150 eleven years later.[24]

The strong impetus for artisan craftsmen such as tailors, tanners, weavers, and leather workers to leave Ireland was, as discussed previously, a result of the decline of Dublin as the fashionable center of the country. With the passage of the Act of Union and with it the shift of the parliament to London, the former legislative seat could no longer support the large number of workers who had catered to the luxurious tastes of Georgian Dublin. The census of 1801 and that of 1821 demonstrate this by decreases in the number of occupations and declines in the multitude of industries which served the gentry class. It is not unlikely to suppose that fashionable clients would have encouraged their favorite hatters or tailors to follow them to London and thus inaugurate a migration network to that capital, which in turn encouraged others to follow.

While London was the most likely destination of Dublin artisans who had formerly catered to the gentry trade, the availability of similar opportunities elsewhere in England also served to attract Irish migrants to become journeymen tailors elsewhere. John Petty, a master tailor of Manchester, estimated that there were approximately 450 Irish journeymen tailors in that city, and that there had been "considerable increase" since 1810.[25] Several other large towns also had considerable numbers of journeymen tailors from Ireland, tending to support the opinion that it was lack of opportunity (although not lack of training in this instance), which propelled Irish persons abroad. The experience of one of Henry Mayhew's informants illustrates how far afield the search for work could take a person. The informant had been trained and worked as a tailor in Cork, travelling first to Waterford, then Wicklow, and lastly to Dublin in search of employment. Finally reaching London, he was no longer working as a tailor, but had been reduced to selling "roots" as a street hawker, aided by his wife and daughter. When questioned why he was working as a street hawker, he said:

> Rayther than put up wid the wages and the *terratement* [said very emphatically] o' thin slop masters at the Aist Ind [the East End was the tailoring section of London which catered to the fashionable] I'd sill myself as a slave. The straits doesn't degrade a man like thim thieves o' the worruld.[26]

He was personally acquainted with ten other Irish artisans who had become street sellers in London, and twenty-five females who had once been in a good trade. Was it independence, or discrimination, or lack of opportunity which reduced them to street trading?

Some small manufacturers recruited regularly in Ireland, according to Mayhew, who believed that they did this because the Irish were a cheaper and more docile labor force. He found a number of instances in which the wives of individuals employing sweated labor in London visited Ireland to recruit women to work in the tailoring trades.[27] Other recruitment was less formal. The owner of a Manchester silk mill who employed 190 Irish girls (mostly as winders of silk) out of a total factory population of 500 said:

> The moment I have a turnout, and am fast for hands, I send to Ireland for 10, 15, or 20 families as the case may be. I usually send to Connaught and get the children, chiefly girls of farmers and cottiers. . . . I provide them with no money. I suppose they sell up what they have, walk to Dublin, pay their own passage to Liverpool, and come to Manchester by railroad, or walk it. In cases of sickness or death I do something for them. . . . I have no agent in Ireland. I sent a man once or twice for this purpose and he found me 60 or 70 hands. I think that more than 400 have come to me from Ireland, many of whom left after they learned their trade.[28]

Although some were recruited directly, as were these or the sweated laborers in London, others brought more marketable skills.

Irish persons who arrived with marketable skills were able to capitalize on this by obtaining employment relatively swiftly, but they had a reputation for not remaining long. As such they were perambulating workers in the classic sense. One example of this was spinners who were relatively well paid. Of the Irish spinners it was said, "They migrate from Belfast to Paisley, from Paisley to Manchester, and from Manchester to Belfast, as it suits their strikings for wages."[29] Arthur Redford called the movement "a progression of skill,"[30] when persons from Ireland, arriving at Liverpool, first travelled to Wigan where they learned to weave calicos, muslins at Bolton, and finally reached Manchester which paid the best wages in the cotton industry.[31] One employer deplored the unwillingness of the Irish to stay long at a particular trade, where he said, "If they get a frame for six months or so they think they are masters of it."[32] Official reports also deplored the "migratory tendencies" of Irish workers, arising from the fact that they moved house so often.[33]

In general it appears that any extensive immigration of Irish persons into industrial and handicraft occupations in Britain was initiated by declines in those trades in Ireland, and facilitated by close connections between the two markets. Ireland continued to produce an abundant population, so that after the introduction and extensive utilization of steam power in Britain it was apparently more advantageous to let the Irish labor force find its way into English mills than to attempt to promote industry in Ireland. Despite the best efforts of such institutions as the Dublin Society which promoted the advantages of the country and sought to devise ways in which industry could be attracted there, the climate of optimistic opinion which had made Ireland appear attractive in the late eighteenth century was gone. After 1800, Ireland's independent legislature was stripped of its powers; her gentry preferred to "cut a dash" in London, and Irish industry did the same.

Relatively skilled artisans were less likely to be temporary migrants. One important factor was that the health of persons who worked in industrial occupations was notoriously bad. One observer said that health of weavers and broguemakers was bad from their confinement in smoky cabins, so that they lived from ten to twenty years less than the average farm laborer.[34] Artisans were thus unlikely to be able to return to farming, even when they had not already lost their access to land. There was one notable exception to this however where a group of weavers from Drogheda migrated abroad every winter. At the turn of the century the weaving industry there had employed about 1,000 looms, so that when trade declined many weavers "abandoned weaving to engage in the provision trade with Liverpool; others had emigrated to Wigan, Manchester and Barnsley."[35] It was believed that approximately four hundred persons left the area between 1831 and 1834. What is of interest is that wages stabilized for the weavers who remained, so that they were the same as wages in Manchester. About one hundred and fifty weavers' families took advantage of the opportunities in both cities by migrating to Lancashire for the winter months because living conditions were more comfortable and the price of coal was lower than in Ireland. Every spring it was said that they returned to their cabins in Drogheda for "more space and purer air."[36]

OWEN PETER MANGAN. The story of Owen Peter Mangan, who first learned machine weaving in Drogheda before emigrating to Lancashire and then to America illustrates an industrial migrant's progression of skill. Born in Cootehill, County Cavan, around 1838, he was fairly typical of the resourceful migrant who by determination, some luck, and talent eventually became a prosperous, successful emigrant.[37] When, late in life, he sat down in Lynn, Massachusetts, to pen his memoir, he described a life of incredible hardship and yet significant achievement.

Ties with the land which drew others back to Ireland were broken for Mangan very early when the family broke up after his father's death. His father had been a moderately successful stock drover who purchased a farm in order to spend more time with his growing family of five sons. When farming proved not to be a full-time occupation, he took up the illegal production of poteen making which, when discovered by the authorities, earned him a prison sentence. In prison he caught a cold and died, leaving Mangan's mother with five boys to rear.

Within six months she was married to the man whom earlier the father had employed to tutor the children. When their new stepfather refused to support them, the family was dispersed. Mangan and his five-year-old brother were fostered out to an old woman who abused them severely, while the other three brothers were sent away to make their own way in the world. At five years of age Mangan ran away seeking his mother, but his stepfather refused to allow him to remain. Once again he was abandoned when the family moved as they were wont to do because his stepfather kept moving from job to job. Until the age of eight he supported himself by various means: selling grass to draymen for their horses, sheltering with an impoverished aunt, and finally by living with the family of Lord Coote's gamekeeper. Once again his mother and stepfather had moved—this time from Baileborough in Cavan, thirty miles away, to Drogheda in Louth. By the time he was twelve he was allowed to remain with his mother because he could now earn enough to help the family, which he did by working in a cotton mill with his stepfather who had secured him the job. Always ambitious, he persuaded the girls who operated the looms to teach him how to weave, and was soon working as a weaver himself.

In 1853, at the age of fifteen, he left home for the last time after a dispute with his mother about the amount of money he brought home to her. Hearing that wages were good in England, he and three friends decided to try their luck finding work there. He found work immediately in Preston in Lancashire, working as a weaver for ten shillings a week, which was four more than his earnings in Ireland. He married at eighteen, his wife an immigrant, from Maynooth in Kildare. They eventually had a family of ten; five born in England and five more after the family's emigration to America.

Mangan never singled out his natal family as unusually cruel, although he does say that throughout his life his friends gave him more assistance than ever his family had, so one can assume that his experience may not have been unusual for stepchildren of families where resources were straitened. Next to the spur of ambition, his wife may have been his greatest asset, and he always gave her full credit for helping him. While living in Preston they opened a dry-goods shop which she kept while he worked in the mills during the day. After work he helped her when he wasn't attending evening classes. Business was good until the late 1860s when because of Fenian activities in England the whole Irish community was regarded with suspicion and his English customers (who he says were the only ones who paid their bills regularly) stopped patronizing him. At this point he began to think about going to America where by this time three of his brothers were. Brother William was prospering as a cooper in Philadelphia and Mangan, believing that his brother would assist him, decided to join him there. After a few weeks Mangan tried to borrow enough money to bring out his family, but was told that in America "every tub stands on its own bottom." With that he left his brother's home and the city of Philadelphia, never to ask his family for anything again.

After a series of jobs, none of which paid enough to enable him to bring out his family, he found employment in Fall River, Massachusetts, through a friend he had met during his stay in England. Fifteen months after arrival in America he brought out his family with one hundred and ten dollars borrowed from a friend — a debt he was proud to repay within three months.

Moving from job to job — only working as a weaver when he could get nothing else because wages in this occupation were low — he continued to do well, finally settling in Lynn, Massachusetts. He sent his oldest son to Holy Cross College in Worcester, Massachusetts, a sure sign of success in the New World. His memoir is almost a case history of the forces which pushed Irish persons out of Ireland, and the energy and enterprise necessary for survival after emigration.

Owen Peter Mangan's life would have been far less successful if he had gone to London rather than Lancashire. Migrants to London were more likely to fall into "a progression of despair," as is clear from the experience of those in the tailoring trades in London. Also, those without kin or friends to assist them lacked an important safety net for survival. Mayhew's work suggests that migrants with no contacts in England generally fell into worse poverty after arrival. One of his informants, a casual laborer who had once been a well-paid cotton spinner, had

lost his job when "self-actors" (machines run by steampower) were introduced in the 1830s. He had been twelve months "knocking about" Manchester without work, and said: "It wants a friend and a character (a
recommendation of good character) to get work," he said.[38] A number
of these were Mayhew's informants in the 1850s.[39]

One, a young man in his late twenties, in England for two years,
had come from better conditions in Ireland than most. He had tilled
forty acres in Kilmeen, County Cork, but said, "I rented my land of a
middleman and he was severe." Why did he leave? "I came to better my
living." The voyage from Cork to Bristol cost twenty-five pence for
himself, his wife, and three children. Finding no work in Bristol he went
on to Cardiff where he worked on the railroad at two shillings sixpence
per day and "did well." Following that he worked with a bricklayer; then
twelve months with a farmer at ten shillings a week and "was comfortable." On reaching London he worked on the docks.[40] He and his wife
went harvesting and received ten shillings per acre for wheat, seven shillings per acre for oats, and two shillings for any other day's work.
Returning to London they fell into destitution and had been forced to
sell their few possessions on the streets. At the time of the interview his
wife and children were lodging in the Union (poor house) to keep them
from starving.[41]

While connections between Manchester and the Irish market created
an information system, this would have been insufficient if strong ties
based on residence and kinship had not existed to maintain a support
system which reduced the worst risks of movement. A network
functioned, facilitating and encouraging migration between the two areas. One informant, remarking on this, said:

> I know that the Irish constantly invite their friends and relations in Ireland,
> and when they come receive and entertain them in their habitations for a
> certain period, or until they can obtain work. . . . Some have been induced
> to come to this country by the great difficulties which they experienced in
> Ireland, and the strong expectation encouraged in their minds by popular
> report that the means of subsistence could be easily obtained in England.[42]

English persons gave grudging admiration to this Irish solidarity.
One informant told Mayhew, "I don't like the Irish, but they *do* stick to
one another far more than we do."[43] It was a familiality and cohesiveness which blunted the worst risks of adjusting to new conditions. According to Mayhew: "The readiness with which young Irish people thus
adapt themselves to all uncertainties and hardships of street life is less to
be wondered at when we consider that the Irish live together, or at any

rate associate with one another in this country, preserving their native tastes, habits, and modes of speech."[44]

While links in the migration stream were often initiated and maintained by familial ties, what of migrants who were not recruited in such direct fashion? It is possible to reconstruct with some accuracy the process by which migrants who were not directly recruited, either by an employer or by kin or friends, were able to find employment, or perhaps to come upon work (as such a process might better be termed) from a number of sources.

The keeper of the Birmingham workhouse believed that it was quite common for the lords mayor of towns in Ireland to pay ship passage to transport redundant laborers to English towns.[45] This story may be a kind of urban myth with which people explain phenomena which they don't understand, and was probably less common than believed. The only documented incidence of such assistance as this was given to a group of weavers in Talbotstown in Wicklow when the manufactories there closed down. As a result of the closure three hundred persons were "compelled to remove to England in search of employment," assisted by Lord Aldborough, a landlord resident in England, and the Stranger's Friend Society of Dublin. The six or seven hundred Bandon weavers who left between 1832 and 1835, "almost all to London and Manchester, [had] their passage paid by public collection." The Bandon Poor Commission paid for two hundred weavers' families to go from Kinalmeaky, and more went for half fare offered by the Steam Packet Company.[46]

The ability of Irish persons to "sniff out" jobs was phenomenal — and often noted. In one case in Scotland, construction on the Caledonian Canal was commenced with the intention of aiding distressed Highlanders. Before this could be done labor contractors brought in Irish workers, who then stayed on as semipermanent inhabitants, or as they were called "exotic crofters," in huts hastily built to accommodate the temporary workers.[47]

Seasonal migrants were more likely to be persons with ties of land and family in Ireland; while landless and unmarried laborers were more likely to linger when greater opportunity presented itself. There is little evidence that migrants who wished to acquire sufficient land so as to enable them to rise into the gentry class achieved this goal very often. Most observers believed that returned migrants often lost their targeted small sums when the increasing costs of leasing land absorbed their savings, leaving them after return worse off than ever, as they were now too old to find employment abroad. One County Galway informant who did not believe that temporary migrants prospered from their sojourn abroad, described the seasonal migrants' return home: "The night they come home there may be half a dozen watching [for] them, expecting to get part of what is due to him; one for con-acre, another for house rent, and another for provisions given on credit, and so on."[48]

Persons whose goals were more modest than such as the fictional hero, Phelim O'Toole's grandfather, described in one of William Carleton's novels raised the family's status in the community after having earned a modest sum from work abroad. The point of the story was that the family also developed unrealistic expectations — "ideas beyond their station" — which eventually caused them to fall back into greater poverty than before. Does this suggest that it was generally believed at the time that migrants failed to succeed?[49]

Unmarried persons wishing to save enough money to lease land were freer to linger abroad. A Birmingham employer of Irish bricklayer's helpers said that many of the men he employed "come for harvest [but] stop to work as masons."[50] Believing that few rose beyond that level of lack of skill he decried what he believed was an inability to commit themselves wholeheartedly to their jobs.[51] What may have appeared to him as a lack of job commitment was more likely an intention to return home by persons who had no incentive to raise their skill levels.

The autobiography of a contemporary Irishman illustrates the situation. In *An Irish Navvy, the Diary of an Exile,* Donall MacAmhlaigh tells a story repeated thousands of times since the first Irish immigrant entered Britain. He says, "This book is an honest account of how the average Irish laborer works, lives in, and makes his contribution to, the development of the country that has given him a good wage for the sweat of his brow."[52]

After demobilization from the First Battalion of the Irish Army in 1951, MacAmhlaigh knocked about Ireland for a while, unable to find employment in the post war period of economic slump. Following the pattern of many before him, he emigrated, attracted by a British Health Service advertisement for stokers. In England he joined his countrymen "without whose help the British Health Service and the building, light engineering and service industries would have ground to a standstill."[53] While unable to consider himself in permanent exile, he nevertheless spoke with bitterness of the necessity that made him leave Ireland to earn a living, and the profound ambivalence with which he and many other Irish persons regard their country, "To be sure, everyone knows that it's the lack of a livelihood that's responsible for us being here; but it's not at all praiseworthy that a man shouldn't stand up for his own country even though it has no place for him."[54] Once there he moved from job to job, lured each time by higher pay, until he settled into employment, sometimes as a navvy, sometimes as a contract construction worker, saying that he preferred irregular employment to more settled work because it permitted him to return to Ireland between jobs.[55]

MacAmhlaigh believed that the majority of the Irish continued to migrate but did not benefit greatly from the effort, believing too that they ruined work conditions by not looking for pay rises or seeking better working conditions. "They used to say that the Irish who came over here long ago ruined the worker's conditions."[56] MacAmhlaigh regarded the English much as had his countrymen of a century ago. One of Mayhew's Irish informants said, "I'm living with these odd people for more than six years now and I don't take to them any better than I did the first day. It's not that I hate them like a number of Irishmen do; indeed, quite otherwise. But they make me tired with their strange ways, and I love to get away from them all the time."[57] What is surprising about MacAmhlaigh's story is that attitudes and experiences have hardly changed from those his countrymen held and experienced a century and more earlier.

As outlined in Chapter Two, in its earliest and broadest sense the migration stream was initiated and largely maintained by a seasonal movement of agricultural laborers seeking work in Britain's burgeoning construction industry and harvest fields. Contemporaries considered the flow fairly undifferentiated but evidence suggests that it was far from random. Mayhew was aware of this when he described Irish seasonal workers: "It appears that for very many years considerable numbers of these [Irish] have annually come to England in the spring to work at hay-harvest, remaining for corn-harvest and hop-picking, and then have carried home their earnings in the autumn, seldom resorting to begging."[58] Increased demand for urban industrial workers encouraged agricultural migrants to become semipermanent emigrants, such as was Mac-Amhlaigh. What determined whether and when this took place was dependent upon the difference between opportunities in England and those in Ireland.

It is doubtful whether the numbers of Irish harvesters in England was very extensive before the end of the eighteenth century.[59] The growth of a really substantial movement was facilitated by the coming of steamship service at the end of the Napoleonic Wars which provided regular and more dependable connections between the two countries.[60] It is certain that the annual movement had become such a well-established element of Irish rural life by the late 1830s that the Commissioners sought to ascertain its incidence.[61] And most considered it inexorable. In 1827 a witness before a Committee on Emigration said that "every decrease in the number coming to England each year would add to the probability of starvation in Ireland."[62]

When seasonal labor in England was integrated with the cultivation and harvest cycle in Ireland migrants could benefit from opportunities in both places.[63] As described in Chapter Two, rural migrants followed a regular progression of work: the conacre crop of potatoes which was the family's subsistence was planted, whatever labor obligation was owed to the landlord from whom they held their lease was fulfilled, and spring planting for whichever local farmers offered employment was completed before migration. Migrants were extremely calculating as well as knowledgeable about the risks of movement, often testifying that they preferred to pay the higher cost of passage by steamship rates because the shorter passage enabled them to conserve on supplies, thereby enabling them to reach England in time to compete for jobs with other casual labor.[64] Mayhew asserted that the Irish were well represented in temporary labor, deliberately seeking it out.

> It is well known that there is a periodical immigration of the Irishmen and women, who clamour for the *casual* employment; others again, leave the towns for the same purpose; the same result takes place also in the fruit and pea-picking season for the London green markets; while in the winter such people return, some to their own country, and some to form a large proportion of the casual class in the metropolis.[65]

Later, by September or October or November they were on their way back to Ireland to rejoin their families and to harvest their potatoes, paying the rent and their creditors with their English earnings.[66]

Those most likely to settle for longer periods of time were leaving declining trades such as weaving and spinning. Irish handloom weavers were attracted to urban Lancashire at a time when English handloom weavers were abandoning the industry in large numbers as a result of drastic wage reductions, although Redford says that 5,000 Irish handloom weavers were settled in Manchester as early as the 1790s, which is well before conditions had declined in either place.[67] Seeking work objectionable to others is consistent with their other behavior, inasmuch as they sought any employment spurned by English workers, but in which employers wished to economize on labor costs.

The state of handloom weaving in Britain in the 1820s and 1830s illustrates the tardiness of the trend to full adoption of machine technology. Despite the fact that power looms were readily available and in operation by the first decade of the nineteenth century, J.H. Clapham maintains that even as late as 1841 neither factory weavers nor journeymen weavers formed large portions of the total weaving population, and in fact there was an increase in the total number of persons employed in handloom weaving, from an estimated 240,000 in 1820 to 250,000 in 1834.[68] The housing conditions of the weavers were deplorable, but understandably so, living as they did on from four to seven or eight shillings a week. Why then, when wages were so low did persons continue to flow into handloom weaving? A contemporary observer, Edward Baines, drew attention to this anomaly, saying that initially the demand for textiles had been so great that, "Weavers were in the utmost request, and their wages rose to a rate exceeding that of any other class of workmen. . . . This induced multitudes to learn the trade, and it continued to attract hands long after the demand was satisfied. An employment so easily learnt, and so handsomely remunerated, became inevitably surcharged with labourers."[69]

Readjustment to peacetime production after 1815 encouraged many disbanded soldiers and sailors to take up handloom weaving because it was known as an easy trade to master, requiring only strength. Competition created by them resulted in wages falling 50 percent in one year— from twenty-four shillings per week in 1815 to twelve shillings per week in 1816.[70] The result was to induce English and Scottish weavers to gradually abandon the trade, while Irish weavers took their places, even though earnings in the trade continued to decline (reaching an average of six shillings sixpence by 1825). It was hardly surprising however that even while declining, the industry still continued to attract workers because, as Baines says, "Throughout the 1830s weavers were never unemployed. The strength of the master is in having the power loom to resort to, as in being able so easily to obtain handloom weavers."[71] Employers were also already feeling the pinch of competition from the American market, which was an additional reason for profit margins to narrow in the 1830s. One manufacturer testified: "I do not think that the manufacturers could afford to give higher wages to weavers than the present rate. Power-loom weaving is a very lean trade for capitalists. Nothing can raise weaver's wages to their former level without materially injuring the trade."[72]

The 1841 *Handloom Weaver's Report* drew attention to the plight of weavers which, while once a trade which commanded respect and a good income, had now become a national tragedy. Clapham says,

> The Commissioners of 1841 recognized the facts and spoke politico-economically, and as it must have seemed brutally, of the problem of supply and demand—"the demand [they had in view handloom weaving of all kinds, not merely of cotton] being, in many cases, deficient, in some cases decreasing, and in still more, irregular, while the supply is, in many branches, excessive, in almost all has a tendency to increase [by the weaver's passionate clinging to his loom and his independence; by the consequent automatic turning of weavers' children into weavers; by the terrible ease with which simple weaving was learnt; and by Irish immigration] and does

not appear in any way to have a tendency to adapt itself to the irregularities of the demand." How should it? How should a fourteen-hour-a-day cellar weaver take up some other job when demand slackened?[73]

Duncan Bythell also says that there is no evidence of a persistent, steady decline of trade, even while long-term trends were unfavorable. Instead, and more usual, was that brief flurries of prosperity encouraged business to pick up, thereby making work more generally available, which then attracted more persons to become weavers.[74]

The Irish, with their gift for underliving the competition[75] were particularly well suited for conditions in spinning and handloom weaving. Spinning had long been a common income supplement for women in rural Ireland; while to a lesser extent weaving was a supplement for men, factors which meant that many arrived with some knowledge and experience. Furthermore both skills were said to be fairly easy to learn, as previous evidence has indicated. It took little capital to either rent or buy a loom, and as long as the demand for cloth remained substantial, looms were plentifully available. Handloom weaving also was an occupation for the whole family: a child as young as six was said to be able to work the loom for about three hours before tiring.[76] During the expansionary years when weaving was a flourishing trade, cellar weaving shops had been built to provide the damp conditions necessary to keep threads supple; later these became relatively inexpensive accommodations sought out by the Irish wishing to live as cheaply as possible by economizing on their housing costs.

Despite the fact that Irish workers were mostly attracted to declining industries such as weaving, or jobs spurned by others, they had long been seen as competitors in the labor market. Dorothy George says that the worst early outbreak of violence between native English workers and Irish workers occurred in 1736 in the Spitalfields area of London when a number of Irish workers, arriving for the hay and corn harvest, "remained to offer themselves at low wages to whoever would employ them." Conflict with the English workers erupted when Spitalfields employers discharged their English employees in order to employ Irish workers. In another instance, when a church was under construction at Shoreditch the master workman discharged workers and took on Irishmen who were willing to work for more than a third less per day, again provoking conflict between the two groups.[77]

Industrial conflict with native workers was a constant fact of life, particularly in the textile districts. Bythell noted at least ten major and extended strikes within the textile regions between 1810 and 1836.[78] And although labor historians usually prefer to emphasize the working population's resistance to machinery, he said that strikes were almost always directed toward "knobsticks" or scabs rather than toward machinery. The extent of the labor unrest tends to explain why strikebreakers were resorted to so frequently because, while at the same time that Irish persons were willing to accept lower wages than their English counterparts, employers sought to hire them as wage cutters and strikebreakers.[79] The owner of the Manchester silk mill, whose labor force was almost two-thirds Irish, acknowledged this when he said, "The moment I have a turnout . . . I send to Ireland."[80] A Scottish shipyard owner also testified that he kept his workers in line by bringing in Irish labor.

> Last August [1833] the sawyers of my yard struck, 14 of whom were Irish. The Irish were not the ringleaders. They were earning from 35s. to 40s. a pair per week, frequently as much as L3. We refused their terms, and employed common labourers, chiefly Irish, to fill the pits; by degrees they learnt the trade, and are now earning from 30s. to 35s. a-week; some come up to 40s. The hands who struck are now begging to be employed on their former wages, and have entirely dissolved the union they formed.[81]

From the employers' view the function of their Irish help was to discipline the English work force.

> The Irish have, in those branches of industry which could be easily taught, either to children or adults, been a check on the combination of the English and Scotch of the western counties, as they could be brought over almost in any numbers, at a short notice, and at little expense. Thus not only can the Irish be put into the place of the natives, if the latter turn out, but the natives sometimes abstain from turning out, in the consciousness that their places can be immediately filled.[82]

In other words, the Irish were a mobile, expendable labor force, who were utilized to satisfy the needs of manufacturers wishing to maximize production. One Manchester manufacturer testified to this in 1834 when he said:

> Ten or twelve years ago we could not have done without Irish; the demand for labour in Manchester could not have been satisfied without them. Not only was there a real scarcity of hands, but the English were so mutinous that nothing could be done with them. The Irish were employed as a check on the combination of the English. Now there is an abundance of English hands, and we could dispense with the Irish.[83]

Official investigations concluded that the majority of Irish persons worked in handloom weaving rather than factories prior to 1850; and when they were employed in factories it was not in spinning, which was well paid, but at the power loom which was not.[84] In fact, two English manufacturers testifying in 1835 believed that they doubted if there were a hundred Irish spinners in the whole country.[85]

The extent to which the Irish labor force was totally quiescent has been the subject of extensive discussion and debate. There is no doubt but that some were extremely vocal. John Doherty, a trade unionist and radical reformer, was one of these. Nevertheless he was an anomaly whose career resembled that of the period after 1850 when migrants tended to become actively involved in political activity. Born in Donegal, he followed a typical pattern of stepwise migration. Leaving Buncrana around 1809 he went first to Larne in County Antrim, and from thence to Manchester at the end of the French Wars. Once in England he joined the Manchester cotton spinners union in 1817, where he soon became a recognized leader. In 1829 he founded the Grand General Union of Spinners and edited a paper, *The Voice of the People*.[86] A hero to his fellow-workers, Doherty was a thorn to employers who considered him a dangerous agitator with his Irish gift of brilliant oratory. While Doherty's career was not at all typical of the usual Irish migrant seeking work in England, it does illustrate why the Irish were believed to play a role in pre-1850 political activity.[87]

Opportunities for machine spinners were different in the west of Scotland where it was said that the aversion of the local people to undertake work in the mills enabled Irish persons to settle and obtain an early hold on factory work there. Irish workers maintained a monopoly there and in 1833 it was said that the Glasgow cotton mills were "almost full of Irish," the spinners being chiefly recruited from Irish born in the neighborhood who had entered the mills as children.[88] The evidence in the Scottish mills is that Irish workers advanced on to the more highly paid skill of spinning, whereas in England this was believed to happen only rarely. The difference between the two groups, the Irish in Western Scotland and the Lancashire Irish, was the contrast between a settled population with a vested interest in advancement in a community to which it now considered itself belonging more or less permanently, and a transient population whose goal was the accumulation of capital, but whose valued communal ties lay elsewhere.[89]

Evidence regarding the incidence of whole families migrating is not conclusive. Seasonal migrants, giving testimony regarding their decision to go or not, indicated frequently that they left their wives at home because they could not get employment in England, or because they could make more by begging or staying on the farm in Ireland.[90] For those for whom such choice was possible, it is not unlikely to expect then that, when there were opportunities for whole families (versus fewer opportunities in Ireland), the productive members would begin to go for relatively permanent settlement. Evidence from the Bombay textile industry regarding seasonal migrants' decisions to bring families bears out that as opportunities for employment of wives and children increased, the fathers (who had earlier been temporary migrants and temporarily employed casual laborers) brought their families who then settled, and became work-life permanent urban residents.[91]

Irish persons abroad were sometimes described as poor parents because they permitted their children to run wild, a story inconsistent with the behavior of children employed in a factory where it would be expected that long tedious hours would have reduced childhood exuberance.[92] It is difficult to know whether such comments proceeded from the usual prejudice against Irish public behavior, or resulted from other factors, such as that Irish children may have been in the streets because they were hawking, a common resort of casual workers in general, and of the Irish in particular, according to Mayhew. If the family intended to remain, would they not also have sought to have their children employed in the factory? Their behavior is consistent with people who needed to earn quick money, and that was hawking or begging.[93]

It was generally believed that Irish women resident in factory districts resisted factory work, and indeed a Manchester workhouse overseer thought them idle because he knew so few to work in factories. Lowe also noted that Irish women did not work in the factories of Manchester-Salford despite the fact that female labor was in great demand.[94] Irish female heads of household were more likely to operate boarding houses than were English women, which lends support to the idea that Irish women preferred to be home-based. However assertions of idleness are belied by other evidence, such as an instance when a Manchester manufacturer imported cotton fibers from Brazil which were so dirty that no one could be found willing to clean them. Irish women were however willing to undertake the laborious chore, and took home bags of fiber to clean. Mayhew said that in London Irish women were street sellers because they lacked skills. He said that they were "unable to do anything else to eke out the means of their husbands or parents. A needle is as useless in their fingers as a pen."[95] The behavior of Irish women was undoubtedly consistent with their skills as well as their goals; Irish women and children came from rural backgrounds where there was little need for sophisticated domestic skills. They were also unlikely to be willing to undertake the kind of commitment implied by factory employment if they intended to return to Ireland soon.[96]

Determining the full range of occupations chosen by the Irish is a complex task, if not impossible, because we know so little of the wide range of ancillary occupations necessary to the nineteenth-century English industrial economy, as was indicated in the previous chapter.[97] But what is important to note here is that many ancillary occupations were seasonal. The question then arises as to the extent to which these occupations were filled by the Irish. One observer believed that most itinerant workers were Irish. Once when he met a wandering laborer, he observed that, "He seemed to be a decent sort of man, and, for a wonder, was not an Irishman."[98] Were these occupations really monopolized by the Irish, or did their distinctive manner of dress and speech only make it appear that way? What proportions of persons may have been Irish who were balancing seasonal labor in these occupations in Britain with agricultural employment at home; and what proportion may have been Irish persons spending a few years migrating around Britain, taking opportunities as they found them? The state of research into such occupations is in a very preliminary stage because the contribution of the Irish to nineteenth-century industrial life is only beginning to be recognized. For that reason it is not surprising that specific Irish contributions are mostly undervalued. Nevertheless all the evidence would suggest that Irish persons were to be found in any kind of outdoor occupation from which they were not actively excluded.

While the Irish tended to be attracted to occupations for which the primary qualification was strength and endurance, two occupations were an exception to this. The first of these was coal mining. Few of the English Irish were to be found as coal miners, even though there were coal mining districts centered around St. Helens and Oldham in Lancashire. Was this a case of exclusion, or did they simply not choose to enter? The answer seems to lie in the nature of mining communities themselves, most of which were in fairly remote areas, away from the urban areas for which most Irish showed a definite preference. But perhaps more significant is the fact that the inhabitants of these regions had developed family traditions which tended to exclude outsiders. Religion may have been another factor. Brian Lewis indicates that Methodism had great appeal to miners, with its message of independence and self-help.[99] The strongly exclusive cultural and religious traditions of this faith may have been an added reason for excluding outsiders who were Catholic. Most importantly, however, the evidence would suggest that mining attracted a more-settled population. Then again, Scotland provides a counter example where employers preferred Irish workers as colliers, for reasons already stated as well as the following: "They are very much disposed to learn anything you put them to; they do not find so many difficulties in beginning anything new. An Irishman who has never seen the mouth of a coal-pit in his life has no hesitation in going down and commencing what you ask him to do. They are, perhaps, quicker at taking anything new than the Scotch, that is, in the same class."[100] The railway was the other industry which did not attract the Irish in great numbers.[101] In 1841 it was estimated that only about 5,000 or one-tenth of the total numbers of railroad workers were Irish.[102] English railway navvies bitterly resented any outside competition, showing their hostility, says Redford, in the frequent outbreaks of fighting between English and Irish navvies.[103]

Any occupation which was seasonal, short term, or which was unattractive to English workers opened opportunities for the Irish, whether male or female. Irishwomen became domestics in English households only late in the nineteenth century when domestic work became less attractive to English women than the alternative of highly paid factory labor. Wherever opportunities for unskilled work existed, abundant numbers of Irish persons could be found. The sugar houses and chemical works of western Lancashire employed considerable numbers of them. An employerer of Irish laborers in Liverpool calculated that there were 500 Irish sugar boilers and another 600 in the chemical works and soaperies.[104]

The general evidence would bear out that it was their endurance and strength which gave Irish persons their initial advantage over the urbanized English when applying for laboring jobs. Mayhew believed this when he said that in their strength "they often resembled the power of a hurricane."[105] In 1844 a Select Committee on the State of Large Towns and Populous Districts reported that "if an extensive drain, or canal, or road, or any other thing that could be done by piecework, were to be constructed, twenty out of every hundred workmen employed on it would be Irish."[106]

J.H. Handley says that seasonal migrants who arrived too early for the general harvest sought other temporary work, subsisting as best they could for two to three weeks until their usual jobs were available.[107] When seasonal laborers wished to remain for a longer period of time there is evidence that there was enough temporary work to induce them to stay. Mayhew says that, "A large class of the Irish who were agricultural labourers in their country are to be found among the men working for bricklayers, as well as among the dock-labourers and excavators, etc. Weed chopping is an occupation greatly resorted to by the Irish in London."[108] When temporary jobs ran out there many alternatives tempting them to linger. "Many of the Irish, however, who are not regularly employed in their respective callings, resort to the streets when they cannot obtain work otherwise."[109]

As noted elsewhere, London street people found harvest employment in the hop fields. John Denvir, the late nineteenth-century Irish journalist, left a richly illustrative account of the Irish in England, which said that the Irish poor had "a kind of mania for hopping and the life it allowed."[110] Harvesting was also the resort of those working in primarily industrial areas. The "English Irish," as they were known locally, contributed their labor to the need for extra hands in Lincolnshire.[111] Mayhew called hopping "the grand rendezvous for the vagrancy of England and Ireland."[112]

Mayhew knew at firsthand that the vagrant life could be precarious; those who followed it for any considerable length of time could fall into appalling poverty, as had many of Mayhew's Irish informants. One woman with four children from "the worst and poorest part" of County Cork, left there "when the Almighty was plazed to deprive me of it" (the home manufacture of flax and wool). Her husband, who had been a miner in Ireland, preceded her to England by eight months. There they survived for three years on what they made at harvest, and lived the rest of the time on her begging. When asked if many other husbands lived on their wife's begging, she replied in her Cork accent, "O Lord, there is many, sir. He never does anything but at the harvest time, and then he works at raping the corrun. I know nothing else that he does; and I bind the sheaves afther him. Why, indeed, we get work then for about a fortnight or three weeks—it don't howld a month."[113]

Mayhew believed that casual labor was primarily induced by seasonal unemployment, and that it played a central role in the phenomena of underemployment which plagued nineteenth-century Britain. Gareth Stedman Jones says that casual labor had the effect of trapping laborers in an economic situation from which there was little chance of escape, because the conditions which promoted casual and inefficient labor in one generation were reproduced in the next.[114] If so, then the migrant who returned to Ireland was escaping a worse fate in evading the trap of such a cycle, but since the worst and greatest impact of the Famine period was on those who were casual laborers, it is difficult to observe long-term trends.

Lowe found that in 1861 laborers were still the largest single occupational grouping of Irish in the seven towns in his study. In Liverpool laborers were 36 percent of Irish heads of households; 20 percent in Manchester; 20 percent in Salford; 18 percent in Oldham; and 20 percent in Preston. In St. Helens and Widnes, both later to industrialize, and thus to require considerable quantities of casual labor, the percentages were 51 and 75, respectively.[115] If the numbers of laborers prior to 1850 could be known, the percentages of Irish laborers may have been closer to that of St. Helens and Widnes.[116] From this, it may then be assumed that from 50 to 75 percent of all Irish persons in urbanizing areas in the pre-Famine period were in casual labor.

It is not surprising that in the expansionary atmosphere of the early nineteenth century, that the building trades would have attracted the largest number of Irish laborers. Industrial expansion required buildings, roads, and warehouses, all of which necessitated a construction industry which was able to keep pace with the demand. It was work which required more physical force than mechanical dexterity or training, and thus attractive to Irish laborers. It was known that in the west of Scotland Irish persons worked in all work executed by contract, work such as excavating earth and breaking stones for roads; the same was true for the northwestern counties of England and in the neighborhoods around London.[117]

The fact that the Irish failed to rise out of unskilled employment was puzzling to contemporary investigators, but was to their employers, sound evidence of their inferiority. One builder said that his Irish workers were "born bricklayer's labourers, and they die bricklayer's labourers."[118] He said that once established in a trade, they monopolized it, a disclosure which would not have surprised Daniel Patrick Moynihan who claimed the prevalence of this trait among the American Irish.[119] Denvir claimed that he never knew a bricklayer's laborer who was not an Irishman.[120] Their success in monopolizing trades was because they kept others out.[121] The owner of two alkali works, one at Liverpool and one at Newton (halfway between Manchester and Liverpool), testified that while in his Liverpool works all but one of his seventy employees were Irish, in Newton only four out of one hundred employees were Irish because "they contended with the English, and wished totally to exclude them,"[122] a disclosure which again bears out the contention that the Irish were employed where they were the most available.

The more likely explanation for lack of mobility among the Irish community was an unwillingness to commit themselves to a job for very long because their sights were elsewhere. However, it is certainly a fact that most males arrived too late in their work-life cycle and without sufficient capital to invest in apprenticeship training. A more compelling reason for their lack of upward mobility was that work abroad was a temporary or stopgap arrangement and thus not worth the investment in either capital or time.[123]

Irish immigrants were strangers, from a country that conveyed contrary images to the public mind. The "good Irish" who did not inconvenience the English government had the faces of angels, but the "bad Irish" who fought savagely against their landlords and the authorities had the faces of menacing apes. In addition most were adherents of a religion

which traditionally had long political ties with Britain's continental enemies. These elements, when added to the suspicion with which the Irish
were treated, increased their vulnerability to unemployment whenever
the labor market was saturated. Furthermore, Irish persons were entering an old society with long-established traditions, one in which they
were yet to establish a secure role for themselves.[124]

Employers were not slow in expressing prejudice against their Irish
workers, sometimes indicating that they would have preferred English
workers, but could not get them. Occasionally, however, employers preferred to employ Irish laborers, although this was a fairly rare occur-
rence. One such was Samuel Holmes, a Manchester builder who, with
his father had employed approximately an average of one hundred Irish
per year for forty years. He preferred Irish to English laborers because,
as he said, he never had any offers to work from English laborers. He
spoke highly of their honesty, faithfulness, and steadiness of work
habits, but compared them unfavorably to Scots workers, whom he said
often prospered because they persevered and stayed on. Comparing the
relative merits of workmen from the three countries he said: "A Scotchman would not go wrong; an Englishman would go on and blunder
through; an Irishman would generally stop."[125]

Irish persons served their fellow migrants in a number of service
occupations. They were hawkers in "old things of all description, bones,
old tools, old clothes." The Irish monopolized hawking in the Western
seaport cities which were engaged in the West Indies and Honduras
trade. It was said that Irish hawkers "turned their hands to every description of low trade which is the fruit of industry and requires almost no
capital."[126]

Irish sellers were perceived as a threat in the Manchester market.
Their monopoly of the trade there was said to have grown from about a
fourth of total numbers in 1820 to about three-quarters of the total
market in 1836. Describing this, Mr. Howarth, the collector of market
tolls, said,

> The Irish live in much worse lodgings and on worse food than the English,
> and they are thus enabled to sell their goods at a lower price; they are
> contented with less profit. They set up their concern gradually, and carry on
> their trade with £2; very few get on and rise to be small shop-keepers. There
> are probably about 400 Irish stall-keepers in the market. They are like the
> Jews, bartering and running down the farmer after they have got possession
> of his stuff, so that he is almost forced to take what they will give. They are
> much harder dealers than the English and get articles at lower prices. The
> opinion of all the collectors is that in time, the Irish will drive out all English
> out of the market.[127]

Mayhew said that in London Irish petty traders drove the Jews out of orange selling, an occupation that once had been a monopoly of young Jewish boys.[128] The way in which the Irish overtook the Jews in the fruit trade was by offering to assist in the coach yards where anyone arriving at or leaving the metropolis was likely to be; it was said that Jewish boys never did this, being only traders. Irish orange hawkers not only sold fruit and small items but were ready to lend a hand to any overburdened coach porter. By Mayhew's time, he said that "no Jews yet vended oranges in the streets, that trade being almost entirely in the hands of the Irish."[129]

Their ability to monopolize trades or market items was attributable to their adaptation to conditions having their roots in the social structure of Ireland. One of these was the cohesion resulting in strong ties binding them together as newcomers in a strange place. This had been noted by De Tocqueville, who expressed amazement at the extent and degree of their willingness to aid each other, behavior which he contrasted with its lack among the rural French.[130] Since one of the characteristics of a chain migration is the development and maintenance of strong ties between migrants, it is hardly surprising that Irish migrants then sustained their cohesiveness, utilizing it to their advantage.

Irish petty traders also showed their great entrepreneurial skills. The agent for the Glasgow and Londonderry Steam Packet Co., a Mr. Cameron, related that he knew of twenty or thirty of them who had been regular traders for the previous five or six years and had done very well dealing in eggs, butter, and fowl. He said, "They show a great fitness for business and alertness in their dealings when they have had any advantages of education, and have learnt writing and arithmetic . . . some of them have a natural ability for dealings. They seem to be in their element when buying and selling."[131]

Another aspect of Irish entrepreneurial skill was the adventure of conning the less nimble-minded English. Carleton tells the story of the pig drover from Connacht who walked his pigs through England to the market. On one occasion, when he could not bear to part with a pig who had become a favorite, he would always drive a bargain for the pig with a farmer long into the evening and, when concluded, ask to stay the night. That night, while the household slept, he would steal away with the pig, to play the same trick on the next unsuspecting farmer.[132]

Conclusions can be drawn which tend to bear out contemporary judgements about the occupations the Irish went into and why. They flowed into those occupations which English workers refused, of whom it was said:

> They [the English] cannot do those kinds of labor which require skill in mechanics or manufacturers and they will not work for the builders or be porters in the docks at Liverpool. When they cannot get steady employment, they are unwilling to put up with such precarious work as that often met with in large towns. The Irish, on the other hand, are more ready and versatile, and importunate, and more accustomed to an uncertain and irregular subsistence.[133]

The foregoing was not intended intended in any way to draw an idealized picture of Irish laborers. The magnitude of the Irish influx was the despair of charity overseers and magistrates. Irish lifestyles were sufficiently different from that of the English living in similar conditions as to make the most sympathetic well-wisher critical of them. They left Ireland because they were not needed, and they arrived where they were needed, taking jobs unwanted by others. Willing to man the lowest echelons of industry and to work harder than anyone else in the same situation, they put to shame their English counterpart who had learned their rights far too well to satisfy some employers. In these circumstances it is hardly surprising that the Irish were loathed by their fellow workers. But as the *Report on the Irish Poor in Britain* has said, an employer of labor

> never considers whether the place suits the individual; he considers only whether the individual suits the place. . . . The interest of the master leads him to look only to the merit in the workman. No one who is at all acquainted with the tone of feeling which prevails among extensive employers of labour in this country, will doubt that they look exclusively to obtaining good labourers on fair terms, and that their choice is swayed by no other consideration whatsoever.[134]

Irish Migrants and Political Activism

While the intention of the majority of Irish migrants in England was to return home, those who remained for any length of time were vulnerable to the political activism of the working classes in the 1830s and 1840s. The Chartism of that period made England a lively place for the Irish who were accustomed to the faction fighting and political dispute which characterized pre-Famine Ireland.

Irish cohesiveness, so beneficial in enabling them to maintain ties with home, was also expressed in a nascent political consciousness then developing in Ireland. Daniel O'Connell, the architect and coordinator of Irish nationalism on the national level, emerged as an influential force in the 1820s. However, long before he appeared on the political scene in

Ireland, there was a widespread awareness of rights and a willingness to agitate for recognition of them. In the countryside this was expressed as agrarian protest against local grievances such as the exactions of landlords; in urban areas it took the form of militant, fiercely protective trade unionism, as cited in the second chapter.

The question arises, then, as to what extent migrants may have brought their inclinations for cohesive action and political agitation with them to England. Prior to 1850, when for the majority, migration was a temporary commitment, most evidence suggests that on the whole and as a group they were not prone either to organizing or joining organizations. One exception to this was recounted by a Manchester builder who said that about seven hundred and fifty Irish bricklayer's helpers in the town had formed themselves into a club. While he said that this club and others like it were, "meant to be sick clubs and for the protection of their wages," he doubted that this was their sole intention in banding together.[135] Nevertheless, evidence suggests that most Irish workers were of a somewhat less mutinous disposition about their rights than were English or Scottish workers, although this is hardly surprising when it is recalled that many had first obtained their jobs as a result of the strike action of other workers. Other evidence, some previously presented, reveals that quiescence could turn to action when Irish workers had secured a firm place in employment. Another Manchester builder believed that the Irish had "a great disposition to turn out." He recalled with bitterness an instance of his Irish laborers holding up a contract to build some warehouses for the railroad company. When they learned that there would be a heavy forfeiture of money if the project was not completed on time they struck in advance for wages which he was obliged to give them.[136]

Rachel O'Higgins, in her study of the influence of the Irish in the Chartist movement, says that Irish working-class exiles exercised an influence out of all proportion to their numbers and that their influence was consistently extremist.[137] Although there is disagreement as to the magnitude of the Irish contribution to political activism in the earlier period, Lowe's research reveals the extent of Irish activism in the later period when they joined the Irish Republican Brotherhood, later called the Fenian Brotherhood, which he terms a paramilitary organization. Its aim of the overthrow of British rule in Ireland was the first cohesive active political participation of the Irish community in Britain, and the Lancashire Irish played a significant role in its activities.[138]

Prior to 1850, however, most organized political activity had little relevance for the Irish, either socially or industrially. Like most recent migrants—and certainly those who did not intend to settle—their intention was to return to Ireland, not to ameliorate their situation in England. In this their behavior is consistent with that of most first-generation immigrants. Political activism, like social delinquency, tends to be a product of the second, not the first generation.

Irish Migrants and the Catholic Church

Catholic clergy who served the migrant community were totally opposed to the Irish involving themselves in any kind of political or trade union activity. Parenthetically, it is of interest to note that the Irish workers who founded the sick club mentioned previously formed it because their parish priest had refused to permit them to participate in English trades union activity.[139]

Their Catholic faith was probably both a strength and a weakness for the Irish community. Communal cohesiveness was undoubtedly reinforced by their adherence to what was regarded by the host community as an alien religion; but their bonds to their faith may also have prevented them from integrating themselves into the wider community. In this they had all the disadvantages of a minority group which disapproves of the majority of the population. It is worth repeating the words of the Irish costermonger cited in Chapter Two who said: "I don't go much among the English streetdealers. They talk like haythens. I never miss mass on a Sunday, and they don't know what the blissed mass manes."[140] Mayhew believed that the Roman Catholic Church, through its effectiveness as an institution, reinforced such attitudes by offering Irish persons in England an institutional alternative to assimilation into the larger community. He said, "It is this the tie of religion, working with other causes, [which] keeps the Irish in the London streets knitted to their own ways, and is likely to keep them so."[141]

Nevertheless, the Limerick costermonger's faithful adherence at the mass was hardly typical of all Irish migrants. Church authorities worried that some in the Irish community were, "released from the check afforded not only by the superintendance of parents, relations, and friends, but also from the influence of their own clergymen, and from the regular performance of their religious duties."[142] Attention has previously been drawn to the fact that the Irish of this period were part of what Emmet Larkin has termed "the pre-Famine generation of non-practising Catholics," characterized by low figures of church attendance.[143] This is hardly surprising as the influx of persons was of such magnitude that chapels could not be built fast enough to serve them.

All of this would change after 1850. Church attendance of the Irish in South Wales after 1850 was estimated by John Hickey to be approximately 40 percent of total numbers resident there at any one time.[144] Lowe's estimate of church attendance is higher — 60 percent — but other factors may explain the 20 percent difference. The first is the obvious fact elucidated by Larkin that four years of disaster had chastened this generation; and the second, more important to this study, is that the migration had stabilized, tending to become more permanent in nature than that of the previous period. There is no comparable data available for the earlier period to permit a reconstruction of church attendance of the Irish in England, but David Miller's study of church attendance in Ireland for that period indicates that perhaps less than 40 percent of Irish Catholics were regular communicants.[145] Such a relatively low church attendance should be regarded as reflecting less upon a lack of piety than from the difficulties encumbering the Irish Church in previous centuries, when the anti-Catholic penal laws made adherence to the faith hazardous. Although the restrictions of the penal laws had long been either held in abeyance or totally abolished by the nineteenth century, neither church accommodations nor clergy could keep pace with the demands of the growing population in Ireland, with the result that persons were unaccustomed to considering church attendance as part of their religious duty. Less important, but still worth noting, was the excuse given by many Irish, that they were reluctant to attend because they did not have suitable clothing, which in the increasing pauperization of the country was no insignificant matter.[146]

By the early nineteenth century the worst of the anti-Catholic passions in Britain had diminished in intensity, at least at the official level. Legislation directed at restricting the civil liberties of Catholics, as well as those of nonconformist religions, had begun to appear embarrassingly out of date to the more liberal thinking which dominated the age, so that almost all were officially lifted when Catholic Emancipation was granted in 1829.[147] But that is not to say that liberal thinking had percolated down to the working classes, and it must be recalled that an important element of eighteenth-century urban disturbances had been their opposition to the threat of papists in their midst. Urban rioting became the means whereby those classes expressed dissent; and rage expressed against Catholics was a part of this. Most outbursts can be regarded as prefranchise expressions of frustration against threats to their livelihood, of which anti-Catholicism was only a part of a larger process of generalized protest against social change which threated them. Nevertheless, in the early years of the nineteenth century, opposition to Catholicism became, if anything, more vocal because of its association with

Irish immigrants and in regions such as Manchester, where many of the earlier generation of handloom weavers had been Protestants who had long-established settled communities, the immigrants fought out their religious differences much as they had in Ireland.

The reaction of the hierarchy of the Catholic Church, both in Ireland and in England, to their tenuous position in British society was to counsel migrants to be quiescent and conciliatory. In England, the only English Catholics able to afford to retain their dissident faith were descendants of the old landed families, located primarily in the north; and these sought to preserve their hard-won privileges by maintaining a low religious visibility. Despite a good deal of generosity on the part of some members of the English Catholic community they were hardly likely to feel any great sense of delight or welcome toward their brethren in religion from Ireland whose poverty was largely considered a national disgrace.[148] Some Catholic priests giving testimony at parliamentary commissions were hardly more charitable, displaying acerbic attitudes toward the appearance and behavior of the immigrant population, and complaining that they lowered the standards of English workers and were altogether a bad influence. One of these, the Rev. Mr. Peach, a Roman Catholic clergyman of Birmingham, said, "A great many Irish are here [in Birmingham] because it would not be safe for them to remain in Ireland, having been engaged in disturbances and breaches of the law. Irish priests, with whom I have talked, had the same opinion, and thought that the scum of the Irish came over."[149]

Despite persons of the ilk of the Rev. Mr. Peach, changed attitudes were in evidence by the 1830s when testimony was given by priests with recognizably Irish surnames. This is also an indication of changes taking place in the hierarchy of the Catholic Church in Ireland, which now considered Lancashire a mission field and the migrants the new heathen to be retained for the Church.

By 1838 the need for new priests had become acute, and the four vicars apostolic issued a joint pastoral letter appealing for funds to help toward educating the clergy essential to the task, and in 1839 All Hallowes' College was founded in Dublin to prepare priests for service abroad. The correspondence between those training the missionary priests and the young priest on the mission field warned them of their responsibility toward the immigrant community. Their message was to confine themselves to bringing religious succor and to not participate in activities of a more secular nature. It is clear from the advice given to the mission priests which appears in their correspondence with their teachers that the priests were aware of, and often sympathetic to labor agitation and political activity among the Irish community. Most missionary priests had grown up in the highly politicized atmosphere of early nineteenth-century Ireland so that when they saw their parishioners exploited and discriminated against, occupying the worst jobs at wages others refused, it is hardly surprising that they sympathized with the plight of the immigrants. Nonetheless, the policy of the Church hierarchy was to be firmly opposed to any agitation whatsoever. Letters from superiors repeatedly cautioned priests against taking "any public part in political movements, whatever your private opinions." Other letters admonished priests to "leave behind your national feelings, try to accommodate to the habits and ideas of the people among whom you have come to live and consider yourselves sent by God to preach the Gospel to Foreign Nations, in place of preaching to their Irish politics."[150] Warned that their role was to protect the flock, they were also told that political activity could only lead to participants being fired, thus making their economic position yet more vulnerable.[151]

While parish priests might have been able to prevent their parishioners from joining English trade unions, they could not stop them from organizing their own clubs. After 1850 the Church appears to have changed its tactic of opposition to fraternal organizations because they grew in numbers and assumed great importance for the immigrant community, many of which were started by the Church for the migrant community, according to Lowe.[152] Clerical opposition to trade unionism, so obdurate in the 1830s and 1840s, still remained high, but the Church appears to have been willing to sponsor substitutes in order to satisfy the needs of the migrant community.

A number of questions regarding the role of the Church are raised by their activities in the Irish community. By providing an alternative to functions which the migrants would otherwise have had to develop for themselves through integration into English society did the Church further retard occupational mobility and assimilation among the Irish? Additionally, did the presence of a growing Catholic Church with a sense of mission retard the integration of Irish migrants into the larger community, thus perpetuating the distinctiveness and separation of Irish persons in the host community? And did the Church, by providing separate denominational schooling for children, thus prevent their assimilation into British society? Since we are discussing very different migrations pre- and post-1850, the application of these questions must be considered separately. Lowe's study of the Irish in Lancashire in the latter period depicts a relatively permanent, even if fluctuating population; one in which the services provided by the Church did however offer alternatives to integration into the larger society. Earlier, the activities of the Church served a more positive function, providing a needed supplement to the scanty charitable institutions available to this largely mobile and fluid population. Those early years of the migration, when Irish persons were a readily exploitable labor force in an economy undergoing profound dislocation in adjusting to unpredictable shifts in demand, there was the need for more institutional aid than could ever be provided by available kinship networks or public institutions. There is no doubt but that the Church provided critically essential services in the early period, but that subsequent to 1850 the social functions of the Church may eventually have become an alternative to assimilation.[153]

Living Conditions and the Social Organization of Irish Migrants

The popular image of conditions during the early years of industrialization depict scenes of extreme deprivation and much human suffering, yet this may be misleading because what attracted the attention of contemporaries then and historians now is not the typical but the unusual. For that reason, the same person who could walk past squalid rural hovels every day without noticing them, could be scandalized by a sight of the less familiar city slum. Similarly, the sight of women and children toiling from dawn to dusk, harvesting in the fields or huddled over looms in dark cottages, prompted less comment than did the sight of women and children tending machines in a factory. Furthermore, those who pay attention to Friedrich Engels and Karl Marx on the horrors of industrialization, all too often have passed over Marx's scorn for the idiocy of the rural life where many in the early industrial labor force originated.

This is not to minimize in any way the poor quality of conditions during the period of early industrialization, because evidence suggests that living standards before the 1850s improved very little, so that the first two generations of the working class paid a heavy price for whatever gains they made as a result of their new opportunities. Few writers have portrayed the scene as vividly as did the historian, E.P. Thompson.

> In fifty years of the industrial revolution the working-class share of the national product had almost certainly fallen relative to the share of the property-owning and professional classes. The "average" working man remained very close to the subsistence level at a time when he was surrounded by the evidence of the increase of national wealth, much of it transparently the product of his own labour, and passing, by equally transparent means, into the hands of his employers. In psychological terms, this felt very much

like a decline in standards. His own share in the "benefits of economic progress" consisted of more potatoes, a few articles of cotton clothing for his family, soap and candles, some tea and sugar, and a great many articles in *The Economic History Review*.[154]

The attempts of early social reformers to ameliorate urban poverty tended to ignore the problems engendered by over-crowded, jerry-built housing, excessive rents, and an absence of public transport which forced workers to locate their housing as close to factories, with all their stench and filth, as possible. These factors exacerbated the difficulties of urban living, with appalling results, especially for the Irish who were at the very nadir of the social hierarchy. One observer described an Irish cellar dwelling (the kind which had originally been constructed for weaving workshops) which he visited in 1849.

> The place was dark, except for the glare of a small fire. You could not enter without stooping in the room, which might be about twelve feet by eight. There were at least a dozen men, women and children on stools, or squatted on the stone floor, round the fire, and the heat and smells were oppressive. This not being a lodging cellar, the police had no control over the masses of rags, shavings and straw which were littered about. There was nothing like a bedstead in the place. Farther back opened a second cellar, strewn with coals and splinters, bits of furze, and intermingled with rags and straw, lay two girls asleep in two corners.[155]

The worst images indicating declines in the standard of living were in housing, which was often squalid in the extreme. But in an era when legislation to ameliorate social ills was considered detrimental to economic progress, there was little for social reformers to do but continue to proliferate parliamentary blue books and in some cases muckraking novels. "In Manchester," Engels wrote in his account of the condition of the working classes in the early 1840s, "the workers have been caged in dwellings which are so wretched that no one else will live in them, and they actually pay good money for the privilege of seeing these dilapidated hovels fall into pieces about their ears."[156]

Lancashire's rapidly growing urban population constantly outstripped the supply of available housing. Squalid housing was a condition of life, seemingly accepted by the poor whose low wages prevented them from paying more, and by the builders whose profits depended upon the construction of the greatest possible number of living spaces in the smallest possible area. However, the extent to which the poor seemed to acquiesce in accepting the kind of conditions so graphically portrayed by Engels may have been mitigated by their belief that the conditions they lived in were temporary—as temporary as the kind of jobs they worked at. In a sort of cynical side note, one might also say that the high mortality rates of the slums must have significantly reduced the average duration of residency for those forced to endure them.

Irish living conditions in England in the nineteenth century were attracting attention in a context of industrial urbanization which was creating critical situations for all the working classes; although in general, the Irish came in for heartier condemnation for their living standards than did English workers, a fact which can be traced to the relative differences in the experiences of the two groups before migration. The 1841 Irish Census found that 83 percent of the total housing stock in Ireland was of such inferior quality as to be almost unfit for human habitation by middle class standards.[157] If these were the living conditions which were the experience of most migrants, then it is hardly surprising that they had to learn not to throw refuse out the door, or store urine to make alkali, or keep pigs in the kitchen. Thus one could say that the Irish gravitated toward poor housing, not because they preferred to live in wretched hovels, but because they needed to economize and to live near where employment was available.

However well we know rural Ireland today with its antiseptically scrubbed farmhouses situated in isolation from each other, the visual landscape was quite different one hundred and fifty years ago. Prior to the Famine the majority of Irish persons were smallholders, cottiers, and squatters; and as such were accustomed to living in crowded communal conditions which were not unlike those which they found in England.[158] Their most sympathetic advocates did not deny that the Irish placed less emphasis on living standards than did the English. Mayhew said that while usually overstatement was natural to the Irish, when it came to their living conditions they tended to understate the facts in discussing them. When he asked one woman if she had a decent room she replied, "Shure thin, and it is dacint for a poor woman." On visiting it, he found it "smoky, filthy, half-ruinous, wretched in every respect."[159]

Mayhew and Engels present two extremes in their descriptions of the Irish. The latter saw in Manchester's Irish squalor a reflection of the depravity of the Irish race in general (an opinion he never changed in a long life of writing as an advocate of the working population); upon observing that poverty of Dublin was as revolting as it was in Manchester he concluded that the "Latin" nature of the Irish national character (feckless, emotional, unpractical) was responsible. The willingness of the Irish to live in the worst accommodations, wear their clothes in tatters, and to live solely on potatoes and drink justified employer exploitation. "What does such a race want with high wages?" he said.[160] To his credit, however, he did believe that the Irish provided a useful "ginger" as an element in Chartist ranks.

In contrast to Engels, Henry Mayhew used the trained eye of a journalist to see what lay behind what could be observed of the living standards of the London Irish. Drawing attention to their public image of slovenliness, he contrasted it with the private evidence which he had collected:

> In all the houses [of the Irish] that I entered there were traces of household care and neatness that I had little expected to have seen. The cupboard fastened in the corner of the room, and stocked with mugs and cups, the mantlepiece with its images, and the walls covered with showy-coloured prints and saints and martyrs, gave an air of comfort that strangely disagreed with the reports of the cabins in "ould Ireland."[161]

Not unlike a nineteenth-century Oscar Lewis, Mayhew said that to understand these people you had to go into their homes and note the touches of care—the shelf with treasured objects and the starched table cloth. Engels and Mayhew saw Irish migrants in two different habitats: Engels in Manchester and Mayhew in London; and in quite dissimilar employment situations. Engels made no effort to enquire, and we cannot know how recently those his observations were based upon had arrived in Manchester, nor how long they would remain, living a precarious existence in housing never intended to enclose so many persons. In contrast, Mayhew saw the Irish in long-established neighborhoods, where if not outwardly attractive, at least had the advantage of some amount of continuity. Lynn Lees's study of the London Irish emphasizes that the community there was relatively permanent (although she does allow for the fact that proximity to Ireland made migration more reversible), a factor that is at variance with the fluid nature of the Manchester Irish prior to 1850.[162]

The two characterizations may then be seen as reflecting the experiences and aspirations of the inhabitants. The majority of Irish persons in Manchester were mostly recent migrants, and would probably only remain if employment continued to be available. In contrast, the majority of Irish persons resident in London had more inducement to remain, even if immiserated in poverty, partly as a result of the wider range of employment opportunities available, and probably because fewer of them had anything to return to at home. If Mayhew's replication of accents was accurate, his direct quotations strongly suggest County Cork origins. Also, almost every person for whom a home county was reported was from the province of Munster. Furthermore, reference to Chapter Two indicates that few persons from Munster were counted as seasonal migrants, all of which suggests that the London Irish were fairly likely to be longer-term residents.

Oscar Lewis, in his study of the culture of Puerto Rican migrants to New York, and Michael Piore, in his study of undocumented aliens in the United States, both demonstrate the effect on people of living as transients. Piore says when migrants do not intend to remain, the nature of their living arrangements reflects their impermanence.[163] The economy of their lifestyle was directed at minimizing expenditure in order to save money to take home.

Despite his middle class origins, Henry Mayhew was able to penetrate the motivations of the inhabitants of the London slums and to fathom that not all slums are alike. In general, there are two widely different kinds of slums: there are the slums in which hope can remain alive and slums where despair is endemic. Slums of hope are those in which the inhabitants retain some degree of autonomy and control over their lives; this may be because those who live in them have alternatives and that they are free to leave when conditions become intolerable; or it may be because the inhabitants come from worse conditions, or have begun to exert some control within that environment and thus need not feel helpless. Slums of despair, on the other hand, are those in which the inhabitants have lost autonomy. Despair mounts when they discover that there are no alternatives, and that they must await a random fate to end the misery in which they have been caught.

The congested living conditions characteristic of the Lancashire area in general did not as yet contain pockets of permanently impacted poverty—the rate at which slum neighborhoods were vacated and refilled in response to fluctuations in economic conditions made this unlikely. Despite the grimness of Engels' portrayal of Manchester and its industrial environs, it did not show a Hogarthian London where the poor preyed upon each other in a hideous struggle for survival. He described a poverty where the poor were robbed by the middle classes— by shopkeepers who sold adulterated goods, and by capitalists who expropriated a worker's labor, giving in return insufficiently to ensure healthy survival. In contrast to this, and despite the fact that some of Mayhew's informants created oases of good housekeeping and thrift in the midst of chaos, the nature of conditions in that city precluded many migrants from much improvement of their situation. London's slums were thus slums of despair while Manchester's slums offered hope—hope of improving one's condition.

In Manchester good housing was in short supply, so that the conditions which appalled visitors were aggravated by the need for inhabitants to overcrowd in order to economize. Survival meant the need to double up, and the Irish were more likely to share housing than the non-Irish, according to Lowe.[164] For example, when 5.5 persons per house was the national average, the Lancashire Irish had 8.7 persons per house. (The non-Irish average for Lancashire was 6.67.) The residents of Liverpool had a particularly high propensity to double up, which is explainable by its status as a port city and the principal place of entry for immigrants who needed shelter until they found their own housing or moved elsewhere, either abroad or inland. Sharing dwellings was also more common among the Irish than among the non-Irish, but both communities shared dwellings more often than did those in the rest of England, as the census indicates. The overall figure for Lancashire was 1.65 households per house for Irish and 1.31 for non-Irish, compared to 1.1 households per house for England and Wales in general. Thus to paraphrase Michael Anderson, while a house of one's own might be a national ideal, other arrangements were important for a large proportion of the population (not only for Irish persons in Lancashire), particularly in the early days of married life and then again later in the life cycle.[165]

While the main streets of Lancashire towns generally appeared fairly respectable, another world lay behind them. Long rows of smoke-blackened terraced cottages were often built back to back, and the enclosed court housing in alleys often contained a dozen or more dwellings.[166] In areas where housing had been erected hastily, roads were unpaved and sewers and gutters were nonexistent. The best-known Irish neighborhood in Lancashire was that of Manchester's Little Ireland, off the Oxford Road in Deansgate. Public health there drew considerable official attention, but despite its name it was not an entirely Irish ghetto, because Lowe's data shows that non-Irish were also resident there.[167] But it was the poorest and the cheapest housing available, so that Irish people clustered there by necessity. In the New Town, in Manchester, which was also known as Irish Town, Engels noted:

> The unpaved alleys lack any form of drainage. The district is infested with small herds of pigs; some of them are penned up in little courts and sties, while others wander freely on the neighbouring hillside. The lanes in this district are so filthy that it is only in very dry weather that one can reach it without sinking ankle-deep at every step. . . . The nearer one gets to the centre of the town, the more closely packed are the houses and the more irregular is the lay-out of the street.[168]

Court dwellings were usually smaller and less expensive, particularly in Liverpool. A four-mile stretch along the Mersey contained 2,500 courts, all constructed before 1846 and condemned for the high mortality rate of those living in them, largely poor Irish.[169] But while Irish persons were more likely to reside in such court dwellings, the proportion of those living in them declined after the midcentury, bearing out that there was some improvement in the living conditions of the Irish, which is another indication of a tendency toward longer-term settlement after the Famine.

Some estimates exist regarding the numbers of those living in cellar dwellings for two periods before the Famine. The first is from 1836, contained in the *Report on the Irish Poor in Britain*. It was estimated that there were 6,000 cellar dwellings, with an average of five inhabitants each, which would mean a population of approximately 30,000 persons.[170] Ten years later the estimate had tripled, reaching a total of 18,000 dwellings, with an estimated average of four persons per dwelling. The breakdown was as follows:

Table 4.5. **Percentages of cellar dwellings in Lancashire, 1845**

Cities	Cellars	Population	Percent of total population
Liverpool	7,892	39,460	20.00
Manchester	4,443	18,217	24.38
Preston	600	2,460	24.39
Wigan	95	276	34.42
Bury	150	615	24.39
Rochdale	457	1,747	26.15
Bolton	1,210	4,961	24.39

SOURCE: *Second Report on the State of Large Towns,* 1845, Parliamentary Papers, p. 372.

Lowe's work indicates that as fast as sanitary inspectors cleared cellar dwellings they were refilled with new inhabitants (some 30,000 persons were ejected in 1847–48 alone).[171]

Immigrants often cluster in a new environment as a way to gain protection and support, thereby modifying the harsher aspects of the move into the new area. In the eyes of observers they are often termed "ghetto-prone." What observers believed was ethnic solidarity on the part of the Irish may have been a result of the need to economize, according to Lowe.[172] In fact, given the fractious nature of Irish rural life, where faction fights were a common feature, it is unlikely that Irish people sought each other out primarily for ethnic solidarity.[173]

The 1851 Census drew attention to the unusually high incidence of single heads of household in the Manchester and Liverpool regions. In a sample enumeration of twenty-eight families in each city, there were eleven single heads of household in Manchester and ten in Liverpool; it is clear that this was a fairly common pattern throughout England, because more than 25 percent of all heads of household were either unknown or absent.[174]

Lowe suggests that the average number of Irish persons per house declined in the post-Famine period. Whereas in 1851 there had been 8.91 persons per house (versus 6.73 for non-Irish) by 1861 this figure had dropped to 7.44 (6.22 for non-Irish).[175] The declines illustrate changed conditions in Lancashire's position in the English economy where total industrial output was expanding beyond textiles, and industrial location was shifting to areas such as Birmingham and southern Wales. After 1850 Lancashire's industrial output stabilized, and the demand for a transient, fluid work force was thereby lessened. Hickey's study of the Irish in southern Wales bears this out when he indicates that whereas only a few Irish came to the Cardiff area before 1850, after that date their numbers increased along with the area's growing industrial prominence, estimating that there were approximately 100,000 Irish resident in southern Wales at any one time during the 1850s.[176]

It is important in looking at what happened to Irish migrants to consider what happened to rural patterns of life after migration, and to consider the extent to which Irish households contained extended family members (that is, grandparents, in-laws, aunts, uncles, etc.). Also, it is useful to examine how Irish living patterns compared with Anderson's observation about non-Irish families in which he believed that urbanization and industrialization had produced a greater degree of kinship interdependence than had existed previously. Lowe found that the Irish were less likely to have extended family members resident (19 percent of Irish households had extended family members resident, whereas 23 percent of non-Irish households had extended residents).[177] The Irish would be expected to have carried over rural patterns of family interdependence, but migrants who intended to stay only temporarily would also be less likely to bring kin. His studies do not suggest that Irish persons generally brought their extended kin with them to Lancashire and that, while they shared housing more than the non-Irish, they were less likely to share it with kin.

The Irish shared housing, either with extended family or with other Irish persons, more than did the general population, and Irish households, when they became lodging houses, took in more people (3.14 lodgers per household) than did those of the non-Irish (2.3 lodgers per household).[178] Irish persons also were more likely to rent tenements and set them up as lodging houses because by doing so they could gain legal settlement in Britain, and thereby become eligible for poor relief.[179] Irish women were also more likely to be reported as keepers of lodging houses, as they were also more likely to have extended family residing with them. For example, 24 percent of households which had extended family resident in them were headed by females, compared with 18 percent for males.[180] A women's income, then, as now, was considerably less than that of a man, so that women who had been widowed or whose husbands were not "on site," found in the lodging house the opportunity to survive as well as to provide a needed service for their own community. (What was perceived as a dislike for factory work among Irish women may also have been that keeping a lodging house provided income, making factory work unnecessary.) Officials believed that many of the heads of Irish families lived from their lodgers and from the work of their children.[181] Their lodgers were generally single Irish persons.

If in Ireland population growth was producing an increasingly large number of sons and daughters who had to leave the land in order to make a living, it follows that Lancashire would have been a place of opportunity for large numbers of unmarried young persons. The lodging houses to which they came provided necessary companionship and mutual assistance for single persons, who had, to some extent, suspended relationships with their kin by migrating. However, the prevalence of boarding houses also points to a migration which was primarily temporary in nature.

The reputation of the Irish for having large nuclear families was not borne out by evidence from post-Famine Lancashire. Irish families were only slightly larger (4.11) than non-Irish families (4.03).[182] Statistics on Irish mortality might, if known, however, change the conclusion; because Liverpool, which had then the highest mortality rate in the country, also had the smallest households in the county of Lancashire. As indicated previously, another reason for Irish migrants to have small families in England was the custom of bringing only those children who could be gainfully employed, which would then result in Irish families appearing to be smaller on census returns. Again, the evidence points to a mobile population who, because they were primarily target workers, travelled with no unnecessary members. Irish parents usually did not approve of the influence of the alien society on their children, expressing their displeasure with the effect which English culture had upon their children; as a result of which they preferred, when able, to send them back to Ireland for their education. The 1841 Census found that of the 34,608 persons not native to Ireland, but resident there when the census was taken, 21,553 were born in England and 8,585 in Scotland. (These figures are exclusive of those persons in the army.) Of the total, 7,025 were less than fifteen years of age. The Census Commissioners were of the opinion that much of this figure represented "the children of Irish parents born during a temporary residence of the latter in England or Scotland, and presumably being educated in Ireland."[183] We do not know either whether the English-Irish married younger than their non-Irish counterparts in Britain, but if they carried over the general trend from Ireland this would have resulted in children disappearing from the enumeration earlier with the result that the family would have appeared smaller.[184]

In rural England, and earlier in rural Ireland, the age at which a farmer's son could marry was largely determined by the age at which he could obtain a share of the family plot of land. In rural Lancashire, as a result of this, marriage tended to be late; in Ireland, alternatives in the form of usable wasteland and a favorable food crop which could be easily grown were strong disincentives to delay marriage so the age of marriage could be expected to have been lower. Among the urbanized Lancashire working class there was considerable motivation to marry. Relatively high wages obtainable by young persons there made it relatively easy for a couple to support themselves and start a family while still fairly young. Owen Peter Mangan, whose story appeared earlier in this chapter, certainly demonstrated this by marrying at eighteen. Ivy Pinchbeck says that a powerful factor in determining the marriage rate was the degree to which women found industrial occupations.[185] Early independence and the expectation that employment opportunities would shrink fairly early was also a strong inducement to marry young. Furthermore, though housing was scarce, the possibility of going into lodgings or sharing with parents after marriage was not a deterrent.[186] Wage labor offered all young people the opportunity of setting up their own households earlier so Irish young persons in Britain may not have differed significantly from their English counterparts.

The relatively high wages available to young persons in urban working-class families led to their growing importance and economic independence within the family. Engels noted the practice of young persons paying parents fixed sums for board and keeping the rest for themselves.[187] Anderson noted that parents paid great deference to their employed children, indicating that it was because children both could and did leave home as young as fourteen years of age, thereby depriving their parents of needed income, and for that reason parents made special efforts to prolong their childrens' stay at home.[188] Charles Booth believed that employment weakened family ties between parents and children. "Nowadays the home tie is broken easily. . . . The growing independence on the part of children is frequently spoken of."[189]

While it is impossible to state with certainty reasons why some observers believed that the behavior of Irish children was worse than that of English children, recent studies of the behavior of immigrant groups provide some explanations for this. Edwin Sutherland says that the immigrant home frequently suffers from a breakdown of parental control because of the ignorance of the parents about conditions in the new area, and the superior knowledge of their children.[190] Irish parents were both less able and had fewer reasons to adjust to new conditions (particularly if they did not intend to remain) than did their children which would have resulted in a confusion of standards for Irish children, with an eventual breakdown of family authority which could show itself as participation in petty crime. John Tobias points to the large number of juvenile criminals in early nineteenth-century Britain which he sees as resulting from failures in the economic and social system to adjust to large increments in population. Population growth resulted in upsurges in the proportion of young persons with insufficient employment to absorb their energies. There was, however, he says, a marked reduction in the number of young criminals, beginning in the 1850s.[191] Irish children may not, then, have been so much worse than their contemporaries, but they may have been more noticeable for peculiarities of speech and dress which resulted in their being singled out for comment. The early years of urban industrialization was a stressful time for all experiencing it, and for those who wished to affix blame the Irish were a clearly recognizable target.

In Ireland life was as uncertain as that depicted in Banfield's Italian village where, as a result of extreme poverty it led to a situation where kin were expected to render service.[192] Observers have noted the system of shared poverty existing in Ireland which resulted in land being excessively subdivided, to the eventual detriment of all. Married children, while living in Ireland, tended to remain geographically close, although living separately.[193] Children who were able, tended to set up house nearby. "It is the general practice with them to divide their land into portions, which are given to their children as they get married. The last married frequently gets his father's cabin along with his portion of the ground and there his parents like to stop, from a feeling of attachment to the place where they have spent their lives."[194] In contrast to relatively callous attitudes of the English toward their families, many observers noted the strong family orientation of Irish migrants. "Children wanting in affection to their parents are very rare indeed." "The tie between parent and child and kindred is of particular force."[195] There were many instances of children enduring considerable hardships to maintain their parents. Obligations were said to extend further than immediate family, often even to fairly distant kin. Such a pattern of kinship obligation is common in traditional societies where the poorer the society and the more irregular the food supply, the more likely it will be that there will be sharing among the community as a whole.

Observers of spending patterns among the immigrants were sometimes critical of the way in which the Irish spent their money. "They are not as good managers as the English. . . . They don't aspire to the same comforts. They live more for the present moment." "The Irish are not good managers. . . . Many who live in squalid filth in cellars are earning good wages."[196] "Altogether, the Irish differ more from the native English or Scotch in their habits with respect to domestic comforts than in any other circumstances. . . . They appear to be scarcely sensible of the inconveniences arising from the crowding of large numbers into small spaces; even when in tolerably easy circumstances they take in lodgers."[197] Comparisons were made with the English or Scots, but the fact that the Irish chose to live differently and spend their money differently was at the core of criticisms of them. As Chapter Two has indicated, however, their spending patterns were consistent with their behavior at home and also consistent with that of modern rural-urban migrants in developing countries where money is hoarded and creature comforts denied in order to have as much as possible to spend at home. Piore says of Hispanic migrants in the United States, "The underlying motivation of the immigrants and the quality of their living standards while in the developed country are also indicated by the quantity of money which they succeed in sending home."[198] Mayhew said of the Irish street people that in their savings habits they were very unlike English costermongers.

> The saving of an Irish street-seller does not rise from any wish to establish himself more prosperously in his business, but for the attainment of some cherished project, such as emigration. . . . They will treasure up halfpenny after halfpenny, and continue to do so for years, in order to send them money to enable their wives and children, and their brothers and sisters, when in the depths of distress in Ireland, to take shipping to England. They will save to be able to remit money for the relief of their aged parents in Ireland.[199]

An important method of saving among the Irish, for whom the institution of a bank was somewhat alien, was membership in burial clubs. Departing from this life in some degree of style was the last dignity afforded to the poor. It was also customary for children to be entered at birth in burial clubs so as to ensure that if the child died the family would have some return for their effort. A Manchester minister who worked among the very poorest persons said that a common question asked about sickly children was, "Aye, aye, that child will not live; is it in the burial club?" Children were sometimes insured in four or five societies; and one man was known to have been insured in nineteen different burial clubs in Manchester.[200] While there is no direct evidence of the Irish actively participating in such clubs, it is most likely that those who were relatively settled would have chosen this additional method of saving money.

Authors of official reports recognized the ethnocentrism which resulted in invidious comparisons between the English and the Irish. They drew parallels between current comments on Irish behavior and what Daniel Defoe had said about the English working man a century earlier. Comparing English workers with their Dutch counterparts, Defoe said,

> Good husbandry is no English virtue. Tis generally said, the English get estates, and the Dutch save them. And this observation I have made between foreigners and Englishman, that where an Englishman earns 20s a-week, and but just lives, as we call it, a Dutchman grows rich, and leaves his children in very good condition. Where an English labouringman, with his 9s. per week, lives wretchedly and poor, a Dutchman with that wages will live very tolerably well, keep the wolf from the door, and have everything handsome about him. In short, he will be rich with the same gain as makes the Englishman poor; he'll thrive when the other goes in rags; and he'll live when the other starves or goes begging. The reason is plain: a man with good husbandry, and thought in his head, brings home his earnings honestly to his family, commits it to the management of his wife, or otherwise disposes of it for proper subsistence, and this man, with mean gains, lives comfortably and brings up a family; when a single man getting the same wages drinks it away at the ale-house, thinks not of to-morrow, lays up nothing for sickness, age, or disaster, and when any of these happen, he's starved and a beggar. This is so apparent in every other place, and I think it needs no explication, that English labouring people eat and drink, but especially the latter, three times as much in value as any sort of foreigners of the same dimensions in the world. The profuse extravagant humour of our poor people in eating and drinking keeps them low, causes their children to be left naked and starving, to the care of the parishes, whenever sickness or disaster befalls the parent.[201]

Irish food preferences remained the same as at home: they continued to eat potatoes and milk, seasoned with an occasional herring. "They increase its quantity, though they do not improve its quality, even when in receipt of tolerably high wages."[202] But while there was some praise that the Irish continued to eat the plain fare of their homeland, Irish expenditures for drink brought criticism. "In general they stint themselves in solid food in order to procure a larger quality of spirits; or at least, if they do not intentionally retrench their meat in order to buy whiskey, they are satisfied to live on the lowest kind of good, and spend all the surplus of their wages in drinking."[203] It is more likely that for the Irish migrant alcohol was a substitute for an inadequate diet. It was readily available from their countrymen who distilled it in great quantities; and it was said to be cheaper to get drunk than to eat. (It was claimed that you could get drunk for a farthing in Manchester.) However, while alcohol could stanch their hunger pangs, hunger also increased a person's susceptibility to drunkenness. A prison keeper testified that, "They get drunk on Saturday evening and Sunday; having eaten little in the week, a small quantity of spirits has much effect on them. Their general habits appear frugal and sparing; they are rarely drunk on weekdays after Monday."[204]

Illicit distillation was apparently unknown among the urban English; they were "generally ignorant of the process of distilling," but it was common among the Irish who had been "much accustomed to it in their own country, especially before the reduction of the duty on spirits." The excise officer at Manchester took great pains to suppress illicit stills there, calculating the annual loss of revenue from illicit distillation at twenty thousand pounds annually in that city alone.[205]

Conclusions to be drawn regarding Irish spending habits are that while visually their mode of life was very unlike that of their somewhat more settled English and Scots counterparts, it was consistent with their aims and intentions, which was to save as much as possible for consumption elsewhere. They lived cheaply and poorly in the cheapest housing; ate cheaply, although not poorly (because a potato diet is both highly nutritious and filling); and they often drank, possibly to staunch hunger and thereby save money otherwise spent on more expensive food.

Another area where the Irish saved money was in the expense of transport. Chapter Two relates how in 1841, when it was known that steamer passage from Drogheda was cheaper than from Dublin, the stream of migrants that year deflected from the usual route through Dublin to go twenty miles north through Drogheda.[206] Walking was the usual mode of passage for them, both in Ireland and in England. Rumors bandied about regarding Irish travelling habits said that the migrants took advantage of the settlement laws which passed vagrants from one county to another in order to rid themselves of the responsibility of supporting the poor. By having themselves passed in this fashion, the Irish were said to joyride merrily about the country at the public's expense. As with many such stories, however, no one knew of this first hand. All the evidence would bear out that for outsiders in Britain, where living was not cheap and native laborers were hostile, there would have been little toleration of much larking about the countryside. There is evidence though that when a poor year reduced earnings, some migrants were forced to take advantage of the vagrancy laws to have their fares home paid for them. It cost Buckinghamshire and Lincolnshire, counties which attracted agricultural harvest laborers from Ireland and Scotland, 14,698 pounds in 1822 and 4,562 pounds in 1827 to remove those declared vagrant from their counties.[207]

Most evidence would indicate that the Irish preferred to pay their own expenses whenever possible. The manager of a number of Irish estates testified that it "appears to be something disgraceful among them [the laborers] to obtain passes but prefer to perform their journey on foot."[208] When unable to pay their expenses seasonal migrants would sometimes strike a bargain with a leader before leaving Ireland who advanced them their expenses, and later often served as banker on the trip, as well as negotiating with employers for work (if they spoke no English). Occasionally the Irish were known to plead poverty at the dock and thus obtain free passage back to Ireland.[209] It is apparent that their actions were aimed at maximizing all possible returns from the migration. Passage back was said to be almost always through Liverpool, by steam packet, as other ports had sailing vessels which took too long, causing their provisions to give out.[210]

It is clear from the evidence that one or more bad years in Britain was sufficient to cause persons to stop going, but that migrants continued going as long as the anticipated gains were perceived to outweigh the losses. Some seasonal migrants were even able to amass considerable sums. Lord Dillon's agent testified to the thrift of tenants from that lord's estates where some had accumulated sums as large as sixty pounds for transmittal home to Ireland.[211] Perry, the steamer company agent, indicated that he knew of considerable savings because seasonal migrants brought the gold earned in England to be exchanged for Bank of Ireland notes in his packet office.[212] When the packet, King George, bound for Dublin from Parkgate went down on 14 September 1807 the passengers "100, mostly poor Irish" were found with considerable sums of gold on their persons when the bodies washed ashore.[213]

While many migrants may have preferred trusting their accumulated sums to reliable persons from home, others did use local banking facilities. The District Provident Society of Liverpool noted that the numbers of depositors had grown in the previous three years, and estimated that "a fair proportion" of depositors were Irish. Table 4.6 illustrates the growth of deposits in two years, which, as years when a cholera epidemic raged in Ireland as well as in English port cities, can scarcely be considered good years.[214]

Table 4.6. Growth of bank deposits, District Provident Society of Liverpool

	1831	1832
Number of depositors	1,224	3,489
Amount of deposits	2,570	5,946
Paid back to depositors	2,086	5,380
Premium allowed to sum at 6d. on 10s. (5%)	£81.10s.9d.	£207.15s.10d.

SOURCE: *Report on the State of the Irish Poor,* p. 11.

The amount repaid relative to deposits suggests a high rate of turnover. While hardly conclusive, this is consistent with retrieval of funds in order to return to Ireland.

Conclusions

While data regarding the migration of Irish persons into urban industrial Britain do not permit a full reconstruction of the situation in the pre-Famine period, some conclusions may be attempted.

What was the place of these Irish migrants in British industrial life? Did their migration tend to increase the inter-regional wage differentials within Britain, as J.H. Hunt has claimed, when he says that, "Not all migrations reduced wage differentials. On the contrary, certain migration streams seemed to have sustained regional wage variations. It has been suggested that Irish immigration into Lancashire in the 1830s and 40s encouraged further expansion in an area where wages were already well above average by relieving bottlenecks in local labour markets."[215] A contemporary Manchester manufacturer bore this out when he said, "The rate of wages instead of being low, is actually high, much higher than the general average of the kingdom. It might with more show of reason be asserted that, where Irish labourers are most numerous, wages are the highest."[216]

The place of the Irish may have best been summed up by the report which investigated their condition in the mid thirties which concluded that, "Their irregular habits and low standard of comfort may have been regretted; but it is to be remembered that these Irish have been, and are, most efficient workmen; that they came in the hour of need, and that they afforded the chief part of the animal strength by which the great works of our manufacturing districts have been executed."[217]

Demographic and economic data in the text of Mitchell and Deane's abstract of British historical statistics indicate that in the decade of the 1830s the growth of the labor force outside agriculture was chiefly in the service sector and not in the manufacturing and mining sector.[218] This would tend to support the hypothesis that during that decade there was an accelerated expansion of the demand for the kinds of jobs which the Irish performed. This would also tend to place their contribution in a much stronger light — which is that of facilitating the expansion of the English economy. By filling the lowest echelons of the work force, and by willingly undertaking employment that others resisted, Irish migrants enabled the English work force to move into higher occupational brackets.

Conclusions

I'm proud of my identity, I'm proud of being Irish. I love Ireland, although I never got anything there. It never done anything for me. But it's the country. When I go back to Ireland on holidays I look around me and think those hills belong to me, and that's my grass, and that's the way I feel. I can't say it, as long as I've been in this country, I can't feel that way, you know. I'll never go back to Ireland, but my spirit is there. That's how I feel about Ireland.

NOREEN HILL
who left Cork to work in England

What later became of migrants who had worked abroad? We know very little because they were, after all, people who left very few tracks, very little evidence of themselves when they moved on. In Ireland they lived in biogradable housing, cabins which disintegrated when the peat fires keeping them dry went out. In England and Scotland the jerry-built housing they inhabited during their brief stays was scarcely more permanent. Nevertheless, despite the lack of evidence for the many, a few left their stories,[1] while of others there are fragments of evidence in records.

A small window opens on the emigrant experience in the *Ordnance Survey Memoirs* for County Derry,[2] which contains names of persons who were seasonal migrants as well as those who left permanently. Some names reappear in a "Missing Friends" information-wanted column. These personal advertisements appeared in the *Pilot,* a Boston newspaper that published ads in which Irish immigrants sought to locate relatives and friends in North America with whom they had lost contact.[3] Searchers reported a wide range of information so as to identify those whom they sought. For that reason the advertisements contain valuable information about the migration patterns of emigrants.

Data from the advertisements for the more than 25,000 persons sought during the first twenty-nine years of the column's existence (1831–1860) also bears out the fact that many of those sought had worked in England or Scotland before emigrating. The majority of persons for whom a port of departure was reported left from Liverpool, despite the fact that fares were higher than from Irish ports. One explanation is that these may have been the more prosperous emigrants who chose to purchase a safer and more predictable journey, but what is equally likely is that these were persons already working abroad.[4] Another indication of connections between the two countries is that the numbers of those departing for America rose considerably during 1840, 1841, and 1842, years when there was no unusual acceleration of distress in Ireland, but there were severe cutbacks in the textile industry in Britain. This would suggest that when migrants who had been working abroad saw their resources shrinking in England as well as in Ireland, they decided to minimize their losses and become permanent emigrants to America.

Linking evidence from the *Ordnance Survey Memoirs* with the Boston *Pilot* "Missing Friends" column bears out that at least two seasonal migrants from County Derry appear to have emigrated to America. Thirty-year-old John Kane, of the parish of Termoneeny, County Derry, appears on a list of seasonal migrants to Scotland. Evidence that he may have emigrated to America appears when a person of that name placed an advertisement on January 6, 1849, in the *Pilot* in search of his niece and nephew, Mary and Patrick Kane, natives of the town of Garvagh. Garvagh, in the parish of Errigal, is sufficiently near Termoneeny to suggest a relationship between them. In the ad John Kane reported their residence as Albany, New York, in November of the preceding year.[5] It is quite possible that this John Kane, giving his address as 104 Tremont Street in Boston, and the earlier John Kane were one and the same person. If so, then the seasonal migrant to Scotland later became the permanent emigrant to America.

Forty years of age when he appeared in the *Memoir* list as a seasonal migrant to Scotland, Thomas Henry of Ballinderry, Kilcronaghan Parish, County Derry, reappeared again a decade later, this time sought in an advertisement placed by his wife in the Boston *Pilot* of July 1, 1848.[6] Mrs. Henry sought her husband, a Thomas Henry of Ballinderry, who was known to have been in New York City in August of 1847. Apparently she had arrived in Boston from Ireland in a debilitated condition and was being detained at the Deer Island Hospital by the Boston immigration authorities; if unsuccessful in locating her husband, it is quite likely that the authorities would then have returned her to Ireland. Again, the similarity of geographical origin would point to the fact that this Thomas Henry is the same person who earlier was a seasonal migrant.

Other life stories and fragments of experiences of individual migrants have appeared earlier. The story of Owen Peter Mangan (see Chapter 4) was taken from the memoir which he wrote in old age. Patrick MacGill of Donegal was another who began as a seasonal migrant and later emigrated to America. Lacking the industrial skills which gave Owen Peter Mangan his rise in the world, MacGill's ticket to posterity was his ability to write effectively. His novel, *Children of the Dead End,*[7] first published in 1914, is believed to be a thinly disguised account of his own experiences as an agricultural migrant, travelling first as a twelve-year old boy from Donegal to work for farmers in County Tyrone as a hired hand, then later to Scotland for work as a "tatie howker" in the potato fields.

The life of Michael Sullivan (see Chapter 2) was lived in conditions which would collapse during the Famine years, but the lives of the others were affected by post-Famine conditions and thus are less representative of the period covered by this study when most migrants had some assurance of returning to a home base. They do however serve to illustrate aspects of the environment of the prior period and to put flesh on this account, which must by necessity be rather lacking in human drama.

No one has portrayed the break which took place as a result of the Famine more vividly than did John Mitchel, that angry Jonathan Swift of the nineteenth century, gifted with intellectual courage. Again, there is the account of the detached observer, and there is also the raw, searing agony of those who experienced it. In June 1847, Mitchel sat down to the task of writing a review of Irish guide books for the Young Irelanders' newspaper, *The Nation,* but was apparently overcome with horror by a Famine scene he had recently witnessed. As one of the founders of the Gaelic League, Arthur Griffiths, wrote of this event: "In it the John Mitchel of 1848 has his birth."[8]

Mitchel had been accustomed to tramping the hills of Ireland and enjoying the hospitality of the local peasantry, but experiencing the following scene he was never again a dispassionate observer of Irish affairs:

> Rise, then, and we shall show you the way through the mountain to seaward, where we shall come down upon a little cluster of seven or eight cabins, in one of which cabins, two summers ago, we supped sumptuously on potatoes and salt with the decent man who lives there, and the black-eyed woman of the house and five small children. We had a hearty welcome though the fare was poor; and as we toasted our potatoes in the greeshaugh, our ears drank in the honey-sweet tones of the well-beloved Gaelic. . . . There is no name for "modern enlightenment" in Irish, no word corresponding with the "masses," or with "reproductive labour"; in short, the nineteenth century would not know itself, could not express itself in Irish. . . . But why do we not see the smoke curling from those lowly chimneys? And surely we ought by this time to scent the well-known aroma of the turf-fires. But what . . . reeking breath of hell is this oppressing the air, heavier and more loathsome than the smell of death rising from the fresh carnage of a

battlefield. Oh misery! had we forgotten that this was the Famine Year? And we are here in the midst of those thousand Golgothas that border our island with a ring of death from Cork Harbour all round to Lough Foyle. There is no need of inquiries here—no need of words; the history of this little society is plain before us. Yet we go forward, though with sick hearts and swimming eyes, to examine the Place of Skulls nearer. There is a horrible silence; grass grows before the doors; we fear to look into any door, though they are all open or off the hinges; for we fear to see yellow shapeless skeletons grinning there; . . . We walk amidst the houses of the dead . . . and there is not one where we dare to enter. We stop before the threshold of our host of two years ago, put our head, with eyes shut, inside the doorjamb, and say . . . "God save all here!"—No answer—ghastly silence, and a mouldy stench, as from the mouth of burial vaults. Ah! they are dead they are dead! the strong man and the fair, dark-eyed woman and the little ones, with their liquid Gaelic accents that melted into music for us two years ago; they shrunk and withered together until the voices dwindled to a rueful gibbering, and they hardly knew one another's faces; but their horrid eyes scowled on each other with a cannibal glare. We know the whole story—the father was on a "public work," and earned the sixth part of what would have maintained his family, which was not always paid him; but still it kept them half alive for three months, and so instead of dying in December they died in March. And the agonies of those three months who can tell?—the poor wife wasting and weeping over her stricken children; the heavy-laden weary man, with black night thickening around him—thickening within him— feeling his own arm shrink and his step totter with the cruel hunger that gnaws away his life, and knowing too surely that all this will soon by over. And he has grown a rogue, too, on those public works; with roguery and lying about him, roguery and lying above him, he has begun to say in his heart that there is no God; for a poor but honest farmer, he has sunk down into a swindling, sturdy beggar. . . . Even ferocity or thirst for vengeance he can never feel again; for the very blood of him is starved into a thin chill *serum,* and if you prick him he will not bleed.

Following the years after the Famine, by mid-century what had been rational exodus became flight. The era of the Great Famine, 1845– 1850, thus marks a critical break between the two periods. Before 1845 the decision to migrate was largely the result of weighing a range of choices available, so that most who left Ireland permanently did so because their ties with the land were no broken. Following the Famine, the available range of choices narrowed so sharply that those who left to work in England or Scotland could entertain little hope of ever living permanently in Ireland again. Seasonal migrants who continued the pattern were caught up in a permanent cycle of poverty. The social and economic needs of the people of the one country complemented the economic needs of the other, with the result that seasonal and temporary migration drew persons from the most isolated regions of Ireland into the mainstream of economic development in mainland Britain.

What gave rise to this was a set of conditions arising largely from economic connections between Ireland and the sister island which had the effect of encouraging the Irish people into a growing dependence on a money economy. Temporary migration began from these connections and functioned to permit Irish persons, while still retaining Ireland as their home base, to migrate abroad to earn the cash to fulfill obligations incurred at home. Migration was both dependent on and facilitated by a potato economy, where they were the subsistence diet for the people in much of the western part of the country. By adjusting the cultivation cycle of potatoes, migrants were able to meet peak demands for their labor elsewhere. Those who depended upon growing a sufficient supply of potatoes for subsistence, or whose access to land depended on their yearly return, migrated seasonally, retaining access through family or kin connections; while those whose goal was capital for a project such as setting up an independent household could remain abroad for a longer period. Ireland's proximity to Britain facilitated and encouraged this pattern of largely temporary migration so that it became systematized into Irish culture, and became, with the passage of time and growing pressures on land and capital, the cornerstone of the social system for large areas of the west of Ireland.

The migrants, while maintaining the equilibrium of the rural Irish social structure by their migrating also filled a vital function abroad. Irish workers became the elastic supply of labor which enabled British industry to respond rapidly and efficiently to changes in the demand for goods and services. Prior to the Famine the rural Irish were primarily peasants in the sense that land was more important than was wage labor. Migration, by providing the necessary injections of cash, facilitated their ability to remain on the land, but as conditions deteriorated causing opportunities to contract, what began as short-term migration began to be gradually supplanted by longer-term migration, ultimately resulting in profound changes in the social structure of the country as it adjusted to a hemorrhage of the young and energetic.

In conclusion, there are a number of somewhat disparate points regarding the process of migration as it relates to these pre-Famine Irish migrants.

1. In addition to an Irish economy exhibiting either the dual structure of Lynch and Vaizey or the strata dualism of Lee in its economic structure, in its relation to the market for migrant labor, Ireland and Britain were a single economy—one in which the wages from Britain

were rechannelled back into maintaining the outmoded and archaic economy of the regions of the west and northwest from which migrants originated.

2. Migration from some districts tended to become habitual as each migrant who left and returned then became the information and communications network of new conditions. He, and to a lesser extent she, was the apostle of migration when opportunities were good in Britain or elsewhere in Ireland, and the Cassandra of it when times were bad. In this way potential migrants could be extremely responsive to changes in conditions. One witness reported seeing in July of 1833 about two hundred workers leaving for the harvest in England. Later in the day he saw them all returning because they had heard there was cholera in England.[9] Pity the harvest laborer who returned home without having earned much! One informant said, "The night they come home there may be half a dozen watching them, expecting to get part of what is due to him: one for conacre, another for house-rent, and another for his provisions given on credit, and so on."[10]

3. The kinship network played a critical role in obtaining jobs abroad, as well as in preserving access to land in Ireland. Damian Hannan's study of contemporary migration from County Cavan emphasizes the importance of kin when he says that less than 4 percent of the migrants in his study had no relatives abroad while 54 percent had more than three relatives abroad.[11]

4. What were the aims of these pre-Famine migrants? Primarily what they sought was to return home to live in some degree of comfort not possible on an Irish income. Probably only the very young were as naively hopeful as the three brothers from Connacht who wished to return with their earnings and become gentlemen. With the wisdom and calculation characteristic of most rural peoples, the aim of the majority of them was to retain that margin of safety which retaining access to land ensured. Having gained that, most probably hoped to live just a little more comfortably.

When it is established that much of pre-Famine migration was circular, commonly accepted conclusions about the nature of Irish migration require modification. It has been said that by migrating the Irish had "to abandon their culture and their country" when they moved to Britain or America.[12] Undoubtedly, those who remained abroad permanently would have had to relinquish some aspects of their culture in order to adapt to a different world, but this does not apply to migrants who continued to circulate between Ireland and Britain. Movement to Britain was relatively short-distance migration, and the evidence would suggest that because of this the migrants did not have to lose either their culture or their country. Nevertheless, extended migration over the course of many years resulted in individuals shifting between two worlds, often not able to fully commit themselves to either, with important consequences. Employers complained of their lack of commitment, priests said that they lacked stability, and the casual forms of employment to which they were attracted prevented them from upgrading their skills. What is more, this is a pattern which has persisted. J.A. Jackson believes that the inability of the Irish to fully detach themselves from Ireland has functioned to retard the integration into the larger society of Britain.[13]

How would Britain's industries have functioned without Irish laborers? Since Irish labor was primarily in the secondary sector it can be assumed that their willingness to perform the vital supportive tasks of that sector facilitated the operations of the rest of the economy. It may be concluded then that without the Irish labor force Britain's industrialization would have followed quite a different course. Factories might have been forced into full mechanization earlier. One wonders, though, who would have done the menial labor which is necessary in any economy? (In contemporary Britain the willingness of East and West Indian immigrants to fill the worst service jobs has either pushed the Irish up into the next echelon of employment, or forced them to return to Ireland for lack of employment because the newcomers are undercutting them in the wage market.)

Ireland did not have the resources to enable her to have her own industrial revolution. She was too near Britain to compete successfully, too vulnerable in capital resources, and possessed few natural resources, except one: Ireland had people – an essential fuel for an industrializing economy – and so a willing population of workers was Ireland's primary contribution to Britain's Industrial Revolution.

In looking at the effect of the migration in this period on Ireland and on the Irish, it is important to evaluate when migration was disruptive of the social system and when it was a process which preserved the system by siphoning off excess population into areas of greater opportunity. In general, seasonal and temporary migration had the effect of injecting needed cash income into the rural economy. In doing so, however, it may have delayed Ireland's transition into a modern land-tenure system (a system which the Famine experience and popular discontent with the land system later forced upon the country) by offering neither tenants nor landlords any incentive to modernize agriculture.

Did migration, then, delay or facilitate Ireland's emergence into the modern world? It is difficult to be certain of this because the Famine intervened, forcibly accelerating changes which were already underway. While the system of land ownership was already being questioned and would eventually have changed, it would have been reform of the land, not the revolutionary action, whereby the British parliament bought out the landlords in a series of land acts.

Returning migrants brought new ideas into Ireland, one of which was the belief that economic salvation was both possible and available nearby, if not at home. The effects of migration also reduced regionalism. The Tipperary countryman who would not tolerate his fellow countrymen from Connacht was forced when he worked alongside him in England to accept their common nationality. Irish nationalism was thus forged out of experiences such as this.

The migrant who lingered abroad was a failed migrant. For them settlement was failure because unless he possessed a readily marketable skill—and most didn't—they were doomed to eventual loss of status in their own eyes. As long as they were temporary migrants they could divorce themselves from the status of the job because they were far from the purview of those whose esteem mattered. However, with the passage of time, and as they remained for longer and longer periods and home ties receded, it became more difficult to separate themselves from the status of their employment which set the stage for frustration resulting in feelings of loss (of status), ultimately resulting in a degree of social disorganization.[14]

Overall it can be said that emigrants are failed migrants—they are failures inasmuch as their original intention was not to settle but to return. So whether the migrant who went abroad remained in Britain for the period of his or her work life or emigrated to America, migration was no longer as functional as prior to 1845 when five out of seven persons returned home within the year.

For those who became militant political radicals (whether as Chartists, as Orangemen, as Fenians, or as members of the Irish Republican Army in the next century) their identity in the new society could be worked out on an institutionalized level. For those who, for one reason or another, did not join the societies or the Church, but remained in Britain feeling blocked and frustrated, pathological drinking was an all too common outlet. Irish communities in Britain have always been said to be characterized by high alcohol consumption. Jackson's studies of the modern Irish in London have concluded that alcoholism, which was the result of poor social adjustment, has been an endemic characteristic of the Irish subculture in that city.[15]

Hannan's studies indicate that for the children of migrants their degree of settlement and assimilation into British society was dependent upon where they had spent their adolescence.[16] If it had been spent in Ireland — and the mid–nineteenth-century census returns indicate that it was common for Irish people in Britain to send their children home to be raised in Ireland — their chances of adopting the new culture was minimal and, again, frustration with consequent social disorganization was often the result.

To what extent then did the Irish, by failing to integrate into British society, fall into a culture of permanent deprivation as described by Handlin and Leibow?[17] From what we know of the Irish in Britain, both then and now, low skills and temporary job attachment kept them in the low-wage occupations and sectors. While some Irish behavior in the earlier period covered by this study falls into such patterns of instability, the extent to which this became a problem is highly correlated with such factors as whether persons who remained in Britain fell into worse poverty or obtained jobs which assured an income sufficient to encourage habits such as thrift, delayed gratification, and marital stability. Here, undoubtedly, the Catholic Church has always played an important role in providing a structure where the immigrants could meet compatriots, save for the future, and educate their children. But it also true that the Church may also have provided an alternative to assimilation into British society. This, however, is less important when one realizes that this was a society which did not welcome the Irish on a personal level, and in which the relative scarcity of opportunities for job advancement may have precluded much opportunity for assimilation anyway.

Studies of Irish immigrants, whether in Britain or in America, almost always emphasize their lack of upward mobility.[18] What we cannot ascertain with any degree of accuracy, however, is how rapid, widespread, and significant was social mobility for the rest of the population. One suspects that occupational mobility gains were small for most of the population, but that peculiarities such as being female, or Black, or Irish, or whatever other characteristic may make a person visually distinctive, can skew judgements about what may be generally happening in terms of mobility. Immigrant populations stand out as long as national characteristics set them apart. Once they have lost (or deliberately discarded) these characteristics because they have become, or wish to become, economically successful, we conclude that assimilation has brought success. Is it not equally possible that it is the deliberate retention of national (and foreign) characteristics which erects barriers to economic success in an economic system that necessitates working toward common goals? A 1969 U.S. ethnic census of the population indicated that those in a self-reported Irish ethnic origin were most likely to be in a lower income bracket than were those who claimed an Italian ethnic origin. Is it possible that this suggests that the poorer Irish may have emphasized their ethnic origins more strongly than did Italians as a means of overcoming their sense of frustration over their low economic status?

In 1880 an Irish journalist, resident in England, mused upon the conspicuous ethnicity of the Irish population when he said: "Recognition is slow to wait upon those who cannot forget that they are Irish, and, save in exceptional instances, the warmth of social welcome is reserved for those who have allowed the ice barrier of their nationalism to melt away."[19]

Migration is always interruptive of individual development, whether positively or in a negative way. Seasonal migrants brought back either money or, in some cases, disappointment. When persons remained and settled, however, some disruption was inevitable. Longer-term emigration placed the individual outside the familiar structured social context which had existed in Ireland. For children, such a process could be relatively disruptive of normal maturation. In urban industrial regions, such as Lancashire, the migrants were to some extent able to reconstruct the functional support system of the kinship network by means of boarding houses run by their countrywomen. The boarding house functioned, thus, to both facilitate temporary migration and to ease the process of transition to urban industrial society if migrants chose to remain longer.

It may be concluded then, that unless the migrant found employment which gave him some assured degree of security, or stayed within the kinship system or within range of his Church, he or she was fairly vulnerable and thus likely to fall into some degree of social disorganization. The adjustment to urban industrialization was undoubtedly stressful and Britain was a hostile atmosphere for strangers. It was a very old society undergoing disruptive transformation itself, with severe consequent readjustments of its social structure. Such a society was unlikely to welcome outsiders, particularly if they arrived with some mistrust for their neighbors.

Did the Irish family's function change with migration? At home, seasonal migration left many families without males for months at a time. In their absence the women were left to make the major decisions of the family. When this took place for extended periods of time and over many years, the result would undoubtedly have been for the woman's role to become more autonomous and the family to become more matrifocal. Does this then possibly lend itself to an explanation for the syndrome of the dominant Irish female—the woman who cannot relinquish her strong influence over her son?

The family in Ireland has always performed a critical role in the process of migration. Migration is, in Jackson's words, "instituted in Irish life, built into it by family obligations, and expressed through remittances and visits home."[20] Conrad Arensberg and Solon Kimball's studies of the country people of County Clare demonstrated that in the 1930s the family in the west of Ireland encouraged potential migrants to leave and facilitated migration through their contacts abroad.[21] Hannan, twenty years later, found that emigration was emptying out the countryside and for that reason families tried to hold back potential migrants, with the result that when it became inevitable that the young must migrate they left with inadequate skills, prepared for little more than unskilled labor.[22]

What effect did temporary migration have on later permanent migration to the New World? Contrary to Oscar Handlin's assertion that the Irish who went to North America had never before left the land, I would suggest that those who worked abroad before permanent emigration to America were no longer peasants. The experience of migration had already thrust them into a modern world from which there was no real retreat. After being treated as strictly *homo economicus* by their British employers, migrants could never again integrate into a system in which the landlord was a sort of demigod. Returning to Ireland with the knowledge gained abroad, they could no longer regard the landlord as a sort of corrupted superior being who could be taught his duty through Whiteboy vengeance.

Ultimately, then, the experience of migration taught the Irish people to take their fate in their own hands. Leaving Ireland they were thrust into the modern world, and the only way that Ireland could remain the traditional world of saints and scholars was to refuse to have these tainted souls back — which, of course, to a certain extent is what did happen.

Notes

Sources frequently cited have been identified by the following abbreviations:

I.F.C.	Irish Folklore Commission
NIPRO	Northern Ireland Public Record Office
PP	Parliamentary Papers
PROI	Public Record Office of Ireland
Report	*Report on the State of the Irish Poor in Great Britain, 1836*

Preface

1. James Boswell, *Life of Johnson,* vol. 1 (London, 1763), p. 425.
2. W. I. Thomas and E. Znaniecki, *The Polish Peasant in Europe and America* (New York, 1927).

1. The Irish in Ireland and England

1. Quoted by V. G. Kiernan, "Britons Old and New," in *Immigrants and Minorities in British Society,* ed. Colin Holmes (London, 1978), p. 23.
2. See Arnold Schrier, *Ireland and the American Emigration, 1850–1900* (Minneapolis, 1958) for an excellent discussion of the custom, pp. 84–92.
3. Patrick MacGill, *Children of the Dead End* (Kerry, 1982), p. 48.
4. As quoted in F. P. Wilson, ed., *The Oxford Dictionary of English Proverbs,* 3d ed. (Oxford, 1970), p. 223.
5. See J. D. Marshall, "The Old Poor Law, 1795–1834," in *Studies in Economic History,* ed. M. W. Flinn (London, 1968) for a discussion of the operations of the old poor law.
6. For a discussion of the shift to industrial work discipline, see "Time, Work-Discipline, and Industrial Capitalism", by E. P. Thompson in *Past and Present,* 38 (December 1967), pp. 56–97.
7. Daniel Defoe, "Giving Alms No Charity and Employing the Poor," in *A Collection of Pamphlets Concerning the Poor* (London, 1704), pp. 83–85. Neil Smelser notes that "the eighteenth was a century of browbeating the poor over lack of discipline, immorality,

theft, drunkenness, holiday-keeping, etc. . . . . Inasmuch as critics blamed poverty and industrial inefficiency on the poor, they were expressing misplaced aggression because the system of production was outmoded." Neil J. Smelser, *Social Change in the Industrial Revolution* (Chicago, 1959, p. 80.

8. Karl Marx, *Capital* (1887, reprint London, 1928).

9. The towns with the highest proportion of Irish-born persons in 1851 were: Liverpool 22 percent, Dundee 19 percent, Glasgow 18 percent, Manchester 13 percent, Paisley 13 percent, and Bradford 9 percent.

10. John Bernard Trotter, *Walks through Ireland in the Years 1812, 1814, and 1817* (London, 1819), p. 21.

11. Frank Thistlethwaite, "Migration from Europe Overseas in the Nineteenth and Twentieth Centuries," in *Congrès Internationale des Sciences Historiques,* ed. V. Rapports (1960). Thistlethwaite estimates that "perhaps a third of United States emigrants reemigrated" (p. 75). Of even greater importance for this study is his assertion that "a significant proportion of the re-emigrants were 'repeaters,' who made a regular practice of temporary migration (p. 77). Narrowing to the period of the 'new' industrial immigration between 1908 and 1923, the figure was as high as 86–89 percent for Balkan peoples, and as low as 5 percent for Jews. Ferenzi relates this to the proportion of males to females in the migration stream. For example, there was a high proportion of males among Greek immigrants and a comparatively low proportion (52 percent) among Jews (Imre Ferenzi, "An Historical Study of Migration Statistics," *International Labour Review,* 20(1929): p. 380).

12. *Report on the State of the Irish Poor in Great Britain, 1836,* App. A, p. 518.

13. David Thomson, *Woodbrook* (London, 1978) p. 252.

14. Donald Bogue, "Internal Migration," in *The Study of Population,* ed. P. M. Hauser and O. T. Duncan (Chicago, 1959).

15. Stephan Thernstrom, *The Other Bostonians* (Cambridge, 1973), pp. 6–7. His primary reason for studying only male immigrants to Boston was, he says, because they were the major breadwinners and carriers of the family's hopes and life chances. Yet in a recent study of the Irish in Lowell, Brian Mitchell found that an Irish father provided only about 60 percent of family income in 1860, so that the role of Irish women was central to employment within the family. Brian C. Mitchell, *The Paddy Camps, the Irish of Lowell, 1821–61* (Chicago, 1988) p. 144. For a retrospective view of Thernstrom, see Edward Pessen, "Poverty and Progress: A Critique," and Michael Frisch, "Poverty and Progress: A Paradoxical Legacy," in *Social Science History,* 10, no.1(Spring 1986):5–22.

16. John Revans, "Poor Laws in Ireland," *The London and Westminster Review,* vol. 25 (July, 1836), pp. 185–86. Despite such inducements to marriage, the poorest Irish peasant was less likely to be married after the 1830s when access to land declined.

17. Robert Redfield, *Peasant Society and Culture* (Chicago, 1956), p. 29; see also Margaret MacCurtain, "Pre-Famine Peasantry in Ireland: Definition and Theme," *Irish University Review* (Autumn 1974), p. 195.

18. James Edmund Handley, *The Irish in Scotland, 1798–1845* (Cork, 1945), p. 48.

19. Michael Hechter, *Internal Colonialism: The Celtic Fringe in British National Development, 1536–1966* (Berkeley, 1975).

20. Friedrich Engels, *The Condition of the Working Class in England* (Middlesex, England, 1987 reprint), p. 124.

21. Henry Mayhew, *London Labour and the London Poor,* vols. 1–4 (New York, 1928 reprint).

22. Eileen Yeo and E. P. Thompson, *The Unknown Mayhew* (New York, 1971).

23. Alexis de Tocqueville, *Journeys to England and Ireland* (New Haven, 1958 reprint).

24. John A. Jackson, *The Irish in Britain* (London, 1963); and Jackson, "The Irish,"

in *London, Aspects of Change,* ed. John A. Jackson (London, 1964). Jackson sees the Irish now resident in Britain as hampered by their belief that they are still only temporary residents. He sees the community's lack of upward mobility and family breakdown as stemming from their inability to assimilate successfully into the host society.

25. Roger Swift and Sheridan Gilley, eds., *The Irish in the Victorian City* (London, 1985). See also Gilley, "English Attitudes to the Irish in England, 1790–1900" in Colin Holmes, ed. *Immigrants and Minorities in British Society* (London, 1978), pp. 81–110; Swift, "The Outcast Irish in the British Victorian City: Problems and Perspectives," in *Irish Historical Studies,* 25, no.99, (May 1987):264–76.

26. M. A. G. O'Tuathaigh, "The Irish in Nineteenth-Century Britain: Problems of Integration," *Transactions of the Royal Historical Society,* 5th ser., vol. 31 (1981).

27. John Denvir, *The Irish in Britain* (London, 1892) and *Life Story of an Old Rebel* (Dublin, 1910).

28. Ibid., pp. 435–37.

29. James Edmund Handley, *The Irish in Scotland, 1798–1845* (Cork, 1945); and *The Irish in Modern Scotland* (Oxford, 1947).

30. Brenda Collins, "Irish Emigration to Dundee and Paisley," in J. M. Goldstrom and L.A. Clarkson, (eds.) *Irish Population, Economy, and Society, Essays in Honour of the Late K. H. Connell* Oxford, 1981, pp. 195–212.

31. Lynn H. Lees, "Social Change and Social Stability among the London Irish" (Ph.D. diss., Harvard University (March 1969). Published as L. H. Lees, *Exiles of Erin: Irish Migrants in Victorian London* (Manchester, 1979).

32. William James Lowe, *The Irish in Mid-Victorian Lancashire: The Shaping of a Working Class Community* (Washington D.C.; American University Press, 1989).

33. Arthur Redford, *Labour Migration in England, 1800–1850* (Manchester, 1926, reprint 1964).

34. Jeffrey G. Williamson, "The Impact of the Irish on British Labour Markets during the Industrial Revolution," in the *Journal of Economic History,* vol. 46(1986), pp. 693–720.

35. Michael J. Piore, *Birds of Passage: Migrant Labor in Industrial Societies* (Cambridge and New York: Cambridge University Press, 1979).

36. Anand A. Yang, "The Optimizing Peasant: A Study of Internal Migration in a Northeast Indian District," (Workshop on the Effects of Risk and Uncertainty on Economic and Social Processes in South Asia, University of Pennsylvania, 1976).

37. J. R. Harris and M. Todaro, "Migration, Unemployment, and Development: A Two-Sector Analysis," *American Economic Review* (March 1971).

38. Brinley Thomas, *Migration and Economic Growth* (Cambridge, 1954).

39. E. P. Thompson, *The Making of the English Working Class* (New York: Random House, 1963).

40. E. J. Hobsbawm, *Labouring Men, Studies in the History of Labour* (New York, 1967).

41. J. H. Clapham, *An Economic History of Modern Britain* (Cambridge, 1926).

42. Carlo M. Cipolla (ed.), *The Fontana Economic History of Europe; 4, The Emergence of Industrial Societies; 3, The Industrial Revolution* (London, 1973).

43. George O'Brien, *The Economic History of Ireland from the Union to the Famine* (London, 1921).

44. L. M. Cullen, *An Economic History of Ireland Since 1660,* (New York, 1972); and *Anglo-Irish Trade, 1660–1880* (New York, 1968).

45. T. W. Freeman, *Pre-Famine Ireland, A Study in Historical Geography* (Manchester, 1957).

46. K. H. Connell, *The Population of Ireland, 1750–1845* (Oxford, 1950). See also

Connell, "The Population of Ireland in the Eighteenth Century" *Economic History Review,* no.16 (1946) pp. 111–24: "Land and Population in Ireland, 1780–1845," *Economic History Review,* no.2 (1950), pp. 278–89; and "Some Unsettled Problems in English and Irish Population History, 1750–1845," *Irish Historical Studies,* no.7 (1951), pp. 225–34.

47. Edward Baines, *A History of the Cotton Manufacture in Great Britain* (London, 1835).

48. L. M. Cullen, "Irish History Without the Potato," *Past and Present,* no.4 (July, 1968) pp. 72–83. For a response, see Joel Mokyr's "Irish History with the Potato," in *Irish Economic and Social History,* vol. 8, 1981, pp. 3–29.

49. P. M. A. Bourke, "The Potato, Blight, Weather, and the Irish Famine" (Ph.D. diss. National University of Ireland, 1965). Fortunately his collected works, many previously unpublished, are published in a collected edition to mark the fiftieth anniversary of the Irish Historical Society and the Ulster Society for Irish Historical Studies as *Essays on the Irish Famine, 1845–49,* Irish Historical Studies, 1938–88: Fiftieth Anniversary Publication (Dublin, 1993).

50. Patrick Lynch and John Vaizey, *Guinness's Brewery in the Irish Economy, 1759–1876* (Cambridge, 1960).

51. Joseph Lee, "The Dual Economy in Ireland, 1800–50," in *Historical Studies,* ed. T. Desmond Williams, vol. 7 (Dublin, 1971), pp 27–30.

52. Raphael Samuel, "Workshop of the World: Steam Power and Hand Technology in Mid-Victorian Britain," *History Workshop,* 3 (Spring 1977); and *Miners, Quarrymen and Saltworkers* (London, 1977); and "Comers and Goers", in *The Victorian City,* H. J. Dyos and M. Wolff, (eds.) (London, 1974).

53. Three Reports of the Commissioners on the Condition of the Poorer Classes in Ireland, the Various Institutions Established by Law for Their Relief, and the Further Remedial Measures for Ameliorating the Irish Poor; Evidence, Appendices and Papers (App. D, E, and F). *Irish Poor in Great Britain.* Sir G. Cornewall Lewis. 15 parts. 1835–36.

54. PP. 1836 Reports from Commissioners, *Poor Laws (Ireland) 3rd Report;* hereafter called "Poor Inquiry."

55. The importance of the belief that any amelioration of Ireland's condition necessitated the introduction of a poor law can be gathered from a society formed in Dublin in the 1820s whose intention it was to "force the issue forward (in parliament)" by collecting funds to send destitute Irish into English industrial districts. PP. 1828, *Report from Select Committee on the Laws Relating to Irish and Scotch Vagrants, July 1828,* vol. 4, p. 15. While there is no evidence of this threat ever having been carried out, it was in fact believed in England to be a common practice of the public authorities in Ireland.

56. Thomas, *Migration,* p. 4.

57. See Edward Gibbon Wakefield, *A Letter from Sydney and Other Writings* (London, 1929) in which, writing from Newgate prison, he convinced the leading economists of the day as well as influencing the policies of several successive governments.

58. *Poor Inquiry,* Supplement to App. A.

59. J. H. Johnson, "Harvest Migration from Nineteenth-Century Ireland," *Transactions of the Institute of British Geographers,* 41 (June 1967).

60. S. H. Cousens, "The Regional Variation in Emigration from Ireland between 1821 and 1841," *Transactions of the Institute of British Geographers,* 37(December 1965), pp. 15–30.

61. S. H. Cousens, "Emigration and Demographic Change in Ireland, 1851–1861," *Economic History Review,* vol. 14, 2d Ser. (August 1961), pp. 275–88; and "The Regional Variations in Population Change in Ireland, 1861–1881," *Economic History Review,* no.22 (December 1964).

62. Brendan M. Walsh, "A Perspective on Irish Population Patterns," *Eire-Ireland,* no.4 (Autumn 1969), pp. 3–21; and "Marriage Rates and Population Patterns in Ireland, 1871 and 1911," *Economic History Review,* no.28 (April 1970), pp. 161–69.

63. Cormac Ó'Gráda, "Seasonal Migration and Post-Famine Adjustment in the West of Ireland, 1850–1880," in "Post Famine, Adjustment: Essays in Ninetenth-Century Irish Economic History," (Ph.D. diss., Columbia University, 1973); and "Seasonal Migration and Post-Famine Adjustment in the West of Ireland" *Studia Hibernica,* no.13 (1973), pp. 48–76.

64. Barbara Kerr, "Irish Immigration into Great Britain, 1798–1838," (B. Litt. thesis, Oxford University, 1954); and "Irish Seasonal Migration to Great Britain, 1800–38," *Irish Historical Studies,* vol. 3 (1942–43.)

65. PP. 1837–8, *Second Report of Commissioners Appointed to Consider and Recommend a General System of Railways for Ireland, HC, 1837–38* (145), 35, pp. 449.

66. *Digest of Evidence taken before Her Majesty's Commissioners of Inquiry into the State of the Law and Practice in Respect to the Occupation of Land.* Parts I & II (London, 1847).

67. *1843 Reports of the Commissioners appointed to take the Census,* June 1841.

68. PP. 1843, Accounts and Papers, Valuations, (Ireland), pp. 1–3. Sir Richard John Griffith (1784–1878) supervised the valuation of Ireland, the primary valuation under the Valuation Act of 1852, which was a relative valuation of property to regulate the taxation of Ireland.

69. H. D. Inglis, *A Tour through Ireland in the Spring, Summer and Autumn of 1834,* 2d ed., 2 vols. (London, 1835).

70. Mr. And Mrs. S. C. Hall, *Ireland: Its Scenery, Character, Etc.,* 3 vols. (London, 1841).

71. Caesar Otway, *A Tour in Connaught* (Dublin, 1839); *Sketches in Ireland* (Dublin, 1839).

72. Giraldus Cambrensis or John of Wales, *Expugnatio Hibernica, The Conquest of Ireland,* edited with translation and historical notes by A. B Scott and F. X. Martin (Dublin, 1978).

73. L. Perry Curtis, Jr., *Apes and Angels, the Irishman in Victorian Caricature* (Washington, 1971).

74. See Patrick F. Murray, "Calendar of the Overseas Missionary Correspondence of the All Hallowe's College, Dublin, 1842–47." (MA thesis, 1956, University College, Dublin.)

75. Desmond McCourt, "The Use of Oral Tradition in Irish Historical Geography," in *Irish Geography,* vol. 6, no. 4 (1972).

76. I am indebted to Cormac Ó'Gráda for translating some accounts from the Irish for me.

77. Irish Folklore Commission, MS 1457, p. 310 (Irish Folklore Commission abbreviated to I.F.C. in later references).

78. I.F.C., MS 404, p. 50.

79. I.F.C., MS 642.

80. Quoted by Maurice Harmon in his introduction to the Mercier Press edition of *Wildgoose Lodge* (Cork and Dublin, 1973), p. xviii.

2. Profile of the Migration: Those Who Left

1. Cormac Ó'Gráda, in Appendix C: "The Income of Agricultural Labourers, 1845–1870, a Tentative Estimate," p. 144, in "Post-Famine Adjustment: Essays in Nine-

teenth-Century Irish Economic History." (Ph.D. diss., Columbia University, 1973).

2. See Figure 2.2, "Average Number of Days per Year when Agricultural Labor was Available."

3. See Ó'Gráda, "Seasonal Migration and Post-Famine Adjustment in the West of Ireland, 1850–1880," in Ó'Gráda, "Essays," pp. 5–38 for an analysis of the role of seasonal migration to England and Scotland in the post-famine years, in which he argues that a persistence of pre-Famine conditions in western districts was due to the persistence of seasonal migration.

4. *Report on the State of the Irish Poor in Great Britain, 1836,* PP. App.G, p. iv. Hereafter referred to as *Report.*

5. There is some evidence that Irish Celts (or Gaels as they called themselves) attempted to travel further westward across the Atlantic. Such attempts culminated in a typically Irish response to history—the mythologizing of the event in a hero-story. The hero, Saint Brendan, made his way it is said to North America (probably Newfoundland) sometime in the sixth or seventh century. Recent interest in the story resulted in a reconstruction of the expedition; the conclusions being that such a voyage was both possible and feasible. Ties between Ireland and Newfoundland have remained strong; in the late 18th century the Irish colony on the island was sufficiently large to warrant a bishop. It was also near enough to Ireland that fishermen migrated seasonally between southern counties such as Waterford and Newfoundland well into the nineteenth century.

6. This is based on the concept of possible responses to inequitable situations as posed by Albert O. Hirshman in *Exit, Voice and Loyalty,* (Cambridge, 1970).

7. See Nicholas P. Canny, *The Elizabethan Conquest of Ireland: A Pattern Established 1565–1576,* (Sussex, 1976) and Brendan Bradshaw, "The Elizabethans and the Irish", *Studies,* Spring 1977, for an examination of Elizabethan attitudes toward Ireland.

8. Brehon law was the ancient Gaelic law.

9. Daniel Corkery, *The Hidden Ireland,* (Dublin, 1924), p. 135.

10. Testimony of Alexander Glendinning, as cited in Ó'Gráda, "Essays," 1973, p. 14, from PP, 1833, V, Q.7616.

11. Digby Beste, *Poverty and the Baronet's Family* (London, 1841) p. 4. I am indebted to the late Prof. Wolfe, Professor of English, Harvard University, for this reference and to the late Aiken McClelland for locating for me the one copy of the book which existed.

12. Ibid., pp. 7–8.

13. Ibid., pp. 10. The author was a recent convert to Catholicism. Since intention in writing the book was to proselytize, the story lacks relevance beyond the above account. The hero was the son of one of the migrants, educated in gratitude by an estate owner after the father lost his life saving the man's son from drowning. The story portrays a romanticized hero, an Irishman raised with an English education, but who later rejects his Englishness and returns to Ireland to liberate his country.

14. See Chapter Four for a discussion of English-born children resident in Ireland. The census commissioners took this to mean that these were the children of Irish parents resident in England.

15. Michael J. Piore, *Birds of Passage,* Chapter 3.

16. L. M. Cullen, *An Economic History of Ireland Since 1660* (New York, 1972) p. 11. See also Cullen, *Anglo-Irish Trade, 1660–1800* (New York, 1968).

17. E. A. Wrigley, "A Simple Model of London's Importance in Changing English Society and Economy, 1650–1750," *Past and Present,* no.37, July 1967, p. 54.

18. J. Houghton, *A Collection of Letters for the Improvement of Husbandry* (London, 1681), pp. 165–66, quoted in Wrigley, "London's Importance" p. 55.

19. Phyllis Deane and W. A. Cole, *British Economic Growth, 1688–1959,* (Cambridge, 1967), p. 75.

20. The Navigation Acts were not aimed at restraining Irish trade or the country's economic development, but reflected the belief that England should receive the full benefit of any trade from Ireland and that England was under no obligation to share its colonial wealth equally with Ireland.

21. Eric L. Almquist, "Mayo and Beyond: Land, Domestic Industry and Rural Transformation in the Irish West" (Ph.D. diss., Boston University, 1977), p. 193. Almquist says that County Mayo landlords sought to promote domestic industry on their estates because they wished to increase the income of their tenants, income which would not hinge solely on improving the traditional husbandry of their tenants, p. 78.

22. Ibid., p. 53.

23. K. H. Connell, "Population", in *Social Life in Ireland 1800–45,* ed. R. B. McDowell (Cork, 1963), p. 88.

24. L. M. Cullen, "Irish History Without the Potato", *Past and Present,* no. 40 (July 1968), pp. 72–83. For the counterargument to Cullen, see Joel Mokyr "Irish History With the Potato," *Irish Economic and Social History,* vol. 8 (1981), pp. 8–29.

25. P. M. Austin Bourke, *The Visitation of God: The Potato and the Great Irish Famine* (Dublin: Lilliput Press, 1993), pp. 11–25.

26. Ibid, p. 12. Salaman suggests that the potato may have proven its worth at this time as a "hidden crop" which could be kept underground, out of sight of troops foraging for food, at a time when Ireland was often subject to bitter conflicts and marauding armies. R.N. Salaman, *The History and Social Influence of the Potato* (Cambridge, 1949).

27. In his study of illicit distillation in Ireland, Connell sees the growth of poteen production as being encouraged by two factors: the relatively greater returns from grain-produced poteen in a country where transport was rudimentary and thus expensive, and the high cost of parliament whiskey which was heavily taxed. K. H. Connell, *Illicit Distillation" in Irish Peasant Society* (Oxford, 1968). He also suggests, but does not develop, the idea that poteen making was winked at by local landlords who acknowledged that its production was a critical supplement to meagre incomes. For example, in 1816 a Sligo rector said that if ownership of a distillery were made a felony the poor of his parish could not pay their rents, p. 26.

28. Bourke, *Visitation,* pp. 16–20.

29. Arthur Young, *A Tour in Ireland,* bk.I, (Dublin, 1780).

30. For a discussion of the practice of booleying, see Breandan MacAodha, "A Booley Place Name in County Tyrone," in *Ulster Folk Life,* vol. 2 (1956) pp. 61–62.

31. The ridges in which potatoes are grown in their Andean homeland appear to be similar to Irish lazybeds, and tuber crops throughout the tropics are planted in ridges or mounds, but according to Bourke the ridge technique in Ireland is certainly older than the cultivation of the potato there because it was used for growing cereal crops from early times. See Bourke, *Visitation.*

32. Estyn Evans, "Lazy-beds" in *Irish Folk Ways* (London, 1957), pp. 140–150.

33. Bourke, *Visitation,* pp. 20–25. The keeping quality of potatoes was always precarious, and potato varieties had a life expectancy of only about twenty years.

34. In this connection the correspondence between Maria Edgeworth and the economist, David Ricardo, is of interest. She writes (June 14, 1847), "The potato for many reasons is not fit to be the staple food of a country—not storable—not employing industry of labour sufficient in its cultivation for the moral purpose—and it brings in the lowest price, affording nothing to fall back upon in case of failure. I have letters of Ricardo's in which all the requisites for a safe national food are ably stated and the potato is lowest in

his scale. . . . I do not consider it as an evil, in itself, but a good that has been abused." (Mansergh, 1965) pp. 289–90, as quoted in Bourke, *Visitation*, p. 27.

35. Edward Wakefield, *An Account of Ireland, Statistical and Political* (London, 1812).

36. Raymond D. Crotty, *Irish Agricultural Production, Its Volume and Structure* (Cork, 1966), p. 28–35.

37. This is an interesting comment on Marxian analysis of class formation and appropriation of surplus value. While the capitalist class may have gained control of the land, thereby alienating peasants as a whole from the means of production, at the same time younger family members were gaining greater control. At one level you could say that exploitation by patriarchy within the family was being superseded by exploitation by capitalists; but the net effect on younger members may have been favorable.

38. Cullen, *Anglo-Irish Trade*, p. 100.

39. The circulation of these notes rose more sharply in Ireland than in England, says Cullen, because agricultural prices rose more rapidly than other prices and the supply of money followed the increase in prices. *Economic History*, p. 102.

40. Ibid. Cullen says that the banking crisis had little effect in the north where landlords had always insisted upon cash rather than notes.

41. The migration of Scots settlers from the province of Ulster to America had been underway since the first of their leases began coming due around 1715. In the following decades increasing numbers of Scots-Irish preferred to sell up and use the accumulated capital for emigration rather than pay the increased cost of leases for their land.

42. Bourke, *Visitation*, p. 31.

43. 1841 Census.

44. Alexis de Tocqueville, *Journeys to England and Ireland* (New Haven, 1958), p. 122.

45. Ibid., p. 44.

46. Hely Dutton, *A Statistical and Agricultural Survey of the County of Galway* (Dublin, 1824), p. 345.

47. See F. J. Carney, "Pre-Famine Irish Population: the Evidence from the Trinity College Estates." *Irish Economic and Social History,* vol. 2 (1975) pp. 35–45.

48. James S. Donnelly, Jr., *The Land and People of Nineteenth-Century Cork* (Boston, 1975), p. 10. The work of W. A. Maguire on the Downshire Estates, where the Hill family held property in counties Down, Antrim, Wicklow, and King's, indicates that by the nineteenth century, while the system of absentee ownership did not necessarily cause wretchedness and exploitation, when the landlord was indifferent or uninterested in the well-being of his tenantry, hard-hearted or corrupt local agents or middlemen still had free rein to wreak havoc. W. A. Maguire, *The Downshire Estates, 1801–1845* (Oxford, Clarendon Press, 1972) and *Letters of a Great Irish Landlord: A Selection from the Estate Correspondence of the Third Marquess of Downshire 1809–1845* (Belfast, H.M.S.O. 1974) See also David Dickson, "Middlemen," pp. 162–85, in Thomas Bartlett and D.W. Hayton, *Penal Era and Golden Age, Essays in Irish History, 1690–1800,* (Belfast, 1979).

49. Catholics were still constrained by the penal laws to lease terms of thirty-one years, which Cullen says were in fact quite long, although contemporaries did not always acknowledge this. Cullen, *Economic History* p. 78. In 1778 the restriction was removed, but did not prove to be of great significance economically as it was becoming by then a custom to grant shorter leases. It did, however, have political significance when voting tenants gave landlords an incentive to accumulate tenants for parliamentary support.

50. Arthur Young, *A Tour in Ireland, 1776–1779,* bk. II, (Dublin, 1780), p. 25.

51. Donnelly, *Cork,* p. 52.

52. Ó'Gráda, "Essays," p. 35.

53. Ibid., p. 81. Cullen says that unchecked subdivision operated primarily in regions where agricultural output for the market was limited or on inferior or upland soil, or newly reclaimed waste land, where commercialized agriculture did not exist. Bourke says that the smallness of holdings has been exaggerated. Census figures have grossly overstated fragmentation, relying as they have on figures based on an English acre, whereas they should have been for an Irish acre which is 1.62 larger than an English acre. P. M. A. Bourke, "The Extent of the Potato Crop in Ireland at the Time of the Famine", in *Statistical Society of Ireland Journal,* vol. 20, pt. II (1959), pp. 20–26. According to Donnelly the fragmentation of holdings in County Cork may not have been as great as in other areas as a result of the prevalence of dairying there which obstructed the progress of the subdivision of land (Donnelly, *Cork,* p. 16.) This did, however, increase the incentive for a more permanent leave-taking from such areas as migrants lost their tie to the land.

54. Patrick Murray, *Maria Edgeworth: A Study of the Novelist* (Cork, 1971), pp. 38–49.

55. Ibid, p. 37.

56. Ibid., p. 38.

57. Caesar Otway, *A Tour Through Connaught* (Dublin, 1839), p. 127.

58. Eric Hobsbawm, *Primitive Rebels* (New York, 1959), pp. 132–146.

59. Henry Mayhew, *London Labour and the London Poor,* bk.I (New York, 1855, reprint 1968), p. 106.

60. See Maureen Wall, *The Penal Laws in Ireland* (Dundalk, 1967), for a discussion of the Penal Laws as operating to prevent political disloyalty.

61. Hely Dutton, *A Statistical Survey of the County of Clare* (Dublin, 1808), p. 50.

62. De Tocqueville, *Journeys,* p. 155.

63. Conacre was the practice of hiring land on which to grow food; known as "taking land in conacre" or "taking potato garden." The land was manured and cultivated by the laborer who often prepared the ground for the landlord's subsequent wheat crop, at no expense to him. Unless there were unusual facilities for a supply of manure or other fertilizer such as seaweed nearby, laborers tended to underfertilize, thereby exhausting the soil. For this reason farmers often forced people to take more valuable ground, paying dearly for it, even though the laborers would probably have preferred cheap, wornout pasture, or unmanured land, according to the authors of the *Devon Digest. Devon Commission Digest,* I, p. 522.

64. Ibid., Pt. K, p. 485.

65. Donnelly, *Cork,* p. 21. The market value of six tons of potatoes (the normal product of an acre), was fifteen pounds. However the dependence on the potato became a desperate gamble as failures multiplied and accelerated. Salaman indicates that there were fourteen partial or complete failures of the crop between 1816 and 1842. Salaman, *Potato,* pp. 603–608.

66. Bourke, *Visitation,* pp. 56, 69.

67. A report said of this: "They are gathering the people like pigeons to get some crumbs for themselves." *Poor Inquiry,* App. C., p. 480.

68. Ibid.; *Poor Report,* App. H, pt. 1, p. 12. The report says that the average employment was about twenty-two weeks of about six working days each, for the whole country, with average wages of about eight and a half pence per day.

69. *Poor Inquiry,* App. A, p. 355.

70. Ibid., Supplement to App. D, p. 164. In addition to there being less employment for men, it also declined for women, as a result of declines in the linen trade. Farmers, who had employed two to three servant maids who could spin sufficient quantities in a week to

pay their wages and diet, now, as a result of declining demand for linen, would no longer employ these women. Ibid., App. C, p. 561.

71. Donnelly, *Cork,* p. 97.

72. Bourke, *Visitation,* p. 92.

73. Ó'Gráda, "Essays," 1973, p. 144.

74. Patrick Lynch and John Vaizey, *Guinness's Brewery in the Irish Economy, 1759–1876* (Cambridge, 1960).

75. *1841 Census,* p. xxxi.

76. Donnelly, *Cork,* p. 43.

77. *Poor Report.,* App. A, p. 356.

78. Ibid., p. 379.

79. Ibid., p. 385.

80. Harriet Martineau, *Irish Economy* (London, 1832), pp. 6–7.

81. Evidence of John Allen Powell, 1828, *Report from Select Committee on the Laws Relating to Irish and Scotch Vagrants,* V. IV, pp. 7–10.

82. PP, 1827, *Evidence of the Select Committee on Emigration,* p. 334.

83. Ibid., p. 444.

84. *Poor Inquiry,* p. 9.

85. Crotty, *Irish Agriculture,* p. 38.

86. *1841 Census,* p. viii. These percentages depend upon the accuracy of the censuses of 1821, 1831, and 1841. The Commissioner believed that 1821 underestimated the population and 1831, which was taken at different times and in different places, probably overestimated the population somewhat. Carney believes that 1831 may have been a more accurate census than it has been considered. F. J. Carney, "Some Notes on the Pre-Famine Population of Ireland", (December 1974), University College, Dublin.

87. See Brendan Walsh, "A Perspective on Irish Population Patterns," *Eire Ireland,* vol. 4, no. 3 (Autumn, 1969), p. 7; and Walsh, "Marriage Rates and Population Pressures: Ireland 1871 to 1911", *Economic History Review,* 2d ser., 23, 1970. He says that trends established in Ireland before the Famine were intensified by the Famine experience and that no new trends were established in the 1840s. See also J. Joseph Lee, "Marriage and Population in Pre-Famine Ireland," *Economic History Review,* 2d ser. vol. 21 (1968), p. 295.

88. Bourke, *Visitation,* p. 33–36.

89. As quoted in Bourke, *Visitation,* p. 36.

90. *Poor Report,* p. 12.

91. Bourke, *Visitation,* p. 38.

92. Mayhew, *London Poor,* Vol. 3, (New York, 1855, reprint 1928). He says that every summer Irish laborers came for work as lumpers from Ireland in the Cork boats. They constituted upwards of a third of the entire work force during the summer months, which was the peak of the seasonal lumber import trade. pp. 288–92.

93. Bourke, *Visitation,* p. 64.

94. The importance of the tenantry as voters had been enhanced in the political sphere as early as 1768 when the Octennial Act of that year made parliamentary elections more frequent and regular, thus making tenants a source of votes, which in turn encouraged landlords to increase the numbers of their tenants. By act of 1778, Catholics were first permitted to take long leases on land, and in 1783 freeholders with land worth forty shillings a year were given the franchise. In this period landlords had to weigh the votes of their tenants, both Catholic and Protestant, against their profits. Later the political worth of a numerous tenantry was reduced when, in 1829, electoral reforms abolished the forty shilling freeholder vote eliminating 78,000 voters from the rolls.

95. *Poor Report,* App. C, p. 480. See also K. H. Connell, "The Colonisation of Waste Land", *Economic History Review,* 2d ser., vol. 3.

96. *1841 Census.*

97. As a result of many of these changes Ireland became the prototype of what would later be called in India a gigantic system of outdoor relief for the younger sons of the upper classes. Ambitious young persons who wished to make a reputation in the government came to Ireland. Persons such as the future prime minister of Britain, Robert Peel, (the Irish always called him "Orange Peel") came early in the century to assume the office of chief secretary for Ireland. As his biographer, Norman Gash has observed, "His lifework was to fashion a viable compromise between the system he inherited and the pressing necessities of the changing world in which he found himself." Norman Gash, *Mr. Secretary Peel* (Cambridge: University Press, 1961), p. 13. Primary among the achievements of his tenure was that he applied his middle-class principles of political economy to develop an outstanding police force. See Galen Broeker, *Rural Disorder and Police Reform in Ireland, 1812–26* (London: Routledge & Kegan Paul, 1970). Ireland was the laboratory in which social improvements were attempted which would be later transferred to Britain. It was also where the defeat of ambitious schemes broke many reputations in that century as Britain was forced to take the blame for Ireland's difficulties.

98. *Second Report . . . on . . . System of Railways for Ireland,* p. 9.

99. Thomas Carlyle, *Chartism* (Boston, 1840), p. 29.

100. See *Devon Report (Occupation of Land in Ireland)* 4 vols., For the testimony of Michael Sullivan see the *Devon Digest,* J. P. Kennedy, (ed.), *Digest of Evidence on the Occupation of Land in Ireland.* (London, 1848), pp. 488–90.

101. Witnesses at such hearings often testified that they had to borrow clothes from friends in order to appear. Others said that it was customary for persons to share clothes to wear to mass.

102. J. C. Curwen, *Observations on the State of Ireland,* vol. 1 (London, 1818), p. 203. While the propensity to migrate permanently from Donegal was lower than that of the rest of Ulster (2.98 versus 4.7), persons lived as potential migrants, prepared for the possibility of departure if opportunities narrowed.

103. Cullen, *Economic History,* p. 111–12.

104. Otway, *Tour,* p. 356.

105. H. D. Inglis, *A Tour Through Ireland in the Spring, Summer and Autumn of 1834,* 2d ed., vol. 1 (London, 1835), p. 86.

106. Rev James Hall, *Tour Through Ireland,* vol. 1 (London, 1813), p. 276.

107. William Forbes Adams, *Ireland and Irish Emigration to the New World from 1815 to the Famine* (New Haven, 1932), p. 35. As Bourke says, "they were below the law and the propertied above it." Bourke, *Visitation,* p. 145.

108. PP. 1843, vol. 51. "Accounts and Papers, Ireland", pp. 1–3. The return is a report of the valuations (the valuation was strictly that of the value of the land and any buildings on it) for every union in Ireland, drawn up by the Poor Law Commissioner's Office, Somerset House, by the Secretary, Edwin Chadwick. It was the first attempt of its kind, being drawn up in the fifth year of the establishment of a poor law in Ireland. I can find no previous scholarly utilization of this report by which to judge its accuracy, although Connell uses the next valuation report (1848) to arrive at some measures of fragmentation of holdings. (Population of Ireland, pp. 164–65.) His valuation figures are sufficiently similar to those of the earlier report that I believe that it can be used with some confidence. In addition, valuation correlates well with the incidence of first class housing.

109. The value of assets per capita were derived by dividing the figures for assessment by county by those for population by county, e.g., the total assessment for Dublin with a

population of 372,700 was 1,219,526. The per capita value then was 3.27. (See Table 2.3, columns 1, 4 and 6.) A previous attempt was made to arrive at per capita valuation figures by dividing total assessment by numbers of ratepayers (column 4 divided by column 2) which produced what appear to be inaccurate numbers of persons per ratepayer (which I would take to be some approximation of a measure of household size); e.g., Dublin numbers of persons per ratepayer was 8.29; Leitrim was 5.30; Cork was 12.88; Monaghan was 5.81; and Donegal was 15.42 which is unlike Connell's estimates of persons per house. (His estimates were as follows: 1821, 5.95; 1831, 6.2; and 1841, 5.9 persons per house.) Ibid., p. 25; *1841 Census*, p. xiii.

110. The source from which Figures 2.2 and 2.3 are derived is the result of data collected by the Poor Inquiry Commissioners. As such it is the best source of consistent information on wages and days worked per year. I have used the information with caution, finding its greatest usefulness in providing an aggregate picture of the conditions of the country, rather than individual regions.

111. Agrarian unrest is the general term applied to the frequently violent secret societies which erupted in the late eighteenth and early nineteenth centuries to form a "standing army of the disaffected." Their aim and determination was to extract justice from landlords for their exactions from the peasants. One landlord called them "midnight legislators." Broeker classified the organizations into three categories: agrarian societies, religious societies, and local faction fighters. See Galen Broeker, *Rural Disorder and Police Reform in Ireland, 1812–36* (London, 1970); see also T. Desmond Williams, *Secret Societies*.

112. In the *1821 Census*, Mayo was one of only six counties, apart from Ulster, in which there were more people returned as being engaged in manufacture, trade, or handicraft than in agriculture. See also Almquist for a study of the decline of domestic industry in Co. Mayo.

113. Old myths underscore the differences between Ulster and the rest of Ireland: the Tain bo Cuailgne, the national epic of Ireland, tells of the fierce animosity which caused Ulster and Connacht to wage war against each other.

114. See E.R.R. Green, *The Lagan Valley: A Local History of the Industrial Revolution* (London, 1949).

115. A town was classified according to the census as any place having more than twenty houses. In Britain in 1851, more than half the population lived in towns, "a situation that had probably not existed before, in a great country, at any time in the world's history." J. H. Clapham, *An Economic History of Modern Britain* (Cambridge, 1926), p. 536.

116. *1841 Census*, p. xiviii.

117. See R. B. McDowell, "Dublin and Belfast—A Comparison," in *Social Life in Ireland 1800–45*, ed., R. B. McDowell (Cork, 1963), pp. 11–24.

118. *1841 Census*, p. xiviii.

119. Cullen, "The Irish Economy in the Eighteenth Century," in *The Formation of the Irish Economy*, L. M. Cullen, ed (Cork, Mercier Press, 1968), p. 21.

120. Cullen, *Economic History*, p. 97–98. Cullen says that this fear was not unrealistic; as indicated, there had been an outflow of capital, and skilled labor from Britain had followed the investment capital. This would be the pattern of industrial development in the north later in the nineteenth century, when the original shipbuilding labor force was brought from Clydeside and Tyneside in the 1850s. Andrew Boyd, *The Rise of Irish Trade Unions, 1729–1920* (Tralee, 1972), p. 97.

121. Cullen, *Economic History*, pp. 95–99.

122. Thomas Newenham, *A View of the Natural, Political, and Commercial Circumstances of Ireland* (London, 1809).

123. This view became more widespread in the pre-independence period of the late 19th and early 20th century. O'Brien's economic history of the period attributes Ireland's economic misfortunes after the Union to the malevolence of English policy. His histories were, however, being written during the politically active period between 1915 and 1928, when Ireland was acutely aware of breaking the English tie, and are thus influenced by the struggle for independence. George O'Brien, *The Economic History of Ireland from the Union to the Famine* (London, 1921), and O'Brien, *The Economic History of Ireland in the Eighteenth Century* (Dublin and London, 1918).

124. Cullen, *Economic History,* pp. 100–103.

125. Maureen Wall, "Catholics in Economic Life", in *The Formation of the Irish Economy,* ed., L. M. Cullen, pp. 37–51.

126. Ibid., p. 48. Daniel O'Connell was a good example of this change of direction; of a Catholic family who had made their money in smuggling, he chose to become a lawyer and was called to the bar in 1798.

127. Clearly the brewing and distilling trades had not yet received the very temporary shock of Fr. Mathew's total abstinence campaign of the 1830s and 1840s.

128. J. M. Goldstrom, "The Industrialization of the North-East", in *The Formation of the Irish Economy,* pp. 101–12. In England the cotton industry gradually declined in areas such as Derbyshire which had been cradles of the industrial revolution in cotton. Cullen, *Economic History,* p. 107.

129. Ibid., pp. 7–8. Cullen says that as industries were already in decline, the removal of tariffs was not solely responsible for difficulties. The poor quality of Irish manufactures and Irish yarns put them at a disadvantage, which was made worse when English manufacturers "dumped" unsold goods at ruinous prices on the Irish market. The Drummond Report indicated that there had been considerable diminution of trade from 1822 at which time there had been 45 manufacturers in or about Dublin with an annual volume output of about 200,000 lbs—now said to have fallen to about 90,000 lbs. It was the opinion of the Commissioners that the former protective duties had paralyzed the Irish woolen industry by restraining healthy competition.

130. PROI, HO Series, *Cloncurry to Peel, 1 Sept. 1826,* cited in Fergus D'Arcy, "Dublin Artisan Activity, Opinion and Organisation, 1820–1850", (MA thesis, National University of Ireland, University College, Dublin, 1968), p. 27.

131. *Freeman's Journal* (28 April 1826), cited in D'Arcy, "Artisan," p. 30. Wages were reduced from approximately 25–30 shillings a week to 12 shillings a week according to the Journal.

132. H. D. Inglis, *Tour 1834,* p. 15.

133. For comparison, the current population density of Java is 80,000 persons per square mile.

134. C. Gill, *The Rise of the Linen Industry* (Oxford, 1925).

135. W.M. Thackery, *The Irish Sketch Book* (London, 1869).

136. D'Arcy, "Artisans," p. 142. By 1800, D'Arcy says, most of the city's 25 guilds were no longer concerned with the affairs of the trades they catered for. D'Arcy says that the objective of Irish trade union activity which grew out of these combinations was less economic and more directed toward the maintenance of their independence and an entire system of order. Ibid., p. 133. Initially, when religious feeling against Catholics was still strong, no guild admitted Roman Catholic merchants or craftsmen, but economic expedience later decreed their gradual entry into economic life. See Wall, *Irish Economy,* pp. 37–51.

137. See Maurice O'Connell, "Class Conflict in a Pre-Industrial Society, Dublin in 1780", *Duquesne Review,* vol. 9, no.1 (Fall 1963). Also, O'Connell, *Irish Politics and*

Social Conflict in the Age of the American Revolution (Philadelphia, 1965). Dublin combinations were sufficiently militant that those who refused to join them were said to be in danger of their lives. PP 1838, *Report on Combinations of Workmen,* p. 18. Skilled workmen reported that they sometimes actually preferred to emigrate to England and take lower wages there than to suffer the tyranny of their combinations at home. Constantia Maxwell, *Dublin Under the Georges* (London, 1940), pp. 213–215.

138. *Report on Combinations,* p. 5. Evidence of James Fagan. Another shipmaster, testifying that laborers demanded at least a third more than their counterpart in England, said that where the average price for labor in England was 2 pounds per ton, in Ireland it was 4 pounds per ton. Ibid., p. 35. A parliamentary commission on union activity reported in 1838 that it was the custom for Dublin masters to increase their profits by training more apprentices than there were entry level positions available. If this was widely practiced, then it resembles a factor which caused the apprenticeship system in London to come to an end, according to M. Dorothy George, *London Life in the 18th Century* (New York, 1965).

139. Cited in Maxwell, *Dublin Under the Georges,* p. 233.

140. Workmen who formed combinations to peg their wages at high level may not have been wholly responsible for inflexible wage levels in Dublin industries. The Dublin Society succeeded in having passed a bill called the Spitalfields Act in 1780 which fixed Dublin weavers' wages at the same rate as those in London. Maxwell, *Dublin Under Georges,* p. 236. By doing so they removed the right of bargaining in a trade particularly subject to fluctuations, thus contributing unwittingly further to difficulties in that industry.

141. *Poor Inquiry,* vol. XXX, App. C, p. 19A. The numbers of those returning themselves as paupers who left Dublin for elsewhere is fairly low (0.64 percent of total migrants) which may indicate that once there, paupers may not have found incentives to leave. The mean for all Ireland was 1.11 percent; the lowest number of migrant paupers was to be found in County Down (0.13 percent) and the highest number of migrant paupers was in Mayo (3.26 percent) (calculated from the *Census,* pp. 448–449).

142. David LaTouche was a Huguenot who first came to Ireland as an officer in the army of William of Orange. Beginning as a manufacturer of silk and poplin, he later founded what became the most important Dublin bank.

143. Maxwell, *Dublin Under the Georges,* p. 245.

144. J. R. Harris and M. Todaro, "Migration, Unemployment, and Development: A Two-Sector Analysis", *American Economic Review* (March, 1971).

145. Frank Thistlethwaite, "Migration from Europe Overseas in the Nineteenth Century and Twentieth Centuries," *Congrès Internationale des Sciences Historiques,* ed. Rapports (1960) pp. 42–43.

146. Lynch and Vaizey, *Guinness's Brewery;* George O'Brien, *The Economic History of Ireland from the Union to the Famine* (London, 1921).

147. J. J. Lee, "The Dual Economy in Ireland, 1800–50," in *Historical Studies,* T. Desmond Williams, (ed.) (Dublin, 1971), pp. 191–201.

148. C. Ó'Gráda, "Rationality, Supply Response, and Dualism in Nineteenth-Century Irish Agriculture," in "Post Famine Adjustment: Essays in Nineteenth-Century Irish Economic History (Ph.D. diss., Columbia University, 1973), p. 44.

149. PP., *Report of the Commission for the Relief of the Distressed Districts in Ireland* (London, 1823), p. 74.

150. Connell, *Population,* p. 84.

151. See Evans, *Irish Folk Ways,* p. 33.

152. F.H.A. Aalen, "Transhumance in the Wicklow Mountains", *Ulster Folklife,* vol. 10 (1964), pp. 65–72.

153. See Edward MacLysaght, *The Surnames of Ireland* (Dublin, 1973), p. xv.

154. See T. W. Freeman, *Pre-Famine Ireland, A Study in Historical Geography* (Manchester, 1957) p. 168.

155. See "Introduction" by Ruth-Ann M. Harris in *The Search for Missing Friends, Irish Immigrant Advertisements Placed in the Boston Pilot, vol I, 1831–1850,* by R. A. Harris and D. M. Jacobs, eds. (Boston, The New England Historic Genealogical Society, 1989); and *The Search for Missing Friends, Irish Immigrant Advertisements Placed in the Boston Pilot, vol. II, 1851–1853,* by R. A. Harris and B. E. O'Keeffe, eds. (Boston, The New England Historic Genealogical Society, 1991). In volume III further analysis of migration patterns to North America shows the steady increase in the proportion of migrants from Munster. Prior to 1839 Munster's share was 44 percent of those in the sample; from 1840–45 it was 47 percent; during the Famine years it was 49 percent; and rose to 56 percent between 1851 and 1857. Although prior to 1850 emigrants from Cork had dominated, the trend overall was for Cork's share to decline over time (from 22 percent; to 19 percent; to 16 percent; and lastly, 17 percent). While the proportions of emigrants from Cork declined, those from the remaining five counties of the province increased. Of these, emigrants from Kerry predominated; Kerry's share was 4 percent prior to 1838, rose to 7 percent between 1840 and 45, then to 9 percent from 1846 to 50, and to 14 percent between 1851 and 1857. See Table 8: County of Origin by Date of Emigration in the "Introduction" by Ruth-Ann M. Harris in *The Search for Missing Friends, Irish Immigrant Advertisements Placed in the Boston Pilot, vol. III, 1854–56,* R. A. Harris and B. E. O'Keefffe, eds. (Boston, The New England Historic Genealogical Society, 1993), p. ix.

156. Details of the occupational groupings are provided in the Appendix to this chapter.

157. Freeman, *Pre-Famine Ireland,* pp. 173–74.

158. Hall, *Tour,* p. 13.

159. This was computed by adding together the last three columns of Table 2.12.

160. *Poor Inquiry,* Supplement to App. X, p. 14.

161. Inglis, *Tour,* p. 84.

162. *Comparative Abstract of the Population of Ireland, 1821 and 1831* (Jan. 30, 1833), pp. 21 and 29.

163. Ibid.; Freeman, *Pre-Famine Ireland,* p. 213.

164. App. A (Supplement).

165. J. H. Johnson, "Harvest Migration from Nineteenth Century Ireland," *Transactions of the Institute of British Geographers,* 41 (June, 1967) pp. 97–112; Ann O'Dowd, *Spalpeens and Tattie Howkers, History and Folklore of the Irish Migratory Agricultural Worker in Ireland and Britain.* (Dublin: Irish Academic Press, 1991), pp. 15–26.

166. Begging was a primarily female occupation. Irish women begging in London testified that pride kept their husbands from begging, but expected their wives to beg. Pride also kept them from begging alms in their home neighborhoods. Revans, the Poor Law Commissioner, said that Irish women always begged elsewhere than their home districts. ("Westminster Review," p. 193) Parenthetically, it is of interest to note what they begged for and where they begged. The evidence is consistent that women and children begged, not for coin, but for potatoes. (The old begged tobacco in addition to potatoes as it was said that they had become accustomed to it in their youth and had become addicted; and their children, upon whom they were now dependent, were so poverty-stricken as to be unable to buy tobacco for them.) It was said that beggars never applied to the houses of the gentry for assistance, but sought it from their own kind. (The gentry were said to have such a fear of disease that they always refused beggars at the door.) Testimony has it that the only class which gave charity were those with ten acres or less, never the more prosperous. It is important to remember that Ireland had never experienced the post-Reformation

rationalization of the distribution of charity as described by Davis. (Natalie Zemon Davis, "Poor Relief, Humanism, and Heresy: The Case of Lyon," *Studies in Medieval and Renaissance History,* vol. 5, (1968, pp. 217–40.) For attitudes in England see David Owen, *English Philanthropy, 1660–1960* (Cambridge, 1964). In Ireland there was a persistence of the belief that charitable giving blessed the giver as much as the receiver (the twentieth century version of this is that the poor give charity in recognition that they too may some day need it). One person who gave regularly said that he considered 150–200 persons a day normal; another in England said that five per day was normal for there.

167. PP. *Commission on Irish and Scotch Vagrants, 1828,* pp. 9–10.

168. Wm. Carleton, "Phelim O'Toole's Courtship", in *Phelim O'Toole and Other Stories,* Maurice Harmon (ed), (Cork, 1973), p. 1. A spalpeen was the generic term for an itinerant laborer and was, by the twentieth century, used as a term of contempt like *amadan* (fool). The degeneration of the word may have had to do with the fact that by the mid-nineteenth century the term was applied to itinerant potato diggers who were on a lower social scale than harvesters. (See Ms 1480, I.F.C., p. 69.) Corkery uses the term spailpin (spalpeen) in the broader 18th-century sense of any wanderer. Corkery, *Hidden Ireland.*

169. *Poor Inquiry,* Supp. to App. C, p. 3.

170. J. M. Synge, *The Works of John M. Synge,* vol. 4 (Dublin, 1910), p. 203.

171. Ibid, p. 209.

172. Calculated from the *1851 Census,* p. xxxix.

3. The Demand for Labor in England

1. *Report on the State of the Irish Poor in Great Britain.* H.C. 1836 (40), p. 1. Hereafter called *Report.*

2. Ibid., *Report,* Evidence of Mr. Whitty, p. 21.

3. David Landes, *The Unbound Prometheus* (Cambridge, 1969), p. 41.

4. Henry Mayhew, *London Labour and the London Poor,* vol. 1 (New York, 1968) pp. 203–4.

5. Raphael Samuel, "Workshop of the World," *History Workshop,* no.3 (Spring 1977), p. 17.

6. The *London Illustrated News* for the years immediately preceding 1851 has the best coverage of the technology of the architecture, as well as the historical development of the idea of the Exhibition.

7. Defoe, "Giving Alms No Charity and Employing The Poor," in *A Collection of Pamphlets Concerning the Poor* (London, 1704), pp. 83–85. Smelser notes that "the eighteenth was a century of browbeating the poor over lack of discipline, immorality, theft, drunkenness, holiday-keeping, etc. In certain respects this was unjustified . . . Inasmuch as critics blamed poverty and industrial inefficiency on the poor, they were expressing misplaced aggression because the system of production was outmoded." Neil J. Smelser, *Social Change in the Industrial Revolution* (Chicago, 1959), p. 80.

8. The Luddites were early nineteenth-century British workers who destroyed labor saving machinery as a protest.

9. Samuel, "Workshop," p. 9.

10. Edward Baines, *History of the Cotton Manufacture of Great Britain* (London, 1835), p. 361.

11. Ibid., p. 362.

12. Samuel, "Workshop," p. 24. Much of the work was done by contract. Growers

needing labor in addition to that of their families employed the poor people of the locality; or for larger jobs would engage labor contractors or itinerant laborers. Irish laborers were employed at the pea-picking at Stokes Poges, Buckinghamshire.

13. Patrick MacGill, *Children of the Dead End* (Kerry, 1982). For a sociological analysis of MacGill's writings, see "Patrick MacGill, The Making of a Writer," by Patrick O'Sullivan in *Ireland's Histories, Aspects of State, Society and Ideology,* S. Hutton and P. Stewart, eds. (London, 1991), pp. 203–322.

14. J. H. Clapham, *An Economic History of Modern Britain* (Cambridge, 1926), pp. 140–42.

15. As quoted in David Morgan, "The Place of Harvesters in 19th Century Village Life," in *Village Life and Labour,* ed. Raphael Samuel (London, 1975), p. 62.

16. Ibid.; Anon., *Stubble Farm,* pp. 209–11, cited in Morgan.

17. R. H. Tawney, *The Agrarian Problem in the Sixteenth Century* (New York, 1912, 1967), p. 104–6.

18. See J. D. Chambers, "Enclosure and Labour Supply in the Industrial Revolution," *The Economic History Review,* 2d Ser., vol. V, No. 3, 1953, pp. 326–27 for a discussion of the effect of enclosure on the landless or semilandless workers who he said were "the real victims of enclosure . . . [For them] enclosure was the last act in the drama of proletarianisation."

19. E. J. Hobsbawm and George Rude, *Captain Swing* (New York, 1968), p. 35.

20. Karl Polanyi considered this Speenhamland System of poor relief as occupying a strategic position in retarding the development of a mobile industrial labor force. Karl Polanyi, *The Great Transformation* (New York, 1944), pp. 77–78. Criticism of this thesis has demonstrated that what was called the Speenhamland system was by no means as widespread in England as he suggested and that it was only occasionally extended to manufacturing districts. Adam Smith believed that the intransigence of the laboring population was due to the operation of the settlement laws, but Eden, a contemporary, differed, saying that the effect of settlement laws in tying laborers to their parishes was much exaggerated. "Increasing wages has always got the man," he said (as quoted in Arthur Redford, *Labor Migration in England, 1800–1850* (Manchester, 1926, 1964) p. 70). Truth undoubtedly lay somewhere between the two extremes and was a mixture of many factors. See Sidney and Beatrice Webb, *English Poor Law History,* (London & New York: Longmans, Green & Co., 1927–29), pt. 1, p. 423 for a discussion of the Speenhamland System. First introduced in Speenhamland, Berkshire, in 1795, at a time of great distress in that county, it provided for a wage subsidy based upon the price of bread. The Webbs say that the situation which faced the government in 1795 forced a choice between regulating the conditions of employment, as had the medieval guilds, or subsidizing employers out of public funds so as to enable industries to be carried on as they were, yet permitting workers to live. Part of the popularity of the Speenhamland system was that it also amounted to a subsidy for the farmer who now had no incentive to raise wages to obtain more or better workers; while for the worker there was no incentive to be productive as the rewards were the same for hard worker as for indolent pauper. While Speenhamland protected the worker from the dangers of the market system, at the same time the agricultural laborer was becoming a rural proletariat and perpetuating that system. The Hammonds say that "The Poor Law which had once been the hospital had now become the prison of the poor. Designed to relieve his necessities, it was now his bondage." J. L. and Barbara Hammond, *The Village Labourer 1760–1832,* vol. 1 (New York, 1911, 1967), p. 166.

21. Clapham, *Economic History,* p. 54. Even while Thomas Malthus was campaigning against the poor law he charged that the Speenhamland system encouraged families to breed recklessly. However Clapham says that the rate of population growth was nearly the

same in Scotland, where there was no Speenhamland system, and may have been even greater in Ireland where there was no poor law at all.

22. Bill Jordan, *Paupers, The Making of a New Claiming Class* (London, 1973), p. 21. J. D. Marshall sees the period between 1815 and 1822 as producing marked changes in attitudes toward the poor on the part of the gentry class. Good harvests lowered wheat prices to half the wartime level and when combined with high expenditures on poor rates, hardened attitudes toward poverty. In the aftermath of the French Wars the pauper was seen as a potential Jacobin, lurking around corners to threaten the serenity of the upper classes. All of this was in spite of the fact that less than twenty percent of those on poor relief were able bodied adults (a total of two percent of the total population). Seventy percent of those on poor relief were unable to work, being children (50%) or aged (15–20%). J. D. Marshall, "The Old Poor Law, 1795–1834," *Studies in Economic History*, ed., M. W. Flinn, (London, 1968).

23. *Report,* testimony of Mr. Guest, cotton manufacturer, p. xxviii.

24. Ibid., p. xxvii.

25. *Report,* p. xxvii.

26. John Saville, *Rural Depopulation in England and Wales, 1851–1951* (London, 1957), p. 38.

27. That is, the local parish was taxed to clear out the indigent by sending them either to areas where work was available, or to the colonies.

28. PP. IV, *Reports from Committees, Emigration from the United Kingdom, 1826,* p. 114.

29. *Report,* App. B, no. 11, p. 187.

30. Redford, *Labour Migration,* pp. 90–95.

31. As quoted in Redford, *Labour Migration,* p. 174.

32. P.P. 1880, XIV, *Factory Inspector's Report for 1879,* p. 54.

33. David Morgan, "The Crowded Fields," in *Village Life,* p. 29.

34. Mayhew, *London Poor,* vol. 2, p. 308.

35. Ibid., p. 311.

36. E. P. Thompson sees this pattern persisting among some self-employed persons such as skilled artisans, artists, writers or students, where discipline is spurred by the need to produce, which provokes the question of whether or not this may be closer to a "natural" work rhythm. See E. P. Thompson, "Time, Work Discipline, and Industrial Capitalism," *Past and Present,* no. 38 (Dec. 1967), pp. 56–97.

37. Ibid.

38. Said by an old potter, "When I was a Child," as quoted in Thompson, "Time".

39. Redford, *Labour Migration,* p. 20; See also Michael Anderson, *Family Structure in Nineteenth Century Lancashire* (Cambridge, 1971), p. 114–15; and Smelser, *Social Change,* p. 200, corroborate that this practice existed. It was common in Lancashire for such persons to employ kin and children as their assistants. In Preston in 1816, 54 percent of the children under eighteen employed in the thirteen mills of that town were employed in this fashion; and 59 percent of those in the surrounding countryside. Anderson believes that Smelser underestimates the importance of this type of recruitment because adolescent weavers became weavers in their own right much sooner than did spinners who usually had to wait until their twenties, which thus gave the proportion of children employed by masters and by operatives a bias in favor of spinners. (Anderson, p. 216, n.19).

40. S. J. Checkland, *The Rise of Industrial Society in England* (New York, 1964), pp. 219–20.

41. Ibid.

42. Anderson, *Family Structure,* p. 29. More than one-quarter of the males in the

thirty-to-forty-year age group which he studied left factory work. This was fewer than the popular image of what was believed to be a common trend but it is nevertheless significant. The workers cited as their reasons for leaving the loss of dexterity or failing eyesight; management cited that character disorders were responsible for employees being discharged. However, in a study of fourteen workers in this age group who left, only six went into lower paying occupations, one took a clerical job and four became self-employed tradesmen.

43. Flora Thompson, *Lark Rise to Candleford* (London, 1939, 1971).

44. Ibid., pp. 21–22.

45. Ibid., p. 63. The widespread consumption of potatoes contrasts with reports from the early nineteenth century when English workingmen refused to eat potatoes because of the connotation with the Irish workingman.

46. Ibid., pp. 28–29. Thompson says that these women prided themselves on the fact that they did not have to work as wage laborers on farms, as many of their mothers and grandmothers had been forced to do previously.

47. Ibid., p. 25.

48. Ibid. In Ireland, where he was referred with respect as the Gentleman Boarder, the pig had the same function. Among English brickmakers in Hertfordshire who kept pigs for protection against winter distress, the pig was known as "Brickies" Bank. (R. Samuel, "Mineral Workers" in *Miners, Quarrymen and Saltworkers,* ed., R. Samuel (London, 1977), p. 5.

49. This was particularly true of the young people, faced with the end of school and the need to find a job.

50. The author was in a position to know about this as she eventually became a postmistress. In contrast, the communication system developed by Irish migrants was an important factor in their willingness to take risks. This is another example of the strength of the Irish traditional system of mutual aid.

51. *Report,* p. xxvii.

52. Charles Booth, *Life and Labour of the People in London* (London, 1892), and B.Seebohm Rowntree, *Poverty, a Study of Town Life* (London, 1901).

53. Anderson, *Family Structure,* p. 29–30; J. O. Foster, "Capitalism and Class Consciousness in Earlier 19th Century Oldham" (Ph.D. diss., University of Cambridge, 1967). Foster also estimated that only about one in seven of all families located in Oldham were ever free from the threat of poverty.

54. Foster, "Capitalism," pp. 31 and 201.

55. *1841 Census of Ireland.*

56. Where eighteenth-century observers had pictured the British workers as in need of improvement and early nineteenth-century observers pictured them as reluctant, by mid-century the picture was very different. By 1860, Mechanics Magazine said, "There is no doubt whatever than the people of England work harder, mentally and physically, than the people of any other country on the face of the earth. Whether we take the town or the country population, the same plodding industry is apparent, and the respites enjoyed by either in the shape of holidays are few and far between." (*Mechanics Magazine,* III, April 1860.) G.D.H. Cole said that what had intervened was that workers had accustomed themselves to industrialization. After 1848, with the exception of a few remaining pockets of rural stagnation, the worker was no longer a peasant at heart, looking back over his shoulder at a way of life that had vanished. (G.D.H. Cole, *A Short History of the British Working Class Movement, 1789–1937* (London, 1925, 1937), p. 11. Following 1841, he says, workers were no longer intent on destroying the capitalist system, but organized their forces through trades unions and cooperative societies. There was also a growing labor surplus in agriculture and an increasing concern for efficient husbandry at the end of the

18th century, all of which must have tightened the screw for those in regular employment, forcing them into more regular habits of industry. A labor surplus was often noted by such as Mayhew. Proponents of child labor were explicit about the socializing influence of early and regular work habits which aided in the eventual production of a disciplined labor force.

"There is considerable use in their being, somehow or other, constantly employed at least twelve hours a day, whether they earn their living or not; for by these means, we hope that the rising generation will be so habituated to constant employment that it would at length prove agreeable and entertaining to them." (*Mechanics Mag.,* April 1860.)

57. *Report,* p. xxxv.

58. See M. C. Buer, *Health, Wealth & Population in the Early Days of the Industrial Revolution* (London, 1926).

59. Redford, *Labour Migration,* p. 12.

60. D. Mazumdar, "Labour Supply in Early Industrialization: The Case of the Bombay Textile Industry," *Economic History Review,* no. 3 (Aug. 1973), pp. 480–82.

61. Ibid., p. 481.

62. Ibid., pp. 481–82. In the spinning sector of Bombay, the number of spindles tended by each operative in 1927 was only 180; in Japan, it was 240; in England it was from 540 to 600; and in the United States, 1,120, which is an indication of the relative low labor intensity of the Bombay factories.

63. Cited in Redford, *Labour Migration,* pp. 22–23. In order to attract a settled labor force various attempts were made by some employers to retain their workers by varying jobs within the factory. Within the factory workers were shifted around as needed to reduce the boredom of monotony. Where factories were a part of a country estate employers found outdoor labor to keep them occupied in slack times. Agricultural workers whose work pattern had been to labor in domestic occupations in slack times were more attracted by factory work when the monotony was relieved by transfers from one job within the factory to another.

64. There existed some reluctance on the part of the settled population to enter factory life which was said to be partly due to visible resemblances between factories and the dreaded workhouse. And since residence in the workhouse also entailed inhabitants working on public works projects, anything faintly resembling these was loathed and resisted. In addition, as much of the early labor supply was recruited from children who had grown up in the workhouse, confusion between the two, and a resistance to working in factories, is understandable.

65. Mayhew, *London Poor,* vol. 2, p. 300. He estimated that only one-third of the London's labor force was fully employed; another one-third was partially employed; and that another third was unemployed throughout the year. (Thus, two-thirds of the labor force was essentially casual labor.) I have seen no studies that attempted to analyze whether he was correct in his estimates, but Samuel has studied the kinds of labor which the casual labor force undertook. In Raphael Samuel, "Comers and Goers," in *The Victorian City,* eds. H. J. Dyos and Michael Wolf (London, 1973), pp. 123–60.

66. Mayhew, *London Poor,* vol. 2, 300. A cautionary note regarding Mayhew's conclusions should be noted: his experience was primarily with highly urbanized London whose industries and labor force were unrepresentative of the whole economy.

67. Ibid., p. 297.

68. Quoted in Samuel, "Comers," p. 132. These workers went to the brickfields in summer.

69. "The Irish in England," *Labour News,* 28 March 1874.

70. Samuel, "Workshop," p. 137. Most London women in casual labor went hop-

picking in Kent during the harvest season. See Orwell's novel of hop-pickers. (George Orwell, *A Clergyman's Daughter* (London, 1935).

71. As quoted in Samuel, "Workshop," p. 147; Williams, *The Liverpool Docks Problem* (Liverpool, 1912), p. 42.

72. Rowland T. Bertoff, *British Immigrants in Industrial America* (Cambridge, 1953), pp. 82–83. In Britain, wages were considerably lower than in the United States, but work was conducted throughout the year, in contrast to the situation in America where the severe winters curtailed work.

73. Mayhew, *London Poor,* vol. 1, 104 and vol. 3, p. 413.

74. Samuel, "Workshop," p. 134.

75. Mayhew, *London Poor,* vol. 2, pp. 297–300.

76. E. J. Hobsbawm, "The Tramping Artisan," *Economic History Review,* 2d ser., vol. 3, no. 3 (1951), pp. 299–320.

77. The definition of an industrial occupation is based on that of Anderson, which includes all of those based in trades geographically separate from the home where some form of manufacture takes place and in which employers claim to employ ten or more persons.

78. A total of 17 percent of males and 38 percent of females in the work force, twenty years of age and over, were engaged in the manufacture of cotton, according to the 1851 Census; a further 5 percent and 6 percent, respectively, were employed in the various processing industries (especially printing and dyeing) and in worsteds and silk. There was also a small but significant engineering, metals and textile machinery industry, which employed a further 3 percent of adult males. (These percentages are drawn from Anderson's calculations.) Factory work, then, was the basis of Lancashire's prosperity, even though at any one time it employed a minority of the total labor force. Anderson's estimates indicate that approximately 7 percent of the total labor force were laborers of some kind, obtaining only casual and irregular employment and earnings at a maximum some fifteen shillings per week. The remainder, which was about half the population, were engaged in trading or artisan occupations, many of them providing services of some kind or another to the cotton trade. Most of the population of the area, then, depended directly or indirectly upon the cotton industry which provided a fairly wide range of employment opportunities.

79. W. E. H. Lecky, *History of Ireland in the Eighteenth Century,* vol. 2 (London, 1913).

80. Raymond Crotty, *Irish Agriculture,* p. 18.

81. Baines, *Cotton,* p. 87.

82. John Aiken, *A Description of the Country from Thirty to Forty Miles Round Manchester* (London, 1795), p. 23.

85. Baines, *Cotton,* p. 337

84. John Burnett, *A History of the Cost of Living* (Harmondsworth, 1969), p. 165.

83. Baines, *Cotton,* p. 339

86. While agriculture declined in importance relative to the gains to be made from industry it is apparent that farming continued in the area because accounts describe the factory workers clearing out to work on the farms at harvesttime.

87. As quoted in Baines, *Cotton,* p. 90.

88. Ibid., p. 92.

89. Ibid., p. 100.

90. Ibid., p. 108.

91. Ibid., p. 160.

92. Ibid., p. 107.

93. See H. B. Rodgers, "The Lancashire Cotton Industry in 1840," *Transactions of the Institute of British Geographers,* no. 28 (1960).

94. Baines, *Cotton,* p. 218.

95. Buer, *Health,* p. 107.

96. As quoted in Steven Marcus, *Engels, Manchester and the Working Class* (New York: Random House, 1974), p. 234.

4. Irish Migrants in England: The Reserve Army

1. Géaroid O'Tuathaigh, *Ireland before the Famine, 1798–1848, The Gill History of Ireland,* no. 9. (Dublin, 1972) pp. 203–7.

2. NIPRO, T2345/2.

3. W. J. Lowe, "The Irish in Lancashire, 1846–71, A Social History," (Ph.D. diss. University of Dublin, Trinity College, 1974).

4. A hundred was a Norman unit of measurement, one hundred spade lengths long by sixty to eighty feet wide.

5. Lowe, "Lancashire," p. 55.

6. See David W. Miller, "Irish Catholicism and the Great Famine," *Journal of Social History,* vol. 9 (1975–6), pp. 81–98. See also Emmet Larkin, "The Devotional Revolution in Ireland, 1850–75," in the *American Historical Review,* vol. 17, no. 3 (June 1972), p. 636.

7. As cited in Barbara Kerr, *Irish Immigration into Great Britain, 1798–1835,* B. Litt. thesis (Oxford, 1954), p. 51.

8. *1841 Census of Ireland,* 1843, p. x.

9. Ibid., p. xxv–xxvi. These totals still underrepresented the total amounts because, as the census takers indicate, they did not enumerate persons taking passage on steam vessels. Evidence from harvest migrants themselves indicate that while more expensive, they preferred steam passage as the voyage was shorter thereby allowing them to conserve on supplies for the trip.

10. Approximately 8,500 persons remained for a longer period of time.

11. As a result of narrowing opportunities for women and thus a diminished role within the family economy, Irish daughters were more expendable within their families than were sons; thus women had fewer reasons to return at the end of the season. This is assuming that the majority of female migrants, having fewer ties, were also more likely to be single. Married migrants testified to the fact that they did not take their wives with them because they could earn more at home from begging. Irish women who have migrated to Britain in the twentieth century are also less likely to return than are males. See, Mary Lennon, Marie McAdam, Joanne O'Brien, *Across the Water, Irish Women's Lives in Britain,* (London, 1988).

12. Ibid.; *1841 Census,* p. xxvi. The census takers were unable to count the numbers of those who returned because, "on their return to Ireland they land in such haste, that all attempts to count them were abandoned. We had not the power of counting them on embarkation at English ports, and the returns of the Steam Packet Companies are not complete." The enumerators assumed, however, that 40,000 of the total 57,651 returned, which is consistent with the figures arrived at by other means.

13. *1841 Census,* p. xxvii.

14. Ibid., p. 14.

15. Ibid., Appendix, p. lxxxvii.

16. Ibid., p. lxxxix. Middlesex, which contained London, had 58,068 Irish persons

resident, 13.9 percent of total, which was the next largest Irish community after that of Lancashire, then Leeds (5,027 Irish persons), and Birmingham (4,683 Irish persons). William Lowe sought a more accurate measurement of total numbers of the Irish in England in order to account for the English-born children of Irish persons. Taking a 100 percent sample of Irish households in the small Merseyside town of Widnes he also enumerated all Irish persons living in non-Irish households in the three census years, 1851, 1861, and 1871. Using the complete information available for the town of Widnes a factor was derived which was then applied to the Irish community of the other six towns included in the study. He found that in 1851 at least 100 non Irish-born Irish were among an Irish-born population of 250. The minimum Irish community in Widnes in 1851 was 350, a factor 1.4 percent larger than the 250 Irish-born reported. Applying this test of multiplying by 1.4 to the 1841 population would increase the total number of persons from 419,256 to 586,958. (This figure is only 62,888 larger than the estimate arrived at by the census commissioners when they attempted to calculate the numbers of children of Irish persons.)

17. See Chapter Three for a description of the range of seasonal employment available in the port of Liverpool.

18. The contrast between the two cities is illustrated by the responses to questions regarding whether or not it would be desirable to put an end to the migration from Ireland. Of the thirteen informants from Liverpool, six gave an outright yes and a seventh said that there would be definite benefits in some areas. When the same question was put to ten Manchester respondents, only three said that the immigration was undesirable, and these were public authorities who in dealing with issues of public relief or crime were thus more likely to be affected by Irish problems.

19. M. D. R. Leys, *Catholics in England, A Social History, 1559–1829* (London, 1961), p. 172.

20. The numbers of these was probably very small because Arthur Young observed at the end of the eighteenth century that the Catholic Irish were unwilling to leave their parishes. Irish labor was considered largely inconsequential. Was this so because Irish persons did not settle, but drifted in and out, accommodating the tempo of their work to the availability of employment? There is a notable lack of first-hand accounts either by migrants or about them. Little notice was taken of them because of their high mobility and there is an ambivalence about the Irish in official records; they are never called immigrants.

21. Arthur Redford, *Labour Migration in England, 1800–1850* (Manchester, 1926, 1964) pp. 33–34.

22. Dorothy George, *England in Transition* (London, 1931, 1969).

23. Redford, *Labour*, p. 33.

24. PP., *Reports, Handloom Weavers*, 1840, p. 657.

25. *Report*, p. 74, Evidence.

26. Henry Mayhew, *London Labour and the London Poor*, vol. 1 (New York, 1968) p. 460. Chapter Two refers to problems within trades in Dublin, where workmen had become extremely militant in protecting the conditions of their work. Despite the existence of Combination Laws (against trade union activity) in Ireland, their enforcement was lax. Irish workers complained that their wage standards were depressed because employers took on too many apprentices. Dorothy George notes this tendency became common in 18th century England when profits could be made from the fees, a factor in the eventual decline of the system. In Ireland, where enforcement laws against Dublin trade union activity was desultory, apprentices who were barred from employment, either by militancy or lack of it, always had the outlet of migration to England; thus there was fewer disincentive for masters to reduce the number of apprentices being trained. George, *England*.

27. Mayhew, *London Labour*, vol. 2, p. 316.

28. *Report,* pp. 68–69. Evidence of James Taylor. His testimony supported other evidence of a fluid work force. It is apparent that he had only the most casual knowledge of the way in which his workers found their way to his factory, or what they did when they left his employment, as frequently happened. His remarks point to a plentiful work force with high mobility.

29. ibid., as quoted in Kerr, *Poor Rates the Panacea for Ireland,* p. 59.

30. Redford, *Labour* p. 36.

31. *Reports of Handloom Weavers,* 1839, pp. 602–7.

32. *Report,* Evidence, p. 17.

33. Raphael Samuel, "Workshop of the World; Steam Power and Hand Technology in Mid-Victorian Britain," *History Workshop,* issue 3 (Spring 1977), p. 127.

34. *First Report from the Commissioners on the Condition of the Poorer Classes in Ireland,* App. A, July 1835. p. 232; App. C., p. 187.

35. Ibid., App. C, p. 46.

36. Ibid.

37. Mangan typescript memoirs, NIPRO, T3258.

38. Mayhew, *London Labour,* vol. 4, p. 103. "The effective arrival of the self-actor during the thirties seems to have driven wages down," Clapham, *Economic History,* p. 551.

39. As the date followed immediately after the Famine one can assume was representative of the only worst years of distress in the pre-Famine period.

40. Mayhew said that the docks were always a good entry level occupation for persons with no friends or kin to get them on their first job. "The London Dock is one of the few places in the metropolis where men can get employment without either character or recommendation, so that the labourers employed there are naturally a most incongruous assembly." *London Labour,* vol. 3, (p. 301.)

41. Ibid., p. 413.

42. *Report,* p. vi., evidence of Dr. Kay of Manchester.

43. Mayhew, *London Labour,* vol. 1, p. 115.

44. Ibid., p. 460.

45. *Report,* p. ii.

46. *Reports from Commissioners,* vol. 5, p xxx; *Poor Laws* (Ireland) 1836, 1st Report, Supplement to App. F. p. 153. No assistence, however, was said to be given to those going to North America, pp. 172,200.

47. *Report on Emigration,* Scotland, 1841, p. 36.

48. *Poor Law Report,* App. A, p. 357.

49. William Carleton, *Traits and Stories of the Irish Peasantry* (London, 1875).

50. *Report,* p. 11, Evidence.

51. While it is difficult to know just what "lack of commitment" meant, it is most likely that they did not remain in his employ. Similar accusations regarding the present-day Irish in Britain bear out that it is a long-standing pattern of behavior. As such it is representative of persons who consider themselves temporary residents.

52. Donall MacAmhlaigh, *An Irish Navvy, The Diary of an Exile* (London, 1964), p ix.

53. Ibid., p. vii.

54. Ibid., p. 85.

55. MacAmhlaigh noted that Irish farmers and laborers made their terms for jobs much as they always have—meeting with an employer in the local pub.

56. MacAmhlaigh, *An Irish Navvy,* p. 137.

57. Mayhew, *London Labour,* vol. 3, p. 375.

58. Ibid., p. 164.

59. J. H. Johnson, "Harvest Migration from Nineteenth-Century Ireland," *Transactions of the Institute of British Geographers* no. 41 (June, 1967), p. 97.

60. The master of the Dublin Steamship and Packet Company said that he carried 200–500 migrants per vessel at five pence per head for deck passengers. They left in May or June, after their crops were planted. He estimated that in the seven years ending in 1833, that he had carried a total of 200,096 persons. PP, *Report from the Select Committee on Irish and Scotch Vagrants,* 1838, p. 10.

61. This figure is a vast underestimate as it was so difficult to count returning migrants. See footnote 12.

62. *Report on Emigration from the United Kingdom,* 1827, p. 336.

63. Previous studies of Irish migration which have focused primarily upon one side or the other have missed the adjustments which the migrants made in correlating seasonal cycles between the two areas. Johnson's study of nineteenth-century harvest migration states that "agricultural work was still their main source of employment." He believed that this was why very few Irish laborers were employed as navvies. Johnson, "Harvest Migration." While it is true that few Irish did become navvies, it is because English laborers were determinedly effective in excluding them from that employment.

64. Migrants testified that they paid the higher fare by steamship because the passage was shorter, thus enabling them to conserve on supplies. Sending remittances was costly, so that seasonal migrants tended either to carry the money or appoint one person of their party as banker.

65. Mayhew, *London Labour,* vol. 2, p. 299.

66. *Inquiry,* App. A (Supplement), p. 172. While it is difficult to document specific groups of migrants, there were exceptions. One was that of a regular migration of masons and stonecutters to Britain, from Little Island off the west coast of County Cork. Although it was impossible to ascertain whether or not this migration was seasonal, it seems unlikely, as it was reported that they sent back remittances to support their families at home.

67. Redford, *Labour,* p. 117.

68. J. H. Clapham, *An Economic History of Modern Britain* (Cambridge, 1926), p. 552–55.

69. Edward Baines, *Cotton,* p. 491.

70. Ibid., p. 492.

71. Ibid., p. 500.

72. *Report,* p. xxxv.

73. Clapham, *Economic History,* p. 552.

74. See Duncan Bythell, "The Handloom Weavers in the English Cotton Industry During the Industrial Revolution: Some Problems," *Economic History Review,* 2d ser., vol. 18, no. 1 (1964), pp. 339–553. Also, Bythell, *The Handloom Weavers* (Cambridge, 1969).

75. Handley provides an unusual measure of weavers' wages, which serves to explain Irish ability to underlive their competitors, when he says that weavers' wages between 1797 and 1804 would buy one hundred pounds of flour; the same amount would buy 142 pounds of oatmeal, 826 pounds of potatoes, and 55 pounds of butcher meat. Decreases in weavers' incomes are illustrated by the fact that between 1804 and 1811 the 826 pounds of potatoes fell to 238 pounds; between 1811 and 1818 this fell again to 131 pounds; between 1818 and 1825 this fell to 198 pounds; and between 1825 and 1834 it reached a low of 83 pounds. J. H. Handley, *The Irish in Scotland* (Cork, 1943), p. 275.

76. As the weaving trade declined, there was, as Clapham has noted, a growing tendency for weavers to send their children into the factories. At the same time, Neil

Smelser says, spinners responded to increases in their wages by withdrawing their children from factory employment. Neil J.Smelser, *Social Change in the Industrial Revolution* (Chicago, 1959) p. 199.

There is some evidence to suggest that the Irish were less reluctant than other groups to let their children work. If so, they were doing no more than any other immigrant group does in order to ensure the family's survival. Oscar Handlin says that Irish parents in Boston sometimes kept their children home from school to work to support the family. Oscar Handlin, *Boston's Immigrants* (New York, 1969). "Putting the children on work" was also a carryover of rural custom where the family worked as an economic unit. This is not to imply that the Irish were lacking in affection for their children; indeed it was often noted that they treated their children much more affectionately than did the English.

77. George, *England,* pp. 113, 120.

78. Bythell, *Handloom Weavers,* p. 229.

79. Contemporary investigators generally assumed that opportunities for Irish employment were largely the result of their role as strike breakers or wage undercutters. This belief is borne out by the silk mill owners' testimony, who recruited Irish in a deliberate attempt to keep his English labor force in line.

80. *Report,* pp. 68–69.

81. Ibid., p. 141. Evidence of Charles Scott, shipbuilder of Greenock, Scotland.

82. Ibid., p. xxxvii.

83. Ibid., p. 64. Evidence of Mr. Potter of Manchester.

84. Ibid., p. vii.

85. Ibid., App. B, pp. 185–87.

86. For a study of John Doherty's career, see R.G.Kirby and A.E. Musson, *The Voice of the People, John Doherty, 1798–1854, Trade Unionist, Radical and Factory Reformer* (Manchester, 1975). See also John Boyle, ed., *Leaders and Workers* (Cork, 1966).

87. For a discussion of the controversy regarding the Irish and political activity, see D. Thompson, "Ireland and the Irish in English Radicalism before 1850," in J. Epstein and D. Thompson, eds., *The Chartist Experience* (London, 1982); J. H. Treble, "O'Connor, O'Connell and the Attitudes of Irish Immigrants towards Chartism in the North of England, 1838–48," in J. Butt and I. F. Clarke, eds., *The Victorians and Social Protest* (Newton Abbot, 1973); John Belchem, "English Working-Class Radicalism and the Irish, 1815–50," in Roger Swift and Sheridan Gilley, eds., *The Irish in the Victorian City* (London, 1985), pp. 85–97; R. A. M. Harris, "The Failure of Irish Republicanism among Irish Migrants in England," *Eire-Ireland* (Winter, 1986); and R.O'Higgins, "The Irish Influence in the Chartist Movement," *Past and Present,* no.20 (1981), pp. 83–94.

88. *Report,* p. v.

89. An Irish priest said, "Our population is a rather floating one, following the up and down . . . of industry." Op. cit., quoted in Samuel, *Miners,* p. 125. Denvir noted that the Irish were the first to settle when there were opportunities and the first to leave when there was a depression. John Denvir, *The Life Story of an Old Rebel* (Dublin, 1910) p. 411. David Fitzpatrick has said that this was also true of the Irish in America who were more sensitive than other ethnic groups to regional economic disparities. While they might be restricted to the worst jobs, nevertheless they clustered in areas where employment was expanding. "In effect, they occupied the worst seats in the best theatres." D. Fitzpatrick, *Irish Emigration, Studies in Irish Economic and Social History,* 1. (Dundalgan, 1984), p. 34.

90. *Irish Poor,* App. C, pp. 355–473.

91. D. Mazumdar, "Labour Supply in Early Industrialization: the Case of the Bombay Textile Industry." *Economic History Review,* no. 3 (August, 1973), p. 489.

92. Until the 1840s the working hours in factories gave neither clerks nor operatives much leisure. In 1850 the Ten Hours Act was amended to create a working day with Saturday afternoon free. J. H. Clapham & M. H. Clapham, "Life in the New Towns," in G.M. Young, *Early Victorian England, Portrait of an Age* (London, 1936, 1971).

93. Irish persons were more likely to resort to begging, than their English counter-parts, combining it with trading or other street activities. (See Chapter Two for a discussion of reasons why begging was more tolerated in Ireland than in England.) If one accepts the concept of stages of modernity, the English were simply further advanced in capitalistic attitudes. Daniel Defoe's descriptions of early eighteenth-century England indicate that begging was common in the earlier period. It may have been the way in which the Irish begged which drew attention. The English begged for a targeted goal (e.g., to get to London), whereas it was more a way of life for the Irish. Note the following from an informant of Mayhew, an experienced tramper, "who apparently had a good education and had seen better days . . . 'The low Irish do better in London. They are the best beggars we have. They have more impudence and more blarney and therefore they do much better than we can at it. . . . The Irish tramp lives solely by begging.'" Ibid., pp. 399–402. In Mayhew's study of vagrants (Bk. 3, pp. 368–429) every street person claimed to have begged at various times.

94. Lowe, *Lancashire,* p. 152.

95. Mayhew, *London Labour,* vol. 1, p. 105.

96. Lynn Lees says that Irish women and children in London were forced onto the labor market to tide families over seasonal unemployment. Lynn H. Lees, *Exiles of Erin, Irish Migrants in Victorian London* (Ithaca: Cornell Univ. Press, 1979). This is consistent with what is known of all working class behavior.

97. See Raphael Samuel, "Mineral Workers" in *Miners, Quarrymen and Saltworkers,* Raphael Samuel, ed. (London, 1977), p. 5.

98. Ibid., p. 152. Samuel has said that the casual wandering trades are all but impossible to document systematically. With that in mind, he was cautious and never attempted to estimate numbers of persons or even their proportions to the total popula-tion.

99. Brian Lewis, *Coal Mining in the 18th and 19th Century* (London, 1971).

100. *Report.* Evidence of Mr. Dixon, p. 114.

101. This is in remarkable contrast to the immigrant Irish in North America who monopolized the early railroad and canal building. Undoubtedly, it is a case of those first to secure jobs thereafter monopolizing the field.

102. *Census of Ireland,* 1841 The report drew attention to the fact that since there were in total about 45,000 laborers in the railway industry, their places were "no doubt extensively filled by Irish labourers." (p. x) Thus Irish workers were substituting for indige-nous labor, which in turn, permitted English workers to rise into relatively higher-paid employment.

103. Redford, *Labour,* p. 141.

104. Ibid., p. 68. Evidence of Mr. Holmes.

105. Some thought that chronic underemployment in Ireland gave young persons the opportunity to develop their strength, in contrast to English children who were inured to hard work from such an early age that they were often unhealthy, their bodies exhibiting stunted growth. Some Irish did arrive in a depleted condition. Speaking of Irish laborers resident in Wigtonshire, a Scotsman said that often upon arrival there was "a want of physical strength in them, on account of the insufficiency of their food in Ireland. When they have been here some time, they are better fed, and become good workmen." Ibid., p. xii.

106. PP, *Reports from Commissioners, Status of Large Towns and Populous Districts,* vol. P. XVII, 1844, p. xv.

107. Handley, *Irish Scotland,* p. 139.

108. Mayhew, *London Labour,* vol. 1, p. 104.

109. Ibid., p. 104. This would suggest that Irish persons with some skills were more likely to resort to such occupations when trade was poor. Mayhew says that he believed that Irish persons who became costermongers belonged to "a better class than Irish laborers." This may demonstrate that agricultural migrants were less likely to become permanent migrants. He estimated that of approximately 30,000 street sellers in London, seven out of twenty were Irish, and three-quarters of these sold only fruit and nuts. Fruit sellers were primarily women and children, while men dealt mostly in fish and vegetables.

110. Denvir, *Life Story,* p. 401.

111. PP, 1893, XXXV, *Royal Commission of Labour, The Agricultural Labourer,* cited in Samuel, *Miners,* p. 133.

112. Mayhew, *London Labour,* vol. 2, 299.

113. Mayhew, vol. 3, p. 414. It is clear that while this husband did not fear hard work, he did fear the loss of status associated with the necessity of begging.

114. Gareth Stedman Jones, *Outcast London, A Study in the Relationship Between Classes in Victorian Society* (Oxford, 1971), p. 95–98. When casual laborers married their standard of living declined with each child, while each extra child increased the need for wives to work.

115. Lowe, *Lancashire,* p. 602.

116. St. Helens and Widnes had only recently become industrialized regions, thus the demand for unskilled labor attracting Irish persons would also be fairly recent.

117. Lowe, *Lancashire,* p. ix. In 1822 the London Mendicity Society adopted a system of employment to utilize the poor in breaking paving stones for the roads at eight pence per ton. Few English persons would accept the job, but the Irish took it cheerfully. The scheme was discontinued when it was discovered from authorities in Cork that it encouraged emigration. When emigration did not cease, the society finally refused to employ new Irish on the jobs. (*Emigration Inquiry,* p. 124.)

118. Ibid., Evidence, p. xv.

119. Daniel Patrick Moynihan would say, as he did of the Irish monopoly and proclivity for politics in the New World, that, having found a good trade, they settled into it and refused to move out. D.P. Moynihan & N. Glazer, *Beyond the Melting Pot* (Cambridge, 1963, 1967).

120. Denvir, *Old Rebel,* p. 50.

121. *Report,* p. 72.

122. Ibid., p. xxix. Testimony of James Muspratt.

123. A Catholic priest who testified that few improved their circumstances by migrating, thought that this was so because they returned before they could prosper. *Report,* p. 23.

124. In contrast, Irish immigrants entering America came to a society sufficiently flexible so as to enable them to make a more distinctive contribution.

125. *Report,* pp. 27–28.

126. Ibid., p. viii; Evidence p. 27.

127. Ibid., Evidence, p. 73.

128. Mayhew, *London Labour,* vol. 1, p. 96. Potatoes, to eat or warm the hands on a cold day were another product which the Irish sold exclusively.

129. Ibid., pp. 196–97. Mayhew noted further that the Irish could underlive the Jews, too, because "they did not, like [them], squander any money for the evening's amusement,

at the concert or the theatre." The Jews were not, however, suffering from their exclusion from the fruit-selling trade. Mayhew found that Jewish orange sellers rarely carried on the trade after the age of twenty-two or three, but that they resorted to a "more wholesome calling" such as the purchase of nuts or foreign grapes at public sales. In addition, those who had formerly sold oranges now sold Bahamas pineapples, and Spanish and Portuguese onions.

130. Alexis de Tocqueville, *Journeys to England and Ireland,* (New Haven, 1958). His stated purpose in visiting Ireland was to discover why the aristocracy, which was in Britain so useful an institution, was in Ireland an instrument of social exploitation.

131. *Poor Inquiry,* p. 111.

132. William Carleton, *Stories,* pp. 344–60.

133. *Report,* Evidence, p. 27.

134. *Report,* p. xvi.

135. *Report,* Evidence, p. 71–72.

136. Ibid., p. 72.

137. R. O'Higgins, "The Irish Influence in the Chartist Movement," *Past and Present,* no. 2, (Nov. 1961), p. 83. She sees the radical activity of the Irish in England springing naturally from the background of Irish society itself with its traditions of organized political opposition to authority.

138. Lowe, *Lancashire,* pp. 507–17.

139. While Lowe contends that only a few Irishmen worked in organizable trades during the early period, the fact of the 750 bricklayers helpers who organized themselves into a club would tend in part to refute this.

140. Mayhew, *London Labour,* vol. 1, p. 106.

141. Ibid., p. 460.

142. *Report,* pp. xvii.

143. Larkin, "Devotional," p. 636. See also, S. J. Connolly, "Catholicism and Social Discipline in Pre-Famine Ireland," in Irish Economic and Social History, IV, 1977, pp. 74–76.

144. John Hickey in a paper on the Irish in Cardiff delivered at the American Conference for Irish Studies, Harrisonburg, Virginia, April 1979. Hickey's work deals primarily with the post-Famine period. The numbers of Irish in Wales in the earlier period was said (in conversation) to be inconsiderable.

145. Miller, "Irish Catholicism," pp. 84–87. If so, they shared their lax attitudes toward the exercise of their religious duties with the English. The census of religion in 1851 confirmed that "a sadly formidable portion of the English people" neglected their spiritual duties by non-attendance at church. *Census of Great Britain, 1851: Religious Worship in England and Wales,* H.C., 1852–53, p. clviii.

146. Laborers attending official enquiries in Ireland often told of having to borrow clothes when giving testimony. Irish parents claimed that they kept their children from attending school or Sunday School because they had no shoes or suitable clothing. When the Irish began wearing shoes and clean clothes, observers concluded that it was an indication of their becoming civilized, a clue to the subtle pressures exercised by the authorities on the immigrant community.

147. I am indebted to the late Aiken McClelland for pointing out that one restriction on Catholics remains; the British monarch is still forbidden to marry a Catholic.

148. See Denis Gwynn, "The Irish Immigration," *Cork University Review,* no. 20 (Winter, 1950), pp. 43–47 for a discussion of the attempts of English Catholic families to relieve the Irish poor, and Gwynn, "The Irish Immigration," in *The English Catholics,* ed., G. A. Beck (London, 1950), pp. 265–90.

149. *Report,* p. 2. While such may have been true of some migrants, it could only have been applied to very few. It is good to keep in mind also what a breach of the law could mean at that time; one of Mayhew's informants had left to escape prosecution for "borrowing" a pipeful of tobacco from his employer. In a society where class enmities were increasing, and where the law was unequally and arbitrarily applied, conflict with the law must have been almost unavoidable.

150. Overseas Missionary Correspondence, All Hallowe's College, Dublin, All Hallowe's, Scotland, WDS 2, 21 April 1843; WDS 24.

151. W. J. Lowe, "The Lancashire Irish and the Catholic Church 1846–71: The Social Dimension," *Irish Historical Studies,* vol. 20, no. 78 (Sept. 1976), pp. 132, 136.

152. Lowe, *Lancashire,* p. 278.

153. Thernstrom, in studying the role of the church among the Boston Irish, reached a similar conclusion. He pointed to the dangers which can result from such an inward-looking ethnic group, where it may develop values which are deviant by the standard of the larger society, or, even if they hold the same values, they may not learn socially acceptable methods of pursuing them. Stephan Thernstrom, *The Other Bostonians* (Cambridge, MA, 1973).

154. E. P. Thompson, *The Making of the English Working Class* (London: 1963), pp. 211–12. For a discussion of wage trends see M. W. Flinn, "Trends in Real Wages 1750–1850," *Economic History Review,* XXIV, 1972, pp. 65–80. Also Joel Mokyr, "Industrialization and Poverty in Ireland and the Netherlands," *Journal of Interdisciplinary History,* X:3 (Winter 1980), p. 430–31.

155. A. B. Reach, *Manchester and the Textile Districts in 1849* (Helmshore Local History Society, 1972). Cited by Lowe.

156. Engels, *English Working Class* (Stanford, 1958), p. 70.

157. *1841 Census of Ireland,* pp. xiv–xvii.

158. For an excellent discussion of the crowded rural Irish landscape, see Oliver MacDonagh, "Irish Emigration to the United States of America and the British Colonies During the Famine," in R. Dudley Edwards and T. Desmond Williams, eds., *The Great Famine: Studies in Irish History 1845–52* (New York, 1957), pp. 383–84.

159. Mayhew, *London Labour,* vol. 1, pp. 465–66.

160. Engels, *Working Class,* p. 124.

161. Mayhew, *London Labour,* vol. 2, 110.

162. Lees, *Exiles of Erin.*

163. Oscar Lewis, *La Vida* (New York, 1965); Michael Piore, *Birds of Passage: Migrant Labor in Industrial Societies* (Cambridge & New York: Cambridge University Press, 1979). If the movement of the migrants was as fluid and transitory as other factors would suggest, then the least possible expenditure on shelter would be desirable. Piore's studies of Latin American migrants working temporarily in the United States indicate that they will seek housing which places the fewest constraints on their movements. In one case, twenty men leased three rooms with eight beds on which they slept in shifts, eating tinned unheated food, working two and occasionally three jobs. (pp. 16–17 of Chap. 3)

Stephan Thernstrom's research on nineteenth-century Boston describes a similar pattern of mobility among newcomers to that city. A crucial characteristic of American urban life was precisely the same pattern of brevity of stay, where "poor people in particular were highly transient leaving a single faint imprint on the census schedule or the city directory files and then vanishing completely." (Thernstrom, *Other Bostonians,* p. 41) Lowe found that names in the census changed almost completely from one decade to the next.

164. Lowe, *Lancashire,* pp. 73, 96.

165. Michael Anderson, *Family Structure in 19th Century Lancashire* (Cambridge, 1971), p. 48.

166. Courts were the vacant areas between and behind houses. Dwellings built in courts were considerably less expensive than were those which faced onto a street. This was also true of the Boston Irish whose addresses often indicated this. (Evidence from *Boston Pilot* "Missing Friends" personals column)

167. Engels' material would suggest that the area was an Irish ghetto before the Famine period.

168. Engels, *Working Class,* p. 65.

169. As cited in Lowe, p. 78, from Farrer and Brownhill, eds., *The Victoria History of the County of Lancaster,* p. 322. In 1851, 12.8 percent of the Irish community were living in courts as compared with 7.6 percent for the general population; Ibid., p. 77.

170. *Report,* p. 56. Evidence of Mr. Robertson, surgeon to the Lying-in Hospital, Manchester.

171. Lowe, *Lancashire,* p. 80.

172. This is not to suggest that no such solidarity existed, but it was, as Anderson suggests, more likely a clustering on the basis of kinship. Anderson, *Family,* pp. 59–62. Irish persons were unlikely to be much more gregarious outside the immediate confines of their family or village in England than they had been in Ireland. However, the experience of migration eventually produced ethnic solidarity.

173. Employers noted that they did not dare employ laborers from areas which were known to be antagonistic. Ireland has experienced only minimal inter-regional migration followed by settlement. The result was that the country consisted of many regions with differing customs and traditions. This, together with the fierce animosities encouraged by ethnic and religious differences, retarded the development of Irish nationalism. It is significant, however, that almost every Irish nationalist of the late nineteenth century had some experience of living abroad.

174. *1841 Census,* p.c. Of the 67,609 total families in England, only 3,503 conformed to the traditional family where husband, wife, and children were present; 24,180 (or about 40 percent) of families were reported as having the head of household either unknown or absent (as 12 percent of these kept servants, it can be assumed that this was a measure of some degree of prosperity, p. xli).

175. Lowe, *Lancashire,* p. 98. The table from which this data was compiled, separated street and court housing, whereas prior data combined them.

176. This issue was raised by Hickey, *Irish in Cardiff.*

177. Lowe, *Lancashire,* p. 86.

178. Ibid., p. 92. While it is true that this was primarily a way to supplement incomes, it also supports the view that a population intending to be transient is more likely to seek temporary housing.

179. *Report,* p. xxiii.

180. We have seen already that Irish women gravitated to towns and cities within Ireland, often working as domestics. In Lancashire, unmarried Irish women were generally unwelcome as domestics because of an already adequate supply of native English. Irishwomen also lacked requisite domestic skills. Fewer Irish households had servants, too, which may indicate use of extended family members to fulfill that function. Lowe, *Lancashire,* p. 93.

181. *Report,* p. xx.

182. Lowe, *Lancashire,* p. 84.

183. *1841 Census,* p. xxv. Of those, by far the largest number were resident in Dublin (one-quarter of the total); Cork and Limerick had the next largest number; and of those born in Scotland, the largest number were resident in Londonderry and Belfast, p. xxiv.

184. The trend to send children back to Ireland for their education may have changed by mid-century as, in 1851, Lowe found that 52 percent of the members of Irish nuclear

families in his Widnes sample had been born in England, (Lowe, p. 114). This figure would also seem to have been the result of relatively permanent settlement on the part of the Lancashire Irish.

185. Ivy Pinchbeck, *Women Workers and the Industrial Revolution* (London, 1969), p. 313. Also, Angus McLaren notes that "Class fertility trends in the 19th century revealed that the families of textile workers—in particular those of Lancashire where the wages of women working outside the home could be high—were conspicuously small . . . the number of children born to each one hundred wives of textile families was until 1881–1886 in fact lower than the rate for every other class except that of the unskilled professionals and businessmen, and was declining." Angus McLaren, "Women's Work and Regulation of Family Size," in *History Workshop,* no. 4 (Autumn 1977), p. 70.

186. The work of Laslett has suggested the predominance of a nuclear family pattern in pre-industrial England. T. P. R. Laslett, *The World We Have Lost,* (London, 1965) and "Mean Household Size in England Since the Sixteenth Century," *Population Studies,* vol. 23, pp. 199–223. Few households contained two parents and their married children, which was the minimum to have been considered extended family. Census data can, of course, be misleading, as it often concealed what may be short term co-residence at critical life periods, such as after marriage or in infirm old age. Also, if death and reproduction rates are high, there may be young families and few old people to reside with the stem family. The result from both the preceding may be a reduction in the propensity of households to contain additional married kin even though co-residence may be important at critical periods in the lives of the population. Even allowing for these factors, co-residence in pre-industrial England was rare. As the 1851 Census reiterates, the goal and national ideal was single family residence, and a considerable proportion of people achieved this.

187. Engels, *Working Class,* pp. 164–65.

188. Anderson, *Family,* pp. 124–25. See also J. A. Banks, "The Contagion of Numbers," in *The Victorian City,* vol. 1, eds., H. J. Dyos and M. Wolff (London, 1973), p. 114.

189. Charles Booth, *Life and Labour of the People in London* (London, 1892) vol. 4, p. 43.

190. Edwin H. Sutherland, *Criminology,* (Philadelphia, 1924), pp. 145–48.

191. John J. Tobias, *Crime and Industrial Society in the Nineteenth Century* (London, 1967), pp. 244–47. Tobias poses the question as to what explanations there may be for why so many of these young criminals made good after transportation to the colonies. Perennial labor shortages in places such as Australia offered abundant employment for such persons. In noting that there was "abundant testimony that the worst juvenile criminals were Irish cockneys" (p. 169), he departs from his otherwise valid argument. See also Gareth Stedman Jones, *Outcast London* (Oxford, 1971).

192. E. C. Banfield, *The Moral Basis of a Backward Society* (New York, 1958).

193. The *1841 Census* reported that 35 percent of all houses in Ireland consisted of only one room.

194. *Poor Inquiry, 1835,* p. 229. Daughters did not conform to this pattern of settlement, as many went to towns and cities in Ireland as servants, a further indication that opportunities were shrinking and family members were looking for alternatives.

195. Ibid., p. 240. It would appear that kinship ties in England were remarkably meagre in the late eighteenth and early nineteenth centuries. There is evidence of a degree of callousness when persons bargained with the poor law authorities for payment for their care of sick and elderly relatives. Certainly such attitudes would have been unthinkable in London's Bethnal Green district in the early 1950s, where Young and Willmott found that the care of the old was exclusive of the availability of available support funds. M. Young and P. Willmott, *Family and Kinship in East London* (London, 1957). The existence of the

poor law, in the earlier period in providing an alternative to the greatest hardships of rural life, may have fostered and encouraged calculating attitudes on the part of those who bargained over the care of their aged.

Anderson's study of family in 19th-century Lancashire demonstrates the changes which industrialization brought about in the kinship structure. He concludes that the working classes have come something like full circle from the pre-industrial kinship structure, then weakened because problems were so great and resources so small, through a functional (functional because of a pooling of resources between kin to overcome uncertainty) traditional kinship system, to a situation where kinship is once again weakened because problems are reduced, resources increased and there are ready alternatives open to all. Anderson, *Family,* p. 179.

196. *Report,* p. x. Evidence of Rev. Mr. Glover, Roman Catholic priest of Liverpool, and of Mr. Macdonald, Roman Catholic Priest of Birmingham.

197. Ibid., p. xi. Evidence of Mr. Aaron Lees, cotton manufacturer of Manchester.

198. Piore, "Birds of Passage," chap. 3, p. 8. See also Piore, "Undocumented Workers and U.S. Immigration Policy," paper prepared for the U.S. Commission on Civil Rights, National Council on Employment Policy, September 1977.

199. Mayhew, *London Labour,* vol. 1, p. 115. Mayhew believed Irish costermongers more provident than were the English; they bought themselves their own vehicles much sooner than did English costermongers.

"A quick-witted Irishman will begin to ponder on his paying 1s.6d. a week for the hire of a barrow worth 20s., and he will save and hoard until a pound is at his command to purchase one himself. While an obtuse English coster (who will yet buy cheaper than an Irishman) will probably pride himself on his cleverness in having got the charge for this barrow reduced, in the third year of its hire, to 1s. a week twelvemonth round." (p. 115)

200. PP., *Report from Select Committee on Internment of Bodies in Towns, 1842,* vol. 10, p. 64.

201. Daniel Defoe, *Giving Alms No Charity* (1704), p. 25–27, quoted in *Report,* p. x–xi.

202. *Report,* p. xxii. The informants could not have known English eating habits very well when the *Report* stated that "In England the working classes in the towns are accustomed to eat meat, if not every day, at least on most days of the week. In Scotland the custom of eating meat has only been introduced within the last ten or twenty years among the working classes, especially in the agricultural districts; nor has it hitherto become near so general as in England, or supplanted the oatmeal porridge which forms the chief food of the Scottish labourers." (p. xii.) Neither Booth's nor Rowntree's budgets of the eating customs of the poor included outlays for meat in the diet. Mayhew said that the Irish diet was the cheapest, estimating that a person could live on less than three shillings per week in 1850 if living on potatoes. Mayhew, I, p. 123.

203. *Report,* p. xii. Contemporary studies of rural Russia and rural South Africa indicate that where transport costs are high, farmers preferred to convert surplus grain into spirits. In nineteenth century Russia landowners either sold the grain alcohol to their peasants or paid it in lieu of wages owed.

204. *Report,* p. 4. Evidence of George Redfern, prison keeper of Birmingham. In the eighteenth century it had been a common custom for wages to be paid in the public house. By the nineteenth century this practice was less common, although the habit of stopping by for a drink (or more) on payday persisted.

205. Ibid., pp. xxiii, 77.

206. *1841 Census,* p. xxvi. The singular thrift and foresight which has so frequently been remarked as characterizing these people is curiously illustrated by this table (showing

the numbers of persons migrating from each port during the census year) in which it will be seen that no less than 12,256 Connacht laborers embarked at Drogheda, and only 8,308 at Dublin. This unusual circumstance is attributed to a small reduction in the fare from Drogheda, a few weeks before the season commenced, which reduction was industriously made known in all the towns though which the stream of labourers was likely to pass in its progress from the west.

207. *Report on Vagrants,* p. 2. Rumors regarding Irish indigence are more likely to be related to the general hardening of attitudes toward the redundant poor which increased in intensity in the 1820s and 1830s, bringing demands for poor law reforms in the latter decade. Some evidence would indicate that some parishes were so anxious to rid themselves of paupers that they passed back to Ireland persons who had been resident in England for as long as twenty years (and were thus entitled to legal settlement). ibid., p. 117. English counties were not the only ones who wished to rid themselves of the indigent poor. The Mendicity Institute in Dublin reported that it had returned 2,130 persons back to England between 1824 and 1833. This would indicate that there may have been considerable numbers of English who had been attracted by opportunities for employment in Ireland, but when the bad time of the 1820s and 1830s intervened, they had fallen into poverty (*Poor Inquiry,* vol. 30, App. C., p. 19a).

208. Ibid., pp. 9–10. Evidence of Jerard Edward Strickland.

209. Ibid., p. 14. Again, there is some evidence to indicate that this happened only during years when their wages in Britain were less than anticipated. One informant from Bristol, a resident of Cork, estimated that about forty out of a hundred persons applied for passage back to Ireland.

210. Ibid., p. 10. Evidence of Samuel Perry, agent for the City of Dublin Steam Packet, was that each vessel could carry 500–700 persons "principally in harvest hire" at anywhere from one shilling to five shillings per head. The regular charge was five shillings, but competition could reduce it to as low as sixpence. His count of the number of deck passengers for recent years which, if representative of total migratory flows, would bear out that much of the migration was circular, was as follows:

	To Dublin	From Dublin
1 Feb. 1830 to 1 Feb. 1831	31,794	31,454
1 Feb. 1831 to 1 Feb. 1832	32,596	39,788
1 Feb. 1832 to 1 Feb. 1833	21,829	20,618
TOTAL	81,219	98,618
Total no. of deckers in 7 years, ending 1 Feb. 1833	200,096	188,988

211. *1828, Report from Select Committee on the Laws Relating to Irish and Scotch Vagrants, 7 July 1828,* vol. 4, pp. 8–9. For the convenience of their tenants some large landowners established a system whereby migrants could transmit their earnings direct to Ireland through the offices of an agent at no cost to themselves. Lord Dillon, who had estates in Roscommon and Mayo, was said to have begun the system around 1803. Sums deposited with his agent had increased from £160 in 1815 to a high of £1,316 in 1825.

212. *Report,* p. 10.

213. *Vagrant,* p. 16.

214. *Report,* p. 11.

215. E. H. Hunt, "How Mobile was Labour in Nineteenth Century Britain?" in J. H. Porter, ed., *Provincial Labour History,* no. 6, *Exeter Papers in Economic History* (Univer-

sity of Exeter, 1972), p. 30; and Hunt, *Regional Wage Variations in Britain, 1850–1914* (Oxford, 1973).

216. *Report,* p. xxxv. Evidence of Mr. R. Hyde Greg.

217. Ibid., p. xxxvii.

218. B. R. Mitchell and P. Deane, *Abstract of British Historical Statistics* (Cambridge, 1962).

5. Conclusions

1. Mary Lennon, Marie McAdam, Joanne O'Brien, *Across the Water, Irish Women's Lives in Britain* (London, 1988) p. 102.

2. The project to collect data for the *Ordnance Survey Memoirs* was begun in 1836, and it is unfortunate that it was never completed because funding was withdrawn.

3. The advertisements, which ran from 1831 through 1916, are being published in a series of volumes by the New England Historical Genealogical Society of Boston, Massachusetts. See R. A. Harris and D. M. Jacobs, eds. *The Search for Missing Friends: Irish Immigrant Advertisements in the* Boston Pilot, *1831–1850,* vol. 1, (Boston, 1989); R. A. Harris and B. E. O'Keeffe, eds. *The Search for Missing Friends,* 1851–1860, vols. 2, 3 and 4 (Boston, 1991, 1993, 1994); and Harris, "Characteristics of Irish Immigrants in North America derived from the *Boston Pilot* "Missing Friends" Columns, 1831–1850," Northeastern University Working Papers in Irish Studies, January 1988.

4. Assisted emigrants usually left through Liverpool also, but since assisted emigration schemes were relatively rare prior to 1850, this would tend to reduce the numbers of these represented among those sought.

5. Harris and Jacobs, *Missing Friends,* vol. 1, p. 337.

6. Harris and Jacobs, *Missing Friends,* vol. 1, p. 291.

7. Patrick MacGill, *Children of the Dead End* (Kerry, 1982).

8. John Mitchel, *Jail Journal,* foreword and appendices by Arthur Griffith (Ireland, 1913, 1983), 409.

9. *Poor Inquiry,* p. 390. It may be assumed that the news conveyed was sometimes what people wanted to hear. Permanent emigration to North America was generally unpopular in the earlier period, and persons often related stories which they had heard of bad conditions in the New World. In one instance, informants from Ballina, one of the most distressed parishes in Co. Mayo, told an investigating committee that, "It is commonly represented here that people are lying in the streets starving in American towns for want of employment." p. 502.

10. Ibid., p. 357.

11. Damian Hannan, *Rural Exodus* (London: Geoffrey Chapman, 1970), p. 158.

12. Lynn H. Lees and John Modell, "The Irish Countryman Urbanized, a Comparative Perspective on the Famine Migration," *Journal of Urban History,* vol. 3, no. 4 (August 1977), p. 396.

13. John Jackson, "The Irish," in Jackson ed, *London: Aspects of Change,* publication of the Centre for Urban Studies (London: MacGibbon and Kee, 1964)

14. Michael Piore, "Undocumented Workers and U.S. Immigration Policy," Latin American Studies Association (Houston, 1977).

15. Jackson, "The Irish."

16. Hannan, *Exodus.*

17. The concept is that there is a whole cultural pattern typified by unstable and

volatile social arrangements which are reflected in labor market behavior (high turnover, weak attachment to job market, highly personalized relationships with supervisors and subordinates on job); and in personal relationships (unstable unions, female heads of household, matrifocal families, intense but brief friendships with other individuals). See Handlin & Elliott Liebow, *Tally's Corner, a Study of Negro Streetcorner Men* (Boston, 1967).

18. Thernstrom certainly emphasizes this in his study of Irish immigrants in Boston, *The Other Bostonians.*

19. J. O'Connor Power, "The Irish in England," *Westminster Review,* vol. 27 (Jan–June 1880), p. 410.

20. Jackson, "The Irish," p. 302. In industries characterized by employing primarily Irish persons the labor turnover is as high as 18 percent each month; and while most of it is among new labor, many of the men had been with the firms for a long time (p. 229). What is not apparent from what he says is whether low job attachment is the result of poor adjustment or because people are choosing to move on.

21. Conrad M. Arensberg and Solon T. Kimball, *Family and Community in Ireland* (Cambridge: Harvard University Press, 1940, 1968).

22. Hannan, *Exodus,* p. 151.

Bibliography

Government Papers

BRITAIN

Devon Report (Occupation of Land in Ireland). Vol. 1: *Report and Evidence,* Pt. I (1845); Vol. 2: *Evidence,* Pt. II (1845); Vol. 3: *Evidence,* Pt. III (1845); Vol. 4: *Appendix to Evidence,* Pt. IV, Index and Map (Pt. V), (1845)

Digest of Evidence taken before Her Majesty's Commissioners of Inquiry into the State of the Law and Practice in Respect to the Occupation of Land. Part I, II. Dublin: Alexander Thom, 1848.

PP 1822, *Report from the Select Committee on the Linen Trade of Ireland.*

PP 1823, *Report of the Committee for the Relief of the Distressed Districts in Ireland,* 7th May 1822. London: William Phillips.

PP 1823, *Report of the Commission for the Relief of the Distressed Districts of Ireland.* London: William Phillips.

PP 1826, *Reports from Committees, Emigration from the United Kingdom.* Vol. IV, 2 Feb. 31–May 1826.

PP 1826–27, "Emigration from the United Kingdom," 1826–27, *Reports from Committees.* Vol. V, nos. 88, 237, 550.

PP 1828, *Report from the Select Committee on That Part of the Poor Laws Relating to Employment or Relief of Able-bodied Persons from the Poor Rate.* Vol. IV, 29 Jan. 28–July 1828.

PP 1828, *Report from the Select Committee on the Laws Relating to Irish and Scotch Vagrants.* Vol. IV, 7 July 1828.

PP 1833, "Account of the Number of Irish Poor Shipped Under Passes from Liverpool to Ireland." *Irish Poor.* Vol. XXXII.

PP 1833, *Report from the Select Committee on Irish Vagrants.* Vol. CCXXXIV, no. 394.

PP 1834, *Report of Select Committee on Handloom Weavers.* Vol. X, no. 556.

PP 1836, *Reports from Commissioners, Poor Laws (Ireland).* 3rd Report, Vol. XXX, Appendix C.

PP 1836, *Poor Inquiry.* Vol. XXXIV, Appendix 11, Part II.

PP 1836, *Third Report of the Commissioners for Inquiring into the Condition of the Poorer Classes in Ireland.* Vol. XXX, Appendix C, Part I. London: W. Clowes & Sons.

PP 1836, *Poor Inquiry (Ireland).* Vol. XXX, Appendix C, Part II.

PP 1836, "Report on the State of the Irish Poor in Great Britain." *Reports from Committee.* Vol. XXXIV, Appendix G.

PP 1837, *Abstract of the Final Report of Commissioners of Irish Poor Inquiry.* London: F. C. Wesley.

PP 1837–38, *Second Report of the Commissioners Appointed to Consider and Recommend a General System of Railways for Ireland.* HC (145), XXXV, 449. Otherwise known as the Drummond Report.

PP 1838, "Combinations of Workmen." *Reports from Committees.* Vol. VIII.

PP 1842, *Report from the Select Committee on Improvement of the Health of the Towns: Effects of Interment of Bodies in Towns.* 14 June. Vol. X.

PP 1843, "Accounts and Papers," *Ireland, 22 Valuations.* Vol. LI.

PP 1844, *Reports from Commissioners for Inquiring into the State of Large Towns and Populous Districts.* Vol. XVII.

PP 1845, *Second Report of Commissioners for Inquiring into the State of Large Towns and Populous Districts.* Vol. I. London: William Clowes & Sons.

Return of Owners of Land of One Acre and Upwards in the Several Counties in Ireland. Presented to both Houses of Parliament. Dublin: Alexander Thom, 1876.

CANADA

Emigration, Index 1851 (C.O. 714/53). 1850–87. Public Archives of Canada.

Montreal Emigrant Society Passage Book for 1832. RG7, G18, Vol. 45. Public Archives of Canada.

Report for the Season of 1842 by James Allison, Emigrant Agent, Montreal. RG7, G18, Vol. 47.

UNITED STATES

U.S. Characteristics of the Population by Ethnic Origin, Nov. 1969. Series P-20, No. 221, April 30, 1971.

CENSUS

Abstract of the Answers and Returns, Census of Ireland, 1821.

Census of Great Britain, 1851. Population Tables. I. Numbers of Inhabitants Report and Summary Tables. 1852, Vols. I & II.

The Census of Ireland for the Year 1851, Part VI. *General Report.* Dublin: Alexander Thom.

Comparative Abstract of the Population of Ireland, 1821 and 1831. Ordered by the House of Commons to be printed. 19 Feb. 1833.

Report of the Commissioners appointed to take the Census of Ireland for the Year 1841. Dublin: Alexander Thom, 1843.

Statistical Abstracts for the United Kingdom from 1849–1863. 11th, 12th, 13th, 14th number. 1964, 1965, 1966, 1967.

Manuscript Material

IRISH FOLKLORE COMMISSION

Ms. 107   Co. Wexford, "A Hiring Fair"
Ms. 404   "Harvester's Death Reported Incorrectly"
Ms. 642   Co. Clare, "Spalpeen Contractor"
Ms. 1396-8   Rathlin Is., "Migration to the Scotch Harvest"
Ms. 1407   Munster, "Emigration Collection"
Ms. 1408   Leinster, "Emigration Collection"
Ms. 1409   Galway, "Emigration Collection"
Ms. 1410   Erris, Co. Mayo, "Emigration Collection"
Ms. 1411   Co. Donegal, "Emigration Collection"
Ms. 1430   "An American Letter"
Ms. 1457   Co. Longford, "Migrants in England Joining Molly M'Guires"
Ms. 1480   "Spalpini," "Harvest Workers"

Taped interview with 87-year-old silk weaver in Dublin Liberties, 1974.

NATIONAL LIBRARY OF IRELAND

Annual Register, liii (1811). "Irish Labourers in England."
Ms. 4579   Draft Petition on Behalf of Irish Paupers in England in the Early Nineteenth Century.
Ms. 8479   Fr. Hickey Papers.
A Hand-list of Irish Newspapers, 1685–1750. Cambridge Bibliographical Society, Monograph No. 4. London: Bowes & Bowes, 1960.
Larcom Letter and Papers.
Walpole Papers.

PRIVATE COLLECTIONS

Overseas Missionary Correspondence, All Hallowe's College, Dublin
Scotland W.D.S. (1)
    W.D.S. (2)
    W.D.S. (3)
Northampton, NOR (1843–73)
Nottingham, NOR (1851–1877)
Plymouth, PLY (1851–1860)
Wales (1842–1848)
The Emigration Commission, E.C. 1–49 (1858–1860)
Lancashire L.N.C. (1), 5 March 1845
Salford Sal. (7a), 3 March 1853

PUBLIC RECORD OFFICE, DUBLIN

Almanack Registry and Directory
The Treble Almanack, Watson's Almanack, Dublin: C. Hope
Quit Rent Office (QRO) Public Record Office
2B.43.122—Kingwilliamstown
2B.44.1—Kilconcourse, King's Co.
2B.43.127—Crown Lands, Ballykilcline, Co. Roscommon
Valuation Office Letter Books, Nos. 1–4, Dublin: Public Record Office

PUBLIC RECORD OFFICE, BELFAST

Carrothers, E. R. "Irish Emigrants Letters from Canada, 1839–1870." Duplicated
and bound in Belfast, 1951.
Colby, Colonel. *Ordnance Survey of the County of Londonderry.* Vol. I. Dublin:
Hodges & Smith, 1837.

ROYAL IRISH ACADEMY

Anonymous. "Account of the Culture of Potatoes," 1796.
Anonymous. *Examinator's Letters, or a Mirror for the British Monopolists and Irish
Financiers.* Dublin: (no publ. indicated), 1786.
Anonymous. *Thoughts on Establishment of New Manufactures in Ireland.* Dublin: P.
Higley, 1782.
Extracts from the Essays of the Dublin Society Relating to the Culture and Manufac-
ture of Flax. 1798.
Hudson Bequest. MS. 24E22. R.I.A. "The Fair Mythology of Ireland." Handwritten
account. 1785.
Letter from Fr. James O'Donel to a doctor in St. Johns', Newfoundland. November
16, 1798.
Locke, John, "Ireland, Emigration and Valuation and Purchase of Land in Ireland."
2nd ed. London: John William Parker & Son. 1853. Halliday Pamphlets 2138,
1853, R.I.A.
Moore's Irish Almanack for the Year 1845. Drogheda: James Duffy, 1845.

Secondary Sources

Aalen, F. H. A. "Transhumance in the Wicklow Mountains," *Ulster Folk Life.* No.
10, 1964.
———. *Man and the Landscape in Ireland.* London: Academic Press, 1978.
Abbott, Edith. *Historical Aspects of the Immigration Problem.* Chicago: University
of Chicago Press, 1926.
Aberle, David F. "Matrilinial Descent in Cross-Cultural Perspective," *Matrilinial Kin-
ship.* David M. Schneider and Kathleen Gough, eds. Berkeley: University of
California Press, 1974.
Adams, William Forbes. *Ireland and Irish Emigration to the New World from 1815 to
the Famine.* New Haven: Yale University Press, 1932.

Adshead, Joseph. *Distress in Manchester.* London: H. Hooper, 1842.

Aiken, John. *A Description of the Country from Thirty to Forty Miles round Manchester.* London: John Stockdale, 1795.

Akenson, Donald Harman. *Small Differences, Irish Catholics and Irish Protestants, 1815–1922.* Kingston & Montreal: McGill-Queen's University Press, 1988.

Alfred, Samuel H.G. Kydd. *The History of the Factory Movement.* 2 vols. New York: Augustus M. Kelley, 1857–1966.

Almquist, Eric L. *Mayo and Beyond: Land, Domestic Industry, and Rural Transformation in the Irish West.* Ph.D. diss., Boston University, 1977.

_____. "Pre-Famine Ireland and the Theory of European Proto-Industrialization: Evidence from the 1841 Census," *Journal of Economic History,* Vol. XXXIX, No. 3 (September 1979).

Amherst, W. J. *The History of Catholic Emancipation.* London: Kegan, Paul, Trench & Co., 1886.

Anderson, Michael. *Family Structure in 19th Century Lancashire.* Cambridge: University Press, 1971.

Anonymous. *An Account of the Culture of Potatoes in Ireland.* London: Shepperson and Reynolds, 1796.

Anonymous. "Poor Laws in Ireland," *The London & Westminster Review.* Vol. XXC, July, 1836.

Anonymous. *Society of Friends: Transcriptions of the Society of the Quakers during the Famine in Ireland.* Dublin: Hodges & Smith, 1852.

Anonymous. *Thoughts on the Establishment of the New Manufacture in Ireland.* Dublin: P. Higley, 1782.

Arensberg, Conrad M. and Kimball, Solon T. *Family and Community in Ireland.* Cambridge: Harvard University Press, 1940, 1968.

Ashton, John. *Chap-Books of the Eighteenth Century.* New York: Benjamin Blom, 1882, 1966.

Ashton, T. S. *An 18th Century Industrialist, Peter Stubbs of Warrington, 1756–1806.* Manchester: Manchester University Press, 1939.

Aspinwall, B. *Politics and the Press, 1780–1850.* London: Home and Van Thal, Ltd., 1949.

Aspinwall, B. and Smith, E. Anthony. *English Historical Documents.* Vol. XI. Douglas, David C., gen. ed. New York: Oxford University Press, 1959.

Aspinwall, B. and McCaffrey, John. "A Comparative View of the Irish in Edinburgh in the Nineteenth Century," in *The Irish in the Victorian City,* Roger Swift and Sheridan Gilley, eds. London: Croom Helm, Ltd., 1985.

Atkinson, A. *Ireland in the Nineteenth Century.* London: Hamilton, Adams & Co., 1833.

Baines, Edward. *History of the Cotton Manufacture of Great Britain.* London: H. Fisher, R. Fisher, & Jackson, 1835.

_____. *History.* Vol II. *Directory and Gazetteer of the County and Palatine of Lancaster.* Liverpool: William Wales & Co., 1825.

Baines, Thomas. *History of the Commerce and Town of Liverpool.* London: Longman, Brown, Green & Longmans, 1852.

Baker, Jane. "Irish in Bristol" in *Irish Family History,* vi, 1990.

Banfield, E. C. *The Moral Basis of a Backward Society.* New York: The Free Press, 1958.

Banks, J. A. "Population Change and the Victorian City," *Victorian Studies*. Vol. XI, No. 3, March 1968.

_____. "The Contagion of Numbers," *The Victorian City, Images and Realities*. Vol. I. Dyos, H. J. and Wolff, Michael, eds. London: Routledge and Kegan Paul, 1973.

Barber, Sarah. "Irish Migrant Agricultural Labourers in Nineteenth Century Lancashire," in *Saothar,* No. 8, 1982.

Barker, T. C. and Harris, J. R. *A Merseyside Town in the Industrial Revolution, St. Helens, 1750–1900*. Liverpool: University Press.

Bartlett, Thomas and Hayton, J. eds. *Penal Era and Golden Age*. Belfast Historical Foundation, 1979.

Barton, John. *Economic Tracts of 1817*. London: W, Mason, 1817; reprint ed., *Condition of the Labouring Classes of Society*. Baltimore: The Johns Hopkins Press, 1934.

Beaumont, Gustave de la Bonniniere. *Ireland, Social, Political, and Religious,* 2 Vols. London: Bentley, 1839.

Beckett, J. C. *A Short History of Ireland*. London: Hutchinson University Library, 1952, 1966.

_____. *The Making of Modern Ireland*. London: Faber, 1966.

Belchem, John. "English Working-Class Radicalism and the Irish, 1815–50," Roger Swift and Sheridan Gilley, eds. in *The Irish in the Victorian City,* London: Croom Helm, Ltd., 1985.

Belchem, John and Buckland, Patrick, eds. *The Irish in British Labour History*. Conference Proceedings in Irish Studies, No. 1, A Publication of the Institute of Irish Studies, University of Liverpool, 1992.

Bell, Jonathan and Watson, Merwyn. *Irish Farming, Implements & Techniques,"* *1750–1900*. Edingburgh: John Donald Publishers, Ltd., 1986.

_____. "The Improvement of Rural Farming Techniques Since 1750: Theory and Practice" in *Rural Ireland, Modernization and Change, 1600–1900*. Patrick O'Flanagan, Paul Ferguson and Kevin Whelan, eds. Cork: Cork University Press, 1987.

Bennett, Christopher. "The Housing of the Irish in London, a Literature Review with some Conclusions," *Irish in Britain Research Forum*. Occasional Papers Series: No. 1. The Polytechnic of North London, Irish Studies Centre, 1988.

Berrier, Robert and Wold, Thomas. "Internal Migration: a Selective Bibliography," working paper publication No.C/75–26, Center for International Studies, M.I.T., Cambridge, Massachusetts, 1975.

Berry, Henry F. *A History of the Royal Dublin Society*. London: Longmans, Green & Co., 1915.

Bertoff, Rowland T. *British Immigrants in Industrial America, 1790–1950*. Cambridge: Harvard University Press, 1953.

Beste, Henry Digby. *Poverty and the Baronet's Family*. London: T. Jones, 1845.

Bevan, G. Phillips. *The Statistical Atlas of England, Scotland, and Ireland*. Edinburgh and London: W. & A.K. Johnston, 1882.

Binford, Henry Co. "Never Trust the Census Taker, Even When He's Dead." *Urban History Yearbook,* 1975.

Black, R. D. Collison. *Economic Thought and the Irish Question, 1817–1870*. Cambridge: University Press, 1960.

_____. *The Statistical and Social Inquiry Society of Ireland, Centenary Volume, 1847–1947,* with indices to the transactions of the society. Dublin: Eason & Son, Ltd., 1947.

Blaug, M. "The Productivity of Capital in the Lancashire Cotton Industry During the 19th Century." *Economic History Review,* 2nd. Ser., Vol. XIII, No. 1, 1960.

Bogan, Bernard. "History of Irish Immigration to England, The Irish in Southwark." *Christus Rex,* Vol. XII, No. 1, January 1958.

Bogue, Donald J. "Internal Migration," in *The Study of Population.* P. M. Hauser and O. T. Duncan, eds. Chicago: University of Chicago Press, 1959.

Bolton, Geoffrey C. *The Passing of the Irish Act of Union, a Study in Parliamentary Politics.* London: Oxford University Press, 1966.

_____. "Some British Reactions to the Irish Act of Union." *Economic History Review,* 2nd Ser., Nos. 1–3, 1965.

Booth, Charles. *Life and Labour of the People in London.* Vol. I. London: Macmillan & Co., 1892.

Booth, Henry. *An Account of the Liverpool and Manchester Railway.* Liverpool: Wales and Baines, 1830.

Boston, Ray. *British Chartists in America, 1839–1900.* Manchester: Manchester University Press, 1971.

Boulding, Elise. "Familial Constraints on Women's Work Roles," in *Women and the Workplace.* Martha Blaxall and Barbara Reagan, eds. Chicago: University of Chicago Press, 1976.

Bourke, P. M. A. "Notes on Some Agricultural Units of Measurement in Use in Pre-Famine Ireland." *Irish Historical Studies,* Vol. XIV, No. 55, March 1965.

_____. "The Agricultural Statistics of the 1841 Census of Ireland: a Critical Review." *Economic History Review,* 2nd Ser., Vol. 18, 1965.

_____. "The Extent of the Potato Crop in Ireland at the Time of the Famine." *Statistical Society of Ireland Journal,* XX, Part iii, 1959.

_____. "The Visitation of God, a Study of the Role of the Potato, Blight and Weather in the Irish Famine of 1846." Unpublished paper, 1965, University College, Dublin, 1965.

_____. "The Scientific Investigation of the Potato Blight in 1845–46," *Irish Historical Studies,* Vol.XIII, No.49, March 1962.

_____. "The Use of the Potato Crop in Pre-famine Ireland," *Journal of the Statistical and Social Inquiry Society of Ireland,* Vol.XII, Pt.6, 1968.

_____. "The Average Yields of Food Crops in Ireland on the Eve of the Great Famine," *Journal of the Department of Agriculture (Ireland),* Vol.LXVI, No.7, 1969.

_____. *Essays on the Irish Famine, 1845–49,* Irish Historical Studies, 1938–1988: Fiftieth Anniversary Publication, Dublin: Lilliput Press, 1993.

Boyce, D. G. "Brahmins and Carnivores: the Irish Historian in Great Britain," in *Irish Historical Studies,* Vol.XXV, No.99, May 1987.

Boyd, Andrew. *The Rise of the Irish Trade Unions, 1879–1970.* Tralee: Anvil Books, 1972.

Boyle, J. W., ed. *Leaders and Workers.* Cork: The Mercier Press, 1966.

_____. "The Agricultural Labourer," unpublished paper.

Brabrook, E. W. *Provident Societies and Industrial Welfare.* London: Blackie and Son, 1898.

Bradshaw, Brendan. "The Elizabethans and the Irish." *Studies,* Spring 1977.

Brailsford, H. N. *The Levellers and the English Revolution.* California: Stanford University Press, 1961.

Briggs, Asa, ed. *Chartist Studies.* London: Macmillan, 1960.

Briggs, Asa. "Cholera and Society in the Nineteenth Century." *Past and Present* No. 19, April 1961.

_____. *Victorian Cities.* New York: Harper and Row, 1963, 1970.

_____. *Victorian People.* Chicago: University of Chicago Press, 1955, 1970.

Brody, Hugh. *Inishkillane, Change and Decline in the West of Ireland.* Bungay, Suffolk: The Chaucer Press, 1973.

Broeker, Galen. *Rural Disorder and Police Reform in Ireland, 1812–36.* London: Routledge and Kegan Paul, 1970.

Brown, Alan A. and Neuberger, Egan, eds. *Internal Migration, a Comparative Perspective.* New York: Academic Press, 1977.

Brown, Lucy. "The Chartists and the Anti-Corn Law League," in *Chartist Studies,* Asa Briggs, ed. London: Macmillan, 1960.

Buchanan, Ronald H. "The Drift from the Land." *Ulster Folklife,* Vol. 6, 1960.

Buer, M. C. *Health, Wealth, and Population in the Early Days of the Industrial Revolution.* London: George Routledge and Sons, 1926.

Burke, Thomas. *Catholic History of Liverpool.* Liverpool: C. Tinling and Co., 1910.

Burn, W. L. *The Age of Equipoise.* New York: W. W. Norton. 1964.

Burnett, John. *A History of the Cost of Living.* Harmondsworth: Penguin Books, 1969.

Butler, Beatrice B. "Thomas Pleasants and the Stone Tenter House 1815–1944." *Dublin Historical Record,* Vol. VII, 1944–45.

_____. "Thomas Pleasants, 1729–1818." *Dublin Historical Record.* Vol. VI, No. 4, 1943–44.

Byrne, Stephen. *Irish Emigration to the United States.* 1873.

Bythell, Duncan. *The Handloom Weavers, a Study of the English Cotton Industry During the Industrial Revolution.* Cambridge: University Press, 1969.

_____. "The Handloom Weavers in the English Cotton Industry During the Industrial Revolution: Some Problems." *Economic History Review,* 2nd Ser., Vol. XVIII, No. 1, 1964.

Cairncross, A. K. *Home and Foreign Investment, 1870–1913,* Studies in Capital Accumulation. Cambridge: Cambridge University Press, 1953.

Cairncross, A. K. and Weber, B. "Fluctuations in Building in Great Britain, 1785–1849." *Economic History Review,* and Ser., Vol. IX, No. 1, 1956.

Cameron, Sir Charles. *Autobiography.* Dublin: Hodges, Figgis & Co., 1920.

Campbell, Mildred. "Of People Either Too Few or Too Many, the Conflict of Opinion on Population and its Relation to Emigration." *Conflict in Stuart England.* Appleton Aiken and Basil Duke Henning, eds. New York: Archon Books, 1970.

Canny, Nicholas P. *The Elizabethan Conquest of Ireland: A Pattern Established, 1565–1576.* Sussex: Harvester Press, 1976.

Carbury, Mary. *The Farm by Lough Gur.* Cork: Mercier, 1973.

Carleton, William. *Traits and Stories of the Irish Peasantry.* London: William Tegg & Co., 1875.

_____. *Phelim O'Toole's Courtship and Other Stories.* Cork: Mercier Press, 1973.

_____. *The Party Fight and Funeral.* Cork: Mercier Press, 1973.

_____. *Wildgoose Lodge and Other Stories*. Cork: Mercier Press, 1973.

Carlyle, Thomas. *Past and Present*. Boston: Charles C. Little and James Brown, 1840.

_____. *Chartism*. Boston: Charles C. Little and James Brown, 1840.

Carney, Francis J. "Pre-famine Irish Population: The Evidence from the Trinity College Estates," *Irish Economic and Social History*, Vol.II, 1975.

Carroll, S. J. "Greenore and the Harvest Men." *Ulster Folklife*, Vol. 7, 1961.

Carrothers, W. A. *Emigration from the British Isles*. London: P. S. King & Son, Ltd., 1929.

Carswell, John. *From Revolution to Revolution, England 1688–1776*. New York: Charles Scribner's Sons, 1973.

Chadwick, Edward. *A Supplementary Report on the Result of Special Inquiry into the Practice of Interment in Towns*. London: W. Clowes & Sons, 1843.

Chambers, J. D. "Enclosure and Labour Supply in the Industrial Revolution." *Economic History Review*, 2nd Ser., Vol. V, No. 3, 1953.

Chambers, J. D. and Mingay, J. E. *The Agricultural Revolution, 1750–1880*. London: Batsford, 1966.

Checkland, J. G. *The Rise of Industrial Society in England, 1815–1885*. New York: St. Martin's Press, 1964.

Chesney, Kellow. *The Anti-Society, An Account of the Victorian Underworld*. Boston: Gambit, Inc. 1970.

Chevalier, Louis. *Laboring Classes and Dangerous Classes in Paris During the First Half of the 19th Century*. Trans. by Frank Jellinck. New York: Howard Fertig, 1973.

Cipolla, Carlo M., ed. *The Fontana Economic History of Europe*. Book 4, 2 vols., *The Emergence of Industrial Societies;* Book 3, *The Industrial Revolution*. London: Collins, 1973.

Clapham, J. H. *An Economic History of Modern Britain*. Cambrige: University Press, 1926.

Clark, G. Kitson. *The Making of Victorian England*. Cambridge: Harvard University Press, 1963.

Clark, Samuel. *Social Origins of the Irish Land War,* Princeton, New Jersey: Princeton University Press, 1964.

Clark, Samuel and Donnelly Jr., James S., eds. *Irish Peasants: Violence and Political Unrest 1780–1914*. Madison, Wisconsin: University of Wisconsin Press, 1983.

Clarkson, L. A. "The Writing of Irish Economic and Social History since 1968," *Economic History Review*, XXXIII, 1, 1980.

_____. "Irish Population Revisited, 1687–1821," in J. M. Goldstrom and L. A. Clarkson, eds., *Irish Population, Economy and Society,* Oxford: Clarendon Press, 1981.

_____. "Conclusion: Famine and Irish History," in *Famine: The Irish Experience, 900–1900*. Margaret Crawford, ed. Edinburgh: John Donald Publishers, 1989.

Clear Caitríona and Johnston, Maírín. *Growing Up Poor*. Galway: Galway Labour History Group, 1993.

_____. "The Homeless Young in 19th Century Ireland" in *Growing Up Poor*. Galway: Galway Labour History, 1993.

Clebert, Jean-Paul. *The Gypsies*. Baltimore: Penguin Books, 1961.

Clifford, Robert. *Application of Barruel's Memoirs of Jacobinism to the Secret Soci-*

eties of Ireland and Great Britain. London: E. Booker, 1798.

Clive, John. *Macaulay, the Shaping of a Historian.* New York: Alfred Knopf, 1873.

Close, Col. Sir Charles. *The Early Years of Ordnance Survey.* Great Britain: Latimer Trend & Co., 1926, 1969.

Cobden, John C. *The White Slaves of England.* Buffalo: Derby, Orton & Mulligan, 1953.

Cobden, Richard. *England, Ireland & America by a Manchester Manufacturer.* 2nd. ed. London: James Ridgway & Sons, 1835.

_____. *The Political Writings of Richard Cobden.* Vol. I. London: William Ridgway, 1867.

Cohen, Jon S. and Weitzman, Martin L. *A Marxian Type Model of Enclosures.* Working paper, Dept. of Economics, M.I.T., no. 118, September 1973.

Colby, Col. *Ordinance Survey of the County of Londonderry (Parish of Templemore).* Dublin: Hodges & Smith, 1837.

Cole, G. D. H. *Introduction to Economic History, 1750–1950.* New York: Macmillan, 1954.

_____. *A Short History of the British Working Class Movement, 1789–1937.* London: George Allen & Unwin, 1925, 1937.

_____. *Studies in Class Structure.* London: Routledge & Kegan Paul, 1955.

Cole, G. D. H. and Postgate, Raymond. *The British Common People, 1746–1946.* London: Methuen, 1961.

Coleman, Terry. *Going to America.* New York: Random House, 1972.

_____. *The Railway Navvies.* New York: Random House, 1965.

Collins, Brenda. "Irish Emigration to Dundee and Paisley During the First Half of the Nineteenth Century," in *Irish Population, Economy, and Society.* J. M. Goldstrom and L. A. Clarkson, eds. Oxford: Clarendon Press, 1981.

_____. "Aspects of Irish Immigration into Two Scottish Towns during the Mid-Nineteenth Century." *Irish Economic and Social History,* Vol. VI, 1979.

Collins, E. J. T. "Migrant Labour in British Agriculture in the Nineteenth Century," *Economic History Review,* 2nd Ser., Vol. XXXIX, No. 1, (February 1976).

Colton, Calvin. *Four Years in Great Britain, 1831–35.* 2 vols. New York: Harper & Bros., 1835.

Connell, John; Dasgupta, B.; Lashley, R.; Lipton, M. *Migration from Rural Areas in the Evidence of Village Studies.* IDS discussion paper, no. 39, January 1974. University of Sussex, Brighton.

Connell, K. H. "The Colonization of Waste Land in Ireland, 1780–1845." *Economic History Review,* 2nd Ser., Vol III, No. 1, 1950.

_____. "The Land Legislation and Irish Social Life." *Economic History Review,* 2nd Ser., Vol XI, No. 1, 1958.

_____. "The History of the Potato." *Economic History Review,* 2nd Ser., Vol. III, No. 3, 1951.

_____. "Land and Population in Ireland, 1780–1845." *Population in History.* D. V. Glass and D. C. E. Eversely, eds. Chicago: Aldine Publishing Co., 1965.

_____. "Some Unsettled Problems in English and Irish Population History, 1750–1845." *Irish Historical Studies,* Vol. VII, No. 28, September 1951.

_____. "Population," in *Social Life in Ireland 1800–45.* R. B. McDowell, ed. Cork: Mercier Press, 1963.

_____. *The Population of Ireland, 1750–1845.* Oxford: Clarendon Press, 1950.

_____. *Irish Peasant Society, Four Historical Essays.* Oxford: Clarendon Press, 1968.

_____. "Illicit Distillation: An Irish Peasant Industry," *Historical Studies,* Vol.3, 1961.

_____. "The Potato in Ireland," *Past and Present,* Vol. XXIII, November 1962.

_____. "Illegitimacy before the Famine," in *Irish Peasant Society: Four Historical Essays,* Oxford: Clarendon Press, 1968.

Connolly, Sean J. "Catholicism and Social Discipline in Pre-Famine Ireland." *Irish Economic and Social History,* Vol. IV, 1977.

_____. *Priests and People in Pre-famine Ireland 1780–1845.* Dublin: Gill & MacMillan, 1982.

_____. "Religion and Society in Nineteenth Century Ireland." *Studies in Irish Economic and Social History,* 3, Dundalk: Dundalgan Press, 1985.

Corkery, Daniel. *The Hidden Ireland.* Dublin: Gill & Macmillan, 1924.

Cornelius, Wayne A. "Urbanization and Political Demand Making: Political Participation among the Migrant Poor in Latin American Cities." Working paper publication No.C/75–26, Center for International Studies, M.I.T., Cambridge, Massachusetts, 1975.

Cousens, S. H. "The Regional Variation in Emigration from Ireland between 1821 and 1841." *Transaction and Papers of The Institute of British Geographers,* No. 37, 1965.

_____. "The Regional Pattern of Emigration during the Great Irish Famine, 1846–51," ibid. No. 38, 1960.

_____. "Migration and Demographic Change in Ireland, 1851–1861," *Economic History Review,* No.19, December 1961

_____. "The Regional Variations in Population Change in Ireland, 1861–1881," *Economic History Review,* No. 22, December 1964.

Craig, Robert and Jarvis, Rupert. *Liverpool Registry of Merchant Ships.* Manchester: University Press, 1967.

Crawford, E. Margaret, ed. *Famine: The Irish Experience, 900–1900.* Edinburgh: John Donald Publishers, 1989.

Crawford, William H. *Domestic Industry in Ireland.* Dublin: Gill & Macmillan, 1972.

_____. "Landlord-Tenant Relations in Ulster, 1609–1820," *Irish Economic and Social History,* Vol. II, 1975.

_____. "The Rise of the Linen Industry," in L. M. Cullen, ed. *The Formation of the Irish Economy.* Cork: Mercier Press, 1969.

_____. "Change in Ulster in the Late Eighteenth Century," in *Penal Era and Golden Age,* Thos. Bartlett and D. W. Hayton, eds. Belfast: Ulster Historical Foundation, 1979.

Crew, David. "Definitions of Modernity: Social Mobility in a German Town, 1880–1901." *Journal of Social History,* Vol. 7, Fall 1973.

Crotty, Raymond D. *Irish Agricultural Production, Its Volume and Structure.* Cork: Cork University Press, 1966.

Cullen, L. M. *Anglo-Irish Trade, 1660–1880.* New York: Augustus M. Kelley, 1968.

_____. *The Formation of the Irish Economy.* Cork: Mercier Press, 1969, 1976, 1979.

_____. *An Economic History of Ireland Since 1660.* New York: Harper & Row, 1972.

_____. "Irish History Without the Potato." *Past and Present,* No. 40, July 1968.

_____. *The Emergence of Modern Ireland 1600–1900*. London: 1981.

_____. "The Hidden Ireland: Re-assessment of a Concept." *Studia Hibernica,* No. 9.

_____. "Problems in the Interpretation and Revision of Eighteenth Century Irish Economic History," *Transactions of the Royal Historical Society,* Vol. 17, 5th series, 1967.

_____. "Population Growth and Diet, 1600–1850," in J. M. Goldstrom and L. A. Clarkson, eds., *Irish Population, Economy and Society.* Oxford: Clarendon Press, 1981.

_____. "Incomes, Social Classes and Economic Growth in Ireland and Scotland, 1600–1900," in David Dickson and T. M. Devine, eds., *Ireland and Scotland: Social and Economic Developments, 1650–1850.* Edinburgh: Donald, 1978.

Cunningham, W. *The Growth of English Industry and Commerce.* Cambridge: University Press, 1925.

Curtis, Edmund. *A History of Ireland.* London: Methuen & Co., 1936, 1968.

Curtis, L. P., Jr. "Anglo-Saxons and Celts, a Study of Anti-Irish Prejudice in Victorian England." Bridgeport: The University of Bridgeport, Conn., 1968.

_____. *Apes and Angels, The Irishman in Victorian Caricature.* Washington: Smithsonian Institute Press, 1971.

_____. *Coercion and Conciliation in Ireland, 1880–1892.* Princeton: Princeton University Press, 1963.

Curwen, J. C. *Observations on the State of Ireland.* 2 vols. London: Baldwin, Cradock & Joy, 1818.

Daly, Mary, "The Development of the National School System, 1831–34," in A. Cosgrove and Donal McCartney, eds. *Studies in Irish History Presented to R. Dudley Edwards.* Dublin: University College, 1979.

_____. *Social and Economic History of Ireland since 1800.* Dublin: Education Co., 1981.

_____. *Dublin, the Deposed Capital: A Social and Economic History, 1860–1914.* Cork: Cork Univ. Press, 1984.

Danaher, Kevin. *The Year in Ireland.* Cork: Mercier Press, 1972.

_____. *In Ireland Long Ago.* Cork: Mercier Press, 1962.

D'Arcy, Fergus. A. "Dublin Artisan Activity, Opinion and Organisation, 1820–1850." Master's thesis, National University of Ireland, University College, Dublin, 1968.

_____. "The Irish in 19th Century Britain: Reflections on Their Role and Experience," in *Irish History Workshop* 1, 1980.

_____. "Wages of Labourers in the Dublin Building Industry," 1667–1918." *Soathar* 14, 1989.

Daniels, Mary. "Exile or Opportunity? Irish Nurses and Wirral Midwives." *Irish Studies Review,* No. 5, Winter 1993.

Dardis, Patrick G. *The Occupation of Land in Ireland in the First Half of the 19th Century.* Dublin: Maunsel & Co., 1920.

Davin, Nicholas Flood. *The Irishman in Canada.* London: Sampson Low, Marston & Co., Toronto: Maclear & Co., 1887.

Davis, G. *The Irish in Britain 1815–1914.* Dublin: Gill and MacMillan, 1991.

Davis, Natalie Zemon. "Poor Relief, Humanism, and Heresy: The Case of Lyon." *Studies in Medieval and Renaissance History,* Vol. V, 1968.

Deane, Phyllis and Cole, W. A. *British Economic Growth 1688–1959.* Cambridge: University Press, 1967.

Defoe, Daniel. "Giving Alms No Charity and Employing the Poor," *A Collection of Pamphlets Concerning the Poor.* London: C. Elliot, T. Kay & Co. 1787.

Delaney, Edward J. and Feehan, John M. *The Comic History of Ireland.* Cork: Mercier Press, 1964, 1969.

Dent, J. Geoffrey. "The Irish Reputation for Healing in Northern England." *Ulster Folklife,* Vol. 14, 1968.

Denvir, John. *The Irish in Britain.* London: Kegan Paul, Trench, Trubner & Co., Ltd., 1892.

_____. *The Life Story of an Old Rebel.* Dublin: Sealy, Bryers & Walker, 1910.

De Tocqueville, Alexis. *Journeys to England and Ireland.* New Haven: Yale University Press, 1958.

Devine, T. M., ed. *Irish Immigrants and Scottish Society in the Nineteenth and Twentieth Centuries.* Edingburgh: John Donald, 1991.

Dickens, Charles. *Sketches by Boz.* London: J. M. Dent & Sons, Ltd., 1912.

_____. *Barnaby Rudge.* London: Collins, no date.

Dickson, David. "Aspects of the Rise and Decline of the Irish Cotton Industry," in L. M. Cullen & T. C. Smouth, eds. *Comparative Aspects of Scottish and Irish Economic and Social History.* Edinburgh: Donald, 1978.

_____. "Middlemen," in Thomas Bartlett and J. Hayton, eds., *Penal Era and Golden Age,* Belfast: Ulster Historical Foundation, 1979.

_____. "A Share of the Honeycomb: Education, Emigration and Women," unpublished paper, Trinity College, Dublin, 1985.

Dickson, David and Devine, T. M., eds. *Ireland and Scotland: Social and Economic Developments, 1650–1850.* Edinburgh: Donald, 1982

Disraeli, Benjamin. *Coningsley.* New York: The Century Co., 1905.

_____. *Sybil, or the Other Nation.* London: Longman, Green & Co., 1882.

Donaldson, Gordon. *The Scots Overseas.* London: Robert Hale, 1966.

Donnelly, James S., Jr. *The Land and People of 19th Century Cork.* Boston: Routledge & Kegan Paul, 1975.

Douglas, J. N. H. "Emigration and Irish Peasant Life." *Ulster Folklife.* Vol. 9, 1963.

Douglas, Roy. *The History of the Liberal Party, 1895–1970.* Madison: Fairleigh Dickinson University Press, 1971.

Doyle, David N., "The Regional Bibliography of Irish America, 1800–1930," *Irish Historical Studies,* XXIII, 91, 1983.

Doyle, Martin, *Cyclopaedia of Practical Husbandry.* Dublin: William Curry, Jr., & Co., 1839.

Drake, Michael. "Population Growth and the Irish Economy," in L.M.Cullen (ed) *The Formation of the Irish Economy.* Cork: Mercier Press, 1969.

Drummond, Henry. *The Condition of the Agricultural Classes of Great Britain and Ireland.* 2 Vols. London: John Murray, 1842.

Dufferin, Lord. *Irish Emigration and the Tenure of Land in Ireland.* London: Willis, Sotheran & Co., 1867.

_____. *Contributions to Inquiry into the State of Ireland.* London: John Murray, 1866.

Duffy, Charles Gavan. *Four Years of Irish History, 1845–1849.* London: Cassell, Pelter, Galpin & Co., 1883.

Dunn, Joseph and Lennox, P. J., eds. *The Glories of Ireland.* Washington: Phoenix, 1914.

Dunraven, Earl of. *The Legacy of the Past Years, a Study of Irish History.* London: John Murray, 1911.

Durkheim, Emile. *The Division of Labor in Society.* New York: 1933.

Dutton, Hely, *Statistical Survey of the County of Clare.* Drawn up for the Royal Dublin Society. Dublin: Graisberry & Campbell, 1808.

_____. *A Statistical and Agricultural Survey of the County of Galway,* drawn up for the Royal Dublin Society. Dublin: The University Press, 1824.

_____. *Observations on Mr. Archer's Statistical Survey of Dublin.* Dublin: Graisberry & Campbell, 1802.

Dyos, H. J. "The Slums of Victorian London." *Victorian Studies.* Vol. XI, No. 1, September 1967.

_____ ed. T*he Study of Urban History.* London: Edward Arnold, 1968.

Dyos, H. J. and Wolff, Michael. *The Victorian City, Images and Realities.* Vol. I & II. London: Routledge & Kegan Paul, 1973.

Eden, Frederick Morton. *The State of the Poor, or a History of the Labouring Classes in England.* Vol. I. London: J. Davis, 1797.

Edgeworth, Maria. *Castle Rackrent. an Hibernian Tale.* London and New York: The Chesterfield Society, 1899.

_____. *The Absentee.* London and New York: Macmillan, 1895.

Edward, R. Dudley & Williams, T. Desmond eds. *The Great Famine: Studies in Irish History, 1845–52.* Dublin: 1956, 1957.

Edwards, Ruth Dudley. *An Atlas of Irish History.* London: Methuen, 1973, 1983.

Elliott, Marianne. "Irish Republicanism in England: The First Phase, 1797–99," in Thomas Bartlett and D. W. Hayton, eds. *Penal Era and Golden Age, Essays in Irish History, 1690–1800,* Belfast: Ulster Historical Foundation, 1979.

Engel, Madeline H. "Case Studies in British Immigration." *International Migration Review.* Vol. III, Spring 1960.

Engels, Friedrich. *The Condition of the Working Classes in England.* Stanford: Stanford University Press, 1958.

Epstein, J. and Thompson, D. eds. *The Chartist Experience: Studies in Working Class Radicalism and Culture, 1830–1860,* London, Macmillan, 1982.

_____. *The Lion of Freedom: Feargus O'Connor and the Chartist Movement, 1832–42,* London, 1982.

Erickson, Charlotte. J. *Invisible Immigrants, the Adaption of English and Scottish Immigrants in 19th Century America.* Florida: University of Miami Press, 1972.

_____. "Immigration from the British Isles to the U.S.A. in 1841: Part I. Who Were the Emigrants?" *Population Studies* 43(3), November 1989.

Evans, E. Estyn. *Irish Folk Ways.* London: Routledge & Kegan Paul, 1957.

Eversley, D. E. C. "Population, Economy and Society." *Population in History.* D. V. Glass and D. E. E. Eversley, eds. Chicago: Aldine Publishing Co., 1965.

Fairchild, Henry Pratt. *Immigration.* New York: Macmillan, 1913.

Falley, Margaret Dickson. *Irish and Scotch-Irish Ancestral Research, a Guide to the Genealogical Records, Records and Sources in Ireland.* 2 vols. Strasburg, Virginia: Shenandoah Publishing House, 1962.

Farnie, D. A. "The Commercial Empire of the Atlantic, 1607–1783." *Economic History Review.* 2nd Ser., Vol. XV, 1962.

Faulkner, H. U. *Chartism and the Churches.* New York: Columbia University, 1916.

_____. *The Chartist Movement in its Social and Economic Aspects.* Frank F. Rosenblatt, ed. *Studies in History, Economics and Public Law.* Vol. LXXIII, No. 1. 1916.

Fay, C. R. *Life and Labour in the 19th Century.* Cambridge: University Press, 1920.

Feingold, William L. *The Revolt of the Tenantry: The Transformation of Local Government, 1872–1886.* Boston: Northeast, June 1984.

Ferenzi, Imre and Willcox, W. *International Migrations.* Vol. 1, *Statistics.* New York: National Bureau of Economic Research, Inc., 1929.

Fielding, Steven. *Class and Ethnicity Irish Catholics in England, 1880–1939.* Buckingham: Open University Press, 1993.

Finnegan, F. *Poverty and Prejudice: Irish Immigrants in York, 1840–75.* Cork: Cork University Press, 1982.

Fitzgerald, Thomas. "The Irish Parish and the Emigrant." *Christus Rex,* October 1956.

Fitzpatrick, David. *Irish Emigration, 1801–1921, Studies in Irish Economic and Social History,* 1. Dundalk, Ireland: Dundalgan Press, 1984.

_____. "Irish Emigration in the Later Nineteenth Century," *Irish Historical Studies,* XXII, 86, 1980.

_____. "The Disappearance of the Irish Agricultural Labourer, 1841–1912," *Irish Economic and Social History,* VII, 1980.

_____. "The Irish in Britain, Settlers or Transient?" In Buckland and Belchem (eds). *The Irish in British Labour History,* Liverpool, Univ. of Liverpool, 1992.

_____. "A Peculiar Tramping People: The Irish in Britain 1800–1871," in *A New History of Ireland,* eds. T. W. Moody, F. X. Martin and J. F. Byrne, No. 5. Oxford: Oxford University Press, 1989.

_____. "Was Ireland Special? Recent Writing on the Irish Economy and Society in the Nineteenth Century." *Historical Journal,* xxxiii, No. 1, 1991.

_____. "Review Article: Women, Gender and the Writing of Irish History." *Irish Historical Studies,* xxvii, 107, 1991.

_____. "The Modernisation of the Irish Female," in *Rural Ireland: Modernisation v. Change 1600–1900.* Patrick O' Flanagan, Paul Ferguson, and Kevin Whelan (eds). Cork: Cork University Press, 1987.

Fitzpatrick, S.J., Joseph P. "The Importance of 'Community' in the Process of Immigrant Assimilation." *The International Migration Review.* Vol. 1, No. 1, Fall 1966.

Flanagan, Very Rev. Canon. *A History of the Church in England.* Vols. I, II. London: Charles Dolman, 1857.

Fleming, Donald and Bailyn, Bernard. *The Intellectual Migration, Europe and America, 1930–1960.* Cambridge: Harvard University Press, 1969.

Flinn, M. W. *The Sanitary Condition of the Labouring Population of Great Britain.* Edinburgh: University Press, 1965.

_____. *British Population Growth 1700–1850.* London: 1970.

_____. "Trends in Real Wages, 1750–1850," *Economic History Review,* 2nd Ser., Vol. XXVII, No. 3 (August 1974).

Folliott, Rosemary. "The Surprising Newspapers of Ennis." *The Irish Ancestor.* No. 2, 1974.

Foot, Paul. *Immigration and Race in British Politics.* England and United States: Penguin Books, 1965.

Foster, Thomas Campbell (The Times Commissioner). *Letters on the Condition of the*

People of Ireland. 2nd edition. London: Chapman and Hall, 1846.

Freeman, T. W. "Historical Geography and the Irish Historian." *Irish Historical Studies.* Vol. V, No. 18, September 1946.

_____. *Pre-Famine Ireland, a Study in Historical Geography.* Manchester: University Press, 1957.

_____. "The Changing Distribution of Population in County Mayo." Paper read to the Statistical and Social Inquiry Society of Ireland, 29th January 1943.

_____. "The Changing Distribution of Population in Donegal, with Special Reference to the Congested Areas." Paper read to the Statistical and Social Inquiry Society of Ireland, 28th November 1940.

_____. "Population Distribution in County Sligo." Paper read to the Statistical and Social Inquiry Society of Ireland, 25th February 1944.

_____. "Emigration and Rural Ireland." Paper read to the Statistical and Social Inquiry Society of Ireland, 25th January 1945.

Fry, J. D. "Irish Famines and the Irish Economy, 1750–1845." Ph.D. diss., Queen's University, Belfast, 1968–69.

Gahan, Robert. "Old Alms-Houses of Dublin," *Dublin Historical Record.* Vol. V. Old Dublin Society, 1942–43.

Gainer, Bernard. *The Alien Invasion, the Origins of the Aliens Act of 1905.* London: Heinemann Educational Books, 1972.

Galloway, Robert L. *A History of Coal Mining in Great Britain.* London: Macmillan & Co., 1882.

Garrard, John A. *The English and Immigration, 1880–1910.* Oxford University Press, 1971.

Gash, Norman. *Reaction and Reconstruction in English Politics, 1832–1852.* Oxford: Clarendon Press, 1965.

Gaskell, Elizabeth Cleghorn. *Mary Barton.* London: J.M.Dent & Sons, Ltd., 1911, 1932.

_____. *Cranford.* New York: Thomas Y. Crowell & Co., no date.

Gaskell, P. *Artisans and Machinery.* New York: Augustus M. Kelley, 1836, 1968.

Gately, Michael O.; Moote, A. Lloyd; and Willis, John E., Jr. "17th Century Peasant Furies: Some Problems of Comparative History." *Past & Present.* No. 51, May 1971.

Gatrell, V. A. C. "Labour Power and the Size of Firms in Lancashire Cotton in the Second Quarter of the Nineteenth Century," *Economic History Review,* 2nd Ser., Vol. XXX, No. 1 (February 1977).

Gaughan, J. Anthony. *Listowel and its Vicinity.* Cork: Mercier Press, 1973.

Geary, R. C. and Hughes, J. J. "Internal Migration in Ireland." Paper No. 54, May 1970. The Economic and Social Research Institute.

George, Dorothy. *England in Transition, 18th Century England.* England: Penguin Books, 1931, 1969.

_____. *London Life in the 18th Century.* New York: Capricorn Books, 1965.

Gill, Conrad. *The Rise of the Linen Industry.* Oxford: Clarendon Press, 1925.

Gilley, Sheridan. "English Attitudes to the Irish in England, 1780–1900," in *Immigrants and Minorities in British Society,* Colin Holmes, ed. London: George Allen & Unwin, 1978.

Gilley, Sheridan and Swift, Roger, eds. *The Irish in the Victorian City.* London: Croom Helm, 1985.

———. *The Irish in Britain, 1815–1939.* Savage, Maryland: Barnes & Noble, 1989.

Gillingham, John. "The Beginnings of English Imperialism." In *Journal of Historical Sociology.* Vol. 4, No. 4, December 1992.

Glass, D. V. "Population and Population Movements in England and Wales, 1700 to 1850." *Population in History.* D. V. Glass and D. E. C. Eversley, eds. Chicago: Aldine Publishing Co., 1965.

Glassford, James. *Notes of Three Tours in Ireland in 1824 and 1826.* No date.

Glazier, Ira (ed). *Migration Across Time and Nations: Population Mobility in Historical Contexts.* New York and London: Holmes and Meier, 1986.

Glynn, Sean. "Irish Immigration to Britain, 1911–1951: Patterns and Policy," *Irish Economic and Social History,* VIII, 1981.

Goldstrom, J. M. "The Industrialisation of the North-east," in *The Formation of the Irish Economy.* L. M. Cullen, ed. Cork: Mercier Press, 1969.

Goldstrom, J. M. and Clarkson, L. A. *Irish Population, Economy, and Society. Essays in Honour of the Late K. H. Connell.* Oxford: Clarendon Press, 1981.

———. "Irish Agriculture and the Great Famine," in J. M. Goldstrom & L. A. Clarkson, eds. *Irish Population, Economy and Society, Essays in Honour of K. H. Connell.* Oxford: Clarendon Press, 1981.

Gordon, Milton M. *Assimilation in American Life: the Role of Race, Religion and National Origin.* New York: Oxford University Press, 1964.

Gow, James. "The Irish Tinkers." *Ulster Folklife.* Vol. 17, 1971.

Green, E. R. R. *The Lagan Valley, 1800–1850: A Local History of the Industrial Revolution. Studies in Irish History,* Vol. III. London: Faber & Faber, 1949.

Green, James R. "The Formation of Working Class Communities in New England During the Nineteenth Century." Manuscript prepared for New England Historical Association meetings, New London, Conn., 13th October 1973.

Gribbon, H. D. "Thomas Newenham, 1762–1831," in Goldstrom, J. M. and Clarkson, L. M., *Irish Population, Economy, and Society.* Oxford: Clarendon Press, 1981.

Griffith, G. Talbot. *Population Problems in the Age of Malthus.* New York: Augustus Kelley, Bookseller, 1926, 1967.

Grigg, David. *Population Growth and Agrarian Change, an Historical Perspective.* Cambridge: Cambridge University Press, 1980.

Grimshaw, Thomas Wrigley. *Facts and Figures About Ireland. Part I, 1841–1890.* Dublin: Hodges, Figgis & Co., 1893.

Grindin, Leo H. *Manchester Banks & Bankers.* Manchester: Palmer & Howe, 1878.

Gugler, Josef and Flanagan, William G. *Urbanization and Social Change in West Africa.* Cambridge: Cambridge University Press, 1978.

Guinnane, Timothy W. "Marriage, Migration and Household Formation: The Irish at the Turn of the Century." (Thesis abstract with comment) *Journal of Economic History,* xlix, 1989.

———. "Intergenerational Transfers, Emigration, and the Rural Irish Household System," *Explorations in Economic History.* 29(4) October 1992.

Guinnane, T., B.S. O'Keen, J. Trussell. "What Do We Know about the Timing of Fertility Transition in Europe," in *Demography* Vol. 31, No. 1, Feb. 1994.

Gwynn, Denis. "The Irish Immigration," in *The English Catholics,* G. A. Beck, ed. London: Burns Oates, 1950.

———. "The Irish Immigration." *Cork University Review.* No. 20, 1950.

Habakkuk, H. J. *American and British Technology in the 19th Century, the Search for Labour-saving Inventions.* Cambridge: Cambridge University Press, 1962, 1967.

Hagan, Everett E. *On the Theory of Social Change.* Homewood, Illinois: The Dorsey Press, 1962.

Halevy, Elie. *England in 1815.* New York: Barnes & Noble, 1913, 1924, 1961.

Hall, Mr. and Mrs. S. C. *Sketches of the Irish Character.* London: M. A. Nattali, 1844.

_____. *Ireland: Its Scenery, Character, and History,* 6 vols. London: How and Parson, 1841.

_____. *Tour Throughout Ireland.* 2 vols. London: R. P. Moore, 1813.

Hammond, J. L. and Barbara. *The Village Labourer 1760–1832.* New York: Augustus Kelley, 1911, 1967.

_____. *The Bleak Age.* London: Longmans, 1934.

_____. *The Skilled Labourer.* New York: Augustus M. Kelley, 1919, 1967.

_____. *The Town Labourer, 1760–1832.* New York: Augustus Kelley, 1967.

_____. *The Rise of Modern Industry.* London: Methuen, 1925, 1947.

Handley, James Edmund. *The Irish in Scotland, 1798–1845.* Cork: Cork University Press, 1945.

_____. *The Irish in Modern Scotland.* Oxford: B.H. Blackwell, Ltd.,1947.

_____. *The Navvy in Scotland.* Cork: Cork University Press, 1970.

_____. *Irish Catholicism in Great Britain.* Vol. VI, *A History of Irish Catholicism.* Dublin: Gill & Son, 1968.

Handlin, O. and Thomas B., eds. *The Positive Contribution by Immigrants.* UNESCO, 1955.

Handlin, Oscar. *Boston's Immigrants.* New York: Atheneum, 1969.

_____. "Historians' Perspectives on the American Ethnic Group." *Daedalus.* Vol. 90, No. 2, Spring 1961.

_____. *Immigration as a Factor in American History.* New Jersey: Prentice-Hall, 1959.

_____. *The Newcomers.* New York: Anchor Books, 1962.

_____. "The Social System." *Daedalus.* Vol. 90, No. 1, Winter 1961.

_____. *The Uprooted.* New York: Grosset & Dunlap, 1951.

Hannan, Damian. *Rural Exodus.* London: Geoffrey Chapman, 1970.

Hansen, Marcus Lee. *The Atlantic Migration, 1607–1860.* New York: Harper &: Row, 1940, 1961.

_____. *The Immigrant in American History.* New York: Harper & Row, 1940, 1964.

Hardiman, James. *A Chorographical Description of West or H-Iar Connaught.* Dublin: for the Irish Archaeological Society, 1846.

Hareven, T. K. "Family Time and Historical Time," *Daedalus,* No. 106, 1977.

Harris, J. R. and Todaro, M. "Migration, Unemployment, and Development: a Two-Sector Analysis." *American Economic Review,* March 1971.

Harris, R. A. M. "The Failure of Irish Republicanism among Irish Migrants in England," *Eire-Ireland,* Winter 1986.

_____. "Seasonal Migration between Ireland and England prior to the Famine," *Canadian Papers in Rural History,* VIII, 1989.

_____. "Characteristics of Irish Immigrants in North America Derived from the Boston Pilot 'Missing Friends' Column," *Working Papers in Irish Studies,* Northeastern University, Boston, Massachusetts, January 1988.

Harris, R. A. M. and Jacobs, D., eds. *The Search for Missing Friends, Irish Immigrant Advertisements Placed in the Boston Pilot, 1831–1850.* Vol. I, Boston: The New England Historic Genealogical Society, 1989.

Harris, R. A. M. and O'Keeffe, B. Emer, eds. *The Search for Missing Friends, Irish Immigrant Advertisements Placed in the Boston Pilot, 1851–53.* Vol. II. Boston: The New England Historic Genealogical Society, 1991.

_____. *The Search for Missing Friends, Irish Immigrant Advertisements Placed in the Boston Pilot, 1854–1856.* Vol. III. Boston: The New England Historic Genealogical Society, 1993.

Harris, R. A. M., *The Search for Missing Friends, Irish Immigrant Advertisements Placed in the Boston Pilot, 1857–1860,* Vol. IV. Boston: The New England Historic Geneaological Society, 1994.

Harris, Rosemary L. "The Ordnance Survey Memoirs." *Ulster Folklife.* Vol. 1, 1955.

Harrison, Brian. *Drink and the Victorians, the Temperance Question in England, 1815–1872.* Pittsburgh: University of Pittsburgh Press, 1971.

Hartwell, R. M. "The Causes of the Industrial Revolution, an Essay in Methodology." *Economic History Review.* 2nd Ser., Vol. XVIII, Nos. 1–3, 1965.

_____. "The Rising Standard of Living in England, 1800–1850." *Economic History Review.* 2nd Ser., Vol. XIII, No. 1, 1960.

Hartwell, R. M. and Currie, R. "The Making of the English Working Class." *Economic History Review.* 2nd Ser., Vol. XVIII, No. 2, 1965.

Hartz, Louis. *The Founding of New Societies.* New York: Harcourt, Brace & World, Inc., 1964.

Hasbach, W. *A History of the English Agricultural Labourer.* London: P. S. King & Son, 1920.

Hastings, G. W., ed. *Transactions of the Dublin 1861 meeting of the National Association for the Promotion of Social Science.* London: John W. Parker, 1862.

Hauser, Philip M. and Duncan, Otis D., eds. *The Study of Population.* Chicago: University of Chicago Press, 1959.

Hawrylyshyn, Oli. "A Review of the Theories of Migration." Master's thesis, Dept. of Economics, M.I.T., September 1971.

Hayden, Mary. "Charity Children in 18th Century Dublin." *Dublin Historical Record.* Vol. V, 1942–43.

Head, George. *A Home Tour Through the Manufacturing Districts of England in the Summer of 1835.* New York: Augustus Kelley, 1836, 1968.

_____. *A Fortnight in Ireland.* London: John Murray, 1852.

Hechter, Michael. *Internal Colonialism: the Celtic Fringe in British National Development, 1536–1966.* Berkeley: University of California Press, 1975.

_____. "Regional Inequality and National Integration: the Case of the British Isles," *Journal of Social History,* Vol. V, No.1, 1971.

Heckethorn, Charles William. *The Secret Societies of All Ages and Countries.* Vols. I and II. New York: University Books, 1965.

Henning, B. S. and Foord, A. S. *Crises in English History, 1066–1945.* New York: Holt, Rinehart & Winston, 1966.

Hewitt, M. "The Effect of Married Women's Employment in the Cotton, Textile Districts on the Home in Lancashire, 1840–1880." Ph.D diss., University of London, 1953.

Hickey, John. "The Origin and Growth of the Irish Community in Cardiff." Ph.D. diss., University of London, 1938.

Higham, John. *Strangers in the Land, Patterns of American Nativism, 1860–1925.* New York: Atheneum, 1955, 1973.

Hill, Christopher. "The Poor and the Parish." *Society of Puritanism in Pre-Revolutionary England.* New York: Schocken, 1964.

_____. *Reformation to Industrial Revolution, the Making of Modern English Society.* Vol. I, 1530–1780. New York: Random House, 1967.

Himmelfarb, Gertrude. "The Culture of Poverty," in Dyos and Wolff, eds. *The Victorian City, Images and Realities,* Vol. 2. London & Boston: Routledge & Kegan Paul, 1973.

Hirschman, Albert O. *Exit, Voice and Loyalty, Responses to Decline in Firms, Organizations and States.* Cambridge: Harvard University Press, 1970.

Hobsbawm, Eric J. *Bandits.* England: Delacorte, 1969.

_____. "Economic Fluctuations and Some Social Movements Since 1800." *Economic History Review,* 2nd Ser., Vol. V, No. 1, 1952.

_____. *Industry and Empire.* Vol. 3, *From 1750 to the Present Day.* Baltimore: Penguin Books, 1968.

_____. *Labouring Men, Studies in the History of Labour.* New York: Anchor Books, 1967.

_____. *The Age of Revolution, 1789–1848.* London: The New English Library, Ltd., 1962.

_____. "The British Standard of Living, 1790–1850," in Arthur J. Taylor, ed. *The Standard of Living in Britain in the Industrial Revolution.* London: Methuen, 1975.

_____. "The British Standard of Living 1790–1850." *Labouring Men.* New York: Basic Books, Inc. Publ., 1964.

_____. "The Tramping Artisan." *Economic History Review.* 2nd Ser., Vol. III, No. 3, 1951.

_____. *Primitive Rebels, Studies in Archaic Forms of Social Movement in the 19th and 20th Centuries.* New York: W. W. Norton & Co., Inc. 1959, 1965.

Hobsbawm, Eric J. and Rude, George. *Captain Swing.* New York: Pantheon Books, 1968.

Hoggart, Richard. *The Uses of Literacy.* Great Britain: Penquin Books, 1957, 1959.

Hollingsworth, Thomas H. *Historical Demography.* Ithaca: Cornell University Press, 1969.

Holmes, C. *John Bull's Island: Immigration v. British Society, 1871–1971.* London: Faber & Faber, 1988.

Hornby-Smith, M. P. and Angela Dale. "The Assimilation of Irish Immigrants in England," *The British Journal of Sociology,* xxxix, No. 4, 1992.

Houston, Cecil J. and William J. Smyth. *Irish Emigration and Canadian Settlement, Patterns, Links and Letters.* Toronto: University of Toronto, 1990.

Hovell, Mark. *The Chartist Movement.* New York: Augustus M. Kelley, 1967, 1918.

Humphreys, Alexander J. *New Dubliners, Urbanization and the Irish Family.* London: Routledge & Kegan Paul, 1966.

Hunt, E. H. *Regional Wage Variations in Britain, 1850–1914.* Oxford: Oxford University Press, 1973.

_____. "How Mobile Was Labour in 19th Century Britain?" *Provincial Labour History,* J. H. Porter, ed. Exeter Papers in Economic History, No. 6. University of Exeter, 1972.

Huntington, S. P. *Political Order in Changing Societies.* New Haven: Yale University Press, 1968.

Hurwitz, Samuel. "The Development of the Social Welfare State in Prewar Britain." *The Making of English History.* Schuyler and Ausubel, eds. New York: Holt, Rinehart & Winston, 1952.

Hutton, A. W., ed. *Young's Tour in Ireland.* Vol. I & II. London: George Bell and Sons, 1892.

Hutton, Sean. "Donal MacAmhlaigh, 1926–1989. An Appreciation of the Man and His Writings." *Irish Studies in Britain,* xiv, 1989.

Illsley, Raymond; Finlayson, Angela and Thompson, Barbara. "The Motivation and Characteristics of Internal Migrants, a Socio-Medical Study of Young Migrants in Scotland." New York: *The Milbank Memorial Fund Quarterly,* Vol. XLI, No. 2, April 1963.

Inglis, Brian. *The Story of Ireland.* London: Faber & Faber, 1946, 1965.

Inglis, Henry D. *A Journey Through Ireland in the Spring, Summer, and Autumn of 1834.* Vol. I & II. London: Whittaker & Co., 1835.

_____. *A Tour Through Ireland in the Spring, Summer, and Autumn of 1834.* 2nd ed. Vol. 1 & 2. London: Whittaker & Co., 1851.

_____. *The Freedom of the Press in Ireland, 1784–1841.* London: Faber & Faber, 1954.

Inoki, Takenori. " 'New' Immigration and U.S. Trade Policy: 1880–1913: An Application of the Stolper-Samuelson Tariff Argument." Paper, no date.

_____. "Aspects of German Peasant Emigration to the United States, 1815–1914." Ph.D. diss. M.I.T., June, 1974.

Irvine, H. S. "Some Aspects of Passenger Traffic between Britain and Ireland, 1820–50," *Journal of Transport History,* IV, 4, 1960.

Isaac, Julius. *Economics of Migration.* New York: Oxford University Press, 1947.

Jackson, John Archer. *The Irish in Britain.* London: Routledge & Kegan Paul, 1963.

_____. "The Irish" in *London, Aspects of Change.* John A. Jackson, ed. Centre for Urban Studies. London: MacGibbon & Kee, 1964.

_____. "The Irish in Britain," in *Ireland and Britain Since 1922.* P. J. Drudy, ed. *Irish Studies, No. 5.* Cambridge: Cambridge University Press, 1986.

Jackson, W. Eric. *Local Government in England and Wales.* Hammondsworth: Penquin Books, 1945, 1951.

Jenkins, Arthur Hugh. *Adam Smith Today.* New York: Kennikat Press, 1948.

Johnson, William. *England As It Is, Political, Social, and Industrial, in the Middle of the 19th Century.* 2 vols. London: John Murray, 1851.

Johnston, Edith Mary. *Ireland in the 18th Century. The Gill History of Ireland.* Vol. 8. Dublin: Gill & Macmillan, 1974.

_____. *Great Britain and Ireland 1760–1800, a Study in Political Administration.* Edinburgh: Oliver & Boyd, 1963.

Johnston, H. J. M. *British Emigration Policy, 1815–1830.* Oxford: Clarendon Press, 1972.

Johnston, J. H. "Harvest Migration from Nineteenth Century Ireland." *Transactions of the Institute of British Geographers,* Vol. 41, June 1967.

_____."Migrant Labour in County Derry During a Pre-Famine Year." *Proceedings of the Royal Irish Academy,* Vol. LX, 1959.

_____. "The Distribution of Irish Emigration in the Decade before the Great Famine." *Irish Geography.* No. 21, 1988.

_____. "The Context of Migration: The Example of Ireland in the Nineteenth Century." *Institute of British Geographers Transactions,* xv, 1991.

Jones, David. *Crime, Protest, Community and Police in Nineteenth Century Britain.* London: Routledge, Kegan & Paul, 1982.

Jones, E. L. "Agriculture and Economic Growth in England, 1660–1750: Agricultural Change" in *Journal of Economic History.* Vol. XXV, No. 1, March 1965.

Jones, Gareth Stedman. *Outcast London, a Study of the Relationship Between Classes in Victorian Society.* Oxford: Clarendon Press, 1971.

Jones, Maldwyn A. *American Immigration.* Chicago: University of Chicago Press, 1960.

Jordon, Bill. *Paupers, the Making of a New Claiming Class.* London: Routledge & Kegan Paul, 1973.

Jordon, W. K. *Philanthropy in England, 1480–1660.* New York: Unwin Bros., 1959.

Kaijage, F. J. "Labouring Barnsley, 1816–1856: a Social and Economic History," Ph.D. diss., Warwick University, 1975.

Kaiyama, Michihiro. "Labor Migration, Umemployment and Capital Accumulation." Discussion Paper No. 14, January 1974. Dept. of Economics, Toboker University, Japan.

Kane, Robert. *The Industrial Resources of Ireland.* Dublin: Hodges and Smith, 1845.

Kay, James Phillips. *The Moral and Physical Condition of the Working Classes Employed in the Cotton Manufacture in Manchester.* London: James Ridgway, 1832.

Kay, Joseph. *The Social Condition and Education of People in England and Europe.* 2 vols. London: Longman, Brown, Green & Longmans, 1850.

_____. *The Social Condition and Education of the People in England.* New York: Harper & Bros., 1863.

Kay-Shuttleworth, Sir James. *Thoughts and Suggestions on Certain Social Problems.* London: Longmans, Green & Co., 1873.

Kelley, Allen C. "International Migration and Economic Growth, Australia: 1865–1935." *Journal of Economic History,* Vol. XXV, No. 3, September 1965.

Kemp, Betty. *King and Commons, 1660–1832.* London: Macmillan & Co., Ltd., 1957.

_____. "Reflections on the Repeal of the Corn Laws." *Victorian Studies.* March 1962.

Kennedy, J. P. *Digest of Evidence Taken Before Her Majesty's Commissioners of Inquiry into the State of the Law and Practice in Respect to the Occupation of Land in Ireland* (Devon Commission). Dublin: Thom, 1847.

_____. *Instruct! Employ! Don't Hang Them!, or Ireland Tranquilized without Soldiers or Enriched without English Capital, Contains Observations on a Few of the Chief Errors of Irish Government and Ireland Proprietors, with the Means of Correction.* London: T. & W. Boone, 1835.

Kennedy, R. J. R. "Single or Triple Melting-Pot? Intermarriage Trends — New Haven,

1870–1940." *American Journal of Sociology.* Vol. XLIX, No. 4, January 1944.

Kennedy, Robert E., Jr. *The Irish Emigration, Marriage and Fertility.* Berkeley & Los Angeles, University of California Press, 1973.

Kennelly, Helen and Danny, "From Roscrea to Leeds: An Emigrant Community" in *Tipperary Historical Journal,* 1992.

Kerr, Barbara M. "Irish Immigration Into Great Britain, 1798–1838." Ph.D. diss., Oxford University, May 1954.

_____. "Irish Seasonal Migration to Great Britain, 1800–1838." *Irish Historical Studies.* Vol. III, No. 12. September 1943.

Kerr, Clark; Harbison, F.; Dunlop, J. T. and Myers, C. A. *Industrialism and Industrial Man.* Ithaca, 1951.

Kerr, D.A. *Peel, Priests and Politics: Sir Robert Peel's Administration and the Roman Catholic Church in Ireland 1841–46.* Oxford: Clarendon Press, 1982.

Kiernan, V.G. "Britons Old and New," in *Immigrants and Minorities in British Society.* Colin Holmes, ed. London: George Allen & Unwin, 1978

Kindleberger, Charles P. *Economic Growth in France and Britain: 1851–1950.* New York: Simon & Schuster, 1964, 1969.

_____. "Mass Migration Then and Now." *Foreign Affairs.* Vol. 43, No.4, July 1965.

_____. *Europe's Post War Growth, The Role of the Labour Supply.* Cambridge: Harvard University Press, 1967.

_____. "Review of Polyani's *Great Transformation*" in *Daedalus.* Winter 1974.

Kingsley, Charles. "Cheap Clothes and Nasty" in *New Miscellanies.* Boston: Ticknor & Fields, 1860.

_____. *Yeast.* New York: Macmillan, 1895.

Kirby, R. J. and Musson, A. E. *The Voice of the People: A Biography of John Doherty, 1798–1854.* Manchester: Manchester University Press, 1975.

Knight, P. *Erris in the Irish Highlands.* Dublin: Martin Keene & Son, 1836.

Knight, Patricia. "Women and Abortion in Victorian England." *History Workshop.* No. 4, Autumn 1977.

Kohl, J.G. *Travels in Ireland.* London: Bruce & Wyld, 1844.

Kuczynski, Jurgen. *Great Britain and the Empire, 1750 to the Present Day.* Vol. I. London: Frederick Muller, Ltd., 1942.

Landes, David S. *The Unbound Prometheus. Technological Change and Industrial Development in Western Europe from 1750 to the Present.* Cambridge: University Press, 1969.

Langer, William L. "Europe's Initial Population Explosion" in *American Historical Review.* Vol. LXIX, No. 1, October 1963.

Lanternari, Vittorio. *The Religions of the Oppressed, a Study of Modern Messianic Cults.* London: Macgibbon & Kee, 1963.

Larcom, Capt. Thomas. "Address on the Conclusion of the 3rd Session of the Dublin Statistical Society." Dublin: Hodges & Smith, 1850.

Larkin, Emmet. *James Larkin, Irish Labour Leader.* Cambridge: M.I.T. Press, 1965.

_____. "The Devotional Revolution in Ireland, 1850–75" in *American Historical Review.* LXXVII, No. 3, June 1972.

_____. "Economic Growth, Capital Investment and the Roman Catholic Church in Nineteenth-century Ireland," *American Historical Review,* Vol.LXXII, No.3, April 1967.

_____. ed., *Alexis de Tocqueville's Journey in Ireland*. Dublin: Wolfhound Press, 1991.

Laslett, Peter. *The World We Have Lost*. New York: Charles Scribner's Sons, 1965.

_____. *Household and Family in Past Time*. Cambridge: University Press, 1972.

Lavery, Felix, ed. *Irish Heroes in the War*. London: Everett & Co., Ltd., 1917.

Lawton, R. "Irish Immigration to England and Wales in the Mid-Nineteenth Century" in *Irish Geography*. Vol. IV, No. 1, 1959.

Lecky, W. E. H. *History of Ireland in the Eighteenth Century*. Vols. I–V. London: Longman's, Green & Co., 1913.

_____. *Leaders of Public Opinion in Ireland*. London: Longmans, Green & Co., 1903.

Lee, J. J. "Irish Agriculture: Review of Articles" in *Agricultural History Review*. Vol. XVII, 1969.

_____. *The Modernisation of Irish Society, 1848–1918*. The Gill History of Ireland. Vol. 10. Dublin: Gill & Macmillan, 1973.

_____. "The Dual Economy in Ireland, 1800–50" in *Historical Studies*. T. T. Desmond Williams, ed. Vol. VIII. Dublin, 27–30 May 1969. Dublin: Gill & Macmillan, 1971.

_____. ed. *Irish Historiography 1970–1979*. Cork: Cork University Press, 1981.

_____. "Money and Beer in Ireland, 1790–1875," in *Economic History Review,* Vol. XIX, No. 1, 2nd series, 1968a.

_____. "Marriage and Population in Pre-famine Ireland," *Economic History Review,* Vol. XXI, 2nd series, 1968a.

_____. "Capital in the Irish Economy," in L. M. Cullen, ed., *The Formation of the Irish Economy*. Cork: Mercier Press, 1969.

_____. "On the Accuracy of the Pre-famine Irish Censuses" in J. M. Goldstrom and L. A. Clarkson, eds., *Irish Population, Economy and Society, Essays in Honour of K. H. Connell*. Oxford: Clarendon Press, 1981.

_____. "Women and the Church since the Famine," in MacCurtain and O'Corrain, *Women in Irish Society, the Historical Dimension*. Dublin: Arlen House, Women's Press, 1978.

Lees, Lynn H. "Social Change and Social Stability Among the London Irish." Ph.D. diss., Harvard University, March, 1969.

_____. "Patterns of Lower Class Life: Irish Slum Communities in Nineteenth Century London." *Nineteenth-Century Cities*. S. Thernstrom and R. Sennet, eds. New Haven, Yale University Press, 1969.

_____. "Mid-Victorian Migration and the Irish Family Economy." *Victorian Studies,* xx, 1976.

_____. *Exiles of Erin, Irish Migrants in Victorian London*. Ithaca, New York: Cornell University Press, 1979.

Lees, Lynn H., and Modell, John. "The Irish Countryman Urbanized" in the *Journal of Urban History,* Vol. 3, No. 4, August 1977.

Leeson, Francis. "Records of Irish Emigrants to Canada in Sussex Archives, 1839–41," *The Irish Ancestor*. No. 1. 1974.

LeFanu, W.R. *Seventy Years of Irish Life*. 2nd ed. London: Edward Arnold, 1893.

Lennon, Mary, McAdam, Marie, and O'Brien, Joanne. *Across the Water, Irish Women's Lives in Britain*. London: Virago Press, 1988

Lewis, Brian. *Coal Mining in the 18th and 19th Centuries.* London: Longman Group, 1971.

Lewis, G. F., ed. *Letters of the Rt. Hon. Sir George Cornewall Lewis.* London: Longmans, Green & Co., 1870.

Lewis, George Cornewall. *On Local Disturbances in Ireland.* London: B. Fellowes, 1836.

———. *On the Government of Dependencies.* Oxford: Clarendon Press, 1841, 1891.

———. "Report on the State of the Irish Poor in Great Britain," Parliamentary Papers, 1836, Vol.XXXIV. Appendix G to the *Report of the Commissioners for Inquiring into the Condition of the Poorer Classes in Ireland.*

Lewis, Michael. *The History of the British Navy.* Fair Lawn, New Jersey: Essential Books, 1959.

Lewis, Oscar. *La Vida.* New York: Random House, 1965.

Lewis, Samuel. *A Topographical Dictionary of Ireland with Historical and Statistical Descriptions.* 2 vols. London: S. Lewis & Co., 1837.

Lewis, W. Arthur. "Economic Development with Unlimited Supplies of Labour." *The Economics of Underdevelopment.* A. N. Agarwala and S. P. Singh, eds. New York: Oxford University Press, 1963.

Leys, M. D. R. *Catholics in England, a Social History, 1559–1829.* London: Longmans, 1961.

Liebow, Elliott. *Talley's Corner, a Study of Negro Streetcorner Men.* Boston: Little Brown, 1967.

Lipson, E. *The Growth of English Society.* London: Adam & Charles Black, 1949.

Lloyd, Christopher. *The British Seaman, 1200–1860.* London: Collins, 1968.

Locke, John. *Ireland's Recovery or the Excessive Emigration and its Reparative Agencies in Ireland.* London: John W. Parker & Son, 1854.

Lodge, J. *Peerage of Ireland.* Dublin 1789.

Longford, Christine. *A Biography of Dublin.* City Biography Series. London: Methuen & Co., 1936.

Lough, T. *England's Wealth and Ireland's Poverty.* London: Putney & Co., 1896.

Lowe, William James. "The Irish in Lancashire, 1846–71: A Social History." Ph.D. diss., University of Dublin, Trinity College, November 1974.

———. "The Lancashire Irish and the Catholic Church, 1846–71: The Social Dimension." *Irish Historical Studies.* Vol. XX, Nol 78, September 1976.

———. "Landlord and Tenant on the Estate of Trinity College Dublin, 1851–1903." *Hermathena: Dublin University Review.* Vol. CXX, July 1976.

———. "Irish Community Life in Lancashire During the Mid-Nineteenth Century." Paper for the American Committee for Irish Studies, 27 April 1979.

———. "Lancashire Fenianism, 1864–71." *Transactions of the Historic Society of Lancashire and Chesire.* Vol. 126, 1977.

———. "Social Agencies Among the Irish in Lancashire During the Mid-Nineteenth Century." *Journal of the Irish Labour History Society. Soathar* 3.

———. *The Irish in Mid-Victorian Lancashire: The Shaping of a Working Class Community.* Washington, D.C.: American University Press, 1989.

Lowe, William James and Haslett, John. "Household Structure and Overcrowding Among the Lancashire Irish, 1851–1871." *Histoire Sociale.* Vol. IX, No. 19, May 1977.

Lucas, A. T. *Furze, A Survey and History of its Uses in Ireland.* Dublin: an Roinn Oideachais, National Museum of Ireland, 1960.

Luing, Sean O. "Some Travellers in Kerry." *Journal of Kerry Archaelogical and Historical Society.* No. 1, 1968.

Lunn, Kenneth. "The Irish in Britain: Some Recent Work." *Saothar,* No. 8, 1982.

Lutz, Vera. *Italy, a Study in Economic Development.* London: Oxford University Press, 1962.

Lynch, A. H. *Measures to be Adopted for the Employment of the Labouring Classes in Ireland.* London: Charles Knight & Co., 1839.

Lynch, Patrick and Vaizey, John. *Guinness's Brewery in the Irish Economy, 1759–1876.* Cambridge: the University Press, 1960.

Lyons, F. S. L. *Ireland Since the Famine.* Glasgow: Collins/Fontana, 1973.

MacAmhlaigh, Donall. *An Irish Navvy, the Diary of an Exile.* London: Routledge & Kegan Paul, 1964.

MacAodha, Brendan. "A Booley Place-name in County Tyrone." *Ulster Folklife.* Vol. 2, 1956.

_____. "Letters from America." *Ulster Folklife.* Vol. 2, 1956.

MacCurtain, Margaret. "Peasantry in Ireland: Definition and Theme" in *Irish University Review.* Autumn 1974.

MacCurtain, Margaret, and O'Corrain, Donncha, eds. *Women in Irish Society, the Historical Dimension.* Dublin: Arlen House, Women's Press, 1978.

MacDonagh, Oliver. *A Pattern of Government Growth, 1800–60, the Passenger Acts and Their Enforcement.* London: Macgibbon & Kee, 1961.

_____. "The Irish Catholic Clergy and Emigration During the Great Famine." *Irish Historical Studies.* Vol. V, No. 20.

_____. "Irish Emigration to the United States of America and the British Colonies During the Famine." *The Great Famine: Studies in Irish History, 1845–1852.* R. Dudley Edwards and T. Desmond Williams, eds. New York: University Press, 1957.

_____. "Sea Communications in the Nineteenth Century." *Travel and Transport in Ireland,* Kevin B. Nowlan, ed. Dublin: Gill and Macmillan, 1973.

_____. "The Irish Famine Emigration to the United States." *Perspectives in American History,* No. X, 1976.

_____. "Emigration and the State, 1833–55: An Essay in Administrative History." *Transaction of the Royal Historical Society,* 5th Vol.

MacGill, Patrick. *Children of the Dead End.* Dingle, Ireland: Brandon Book Publishers, 1914, 1982.

_____. *Glenmornan.* London: Caliban Books, 1983.

_____. *The Rat Pit.* London: Caliban Books, 1915, 1983.

_____. *Lanty Hanlon.* London: Caliban Books, 1983.

_____. *Moleskin Joe.* London: Caliban Books, 1983.

MacGowan, Michael. *The Hard Road to Klondike.* Translated by Valentine Iremonger. London: Routledge & Kegan Paul, 1962, 1977.

MacKenzie, Norman. *Secret Societies.* London: Aldus Books, 1967.

MacLysaght, Edward. *The Surnames of Ireland.* Dublin: Irish University Press, 1973.

Madden, Richard Lee. *The History of Irish Periodical Literature.* 2 vols. London: T. C. Newby, 1867.

Maguire, T. F. *The Industrial Movement in Ireland as Illustrated by the National*

Exhibition of 1852. Cork: John O'Brien, 1853.

Mahon, Brid. *A Background to Donegal Tweed.* Dublin: Report for Coras Trachtala, The Irish Export Board, September, 1964.

Maine, Sir Henry Sumner. *Lectures on the Early History of Institutions.* London: John Murray, 1875.

Malcomson, A. P. W. "Absenteeism in Eighteenth Century Ireland." *Irish Economic and Social History.* Vol. 1, 1974.

Malthus, Thomas R. *An Essay on the Principle of Population,* 6th ed. 2 vols. London: Murray, 1826.

Mangalam, J. J. and Morgan, Cornelia. *Human Migration, a Guide to Migration Literature in English (1955–1962).* Lexington: University of Kentucky Press, 1968.

Mangalam, J. J. and Schwarzweller, Harry K. "Some Theoretical Guidelines Toward a Sociology of Migration." *International Migration Review.* Vol. IV, Spring 1970.

Mannion, John J. *Irish Settlements in Eastern Canada, a Study of Cultural Transfer and Adaptation.* Toronto: University of Toronto Press, 1974.

Marshall, Dorothy. *The English Poor in the 18th Century, a Study in Social and Administrative History.* London: George Routledge & Sons, Ltd., 1926.

_____. *Eighteenth Century England.* London: Camelot Press, 1962.

Marshall, J. D. "The Old Poor Law, 1795–1834." *Studies in Economic History.* M. W. Flinn, ed. London: Macmillan, 1968.

Martin, R. M. *Ireland Before and After the Union.* London & Dublin: J. B. Nichols and Sons, 1848.

Martineau, Harriet. *A Manchester Strike.* London: Charles Fox, 1834.

_____. *Letters from Ireland.* London: Charles Fox, 1852.

Marx, Karl. *Capital.* London: Allen & Unwin, 1867, 1928.

Marx, Karl, and Engels, Frederick. *On Ireland, Ireland and the Irish Question.* London: Lawrence & Wishart, 1971.

Mason, William Shaw. *A Statistical Account or Parochial Survey of Ireland.* 2 vols. Dublin: Graiberry & Campbell, 1814.

Mathias, Peter. *The First Industrial Nation, an Economic History of Britain, 1700–1914.* New York: Charles Scribner's Sons, 1969.

Maunsell, Robert. *A Late Professional Gentleman's Recollections of Ireland.* Windsor: Printing Works, 1845.

Maxwell, Constantia. *Country and Town in Ireland under the Georges.* Dundalk: Dundalgan Press, 1949.

_____. *Dublin under the Georges, 1714–1830.* London: George G. Harrap & Co., Ltd., 1940.

_____. *The Stranger in Ireland.* London: Jonathan Cape, 1954.

Mayhew, Henry. *London Characters.* London: Chatto & Windus, 1874.

_____. *London Labour and the London Poor.* Vols. I-IV. New York: Dover Publications, 1968.

_____. *The Fear of the World; or, Living for Appearances.* New York: Harper & Bros., 1850.

Mayhew, Henry, and Binney, John. *The Criminal Prisons of London and Scenes of Prison Life.* London: Charles Griffin & Co., 1862.

Mazumdar, D. "Labour Supply in Early Industrialization: the Case of the Bombay Textile Industry." *Economic History Review.* No. 3, August 1973.

McAlpin, Michelle Burge. "Dearth, Famine and Risk: The Changing Impact of Crop Failures in Western India, 1870–1920," *Journal of Economic History.* Vol. xxxix, No. 1, 1979.

McCarthy, J. G. *Irish Land Questions.* London: B. Nichols & Sons, 1839, 1870.

McConville, P. "Emigration from Ireland: Figures and Facts." *Christus Rex.* October 1956.

McCord, Norman. *The Anti-Corn Law League, 1838–1846.* London: Allen and Unwin, Ltd., 1958.

McCourt, Desmond. "Infield and Outfield in Ireland." *Economic History Review.* 2nd Ser., Vol. XII, No. 1, 1954.

_____. "The Use of Oral Tradition in Irish Historical Geography." *Irish Geography.* Vol. VI, No. 4, 1972.

McDowell, R. B. "Dublin and Belfast – a Comparison." *Social Life in Ireland, 1800–45.* R. B. McDowell, ed. Cork: Mercier Press, 1963.

_____. *Public Opinion and Government Policy in Ireland, 1801–46.* London: Faber & Faber, 1952.

_____, ed. *Social Life in Ireland, 1800–45.* Published for the Cultural Relations Commission of Ireland, in association with Radio Eireann, by Colm O Lochlainn. Dublin: 1957.

McHugh, R. J. "William Carleton: A Portrait of the Artist as Propagandist," *Studies,* xxvii, 1938; "Maria Edgeworth's Irish Novels," *Studies,* xxvii, 1938.

McKay, Robert. *An Anthology of the Potato.* Dublin: Allen Figgis & Co., 1961.

McKernan, Ann. "War, Gender and Industrial Innovation: Recruiting Women Weavers in Early Nineteenth Century Ireland." *Journal of Social History* (forthcoming).

McLaren, Angus. "Women's Work and Regulation of Family Size." *History Workshop.* No. 4, Autumn 1977.

Merton, Robert K. *Social Theory and Social Structure.* New York: Free Press, 1968.

Mill, John Stuart. *Chapters and Speeches on the Irish Land Question.* London: Longman's, Green, Reader & Dyer, 1870.

_____. *John Stuart Mill on Ireland,* R. N. Lebow, ed. Philadelphia: Institute for Study of Human Issues, 1979.

Miller, David. "Irish Catholicism and the Great Famine." *Journal of Social History.* Vol. IX, No. 1, Fall 1975.

Miller, Kerby A. *Emigrants and Exiles, Ireland and the Irish Exodus to North America.* Oxford: Oxford University Press, 1985.

_____. "Emigrants and Exiles: Irish Culture and Irish Emigration to North America, 1790–1922," *Irish Historical Studies,* XXII, 86, 1980.

Minchenton, Walter. "The Merchants in England in the 18th Century." *The Entrepreneur,* papers presented at the Annual Conference of the Economic History Society at Cambridge, England, April 1957.

Mitchell, Arthur. *Labour in Irish Politics, 1890–1930.* New York: Harper & Row, 1974.

Mitchell, Brian C. *The Paddy Camps: The Irish in Lowell, 1821–61.* Urbana and Chicago: University of Illinois Press, 1988.

Mitchell, Brian (ed). *Irish Emigration Lists, 1833–39.* Baltimore: Genealogical Publishing, 1989.

Mitchison, R. and P. Roebuck (eds), *Economy and Society in Scotland and Ireland,*

1500–1939. Edinburgh: John Donald, 1992.

Moch, Leslie Page, *Moving Europeans: Migration in Western Europe Since 1650,* Bloomington: Indiana Univ. Press, 1992.

Mokyr, Joel. "Industrialization and Poverty in Ireland and the Netherlands," *Journal of Interdisciplinary History,* Vol. X, No. 3, (Winter 1980).

_____. "Irish History with the Potato," *Irish Economic and Social History,* Vol. VIII, 1981.

_____. *Why Ireland Starved: A Quantitative and Analytical History of the Irish Economy, 1800–1850.* London: George Allen & Unwin, 1983.

Mokyr, Joel, and O'Gráda, Cormac. "Emigration and Poverty in Pre-Famine Ireland," *Explorations in Economic History,* Vol.19, No.4, October 1982.

Mol, J. J. "Immigrant Absorption and Religion." *International Migration Review.* Vol. 5, Spring 1971.

Moller, Herbert, ed. *Population Movements in Modern European History.* New York: Macmillan Co., 1964.

Monaghan, John J. "The Rise and Fall of the Belfast Cotton Industry." *Irish Historical Studies.* Vol. III, No. 9, March 1942.

Moody, T. W., ed. *Irish Historiography 1936–70.* Dublin, 1971.

Moody, T. W., and Beckett, J. C., eds. *Ulster Today.* London: The British Broadcasting Corp., 1957.

Moore, W. E., and Feldman, A. S., eds. *Labor Commitment and Social Change in Developing Areas.* New York, 1960.

Morehouse, Frances. "The Irish Migration of the Forties." *American Historical Review,* Vol. XXXIII, No. 39.

Morrison, Arthur. *A Child of the Jago.* London: Macgibbon & Kee, 1896, 1969.

_____. *Tales of Mean Streets.* Leipzig: Bernard Tauchnitz, 1895.

Morton, A. L. and Tate, George. *The British Labour Movement.* New York: International Publ., 1957.

Moyles, M. G., and de Brun, Padraig. "Charles O'Brien's Agricultural Survey of Kerry, 1800." *Journal of the Kerry Archaeological and Historical Society,* No. 1, 1968; Part I & II, No. 2, 1969.

Moynihan, D. P. and Glazer, N. *Beyond the Melting Pot.* Cambridge: M.I.T. Press, 1963, 1967.

M'Parlan, James. *Statistical Survey of the County of Mayo,* for the Dublin Society. Dublin: Graisberry & Campbell, 1802.

_____. *Statistical Survey of the County of Donegal.* Dublin: Graisberry & Campbell, 1802.

_____. *Statistical Survey of the County of Leitrim.* Dublin: Graisberry & Campbell, 1802.

_____. *Statistical Survey of the County of Sligo.* Dublin: Graisberry & Campbell, 1802.

Mulvey, Helen F. "Modern Irish History Since 1940: A Bibliographical Survey (1600–1922)." *Changing Views on British History.* Elizabeth Chapin Furber, ed. Cambridge: Harvard University Press.

Murphy, Michael J. *Tyrone Folk Quests.* Belfast: Blackstaff Press, 1973.

Murray, A. E. *Commercial and Financial Relations Between England and Ireland from the Period of Restoration.* London: P. S. King & Son, 1907.

Murray, Patrick F. "Calendar of the Overseas Missionary Correspondence of the All

Hallowe's College, Dublin, 1842–77." Master's thesis, Autumn, 1956, University College, Dublin.

_____. *Maria Edgeworth: A Study of the Novelist*. Cork: Mercier Press, 1971.

Musson, A. E. *The Voice of the People, John Doherty, 1798–1854, Trade Unionist, Radical and Factory Reformer*. Manchester: Manchester University Press, 1975.

Neale, R. S. *Class and Ideology in the 19th Century*. London: Routledge & Kegan Paul, 1972.

Nelli, Humbert S. "Italians in Urban America: A Study in Ethnic Adjustment." *International Migration Review*. Vol. I (new series), No. 3, Summer 1967.

Newenham, Thomas. *A Statistical and Historical Inquiry into the Progress and Magnitude of the Population of Ireland*. London: C.& R. Baldwin, 1805.

_____. *A View of the Natural, Political and Commercial Circumstances of Ireland*. London: Cadell & W. Davies, 1809.

Nicholas, S., and Shergold, P. "Intercountry Impact of Emigration: Prefamine Ireland and England, 1817–1839," Paper, University of New South Wales, Kensington, Australia.

_____. "Human Capital and the Pre-Famine Irish Emigration to England," *Explorations in Economic History* 24(2), April 1987.

Nicholls, George. *Three Reports on the Irish Poor Laws*. London: W. Clowes & Sons, 1838.

Nicholson, Asenath, *Ireland's Welcome to the Stranger, or Excursions through Ireland in 1844 and 1845*. London: Gilpin, 1847.

_____. *A History of the Irish Poor Law*. London: John Murray, 1856.

Nolan, William, (ed). *The Shaping of Ireland, The Geographical Perspective*. Dublin: Mercier Press, 1986.

Nowlan, Kevin B. *The Politics of Repeal: A Study in the Relations Between Great Britain and Ireland*. London: Rontledge & K. Paul, 1965.

O'Brien, Conor Cruise. *States of Ireland*. New York: Vintage Books, 1972, 1973.

O'Brien, George. *The Economic History of Ireland in the Seventeenth Century*. New Jersey: Augustus M. Kelley, 1919, 1972.

_____. *The Economic History of Ireland in the Eighteenth Century*. Dublin & London: Maunsel & Co., Ltd., 1918.

_____. *The Economic History of Ireland from the Union to the Famine*. London: Longmans, Green & Co., 1921.

O'Brien, R. B. *Dublin Castle and the Irish People*. Dublin: M. H. Gill & Sons, Ltd., 1909.

_____. *Thomas Drummond: Life and Letters*. London: Kegan Paul, Trench, Trubner & Co., 1889.

O'Brien, W. P. *The Great Famine in Ireland, and a Retrospect of the Fifty Years 1845–95, and a Sketch of the Congested Districts*. London: Clery & Co., 1896.

O'Connell, Daniel. *On the State of the Irish Peasantry, 1825*. Report from the Select Committee on the State of Ireland, 1825. Parliamentary Papers. V. VIII. 1825.

O'Connell, John. *The Repeal Dictionary*. 2 vols. Dublin: J. Browne, 1845.

O'Connell, Maurice. "Class Conflict in a Pre-Industrial Society." *Duquesne Review*, Vol. 9, No. 1, Fall 1963.

_____. *Irish Politics and Social Conflict in the Age of the American Revolution*. Philadelphia: University of Pennsylvania Press, 1965.

O'Connor, Kevin, *The Irish in Britain*. Dublin: Gulf & Macmillan, 1974.

O'Day, (ed). *A Survey of the Irish in England, 1872* by Hugh Heinrick. London: Hambledon, 1990.

O'Donovan, John, *The Economic History of Livestock in Ireland.* Cork: Cork University Press, 1940.

O'Dowd, Anne. *Spalpeens and Tattie Howkers, History and Folklore of the Irish Migratory Agricultural Worker in Ireland and Britain.* Dublin: Irish Academic Press, 1991.

_____. *Meithal, A Study of Co-operative Labor in Rural Ireland.* Dublin: Bhéaloideas, 1981.

O'Faolain, Sean. *King of the Beggars,* a Life of Daniel O'Connell. New York: Viking Press, 1938.

O'Farrell, Patrick. *Ireland's English Question.* London: Oxford University Press, 1971.

_____. *England and Ireland since 1800.* London: Oxford Univesity Press, 1975.

O'Flanagan, Patrick, Paul Ferguson and Kevin Whelan (ed). *Rural Ireland, Modernisation and Change, 1600–1900.* Cork: Cork University Press, 1987.

O'Gráda, Cormac. "A Note on Farm Inheritance in Southern Ireland, 1900–1930." Paper, December 1978.

_____. "Post-Famine Adjustment: Essays in Nineteenth-Century Irish Economic History," Ph.D. diss., to Columbia University, New York, 1973.

_____. "A Note on 19th Century Irish Emigration Statistics." *Population Studies,* Vol. 29, No. 1, 1975.

_____. "The Beginnings of the Irish Creamery System, 1880–1914." *Economic History Review,* 2nd Ser., Vol. XXX, No. 2, May 1977.

_____. "The Owenite Community at Ralahine, County Clare, 1831–33: a Reassessment." *Irish Economic and Social History.* Vol. I, 1974.

_____. "Some Aspects of 19th Century Irish Emigration." L. M. Cullen and T. C. Smout, eds., *Comparative Aspects of Scottish and Irish Economic and Social History.* Edinburgh, 1977.

_____. "Inheritance, Emigration, and Fertility: Ireland 1850–1920," paper presented to the Franco-Irish Conference on Rural Communities, Paris, March 1982.

_____. "Eighteenth-Century Irish Population: Old Sources and New Speculations," paper on research in progress with Stuart Daultry and David Dickson. February 1980.

_____. "Technical Change in the Mid-Nineteenth Century British Cotton Industry: A Note," *Journal of Economic History,* Vol. 13, No. 2, Fall 1984.

_____. *Ireland Before and After the Famine: Explorations in Economic History, 1800–1925.* Manchester, Mass. Univ. Press, 1988.

_____. *The Great Irish Famine,* London: Macmillan, 1989.

O'Grady, Anne. "Irish Migration to London in the 1940s and 50s," Irish In Britain Research Forum. Occasional Papers Series: No.3. PNL Press. 1988.

O'Higgins, Rachel. "The Irish Influence in the Chartist Movement." *Past & Present.* No. 20, November 1961.

O'Neill, Francis. *Irish Folk Music.* Darby, Pa.: Norwood Editions, 1910, 1973.

O'Neill, Kevin. *Family and Farm in Pre-Famine Ireland: the Parish of Killashandra.* Wisconsin: University of Wisconsin Press, 1984.

O'Rourke, J. *The History of the Great Irish Famine of 1847.* Dublin: M'Glashan & Gill, 1875.

O'Rourke, Kevin. "Rural Depopulation in a Small Open Economy: Ireland 1856–1876." *Explorations in Economic History.* 28(4) October 1991.

O'Suilleabhain, Sean. *A Handbook of Irish Folklore.* Published by the Educational Company of Ireland, Ltd. for the Folklore of Ireland Society, 1942.

O'Sullivan, Denis M. "The Causes, Development and Relief of Distress in Mayo in 1831." Master's thesis, University College, Dublin, September 1968.

O'Sullivan, Patrick (ed). *The Irish Worldwide: History, Heritage, Identity,* 6 vols. Leicester: Leicester University Press (forthcoming).

———. *Patterns of Migration,* Vol. I of *The Irish Worldwide.* New York: St. Martin's Press, 1992.

O'Sullivan, Patrick MacGill, "The Making of a Writer" in *Ireland's Histories, Aspects of State, Society and Ideology.* Sean Hutton & Paul Stewart, eds. London: Routledge, 1991.

———. *The Irish in New Communities: The Irish Worldwide: History, Heritage, Identity,* Vol. II. Leicester: Leicester University Press, 1992.

O'Tuathaigh, M. A. G. *Ireland before the Famine, 1798–1848, The Gill History of Ireland,* No. 9. Dublin: Gill & Macmillan, 1972.

———. "Ireland, 1800–1921," in J. J. Lee, ed., *Irish Historiography, 1970–79.* Cork: Cork University Press, 1981.

———. "The Irish in Nineteenth-Century Britain: Problems of Integration," *Transactions of the Royal Historical Society,* XXXI, 1981.

———. "The Irish in Nineteenth-Century Britain: Problems of Integration," in Sheridan & Gilley, eds., *The Irish in the Victorian City.* London: Croom Helm, 1985.

Otway, Caesar. *Sketches in Erris and Tyrawly.* 2nd ed. Dublin: William Curry, Jun. & Co., 1841.

———. *Sketches in Ireland, Descriptive of Donegal, Cork, and Kerry.* 2nd ed. Dublin: William Curry, Jun. & Co., 1839.

———. *A Tour in Connaught: Sketches of Clonmacnoise, Joyce County, and Achill.* Dublin: William Curry, Jun. & Co., 1839.

Owen, David. *English Philanthropy, 1660–1960.* Cambridge: Belknap Press, 1964.

Paterson, T. G. F. "Family Composition and Occupations in Kilmore, Co. Armagh, 1821." *Ulster Folklife.* Vol. 7, 1961.

Perkin, Harold. *The Origins of Modern English Society, 1780–1880.* London: Routledge & Kegan Paul, 1969.

Peter, A. *Sketches of Old Dublin.* Dublin: Sealy, Bryers & Walker, 1907.

Petty, William. "The Political Anatomy of Ireland," in C. H. Hull, ed., *The Economic Writings of Sir William Petty.* Cambridge: Cambridge University Press, 1899; originally published, 1672.

Pfautz, Harold W., ed. *Charles Booth on the City: Physical Pattern and Social Structure.* Chicago: University of Chicago Press, 1967.

Piercy, Frederick Hawkins. *Route from Liverpool to Great Salt Lake Valley.* Fawn M. Brodie, ed. Cambridge: Harvard University Press, 1962.

Pim, Jonathan. *Condition and Prospects of Ireland.* Dublin: Hodges & Smith, 1840.

Pinchbeck, Ivy. *Women Workers and the Industrial Revolution.* London: Frank Cass & Co., 1969.

Piore, Michael J. "Undocumented Workers and U.S. Immigration Policy." Paper presented to Panel of Latin American Studies Association Conference, Houston, November 4, 1977.

_____. "Birds of Passage and Promised Lands: Long Distance Migrants and Industrial Societies." Manuscript, April 1978.

_____. *Birds of Passage: Migrant Labor in Industrial Societies*. Cambridge, New York: Cambridge University Press, 1979.

Plummer, Alfred. *Bronterre*. Toronto: University of Toronto Press, 1971.

_____. "The Place of Bronterre O'Brien in the Working Class Movement." *Economic History Review*. Vol. II, 1929–30.

Polanyi, Karl. *The Great Transformation*. New York: Rinehart & Co., 1944.

Pollard, Capt. H. B. C. *The Secret Societies of Ireland, Their Rise and Progress*. London: Philip Allan & Co., 1922.

Pollard, Sidney. *The Industrialisation of Europe, 1760–1970*. Oxford: Oxford University Press, 1981.

_____. *The Integration of the European Economy since 1815*. London: The University Association for Contemporary European Studies, 1981.

_____. *A History of Labour in Sheffield*. Liverpool: Liverpool University Press, 1959.

Pomfret, John E. *The Struggle for Land in Ireland, 1800–1923*. New York: Russell & Russell, 1930, 1969.

Porter, J. H., ed. *Provincial Labour History*. Exeter Papers in Economic History. No. 6. Exeter: University of Exeter, 1972.

Portes, Alejandro. "Return of the Wetback." *Society*. Vol. II, No. 3, March/April 1974.

Post, John D. *Food Shortage, Climatic Variability, and Epidemic Disease in Preindustrial Europe*. Ithaca, N.Y: Cornell University Press, 1985.

_____. *The Last Great Subsistence Crisis in the Western World*. Baltimore: University of Baltimore Press, 1977.

Postgate, R. W. *The Builders' History*. London: The Labour Publishing Co., 1923.

Power, J. O'Connor. "The Irish in England." *The Fortnightly Review*. Vol. XXVII, June 1, 1880.

Power, Patrick C. *Sex and Marriage in Ancient Ireland*. Dublin & Cork: Mercier Press, 1976.

Prendeville, P. L. "A Select Bibliography of Irish Economic History, Part One." *Economic History Review*. Vol. III, No. 2, October 1931.

_____. "A Select Bibliography of Irish Economic History." *Economic History Review*. Vol. III, No. 3, April 1932.

_____. "A Select Bibliography of Irish Economic History." Part Three. *Economic History Review*. Vol. IV, 1932–34.

Proceedings of the World Population Conference. Vol. IV. *Selected Papers and Summaries. Migration, Urbanization, Economic Development*. New York: United Nations, 1967.

Procter, Richard Wright. *Memorials of Bygone Manchester*. Manchester: Palmer & Howe, 1880.

_____. *Memorials of Manchester Streets*. Manchester: Thomas Sutcliffe, 1874.

Prothero, Iowerth. "Chartism in London." *Past & Present*. No. 44, 1969.

Pym, Jonathan. *Condition and Propects of Ireland*. Dublin: Hodges & Smith, 1840.

Quennel, Peter, ed. *Mayhew's Characters*. London: Wm. Kimber, 1951.

Ranis, Gustav. "Economic Dualism at Home and Abroad." *Public Policy*. Fall 1969.

Ravenstein, E. J. "The Laws of Migration." *Journal of the Royal Statistical Society*.

Vol. XLVII, No. 2, 1885–1889.

Reach, A. B. *Manchester and the Textile Districts in 1849.* C. Aspin, ed. Helmshore Local Historical Society, 1972.

Read, Donald and Glasgow, Eric. *Feargus O'Connor, Irishman and Chartist.* London: Edward Arnold, 1961.

Redford, Arthur. *Labour Migration in England, 1800–1850.* Manchester: Manchester University Press, 1926, 1964.

_____. *Manchester Merchants and Foreign Trade, 1794–1858.* Vol. I & II. Manchester: Manchester University Press, 1934.

_____. *The Economic History of England (1760–1860).* London: Longmans, Green & Co., 1931.

Reynolds, Reginald, ed. *British Pamphleteers.* Vol. II. London: Allan Wingate, 1951.

Richardson, Alan. "A Theory and a Method for the Psychological Study of Assimilation." *International Migration Review.* Vol. II, No. 1,

Richardson, Benjamin Ward. *The Health of Nations, a Review of the Work of Edwin Chadwick.* Vol. I & II. London: Longmans, Green & Co., 1887.

Rodgers, H. B. "The Lancashire Cotton Industry in 1840." *Transactions of the Institute of British Geographers,* No. 28, 1960.

Rosen, Bernard. "Race, Ethnicity, and the Achievement Syndrome." *American Sociological Review.* Vol. 24, No. 1, February 1959.

Rowntree, B. Seebohm. *Poverty, a Study of Town Life.* London: MacMillan & Co., 1901.

Royle, Stephen A. "Irish Manuscript Census Records a Neglected Source of Information," *Irish Geography,* Vol. XI, 1978.

Rude, George. *The Crowd in History, 1730–1848, a Study of Population Disturbances in France and England.* New York: John Wiley & Sons, 1964, 1966.

_____. "English Rural and Urban Disturbances on the Eve of the First Reform Bill, 1830–31." *Past & Present.* No. 37, July 1967.

_____. *Wilkes and Liberty.* Oxford: Clarendon Press, 1962.

Ryan, W. P. *The Irish Labour Movement.* Dublin: Talbot Press, 1919.

Sadler, Michael Thomas. *Ireland, its Evils and their Remedies,* 2nd ed. London: Murray, 1829.

Salaman, Redcliffe N. *The History and Social Influence of the Potato.* Cambridge: Cambridge University Press, 1947.

Samuel, Raphael. "Mineral Workers" in *Miners, Quarrymen and Saltworkers,* Raphael Samuel, ed. London: Routledge & Kegan Paul, 1977.

_____. "Workshop of the World; Steam Power and Hand Technology in Mid-Victorian Britain." *History Workshop.* Issue 3, Spring 1977.

_____. "Comers and Goers," in *The Victorian City.* H. J. Dyos and M. Wolff, eds. 2 vols. London: Routledge & Kegan Paul, 1973.

_____. "The Roman Catholic Church and the Irish Poor," in Swift & Gilley, eds., *The Irish in the Victorian City.* London: Croom Helm, 1985.

Sanderson, F. E. "The Development of Labour Migration from Nyasaland, 1891–1914." *Journal of African History.* Vol. II, No. 2, 1961.

Sanderson, Michael. "Education and the Factory in Industrial Lancashire." *Economic History Review.* 2nd Ser., Vol. XX, No. 1, April 1967.

Saunders, Harold. "Human Migration and Social Equilibrium." *Population Theory and Policy,* Jos. J. Spengler and Otis D. Duncan, eds. Glencoe: The Free Press, 1956.

Saville, John. *Rural Depopulation in England and Wales, 1851–1951.* London: Routledge & Kegan Paul, 1957.

Schmitt, D. *The Irony of Irish Democracy.* Boston, Massachusetts: Northeastern University Press, 1974.

Schrier, Arnold. *Ireland and the American Emigration 1850–1900.* Minneapolis: University of Minnesota Press, 1958.

Scott, Franklin D. *Emigration and Immigration.* New York: Macmillan Co., 1963.

_____. *The Peopling of America: Perspectives on Immigration.* Washington: American Historical Association, 1963, 1972.

_____, ed. *World Migration in Modern Times.* Englewood Cliffs, New Jersey: Prentice-Hall, Inc., 1968.

Scott, Norman and Gras, Brian. *A History of Agriculture in Europe and America.* New York: F. S. Crofts & Co., 1925.

Semmel, Bernard, ed. *Occasional Papers of T. R. Malthus.* New York: Burt Franklin, 1963.

Sengstock, Mary C. "Differential Rates of Assimilation in an Ethnic Group: In Ritual, Social Interaction and Normative Culture." *International Migration Review,* Vol. III, No. 2, Spring 1969.

Senior, William Nassau. *Journals, Conversations and Essays Relating to Ireland,* 2 vols. London: Longmans, Green & Co., 1868.

_____. "Two Lectures on Population, to which is Added a Correspondence between the Author and the Rev. T. R. Malthus,1829." *Journals of Ireland,* 1867.

Seward, W. W. *Topographia Hibernica.* Dublin: Alexander Smart & Co., 1797.

Slosson, Preston William. *The Decline of the Chartist Movement. Studies in Historic, Economic and Public Law.* Vol. LXXIII. London: Cass, 1967.

Smelser, Neil J. *Social Change in the Industrial Revolution.* Chicago: University of Chicago Press, 1959.

Smiles, Samuel. *Thrift.* New York: Harper & Bros., 1876.

_____. *Duty.* New York: Harper & Bros., 1881.

_____. *Character.* London: John Murray, 1871.

_____. *Brief Biographies.* Boston: Tichnor & Field, 1861.

Smith, Adam. *The Wealth of Nations.* Book I. New York: Modern Library, 1948.

Solar, Peter M. "Harvest Fluctuations in Pre-Famine Ireland: Evidence from the Belfast and Waterford Newspapers." *Agricultural History Review,* xxxvii, No. 2, 1989.

Solberg, Carl. *Immigration and Nationalism, Argentina and Chile, 1890–1914.* Austin: University of Texas Press, 1970.

Solow, Barbara L. *The Land Question and the Irish Economy, 1870–1903.* Cambridge: Harvard University Press, 1971.

_____. "A New Look at the Irish Land Question," *Economic and Social Review,* Dublin, Vol.12, No.4, July 1981.

Somerwell, D. C. *English Thought in the 19th Century.* New York: Longmans, Green & Co., 1929.

Sorokin, Pitirim. *Social and Cultural Dynamics.* London: Collier-Macmillan, Ltd., 1941, 1959.

Spengler, Joseph J. and Duncan, Otis D., eds. *Population Theory and Policy*. Glencoe: The Free Press, 1956.

Stanley, W. *Commentaries on Ireland*. Dublin: Richard Milliken & Son, 1833.

Steele, E.D. "The Irish Presence in the North of England, 1800–1922," *Northern History*, XII, 1976.

Stephenson, George M. *A History of American Immigration, 1820–1924*. Boston: Ginn & Co., 1926.

Strauss, Eric. *Irish Nationalism and British Democracy*. New York: Columbia University Press, 1951.

Sullivan, Dennis B. "Irish Intellect in England." Lecture to the Irish Literary Association, May 1871.

Surtees, Robert Smith. *Hillingdon Hall, or the Cockney Squire*. London: John C. Nimmo, 1888.

Sutherland, Edwin H. *Criminology*. Philadelphia: J. B. Lippincott, 1924.

Swift, Jonathan. *A Modest Proposal* in *Irish Tracts, 1728–1733*, Herbert David, ed. *The Prose Works of Jonathan Swift*. Vol. 12. Oxford: Blackwell, 1955.

Swift, Roger. "The Historiography of the Irish in Nineteenth Century Britain: Some Perspectives," in Buckland and Belchem (eds). Liverpool: Univ. of Liverpool, 1992.

_____. "The Outcast Irish in the British Victorian City: Problems and Perspectives," *Irish Historical Studies* xxv, No. 99, May 1987.

Swift, Roger and Gilley, Sheridan. *The Irish in the Victorian City*. London: Croom Helm, 1985.

_____. "The Outcast Irish in the British Victorian City: Problems and Perspectives," *Irish Historical Studies*, XXV, No. 99, May 1987.

Synge, John M. *The Works of John M. Synge*. Vol. 4. Dublin: Maunsel & Co., 1910.

Tawney, R. H. *The Radical Tradition*. New York: Minerva Press, 1964.

_____. *The Agrarian Problem in the Sixteenth Century*. New York: Harper & Row, 1912, 1967.

_____. *Religion and the Rise of Capitalism*. New York: Harcourt Brace, 1926.

Taylor, Philip A. M. *The Industrial Revolution in Britain, Triumph or Disaster?* Boston: D. C. Heath, 1958.

_____. *The Distant Magnet: European Emigration to the US*. New York: Harper & Rox, 1971.

Taylor, Seamus. "Smalltown Boys and Girls, Emigrant Irish Youth in London," Irish in Britain Research Forum. Occasional Papers Series: No. 2. PNL Press, 1988

Thackeray, William. *The Irish Sketch Book, 1843*. London: Smith, Elder & Co., 1901.

Thernstrom, Stephan. *The Other Bostonians: Poverty and Progress in the American Metropolis, 1880–1970*. Cambridge, Mass.: Harvard University Press, 1973.

Thistlethwaite, Frank. "Migration from Europe Overseas in the Nineteenth and Twentieth Centuries," Kingsley Davis, ed.

Thom's Directory of Ireland, 1847, and Subsequent Years. Dublin: Alexander Thom, 1848 and subsequent years.

Thomas, Brinley. "International Migration" in *The Study of Migration*. P. M. Hauser and O. T. Duncan, eds. Chicago: University of Chicago Press, 1959.

_____. *Migration and Economic Growth*. Cambridge: University Press, 1954.

_____. *Migration and Urban Development, a Reappraisal of British and American Long Cycles*. London: Methuen & Co., Ltd., 1972.

Thomas, Dorothy Swaine. *Research Memorandum on Migration Differentials*. New York: Social Science Research Council, 1938.

Thomas, Keith. "Work and Leisure in Pre-Industrial Societies." *Past and Present*. No. 29, December 1964.

Thomas, W. I. and Znaniecki, F. *The Polish Peasant in Europe and America*. New York, 1927.

Thompson, Dorothy. "Ireland and the Irish in English Radicalism before 1850" in *The Chartist Experience: Studies in Working Class Radicalism and Culture, 1830–60*. James Epstein and Dorothy Thomspon, eds. London: Macmillan, 1982.

Thompson, E. P. *The Making of the English Working Class*. New York: Random House, 1963.

_____. "The Moral Economy of the English Crowd in the 18th Century." *Past & Present*. No. 50, February 1971.

_____. "Time, Work-Discipline, and Industrial Capitalism." *Past & Present*. No. 38, December 1967.

Thompson, Flora, *Lark Rise to Candleford*. London: Penguin Books, 1939, 1974.

Thomson, David, with McGusty, Moyra. *The Irish Journals of Elizabeth Smith 1840–1850*. Oxford: Clarendon Press, 1980.

Thureau-Dangin, Paul. *The English Catholic Revival in the 19th Century*. London: B. T. Batsford, 1967.

Thurneysen, R.; Power, N.; Dillon, M.; Mulchrone, K.; Binchy, D. A.; Knoch, A. and Ryan, J. *Studies in Early Irish Law*. Published by the Royal Irish Academy. Dublin: Hodges Figgis & Co., 1936.

Tighe, Robert Stearne. *Observations and Reflections on the State of Ireland*. Dublin: William Porter, 1804.

_____. *Statistical Observations Relative to the County of Kilkenny*. Dublin: Graisberry & Campbell, 1802.

Tobias, John J. *Crime and Industrial Society in the 19th Century*. London: B. T. Batsford, 1967.

Todaro, Michael. "Migration and Economic Development: A Review of Theory, Evidence, Methodology, and Research Priorities." World Employment Programme, Population and Migration Research Project. June 1975.

Todd, William G. *The Irish in England,* reprinted from *The Dublin Review*. London: Charles Doman, 1857.

Torrens, R., Esq. *Ireland Saved Without Cost to the Imperial Treasury*. Pamphlet. London: James Ridgway, 1847.

Townsend, Joseph. *A Dissertation on the Poor Laws, by a Well-Wisher to Mankind*. Berkeley: University of California Press, 1786, 1971.

Townsend, Rev. Horatio. *Statistical Survey of the County of Cork*. Dublin: Graisberry & Campbell, 1810.

Trainor, Brian, *The Ordnance Survey Memoir for the Parish of Antrim, 1830–40*. Belfast: Northern Ireland Public Record Office, 1969.

Treble, J. H. "Irish Navvies in the North of England 1830–50," *Transport History,* VI, No.3, 1973.

_____. "O'Connor, O'Connell and the Attitudes of Irish Immigrants towards Chartism in the North of England 1838–48," in J. Butt and I. F. Clarke (eds.). *The Victorians and Social Protest: A Symposium*. Newton Abbot, England: David & Charles, 1973.

Trench, W. S. *Realities of Irish Life*. London: Longmans, Green & Co., 1868.

Trevelyan, C. E. *The Irish Crisis*. London: Longman, Brown, Green and Longmans, 1848.

Trotter, John Bernard. *Walks Through Ireland in the Years 1812, 1814, 1817*. London: Sir Richard Phillips & Co., 1819.

Truxes, Thomas M. *Irish-American Trade, 1660–1783*. Cambridge: Cambridge University Press, 1988.

Tuckett, John D. *A History of the Past and Present State of the Labouring Population*. Vol. 1 & 2. Shannon: Irish University Press, 1846, 1971.

Tylecote, Mabel. *The Mechanics Institute of Lancashire and Yorkshire Before 1851*. Manchester: Manchester University Press, 1957.

Ulster Dialects. Ulster Folk Museum publication, published for Her Majesty's Stationery Office. Belfast: Bell, Logan & Carswell, Ltd. 1964.

Vaughan, W. E. "A Study of Landlord and Tenant Relations in Ireland Between the Famine and the Land War, 1850–78." Ph.D. diss. University of Dublin, Trinity College, 1974.

———. "Landlord and Tenant Relations in Ireland between the Famine and the Land War, 1850–1878," in L. M. Cullen and T. C. Smout, eds. *Comparative Aspects of Scottish and Irish Economic and Social History, 1600–1900*. Edinburgh: Donald, 1978.

Vaughan, W. E. and Fitzpatrick, A. J. *Irish Historical Statistics: Population, 1821–1971*. Dublin: Royal Irish Academy, 1978.

Veroff, J., Gurin, G., and Feld, S. "Achievement, Motivation and Religious Background." *American Sociological Review*. Vol. 27, No. 1, February 1962.

Wagley, Charles and Harris, Marvin. *Minorities in the New World, 6 Case Studies*. New York: Columbia University Press, 1958.

Wakefield, Edward Gibbon. *A Letter from Sydney and Other Writing*. London: Dent, 1812, 1929.

———. *An Account of Ireland, Statistical and Political*. 2 vols. London: Longman, Hurst, Rees, Orme, & Brown, 1812.

Wall, Maureen. *The Penal Laws, 1691–1760*. Dublin: Dublin Historical Association, 1961, 1967.

———. "Catholics in Economic Life." In *The Formation of the Irish Economy*. L. M. Cullen, ed. Cork: Mercier Press, 1969.

Wallas, Graham. *The Life of Francis Place, 1771–1854*. New York: Alfred Knopf, 1898, 1919.

Walsh, Brendan. "A Perspective on Irish Population Patterns." *Eire-Ireland*. Vol. IV, No. 3, Autumn 1969.

———. "Marriage Rates and Population Patterns in Ireland, 1871 and 1911," *Economic History Review*, No. 28, April 1970.

———. "Trends in Age at Marriage in Post War Ireland." *Demography*. Vol. 9, No. 2, May 1972.

Walshaw, R. S. *Migration to and from the British Isles, Problems and Policies*. London: Jonathan Cape, 1941.

———. *Migration To and From Merseyside*. Liverpool: University Press, 1938.

Wannan, Bill, ed. *The Wearing of the Green, the Lore, Literature, Legend and Balladry of the Irish in Australia*. Melbourne: Landsdowne Press, 1965.

Watkins, E. I. *Roman Catholicism in England from the Reformation to 1950*. London: Oxford University Press, 1957.

Watson's Almanack and Directory for 1844. Dublin: C. Hope, 1844.

Watt, Hugh. *The Practice of Banking in Scotland and England*. London: Simpkin & Marshall, 1833.

Wearmouth, Robert F. *Methodism and the Working-Class Movements in 1800–1850*. Clifton, New Jersey: Augustus Kelley, 1937, 1972.

Webb, R. K. *The British Working Class Reader*. London: George Allen & Unwin, 1955.

_____. *Modern England, from the 18th Century to the Present*. New York: Dodd, Mead & Co., 1968.

Webb, Beatrice and Sidney. *English Poor Law History*. London and New York: Longmans Green & Co., 1927–29.

Weber, Adna Ferrin. *The Growth of Cities in the 19th Century*. New York: Macmillan Co., 1899.

Webster, Nesta H. *Secret Societies and Subversive Movements*. 2nd ed. London: Boswell Printing and Publishing Co., Ltd., 1924.

Weld, Isaac, *Statistical Survey of the County of Roscommon*. Dublin: Graisberry, 1832.

Werly, John W. "The Irish in Manchester, 1832–49," *Irish Historical Studies,* Vol. XVIII, No. 71, March, 1973.

Whalen, William J. *Handbook of Secret Organisations*. Milwaukee: Bruce Publishing Co., 1966.

White, Terence De Vere. *The Story of the Royal Dublin Society*. Tralee: The Kerryman, 1955.

Wiggins, John. *The "Monster" Misery of Ireland, A Practical Treatise on the Relationship of Landlord and Tenant*. London: Richard Bentley, 1844.

Wilcox, Walter F., ed. *International Migrations*. Vol. II. *Interpretations*. New York: National Bureau of Economic Research, 1931.

Williams, Gwym A. *Artisans and Sans-Culottes*. New York: W. W. Norton & Co., 1969.

Williams, T. Desmond, ed. *Secret Societies in Ireland*. Dublin: Gill & Macmillan, 1973.

Williamson, Jeffrey G. "The Impact of the Irish on British Labour Market during the Industrial Revolution," in *Journal of Economic History,* XLVI, September 1986.

_____. "Migration to the New World: Longterm Influences and Impact," *Explorations in Economic History,* XI, 4, 1974.

_____. "Irish Immigration, Elastic Labor Supplies and Crowding Out During the British Industrial Revolution." Discussion paper of the Harvard Institute for Economic Research, No. 1085 Sept. 1984. Cambridge, Mass. 1984.

Wilson, Charles. *England's Apprenticeship, 1603–1763*. New York: St. Martin's Press, 1965, 1966.

Wolf, Eric. *Peasant Wars of the 20th Century*. London: Faber & Faber, 1969.

Wolff, K. H. (trans.) *The Sociology of George Simmel*. Glencoe, Illinois: The Free Press, 1950.

Wolpe, Howard. *Urban Politics in Nigeria: A Study of Port Harcourt*. Berkeley:

University of California Press, 1974.

Woodbridge, George. *The Reform Bill of 1832*. New York: Thomas Y. Crowell Co., 1970.

Woodham-Smith, Cecil. *The Great Hunger, Ireland 1845–1849*. New York: Harper & Row, 1962.

Wright, J. F. "British Economic Growth, 1688–1959." *Economic History Review,* 2nd Ser, Vol. XVIII, No. 1–3, 1965.

Wrigley, E. A. "A Simple Model of London's Importance in Changing English Society and Ecomony 1650–1750." *Past & Present.* No. 37, July 1967.

_____. *Population and History.* New York: McGraw-Hill Book Company, 1969.

Wrong, Dennis H. *Population and Society.* New York: Random House, 1956, 1969.

Yang, Anand A. "The Optimizing Peasant: A Study of Internal Migration in a Northeast Indian District." Workshop on the effects of risk and uncertainty of economic and social processes in South Asia. University of Pennsylvania, November 10–12, 1973.

Yeo, Eileen and Thompson, E. P. *The Unknown Mayhew.* New York: Pantheon Books, 1971.

Young, Arthur. *A Tour in Ireland.* Vol. 1, Dublin. printed by George Bonham for Messrs. Whitestone, Sleater, Sheppard, Williams, Burnet, Wilson, Jenkins, Wogan, Vallance, White, Beatty, Byrne, Burton, 1780.

Young, G. M. *Victorian England, Portrait of an Age.* Oxford University Press, 1936, 1971.

Young, M. and Willmott, P. *Family and Kinship in East London.* London, 1957.

Ziegler, Benjamin M., ed. *Immigration: An American Dilemma.* Boston: D. C. Heath & Co., 1953.

Index

ISBN 0-8138-1422-7

90000>

9 780813 814223